Java

an object first approach

Java
an object first approach

FINTAN CULWIN

SOUTH BANK UNIVERSITY

PRENTICE HALL

LONDON NEW YORK TORONTO SYDNEY TOKYO SINGAPORE

MADRID MEXICO CITY MUNICH PARIS

First published 1998 by
Prentice Hall Europe
Campus 400, Maylands Avenue
Hemel Hempstead
Hertfordshire, HP2 7EZ
A division of
Simon & Schuster International Group

Typeset in 9.75/12pt Galliard
by Mathematical Composition Setters Ltd

Printed and bound in Great Britain by
The Bath Press, Bath

Library of Congress Cataloging-in-Publication Data

Available from the publisher

British Library Cataloguing in Publication Data

A catalogue record for this book is available from
the British Library

ISBN 0-13-858457-5

1 2 3 4 5   02 01 00 99 98

... at last one
for Melissa ...

Contents

Preface

Java has exploded from its origins as an obscure, and shelved, software engineering project to provide an environment for the production of software to control domestic appliances, into a commercial product which has featured in mass circulation publications such as *Time* magazine and the London *Times*. This popular interest in a programming language is unprecedented and is indicative of a more intense interest within the computer industry.

The reasons for this outburst of interest are still not very well understood but seem related not only to Java's facility for use with the World Wide Web but also to its addressing many of the deficiencies of the existing industry standard languages, C and C++. The production of software, as will be explained, is a complex and tortuous task which can be either assisted or impeded by the language which is used. Both C and C++ were languages which evolved into their final forms rather than being designed. In particular the object oriented facilities added to C to produce C++ resulted in a language which is complex, convoluted, inelegant and insecure. Java has taken the essential syntax of the C family of languages but by not insisting upon being backwardly compatible with C has been able to remove many, but not all, of these problematic features. This partially explains why software engineers are so interested in Java and supplies a partial rationale for this book.

This book attempts to introduce the processes required for the production of software artefacts using Java, from a rigorous software engineering and object oriented perspective. If the processes for developing software are poorly understood and contentiously debated then the processes for the education and training of software developers are extraordinarily unclear and explosively argumentative. The approach taken in this book is that the concept of an object, in the form of a class declaration, is fundamental to effective software and that its production must be accomplished by a defined process involving its prior design and subsequent testing.

This pedagogic approach is not universally accepted and many would regard it as being appropriate only for the second stage of software development education after other, supposedly more fundamental, concepts have been established. However, the contents of this book have been designed so that they can be used as the basis of either a first or second course in software development.

There are a number of possible paths through the contents of this book, all of which should start with Chapters 1 to 7 which introduce the fundamental concepts of object oriented software development with Java. For readers who have not had an initial software development course Appendix A summarizes the nature of the non-object primitive types which will be encountered. Following this introductory part Chapter 8 introduces the topic of concurrent processes which, prior to Java, had been regarded as an advanced topic. Java's facilities for concurrent processes allow this important topic to be introduced at a much earlier stage and its positioning at this location in this book reflects its importance.

Chapters 9 and 12 introduce communication between a software artefact and external devices. Chapter 9 restricts itself to the keyboard and the display, while Chapter 12 extends this to other external resources such as disk files. Chapters 10 and 11 are provided in order that the processes involved in the testing of software can be introduced. Chapters 13 to 15 introduce data structures which allow significant quantities of information to be stored and manipulated within an artefact.

The topic of graphical user interfaces (GUIs) and the use of Java to supply interactive content for World Wide Web pages have been deliberately left to the last chapter, Chapter 16, where only a brief introduction is provided. The production of such artefacts requires the developer to have a high level of skill and understanding of the software development process. Approaches to software development education which commence with these facilities, or introduce them at a much earlier stage, result in programmers who produce poorly engineered artefacts which have limited functionality and usability. A follow-on book to this is currently being written and will provide the basis on which this topic can be adequately explored.

The contents of the present book are consolidated, following Chapter 16, with a case study illustrating how a more realistic artefact can be designed and produced, and a glossary which provides an admittedly terse definition of the technical terms used in the book. Appendix A supplies details of Java's primitive types and Appendix B contains the source code which, for various reasons, was omitted from the body of the book. Appendix C contains a summary of the design notation used throughout the book, which consists of JSP schematics for the detailed design of the actions and UML conventions for almost all other aspects. The single exception is that OMT style class diagrams have been used in preference to UML style class diagrams for reasons explained at the start of section C1.2 in Appendix C.

In its brief history Java has already two invocations. The core language is stable and unlikely to change significantly but its environment includes a large number of pre-supplied classes. The first release of these classes, as part of the 1.0 Java Development Kit (JDK), was supplanted within a year by an improved 1.1 release. There are only two places in this book where the 1.1 release is required: Chapter 16 where the 1.1 JDK addressed some very significant shortcomings in Java's user interface capabilities, and in Chapter 13 where a very minor improvement to the Arial class was supplied. A work-around for the Arial facility is provided in section B1.3 in Appendix B but, unfortunately, there is no sensible work-around for Chapter 16 which requires the 1.1 JDK release.

The typographic convention adopted is to use *normal text bold italic* whenever a new technical term is introduced, or its meaning significantly elaborated. A sans serif typeface (Arial) is used for any Java terms with **bold sans serif** for reserved words and *italic sans serif* for developer decided terms. Program listings are in a monospaced font (`Courier`) with preceding four digit line numbers. Phrases from design schematics which do not directly translate into program terms are presented in *normal italic*.

Whilst I was writing my previous book I promised my family that I would take a break before even contemplating writing another one, a promise which I broke before I had completely finished it. As usual they forgave me and provided their usual level of support and hot coffee, whilst I struggled in the attic with the intricacies of Java and

English syntax and semantics. Peter Chalk again, masochistically, volunteered to read and critique each and every chapter as it was written and rewritten, assisted by Christine Faulkner for aspects concerned with user interface considerations. Various groups of students at South Bank were subjected to parts of the book as it was written and many people provided comments as interim chapters were published on the World Wide Web. Ian Marshall, a South Bank undergraduate student, supplied the case study reworking his excellent first year Ada assignment. At Prentice Hall Jackie Harbor and Derek Moseley provided efficient and effective support. However, it is inevitable that some errors and typos are present in this book and the Web site below will contain an erratum. Should you notice an error please e-mail me at the address below in order that I can add it to the list. Otherwise the Web site contains all the source code presented in the book and visiting it is clearly preferable to retyping it.

Fintan Culwin
fintan@sbu.ac.uk
http://www.scism.sbu.ac.uk/jfl

Chapter one

Two initial applications

This book is concerned with the production of *software artefacts* using the programming language Java, a process known as *software development*. Software artefacts include programs which enable a user to perform some specified task and components which are intended to be used in their construction. Software development is an engineering process which ensures that the artefacts are produced with due regard to their required quality. Most significantly the engineering process requires the production of a design prior to the production of a program and the testing of the artefact to assure its quality when it is developed.

Java is a programming language which assists in the development of quality artefacts by providing an environment which supports sound software engineering principles and prevents many of the most obvious flaws which have permeated programs produced using older languages. It also includes support for the production of small applications, called *applets*, which can be transmitted across the Internet and executed within World Wide Web browsers.

It is possible for small programs, which are only intended to be used by the developer to perform a simple task, to be produced without following a defined development process. However, most applications are produced by a team of developers and are intended to be used to perform complex tasks by a wide range of users. The techniques which can be used for the development of small programs are not suitable for the production of complex applications.

When a novice developer is producing their first programs there is a great temptation to concentrate upon the program code and to avoid the other aspects, such as design, which seem irrelevant. This is a very short sighted and dangerous approach as it will establish habits which subsequently have to be unlearned, and unlearning incorrect skills is much more difficult than learning the correct skills in the first place.

There are many other considerations concerned with the software development process which could be presented and discussed before the production of software is introduced. However, as the philosophy of this book is concerned with active learning this chapter will shortly continue with the production of two initial applications.

There are many concepts introduced in the rest of this chapter and two strategies are suggested to deal with its complexity. The first is to complete all the exercises at the end of the chapter, carefully following through all the design and production stages described in the chapter. The second suggestion is to return to this chapter after finishing the second chapter, and the third chapter, etc., in order to consolidate and extend the initial understanding obtained when it is followed through for the first time. Gaining a complete understanding of a concept takes time and effort. An initial understanding may well be fuzzy and partial but it should become clearer and more complete through careful consideration and practical activities which lead to active learning:

> It is not possible to learn how to develop software just by reading this book; it is also necessary actually to develop some software.

1.1 ▊ The *UltimateQuestion* application

The first application which will be introduced will state the question to life, the Universe and everything as first stated by Douglas Adams in *The Hitch-Hikers Guide to the Galaxy*. The first stage in the production of any software artefact is to establish exactly what it is supposed to do, a process known as *specification*. The specification for the *UltimateQuestion* program is that, when executed, it will produce the following output on the computer's screen:

```
What is the answer to,
life the Universe and everything?
```

The source code of a Java program, called *UltimateQuestion*, which satisfies this requirement might be as follows:

```
0001 // Filename UltimateQuestion.java.
0002 // Initial Java program written for
0003 // the JOF book chapter 1 - see text.
0004 //
0005 // Fintan Culwin, v0.1, August 1997.
0006
0007 public class UltimateQuestion {
0008
0009    public static void main( String args[]) {
0010
0011    String secondLine = "life, the Universe and everything?";
0012
0013       System.out.println();
0014       System.out.println( "What is the answer to," );
0015       System.out.println( secondLine);
0016    } // End main.
0017
0018 } // End UltimateQuestion.
```

The program listings which are presented in this book use **bold type** to indicate words which are reserved by Java for its own use; these are known as *reserved words*. *Italic type* is used to indicate names which have been chosen by the developer; the rules for choosing names will be given below. Other terms, in normal type, are used for facilities which are supplied by the Java environment but are not strictly part of the language. These conventions are intended to make the printed listings more informative and should not be used for listings which are intended to be used for production.

Likewise the line numbers at the start of each line are used to make it easier to indicate which line is being described and should not be included in listings which are intended to be used for the construction of artefacts. A version of the listing which could be used would appear as follows:

```
// Filename UltimateQuestion.java.
// Initial Java program written for
// the JOF book chapter 1 - see text.
//
// Fintan Culwin, v0.1, August 1997.

public class UltimateQuestion {

   public static void main( String args[]) {

   String secondLine = "life, the Universe and everything?";

      System.out.println();
      System.out.println( "What is the answer to," );
      System.out.println( secondLine);
   }  // End main.
} // End UltimateQuestion.
```

When a term from a program listing is used in the text a sans serif font will be used and if the term is chosen by the developer then this font will be italicised. ***Bold italics*** will be used when a technical term is introduced for the first time or when its meaning is significantly elaborated.

The first five lines of this listing all start with a double slash (*//*), which tells Java to ignore the rest of the line. The purpose of these lines is to inform anyone reading the listing of what it contains, who wrote it, where they wrote it, when they wrote it and possibly many other details as well. Lines, or parts of lines, which are included for the benefit of readers and ignored by Java are known as *comments*. All program listing files should always start with a series of similar comments identifying who, what, where, why, when, etc. Throughout the listing blank lines are occasionally inserted in order to make the listing easier to read; these lines, e.g. line 0008, will also be ignored by Java.

Line 0007 is the start of the declaration of a **class** called *UltimateQuestion*. Almost everything in Java has to be a part of a class and the name of the class dictates what name must be used to store the file on the computer's disk. So, as this file contains the declaration of the *UltimateQuestion* class, the filename used to store this listing must be *UltimateQuestion.java* as noted on line 0001 of the listing. The final character on line 0007 is an opening brace ({) which marks the start of its declaration and is matched by the closing brace (}) on line 0018. Everything between these opening and closing braces is the *UltimateQuestion* class.

This class contains the declaration of a single *action*, called *main()* between lines 0009 and 0016. A class which is intended to be used as a program must contain the declaration of a *main* action, and this declaration must appear exactly as shown on line 0009 if Java is to be able to find and execute it. The first term on the line, **public** makes the declaration visible outside the class, otherwise it would be invisible and so Java would be unable to find it for execution. The two next terms, **static** and **void** are required for reasons which will be explained later in this chapter and in the next.

The term *main* is shown in italics even though the developer has no choice about what this action is called. Although line 0009 must appear exactly as shown in the listing the contents of the *main()* action, between lines 0009 and 0016, are provided by the developer and not by Java. So this is a developer supplied *main()* action, not a main() action supplied by Java, and consequently italics are used to indicate this. The main action is followed by a pair of round brackets (), which enclose the **arguments** to the action. For a *main* action the arguments must appear exactly as shown; the meaning and use of these arguments will be fully explained in a later chapter.

The final term on line 0009 is an opening brace ({), which marks the start of the declaration of the *main()* action and is matched by a closing brace (}) on line 0016. The closing brace on line 0016 is the end of the *main()* declaration and the closing brace on line 0018 is the end of the *UltimateQuestion* declaration. Braces are used to delineate the opening and closing of many Java structures and, if care is not taken, it is very easy to arrive at listings which might contain something like the following:

```
}
   }
      }
         }
```

which is very difficult for anyone to understand. To avoid this possibility two techniques are suggested. The first is to label every closing brace with a comment, so line 0016 of the listing is commented as the end of the *main()* action and line 0018 as the end of the *UltimateQuestion* class. The second technique is indentation, which means moving the text of the lines to the right by three spaces. So in the *Ultimate-Question* listing everything which is part of the class declaration, between lines 0007 and 0018, is indented. Likewise the contents of the *main()* action, apart from line 0011, are further indented. By using these conventions the confusing closing braces above might appear as follows:

```
         } // End something.
      } // End someOtherThing.
   } // End penultimateThing.
} // End lastThing.
```

which is still confusing, but hopefully less so!

An action declaration, like *main()*'s action declaration, between lines 0009 and 0016 can contain two types of **statements**. That is, statements which declare the existence of **objects** and statements which declare what is to be done with the objects, known as **steps**. To assist in making this distinction clearer the object declarations are all collected together at the start of the action, are not indented and are followed by the action's steps which are indented. So the *main()* action in this listing contains a single object declaration on line 0011 followed by three steps on lines 0013 to 0015.

The declaration on line 0011 states that a String object called *secondLine* containing the information "life, the Universe and everything?" is required by *main()*. A String is a sequence of individual characters which together form a word, phrase or sentence. One way of visualizing what happens in line 0011 is that an object with the following structure is created:

secondLine
life, the Universe and everything?
String

The upper part of the structure diagram indicates the name of the object, in this example *secondLine*, and, by the use of italics, indicates that it has been chosen by the developer. The lower part of the structure diagram indicates what type of object this is, in this example a String. The middle part of the structure diagram indicates the value of the object and as this is a String it has to be a sequence of characters, as shown. The opening (") and closing (") *string quotes* have not been stored as part of its value. They are required in a listing only to mark the start and end of a String, but are discarded by Java when the String is stored.

All three steps of the *main()* action, on lines 0013 to 0015, are instructions to Java to output something onto the computer's display. The phrase System.out.println(...) means send what follows, inside the round brackets, to the next line of the display. On line 0013 the brackets are empty and this will cause an empty line to be sent to the screen. This causes a blank line to appear on the screen before the rest of the output from this program.

On line 0014 the round brackets contain a string contained between string quotes. Java will again strip the quotes from the string and send it to the next line of the display, producing the first line of output required by the specification. On line 0015 the contents of the brackets are not enclosed by quote marks and so Java knows that this is not a simple string to be output. Instead Java attempts to determine what it might mean. The phrase *secondLine* is known to Java from the declaration on line 0011 and its value is retrieved from the object and output. As shown in the visualization above, this is the sequence of characters which form the second line of the required output, completing the specification.

Before leaving the detailed consideration of this listing, the semicolons (;) which terminate every statement, on lines 0011, 0013, 0014 and 0015, should be noted. Just as a sentence is terminated with a full stop, so every statement which forms an object declaration or a step in a Java action must be terminated with a semicolon.

The listing, as shown above, is written in a form which a Java developer can read and understand. However, it is not yet in a form which the computer can understand. In order to transform it from a form which a human can understand into a form that a computer can understand it has to be *compiled*.

The first stage of the compilation process is to make sure that the listing is written exactly to Java's syntax rules. If a sentence in this book is *exactly written not* to the rules of English a human can still, in most cases, understand its meaning (can't you ☺). Unfortunately computers cannot do this and the compiler will not continue if it discovers a *syntax error*, stopping at this stage with the best explanation of the errors it has found.

Even if the listing does conform to Java's syntax rules the instructions contained in the listing may not be what are required by the program's specification. This is analogous to an English sentence which seems grammatically correct but which contains nonsense: for example, 'T' was brillig and the slivey tove'; or 'When reading this book make sure that you keep your eyes closed.' Java will attempt to do whatever these instructions seem to mean, even if it is nonsense, and fail to do whatever the developer intended. Errors of this form are known as *semantic errors*.

The way in which the program listing above is entered into a computer and compilation subsequently attempted, with syntax errors being reported, or eventually, when all such errors have been removed, the way in which the program is executed, differ widely from computer system to computer system and from compiler to compiler. The first exercise at the end of this chapter will require these details to be discovered. It is suggested that this exercise is attempted at this stage before continuing with the rest of this chapter.

1.2 ▓ The *UltimateAnswer* application

The *UltimateQuestion* application, as presented above, was a very unusual Java program as it consisted of a single class which contained a single action. It would be much more typical for a program to be constructed from a number of different classes each of which contained a number of different actions. In order to move towards this situation a program will be developed in this part of the chapter which contains two classes, each of which contains a single action. The next chapter will continue with programs which contain more than two classes, each of which may contain more than a single action.

The specification for this application, called *UltimateAnswer*, is to provide the answer to the *UltimateQuestion* as asked in the previous section. When executed this application is to produce the following output:

```
The answer to life,
the Universe and everything is forty two.
```

This application will be constructed from two classes, one called *TheAnswer* which knows the value of the ultimate answer and one called *UltimateAnswer* which will communicate it to the user. This is a commonplace architecture where the detailed computation of some information, for example the number of people in a room or the value of an amount of British pounds in American dollars or the visualization of the inside of a human skull from a CAT scan, etc., is supplied by one class and the interaction with the user is handled by a second class. The relationship between the classes can be illustrated by an ***object instance diagram***, as shown in Figure 1.1.

The rectangular boxes at the top of the diagram represent the classes which are being used and the hexagonal boxes at the bottom instances of these classes. The diagram indicates, on the right, that the application object, known as the ***client program***, is an instance of the *UltimateAnswer* class. Similarly the left of the diagram indicates that a single instance of the *UltimateAnswer* class called ***anAnswerObject*** is required. The

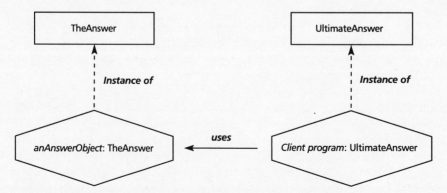

Figure 1.1 Instance diagram for the *UltimateAnswer* application.

anAnswerObject exists in the program in order that the client program can ask it for the value of the ultimate answer. Thus the client program makes use of the *anAnswer-Object* instance as indicated by the arrow connecting them; alternatively the client program can be regarded as a *client* of the *UltimateAnswer* class and its instance.

The most appropriate way of constructing this application is to design and implement the *TheAnswer* class before considering its client. A *class* can be thought of as a pattern or blueprint from which any number of *instances*, known as *objects*, of the class can be produced.

1.3 ▥ The *TheAnswer* class

A class is designed using a *class diagram* which can be thought of as an expansion of the rectangular boxes used in Figure 1.1. The class diagram for the *TheAnswer* class is given in Figure 1.2.

The diagram states that the class of objects called *TheAnswer* provides a single action called *theAnswerIs*, which supplies an item of data identified as *ultimate*. A listing of the implementation of this design is as follows:

```
0001 // Filename TheAnswer.java.
0002 // Initial Java object written for the JOF
0003 // book chapter 1 – see text.
0004 //
0005 // Fintan Culwin, v0.1, August 1997.
0006
0007 public class TheAnswer {
0008
0009    public String theAnswerIs() {
0010       return "forty two";
0011    } // End theAnswerIs.
0012
0013 } // End TheAnswer.
```

Again, the first five lines of this listing are the who, what, where, why, when comments. The first comment identifies the name of this file as *TheAnswer.java*, which indicates that it should contain the declaration of the *TheAnswer* class. Line 0007 contains the start of the class declaration, which extends as far as the end of the file on line 0013. This class is specified as **public** to make it visible outside this file in order that the client class can see it.

The class diagram indicates that the *TheAnswer* class provides a single action called *theAnswerIs()*. This action is declared within *TheAnswer*'s declaration on lines 0009 to 0010 and is indented to emphasize that it is contained within the class declaration.

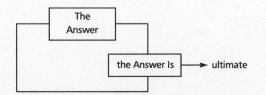

Figure 1.2　The *TheAnswer* class diagram.

Line 0009 states that this is the **public** declaration of an action called *theAnswerIs()* which will supply a String value to any client which asks for it. The **public** modifier indicates that it is visible outside the class, String that it returns a String value and the empty round brackets () that it is an action requiring no arguments. The first line of an action declaration, which states it name, visibility modifiers, the type of value which it returns and its arguments, is known as an action's *signature*. The opening brace on line 0009 and the commented closing brace on line 0011 delineate the extent of the declaration. The steps which comprise a declaration are enclosed between the two braces and, in this case, consist of a single **return** statement, on line 0010. A **return** statement is used to indicate the value which will be supplied when the action is activated. In this action the String value "forty two" will always be supplied. The semicolon (;) at the end of the line terminates the single statement of the action.

This completes the declaration of the *TheAnswer* class which by itself cannot actually do anything. In order for it to be used a client program which asks for its services has to be produced. The provision of a suitable client program is the responsibility of the *UltimateAnswer* class whose design and construction will be described next.

1.4 ▓ The *UltimateAnswer* class

The *UltimateAnswer* class has a single purpose in this application: to provide a client program which makes use of a *TheAnswer* object; its class diagram is given in Figure 1.3.

This diagram indicates that the class supplies a single action called *main()*, which requires arguments to be supplied to it and does not supply any information. An action called *main()*, with a strictly required signature, is recognized by Java as a *client program* and, as explained above, Java will automatically execute it when the program starts running. The implementation of this design is as follows:

```
0001 // Filename UltimateAnswer.java.
0002 // Initial Java client program written for
0003 // the JOF book chapter 1 - see text.
0004 //
0005 // Fintan Culwin, v0.1, August 1997.
0006
0007 import TheAnswer;
0008
0009 public class UltimateAnswer {
0010
0011     public static void main( String args[]) {
0012
0013     TheAnswer anAnswerObject = new TheAnswer();
0014
0015        System.out.println();
0016        System.out.println( "The answer to life,");
0017        System.out.print( "the Universe and everything is ");
0018        System.out.print( anAnswerObject.theAnswerIs());
0019        System.out.println( ".");
0020     } // End main.
0021
0022 } // End UltimateAnswer.
```

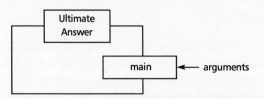

Figure 1.3   The *UltimateAnswer* class diagram.

Lines 0001 to 0005 are again the header comments which identify who, what, why, where, when, etc., for this program file. The *UltimateAnswer* class is declared between lines 0009 and 0022. Before this line 0007 states that this class makes use of the *TheAnswer* class using the Java **import** statement, as indicated on the instance diagram in Figure 1.1.

The declaration of the *main()* action is between lines 0011 and 0020. Line 0011 contains the signature required for a *main()* action if it is to be found and used by Java as a program.

Line 0013 is required to create an instance of the *TheAnswer* class which can be used by the *main()* action. The first part of the line, *TheAnswer anAnswerObject*, states that an object of the *TheAnswer* class will be required and that it will be referred to as *anAnswerObject* in this action. However, it does not actually create an instance of the class. The **new** *TheAnswer()* part of the line actually creates the instance by using the constructor action *TheAnswer()*. This action is not explicitly provided by the *TheAnswer* class declaration so a suitable constructor action is automatically supplied by Java. More complex class declarations will have to provide one, or more, constructors; this will be further explained in the next chapter. The process of creating an instance of a class in this way is known as *instantiation*.

The statements which form the *main()* action, given on lines 0015 to 0018, make use of the *System.out.println()* as in the *UltimateQuestion* application, and also of the *System.out.print()* action. The difference between a *println()* and a *print()* action is that *println()* will complete a line of output and move onto the next line of the screen; *print()* will not advance to the next line, so subsequent output will appear on the same screen line.

Line 0015 is again included to provide a blank line on the screen before the rest of the output from this application appears. Line 0016 provides the first line of output required by the specification and line 0017 the first part of the second line. As line 0017 uses a *print()*, as opposed to a *println()*, action subsequent output from the program will appear on the same line on the screen.

The argument to the *println()* action on line 0018 is not enclosed in quotes and this indicates to Java that it should attempt to work out what the argument means, and then output that meaning. The argument, *anAnswerObject.theAnswerIs()*, indicates that the *theAnswerIs()* action of the *anAnswerObject* instance should be asked to provide its meaning. As explained above *theAnswerIs()* will always **return** the value "forty two" and this, stripped of its opening and closing string quotes, will be output to the screen. The last action, on line 0019, outputs a full stop (.) completing screen output, before the *main()* action and thus the program finishes.

By considering the sequence of output which is produced by the actions on lines 0015 to 0019 it can be shown that the program will produce on the screen exactly what is required to satisfy its specification.

1.5 ▨ Action designs using JSP notation

The two actions which have been introduced above, the *theAnswerIs()* and the *main()* actions, have been presented without a design and for actions as simple as these this is probably acceptable. However, many, if not most, actions will be more complex than these and the production of a design is an essential prerequisite to their successful construction. The design notation which will be used for actions in this book is a modified form of Jackson Structured Programming (JSP) notation. The JSP design for the *TheAnswer theAnswerIs()* action is as follows:

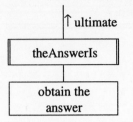

The first level of this design indicates that the action *theAnswerIs()* will supply a single piece of information identified as *ultimate*. The double vertical lines indicate that this action is a part of the software artefact which is currently under construction and is not pre-supplied by Java or being reused from a previously developed class. The second level of the design indicates that it is implemented in a single step which obtains the answer.

The design of the *UltimateAnswer main()* action is as follows:

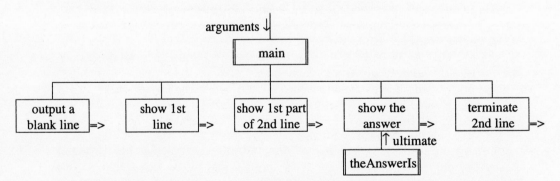

This diagram indicates that the *main* action requires arguments, although in this program it does nothing with them. The second level indicates that it is composed of five steps each of which produces some output, as indicated by the arrows (=>) at the right of each step. These five steps define a sequence which will be followed by Java from left to right. The fourth step, identified as *show the answer*, makes use of an action called *theAnswerIs()* to obtain a value called *ultimate* which is output onto the screen.

1.6 ▨ Names in programs

In the program listings presented above the developer had to invent names for various things. This part of the chapter will introduce the Java rules and style conventions

Table 1.1 Java's reserved words.

abstract	boolean	break	byte	byvalue	case
case	catch	char	class	const	continue
default	do	double	else	extends	false
final	finally	float	for	future	generic
goto	if	implements	import	inner	instanceof
int	interface	long	native	new	null
operator	outer	package	private	protected	public
rest	return	short	static	super	switch
synchronized	this	throw	throws	transient	true
try	var	void	volatile	while	

Table 1.2 Java's commonest pre-declared terms.

append	clone	equals	finalize	getClass
hashCode	insert	interrupt	length	notify
print	println	read	resume	run
sleep	start	stop	suspend	toString
wait	write	valueOf	yield	

which must, or should, be followed when names are chosen. The most fundamental of these conventions, which should be taken as a rule, is that names should always be as meaningful as possible, even though this might mean more typing. It is usual for names to be made up from more than one word and to be joined together using an *InitialCapitals* convention.

The only Java rule for names is that Java's reserved words cannot be used as names. A list of all Java's reserved words is given in Table 1.1.

Some other words identify facilities which are supplied by the Java environment and although they could be used as names, they should not be used as such unless it is intended to change their meaning or to give them an additional meaning. A list of the most common of these terms is given in Table 1.2.

The names which are chosen for classes should use a complete *InitialCapital* convention; names which are chosen for actions and for data attributes should use a partial *followingCapital* convention, i.e. initial capitals for all but the first word. Some data attributes have values which cannot be changed; these are known as class constants and should use an *ALL_CAPITALS* convention using underscores (_) to connect the separate words. Data attributes and class constants will be introduced in the next chapter.

Summary

- The software development process starts with a precise specification of what a software artefact is to do.

- To deal with complexity software artefacts are produced from a number of different objects each of which is an instance of some class.

- Objects are designed using *class diagrams* which show what services an instance of the class being designed will offer its clients.

- An *instance diagram* illustrates the actual object instances which are used in a client program.

- Each class is defined in a separate source code file which contains the declarations of the actions which it supplies.

- The first line of an action declaration which states the action's visibility, return type, name and arguments is known as its *signature*.

- A class offering an action called *main ()* with a strictly defined signature will become the *client program* where execution of the program starts.

- Actions are designed, and documented, using JSP notation.

- The choice of names and the layout of the source code within program files is subject to a set of rules and conventions.

Exercises

1.1   In order to participate in active learning it will be necessary to develop Java programs. Obtain a copy of the *UltimateQuestion* file from this chapter, or even type it in by hand, and make sure that you can compile and execute the resulting program.

1.2   A large number of technical terms have been introduced in this chapter; they are highlighted in the text by the use of *bold italics*. Produce a glossary of terms using your own words to explain their meanings. Do not worry if your understanding of some of the explanations is vague, but return to the declarations after the next chapter and clarify them further.

1.3   Adapt the listing of the *UltimateQuestion* class so that it makes use of two String instances, one for each line of the output. Then adapt it again so that it makes no use of any *String* objects, specifying each line of output in quotes as an argument to *println ()*. Is there any way that a user of the program could know which technique was used?

1.4   Obtain a copy of the *UltimateAnswer* and *theAnswer* files from this chapter, or even type them in by hand, and make sure that you can compile them and execute the resulting program.

1.5   Adapt the designs and the source code from this chapter so that a class called *MyDetails* offers two actions called *myNameIs ()* and *myPhoneNumberIs ()*, both of which should return Strings. The client should be called *MyDetailsClient* and when executed it will output your name and phone number with suitable messages. Design, build and demonstrate this class.

Chapter two

An overview of classes

This chapter will continue the introduction to classes by developing and explaining a second, rather trivial, application which is intended to present and explain the concepts of *data attributes*, *class wide actions*, *instance actions*, *class constants* and *constructors*, which were mentioned or briefly introduced in Chapter 1. The application is described as trivial only in the sense that it does not do anything useful; its conceptual understanding is anything but trivial.

The classes presented in the previous chapter contained only a single action which always returned the same information. By adding *data attributes* to a class declaration it is possible for each instance to maintain information about its own state and to change this information as its actions are used. The *main()* action from the client class in Chapter 1 was described as a *class wide* action, which means that it is associated with the entire class and can be used without having first to declare an instance of the class. The alternative possibility is to have *instance actions* where the action can only be used by first declaring an instance of the class.

The distinction between class wide and instance actions is related to the distinction between *class wide data attributes* and *instance data attributes*. There is only one copy of a class wide attribute for the entire class, and it can be accessed by any instance or class wide action. Instance attributes have one copy per instance of the class and can only be accessed by instance actions. A class wide attribute can also be declared to have a constant value, in which case it is known as a *class constant*, and unlike a class or instance variable attribute its value cannot be changed by any actions.

All the advice which was given at the start of Chapter 1 concerning how to approach that chapter can be repeated for this chapter. A full understanding of the concepts in this chapter is unlikely to be obtained when it is followed for the first time. It will take time and effort to assimilate and accommodate these concepts. It will also be of benefit to revisit this chapter after Chapter 3 has been completed, in order to consolidate the initial understanding.

2.1 ▪ The design of the *Friend* class

In order to give a practical introduction to these concepts, a class whose major purpose is to illustrate their properties will be designed, developed and described. An associated client program will then illustrate the concepts by using its actions. The class is intended to store and manipulate details of a *Friend*; its class diagram is shown in Figure 2.1.

This class diagram differs from the diagrams given in the previous chapter not only by having more actions, but also by giving some indication of its internal structure and

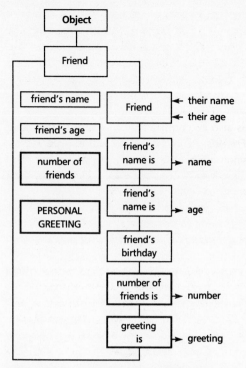

Figure 2.1   The *Friend* class diagram.

by indicating, at the top, that it is an extension of the Java **Object** class. The purpose of a class diagram is first to assist a developer with the design of the class and, second, to inform a developer wanting to use the class of the actions, and other resources, which it makes publicly available.

Any parts of the design which are shown on the right are considered fully public and can be used by any client of the class. Any parts which are fully contained within the diagram are fully private and are the sole concern of the class. They need not be shown and, in some circumstances, the implementation of the class need not actually use them. They are only present in the final version of the class diagram to assist with its understanding.

On this diagram there are four private attributes and as they have single lined boxes and are expressed with noun phrases, they are assumed to be data attributes. The first two, shown in normal lined boxes, are instance variable attributes named *friendsName* and *friendsAge*. The last two, shown in heavy lined boxes, are class wide attributes named *numberOfFriends* and *PERSONAL_GREETING*. The use of capitalization indicates that the last of these attributes is a constant attribute; the others are variable.

The first action on the design is called *Friend()*, which is also the name of the class. This indicates that it is a ***constructor*** for the class. The purpose of a constructor is to place the class instance into a well defined initial state when it is created; this usually involves setting the values of some, or all, of the instance data attributes. There are two instance data attributes in this design and the *theirName* and *theirAge* data flows into the constructor indicate that the value of the attributes will be specified by these arguments when the constructor is used.

The next two actions contain verb phrases which end in the term *Is* which, by the convention used in this book, indicates that they are ***enquiry actions*** retrieving the value of a private data attribute on behalf of a client. The *friendsNameIs()* action will return the name of the friend and the *friendsAgeIs()* their age, as shown by the data flow originating from the action. The remaining instance action is the *birthday()* action which requires no arguments and supplies no data. Its purpose is to record the birthday of a friend by increasing the *friendsAge* instance attribute by 1.

The next action, *numberOfFriendsIs()*, is also an enquiry action returning the value of the class wide data attribute *numberOfFriends*. Likewise the last action *greetingIs()* returns the personal greeting to be used when addressing a friend, stored in the class wide constant *PERSONAL_GREETING*. As these two actions are class wide, as opposed to instance, actions, they are shown in heavy lined boxes.

2.2 ▓ The first part of the implementation of the *Friend* class

The class diagram design above indicates that the class contains four private data attributes, a constructor and five other actions. In order to make the description of the source code more convenient each of these three sections will be presented and discussed in turn. The listing as far as the end of the declaration of the data attributes is as follows:

```
0001 // Filename Friend.java.
0002 // Second Java object written for
0003 // the JOF book chapter 2 - see text.
0004 //
0005 // Fintan Culwin, v0.1, August 1997.
0006
0007 public class Friend extends Object {
0008
0009 private String friendsName = null;
0010 private int    friendsAge  = 0;
0011
0012 private static int          numberOfFriends  = 0;
0013 private static final String PERSONAL_GREETING = "My Dear Friend";
```

The first five lines are the expected file header comments which are followed by the start of the declaration of the class, all of which are comparable with the two classes which were introduced in Chapter 1, differing only on line 0007 where *Friend* is stated to be an extension of the **Object** class. This is not technically necessary as all classes are automatically assumed to be extensions of the **Object** class unless otherwise stated. However, it is regarded as better style to indicate this explicitly rather than rely upon the reader of the class declaration having to remember it.

The two instance data attributes, *friendsName* and *friendsAge*, are declared on lines 0009 to 0010. They are both declared with the modifier **private** to indicate to Java that they are totally contained, or ***encapsulated***, within the class and cannot be seen by clients of the class. The first, *friendsName*, is declared to be an instance of the **String** class, as introduced in the previous chapter, but in this example it is not given a value as this is the responsibility of the constructor, as will be explained below. Instead its default value of **null** is explicitly stated. All instances of any class have a default value, identified as **null**, upon declaration.

The declaration of the instance attribute *friendsAge*, on line 0010, states that it is of the **int** type. Instances of the **int** type are technically not instances of a class but of a *primitive type*. Primitive types, which are part of the Java language, take less resources than class instances. Primitive **int**s are suitable for use where a numeric value, which has no decimal parts, needs to be stored. The final term, '=0', is not strictly required as all **int**s have the default value 0 when declared, unless a different value is specified. However, it is regarded as good style always to indicate the value upon declaration and not to rely upon the default. A fuller description of the properties of the primitive Java **int**eger types can be found in Appendix A1.

The declaration of the class wide attributes follows on lines 0012 and 0013. These are both declared with the modifier **private** for the same reasons as described above. They also both have the modifier **static** to indicate that they are class wide, as opposed to instance, attributes. The *PERSON_GREETING* attribute also has the modifier **final** to indicate that its value cannot be changed once it has been established in the declaration.

On line 0012 the *numberOfFriends* attribute is declared to be of the **int** type as it too will store a numeric value, with no decimal parts, recording the number of instances of the class which have been constructed, as will be described below. The final term, '=0', is not strictly required for the same reasons as described above for the *friendsAge* attribute.

The declaration of the *PERSON_GREETING* attribute on line 0013 indicates that it is an instance of the String class. As this declaration uses the **final** modifier it has to specify what its value is and, once specified upon declaration, it cannot be changed. The value is indicated by the String literal at the end of the line, as explained in the previous chapter.

The four declarations have been laid out to emphasize readability. It is not required that the instance attributes are separated from the class wide attributes by a blank line, nor that the names are aligned in a single column, nor that the initial values are likewise aligned. However, it is much easier to read the declarations if this convention is followed. The design of the constructor action is as follows:

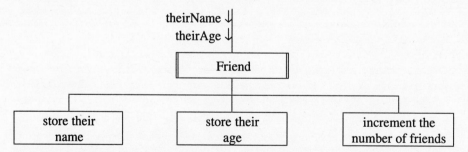

The design indicates that the constructor is a sequence of three activities, first to store *theirName*, then to store *theirAge* and finally to increment the count of the number of friends. The implementation of this design is as follows:

```
0015        public Friend( String theirName,
0016                       int    theirAge) {
0017
0018            friendsName = new String( theirName);
0019            friendsAge  = theirAge;
0020            numberOfFriends++;
0021        } // End Friend constructor.
```

The declaration of a constructor is very similar to the declaration of an action, but only a single modifier specifying its visibility, either **public** or **protected**, is allowed. In this example the constructor requires **public** visibility, in accord with its class diagram. The declaration continues with the name of the constructor which must be the same as the name of the class, in this example *Friend*. The signature of the constructor, on lines 0015 and 0016, indicates that it requires two arguments. The first is an instance of the String class and will be known as *theirName* within the constructor; the second is of type **int** and will be known as *theirAge*. When there is more than one argument in a signature they are separated by commas (,) as shown at the end of line 0015. Placing them on separate lines and aligning the names has been done to improve the readability of the listing.

The body of the constructor commences on line 0018 with the construction of a **new** String containing a copy of the contents of the String passed to the constructor in the *theirName* argument. When the *friendsName* attribute was declared on line 0009 it was noted that, unlike the Strings from the previous chapter, it was not given a value. Its value is specified here upon construction, using a similar technique to that used to specify String values in the previous chapter. The effect is that the *friendsName* attribute will contain a copy of the name passed as the first argument of the constructor.

The second line of the constructor, line 0019, initializes the value of the other instance attribute, *friendsAge*, by *assigning* the value of the **int** argument *theirAge* to it, replacing its default value. The line *friendsAge = theirAge* can be read as 'change the value of the variable *friendsAge* to whatever value is in the argument variable *theirAge*'. It is not necessary, or possible, to construct a **new int** instance as **int**s are, as noted above, of a primitive type and are not instances of a class which would require construction.

The final action of the constructor, on line 0020, is to increment by 1 the *numberOfFriends* class wide attribute. This is accomplished by use of the **int** *post increment operator* (++) described more fully in Appendix A1. The effect is to increase the integer value stored in *numberOfFriends* by 1 every time the constructor is used. So after the constructor has been called for the first time its value will change from 0 to 1, on the second time to 2, and so on.

At this stage only one of the instance actions will be implemented in order that the first part of the client demonstration program can be presented. The *friendsNameIs()* action is not sufficiently complex to require a design; its implementation is as follows:

```
0024      public String friendsNameIs() {
0025         return friendsName;
0026      } // End friendsNameIs.
```

This is comparable with the *theAnswerIs()* action from the previous chapter. It is implemented as a single **return** statement which supplies the *friendsName* instance attribute to a client.

2.3 ▧ The start of the demonstration client

Before continuing with the description of the implementation of the remaining *Friend* actions the first part of a demonstration client for it, and its output, will be presented. As with the *UltimateAnswer* class from the previous chapter the only purpose of the *FriendDemo* class is to supply a client program so that the actions of the *Friend* class can be demonstrated. The class diagram for the *FriendDemo* class would not differ significantly from that of the *UltimateAnswer* class and will not be presented here.

The *main()* client program action in this class is significantly more complex than the previous *main()* action. The first major difference is that in order to demonstrate and explain the nature of instance attributes and actions, two instances of the *Friend* class will be required. The instance diagram for this program is shown in Figure 2.2.

The diagram shows that the client program of the *FriendDemo* class will make use of two instances of the *Friend* class, called *myFriend* and *myOtherFriend*. The high level design of the *main()* action is as follows:

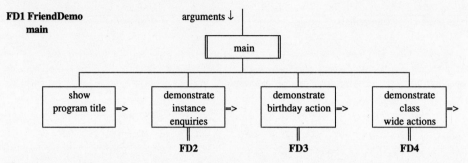

The title on this design indicates that it is the first of a series of designs for the *FriendDemo* (FD1) and that it describes the *main()* program action. The design indicates that the program is a sequence of four steps concerned with showing the program title, demonstrating the instance enquiry actions, demonstrating the birthday action and demonstrating the class wide actions. Each of the latter three of these steps is sufficiently complex to require its own design and these have been cross-referenced to this design as FD2 to FD4. A partial design of the *demonstrate instance enquiries* design stage is as follows:

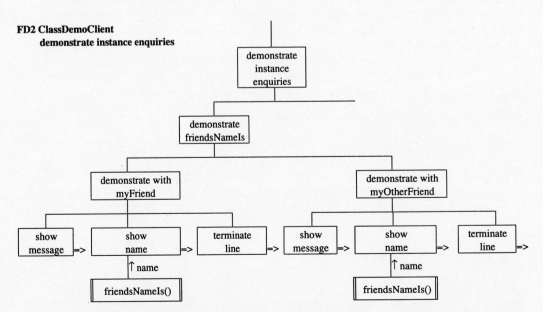

The design indicates that the first part of demonstrating the instance enquiry actions is to demonstrate the *friendsNameIs()* action. To do this it is first demonstrated with the

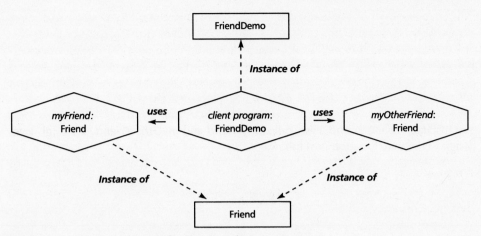

Figure 2.2 Instance diagram for the *FriendDemo* program.

MyFriend instance and then demonstrated with the *myOtherFriend* instance. Each of these demonstrations consists of showing a message, then showing the name which involves a call of the *friendsNameIs()* action and finally terminating the line of output on the screen. The implementation of the *FriendDemo* class as far as the end of this design fragment is as follows:

```
0001 // Filename FriendDemoClient.java.
0002 // Client program to demonstrate the Friend class.
0003 // Written for the JOF book chapter 2 – see text.
0004 //
0005 // Fintan Culwin, v0.1, August 1997.
0006
0007 import Friend;
0008
0009 public class FriendDemo {
0010
0011     public static void main( String args[]) {
0012
0013     Friend myFriend      = new Friend( "Arthur Dent",  32);
0014     Friend myOtherFriend = new Friend( "Ford Prefect", 45);
0015
0016         System.out.println( "\n\t\tThis is the Friend Demo Client\n");
0017
0018         System.out.print(   "Illustrating the friendsNameIs() ");
0019         System.out.println( "action of the myFriend instance.");
0020         System.out.print(   "The name should be Arthur Dent ... ");
0021         System.out.print(   myFriend.friendsNameIs());
0022         System.out.println( ".");
0023
0024
0025         System.out.print(   "\nIllustrating the friendsNameIs() ");
0026         System.out.println( "action of the myOtherFriend instance.");
0027         System.out.print(   "The name should be Ford Prefect ... ");
0028         System.out.print(   myOtherFriend.friendsNameIs());
0029         System.out.println( ".");
```

The first five lines of the listing are the expected header comments and are followed by the **import**ation of the *Friend* class on line 0007 before the required signature of the *main()* action on line 0011 is declared. On lines 0013 and 0014 two instances of the *Friend* class, called *myFriend* and *myOtherFriend*, are declared and constructed. The first term on each line, e.g. *Friend myFriend*, declares a variable which can designate an instance of the *Friend* class, but does not actually construct an instance of the class. This is accomplished by the remainder of the line, e.g. = **new** *Friend("ArthurDent", 35)*, which is a call of the constructor indicating that the name to be associated with this instance is *Arthur Dent* and that he is 35 years old. The second instance, *myOtherFriend*, is constructed with the details of *Ford Prefect* who is 45 years old.

Line 0016 implements the design stage *show program title*, using the System.out.println() action. The string argument which is supplied to this action contains a number of *formatting codes* which are included to make the output more acceptable to the user. Formatting codes consist of a backslash (\) followed by a single letter code: the **\n** code means output a *newline* at this point and the **\t** code means output a *tab*. So the argument to println() will be output as a newline, two tabs, *This is the Friend Demo Client* and a newline. This will be followed by an additional newline as the println() action is being used and the output will appear to the user as follows:

```
     This is the Friend Demo Client
```

Lines 0018 to 0022 implement the *demonstrate with myFriend* part of the *demonstrate friendsNameIs* design stage. Lines 0018 to 0020 implement the *show message* part of the design, indicating to the user what is happening and what should be seen next. Line 0021 implements the *show name* design stage by using the System.out.print() action which will output the String value returned from the *friendsNameIs()* action of the *myFriend* instance. The System.out.println() call on line 0022 completes this line of screen output by terminating it with a full stop.

If everything is working correctly then the constructor should have stored the name "Arthur Dent" in the *myFriend* instance, which should be returned by its *friendsNameIs()* action and output to the screen. The output produced by this client as far as this point in the listing is as follows:

```
                 This is the Friend Demo Client


     Illustrating the friendsNameIs() action of the myFriend instance.
     The name should be Arthur Dent ... Arthur Dent.
```

This seems to indicate that, so far, everything seems to be working correctly. Lines 0025 to 0029 are essentially identical to lines 0018 to 0022, but use the *friendsNameIs()* action of the *myOtherFriend* instance. This should retrieve and output the name "Ford Prefect"; the output from this part of the client indicated that it did so:

```
Illustrating the friendsNameIs() action of the myOtherFriend instance.
The name should be Ford Prefect ... Ford Prefect.
```

Taken together these two demonstrations indicate that each instance of the *Friend* class has its own *friendsName* attribute which is distinct from any *friendsName* attribute associated with any other instance of the class.

2.4 ▒ The remaining actions of the *Friend* class

The second instance enquiry action, *friendsAgeIs()*, is essentially identical to the *friendsNameIs()* action above, but it has to indicate that it returns a value of the **int** type and is implemented as a **return** of the *friendsAge* instance attribute:

```
0028       public int friendsAgeIs() {
0029          return friendsAge;
0030       }// End friendsAgeIs.
```

The final instance action, *birthday()*, does not have any data flow. Its purpose is to record the friend's birthday by incrementing the value of the *friendsAge* instance attribute by 1. Its implementation is as follows:

```
0033       public void birthday() {
0034          friendsAge++;
0035       } // End birthday.
```

The signature indicates by the use of empty brackets that the action requires no arguments and so has no data flow. The use of the reserved word **void** where the returned type, which would indicate an output data flow, would be indicates that there is no output data flow. The *friendsAge* attribute is incremented by 1, on line 0034, using the post-increment operator as described above.

The next action is the class wide enquiry action, *numberOfFriendsIs()*, which returns the value of the class wide *numberOfFriends()* attribute. It implementation is as follows:

```
0038       static public int numberOfFriendsIs() {
0039          return numberOfFriends;
0040       } // End numberOfFriendsIs
```

The signature of the action, on line 0038, starts with the word **static** which indicates that this is a class wide action. It is the absence of the **static** modifier which indicates that the previous actions are instance actions. The remaining parts of the action are essentially identical with the previous actions. The last action of the class, *greetingIs()*, contains no surprises, returning the value of the class wide constant *PERSONAL_GREETING*, and following its declaration the class declaration is concluded.

```
0042       static public String greetingIs() {
0043          return PERSONAL_GREETING;
0044       } // End greetingIs.
0045
0046       } // End Friend.
```

2.5 ▒ The completion of the *FriendDemo* class

The design of the missing part of the *demonstrate instance enquiries* actions, whose first part was presented above, is as follows:

FD2 ClassDemoClient
    demonstrate instance enquiries

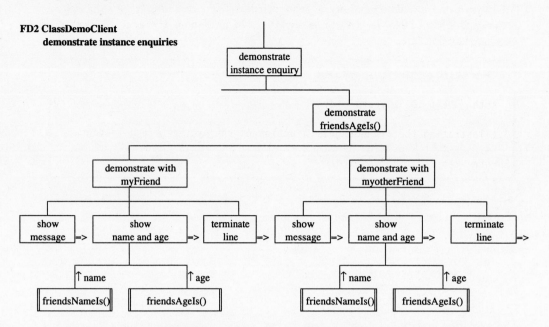

The design is comparable with the demonstrate *friendsNameIs()* above, demonstrating the use of the *friendsAgeIs()* instance actions with each of the *myFriend* and *myOtherFriend* instances. The *friendsNameIs()* action is called again, partly to make the output more meaningful and also to demonstrate that the previous call of *friendsNameIs()* has not changed the value of the attribute. The implementation of this design is as follows:

```
0031        System.out.print(    "\nIllustrating the friendsAgeIs() ");
0032        System.out.println( "action of the myFriend instance.");
0033        System.out.println( "Arthur Dent should be 32 years old ... ");
0034        System.out.print(    myFriend.friendsNameIs() +
0035                             " is "                    +
0036                             MyFriend.friendsAgeIs());
0037        System.out.println( " years old.");
0038
0039        System.out.print(    "\nIllustrating the friendsAgeIs() ");
0040        System.out.println( "action of the myOtherFriend instance.");
0041        System.out.println ( "Ford Prefect should be 45 years old ... ");
0042        System.out.print(    myOtherFriend.friendsNameIs() +
0043 .                           " is "                    +
0044                             myOtherFriend.friendsAgeIs());
0045        System.out.println( " years old.");
0046
```

On lines 0034 to 0036 a single System.out.println() action is used to output a sequence of items of data which are joined to each other by use of the String catenation operator (+). On line 0034 the *myFriend friendsNameIs()* action is used to obtain the name of *myFriend* as a String. On line 0035 this String is joined with the String "is" which itself is subsequently joined to the age returned by the *myFriend friendsAgeIs()* action. The *friendsAgeIs()* action returns an **int** value which, within the argument to a System.out.println() action call, is automatically converted to a String before catenation.

Lines 0042 to 0044 do the same for the *myOtherFriend* instance. The output produced by these steps is as follows:

```
Illustrating the friendsAgeIs() action of the myFriend instance.
Arthur Dent should be 32 years old ...
Arthur Dent is 32 years old.

Illustrating the friendsAgeIs() action of the myOtherFriend instance.
Ford Prefect should be 45 years old ...
Ford Prefect is 45 years old.
```

This seems to indicate that the actions are working correctly. The *demonstrate birthday action* part of the design is as follows:

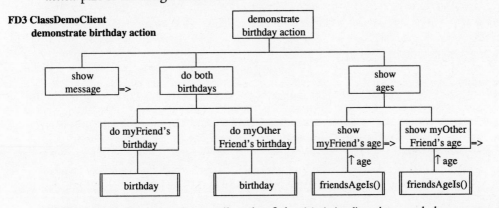

FD3 ClassDemoClient demonstrate birthday action

The basis of the design is to call each of the *birthday()* actions and then to use the *friendsNameIs()* action to demonstrate that the age recorded within the instance has increased by one year. The implementation of this design is as follows:

```
0047        System.out.print(   "\nIllustrating the birthday() actions");
0048        System.out.println( "of both instances.");
0049        myFriend.birthday();
0050        myOtherFriend.birthday();
0051        System.out.print(   "The ages should now be 33 and 46 ... ");
0052        System.out.print(   myFriend.friendsAgeIs() +
0053                            " "                      +
0054                            myOtherFriend.friendsAgeIs());
0055        System.out.println( ".");
```

Following the introductory message on lines 0047 and 0048, the *myFriend* and *myOtherFriend birthday()* actions are called on lines 0049 and 0050. The two *friendsAgeIs()* actions are called in the argument to the System.out.println() action on lines 0052 to 0054. The two **int** values returned from these calls are automatically converted to Strings and catenated together. The output from this fragment is as follows:

```
Illustrating the birthday() actions of both instances.
The ages should now be 33 and 46 ... 33 46.
```

The final design fragment is *demonstrate class wide actions*:

FD3 FriendDemo client
      demonstrate class wide actions

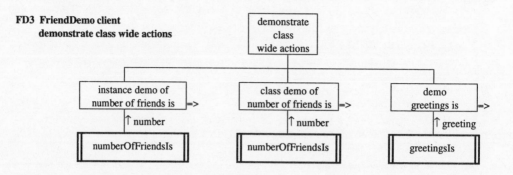

The design indicates that the *numberOfFriendsIs()* action will be demonstrated twice, once via an instance of the *Friends* class and once, class wide, via the *Friends* class. The *greetingIs()* action will be demonstrated once via a class wide action call. The use of bold boxes indicates that class wide, as opposed to instance, actions are being called. The implementation of this design is as follows.

```
0057        System.out.println( "\nIllustrating the class wide numberOfFriendsIs()");
0058        System.out.println( "action, called via the myFriend instance.");
0059        System.out.print(   "The value should be 2 ... ");
0060        System.out.print(   myFriend.numberOfFriendsIs());
0061        System.out.println( ".");
0062
0063        System.out.println( "\nIllustrating the class wide numberOfFriendsIs()");
0064        System.out.println( "action, called via the Friend class.");
0065        System.out.print(   "The value should be 2 ... ");
0066        System.out.print(   Friend.numberOfFriendsIs());
0067        System.out.println( ".");
0068
0069        System.out.println( "\nIllustrating the class wide greetingIs()");
0070        System.out.println( "action, called via the Friend class.");
0071        System.out.print(   "The greeting is ... ");
0072        System.out.print(   Friend.greetingIs());
0073        System.out.println( ".").
0074     } // End main.
0075
0076 } // End FriendDemo.
```

On line 0060 the class wide *numberOfFriendsIs()* action is called via the *Friend* instance *myFriend()*. As two instances of the *Friend* class have been previously constructed on lines 0013 and 0014, this should indicate that there are two instances of the *Friend* class in existence. On line 0066 the same action is called using the *Friend* class itself, not an instance of the class. This is only possible with class wide actions and it is usual for class wide actions to be called only in this way. The output from this call should still indicate that two *Friend* instances exist. The final demonstration is a class wide call of the *greetingIs()* action and, as this is a class constant enquiry action, it will always return the same greeting. The output from this fragment, completing the demonstration, is as follows:

```
Illustrating the class wide numberOfFriendsIs()
action, called via the myFriend instance.
The value should be 2 ... 2.

Illustrating the class wide numberOfFriendsIs()
action, called via the Friend class.
The value should be 2 ... 2.

Illustrating the class wide greetingIs()
action, called via the Friend class.
The greeting is ... My Dear Friend.
```

Summary

▨ Class declarations can include *data attributes* as well as actions.

▨ Actions can be *instance actions* or *class wide* actions.

▨ Class wide actions are usually called using the name of the class, instance actions are called using the name of an instance of the class.

▨ Data attributes can be *instance attributes*, *class attributes* or *class constants*.

▨ Every instance of a class has its own copy of instance attributes, but there is only one copy of class attributes or class constants per class.

▨ Data attributes are usually declared totally **private**.

▨ Constructors are used to place a class instance into a well defined initial state.

▨ Numeric values, without any decimal parts, can be represented by variables of the primitive **int** type.

Exercises

2.1 Return to the glossary which was produced in Exercise 1.1. Review the definitions of any terms which were introduced in Chapter 1 to see if your understanding has changed. Add the new terms from Chapter 2.

2.2 Adapt the client program developed in this chapter to make use of, and demonstrate, three instances of the *Friend* class.

2.3 Adapt the program from Exercise 2.2 so that a class wide call of the *numberOfFriendsIs()* action follows each call of the constructor. Output the value returned each time to demonstrate that it is actually counting the number of instances constructed.

2.4 Extend the *Friend* class so that it stores the phone number of the friend; this can be suitably represented as a String. Change the signature of the constructor to require a phone number and provide a *phoneNumberIs()* action. Make suitable changes to the *FriendDemo main()* action to demonstrate that the changes seem to be implemented correctly.

2.5 Find out what happens if a call of an instance action is made with a variable which does not yet designate a constructed instance. Then demonstrate that it is possible to use a class wide action without constructing an instance of the class.

2.6 A burger can be *meat*, *fish* or *vegetarian* and can be served with a *baked potato* or *french fries*. Design, implement and demonstrate a *Burger* class which encapsulates the *burgerKind* and *sideDish* attributes.

Chapter three

The start of the *Counters* class hierarchy

This chapter will introduce the construction of a collection of classes known as the Counters *class hierarchy*. This collection of classes will subsequently be built upon in the following two chapters to illustrate the development of a class's functionality by extension. *Development by extension* is probably the single most useful technique available to a developer, for reasons which will be explained below.

Although the concept of development by extension may initially seem very complex, it is fundamental to all that follows. Consequently it is important that the contents of these chapters are thoroughly assimilated before proceeding. Each chapter is divided into sections which present one step in the production of the hierarchy, and each section should be well understood before proceeding to the next. Having absorbed the contents of the sections and of each chapter the only way of ensuring that they are fully understood is to complete the exercises presented at the end of the chapters.

3.1 ▥ Class hierarchies

In a class hierarchy the eventual complexity of a class which will be used by a program client is built up in a number of stages. The intention is that although the eventual class will be complex, each of the classes from which it is built up will be relatively simple. It is easier to build a number of small simple classes than it would be to build a single complex class.

The second major reason for building a class hierarchy is that it is often the case that a number of closely related classes are required. If each of these were built as a single complex class then there would be much duplication between them. When the related classes are implemented as a class hierarchy then those aspects of the classes which are common can be implemented in the supporting classes and shared between the classes required by the clients.

Using a class hierarchy makes *debugging* easier. Software rarely works correctly when it is first compiled, and running the program will indicate that something is wrong. With a class hierarchy it is hoped that the symptoms will indicate which class in the hierarchy is faulty and, as the class is relatively simple, it should be easy to fix.

The initial version of a successful application is rarely the last version and either bugs which are not immediately apparent will be discovered or changes and enhancements will be required. The use of a class hierarchy will allow these *maintenance* changes to be more easily implemented. If additional functionality is required in an application then what is the final class in a class hierarchy can be used as a supporting class in an extended hierarchy whose new class, or classes, build upon the existing hierarchy.

Reuse is closely related to maintenance. It is often the case that a new application shares much in common with existing applications but differs in some respects. With a class hierarchy it is possible that some, or most, of the existing hierarchy can be used with the new application and only a few new classes need to be added. This can be taken one stage further and *repositories* of existing classes can be used as the starting point from which the development of an application should proceed.

3.2 ▩ The *Counters* class hierarchy

The hierarchy which will be used as an initial example in this, and the next, chapter is concerned with the implementation of a software model of a *mechanical click counter*. These devices consist of a digital display and two buttons. One button, the *reset* button, resets the counter to zero, and the other button, the *counting* button, will increment the value on the display by 1. These devices are sometimes used to count the number of people who are entering a building or the number of vehicles which are passing a particular point, events known as *occurrences*.

The functionality of the hierarchy which will be developed here extends this concept a little further, most obviously by the provision of an *uncounting* facility which will decrement the value. More significantly the behaviour of the counter at the limits of its range will be modelled in three different ways. Most mechanical counters are limited to three digits and can count from 000 to 999. If the *counting* button is pressed when the counter is displaying 999 the value displayed will *roll over* back to 000. It is also possible that pressing the counting button at this stage might have no effect upon the display or might give some kind of warning that the occurrence has not been counted.

The three different possibilities, known as the *RollOverCounter* class, the *StoppingCounter* class and the *WarningCounter* class respectively, will share two common supporting classes. The simplest class, known as the *BasicCounter* class, will supply the ability to count and uncount occurrences without any obvious limits on its range. An extension to this class, known as the *LimitedCounter* class, will place a limit upon the range of values which can be counted but will not enforce them in any way. The relationships between the five classes can be illustrated by a *class hierarchy diagram*; the diagram for the *Counters* classes is given in Figure 3.1.

The *root* of the hierarchy is the *BasicCounter* class and it has a single *child class* called *LimitedCounter*. Correspondingly the *BasicCounter* class is known as the *parent class* of the *LimitedCounter* class. Both of these classes are never intended to be used directly by a client program and this is indicated by the dotted box. The three child classes of the *LimitedCounter* class (*RollOverCounter*, *StoppingCounter* and *WarningCounter*) are shown in solid boxes as they are intended to be used directly by

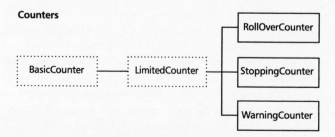

Figure 3.1   The *Counters* class hierarchy diagram.

clients. The parent relationship is transitive, so the *LimitedCounter* class is the parent of the three non-abstract classes as, under some considerations, is the *BasicCounter* class.

All five of these classes, and any other counting classes which might be added in the future, are collected together in a **package** called *Counters*. This is indicated on the top left hand corner of the diagram. This chapter will introduce the *BasicCounter* and *LimitedCounter* classes; the following chapter will introduce the three remaining classes.

3.3 ▨ The design of the *BasicCounter* class

The intention of the *BasicCounter* class is to provide fundamental counting behaviour to its child classes. To achieve this the class will have to provide methods which can *count()* an occurrence, *unCount()* an occurrence and inform other classes how many occurrences it has counted. Additionally it will have to be constructed to allow its child classes to set the number of occurrences counted to an arbitrary value and to *reset()* the counter to its initial state. This is summarized in the *BasicCounter* class diagram shown in Figure 3.2.

The diagram identifies the class being designed as *BasicCounter* and it also indicates that it is an extension of the Java **Object** class. The dotted lines used to define the limits of the class indicate that this is an abstract class, in accord with the class hierarchy diagram presented in Figure 3.1

The resources shown on the right of the diagram are regarded as being fully public and can be seen, and used, by any clients of this class. The resources shown on the left of the diagram are regarded as being only partially public, known as **protected**. Protected resources can only be seen, and used, by a defined set of clients, most usually only those classes which are descended from the class. Any components shown totally enclosed within the diagram are regarded as being totally private to the class and are the sole concern of the class being designed. It is not required that the class is actually implemented using these private components; they might only be shown in order to help a client developer's understanding of the class.

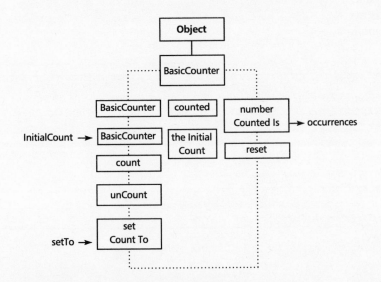

Figure 3.2   The *BasicCounter* class diagram.

The first protected action is a constructor, identified as such by having the same name as the class being designed. The purpose of a constructor is to create an instance of the class and initialize it into a well defined state. The constructor takes a single (**integer**) argument shown as *initialCount*, and will set the newly constructed object to a state where it has counted *initialCount* occurrences.

The next two protected actions will *count()* and *unCount()* an occurrence respectively. This is followed by the last partially private action called *setCountTo()* which requires a single argument: an integer called *setTo*. This action can be used by a child class to set the number of occurrences counted to the value of *setTo*.

The first public action is an enquiry action called *numberCountedIs()* which will inform a client of the current number of occurrences counted. Public actions of a class are inherited as public actions of all its child classes. Thus the abstract *LimitedCounter* class on the class hierarchy diagram, and the three non-abstract classes, will all make a public *numberCountedIs* action available to their clients. The remaining public action, *reset()*, will restore the counter to its initial state.

The private component *counted* suggests to a developer reading this diagram that the class contains a single data attribute which is used to store the value of the number of occurrences counted. The other private attribute, *theInitialCount*, is used by the *reset()* action to restore the counter to its initial state. The full reasoning for all these design decisions will only become apparent when the entire hierarchy is reviewed at the end of the next chapter.

3.4 ▓ The implementation of the *BasicCounter* class

The implementation of this design as a Java class file might be as follows:

```
0001  // Filename Counters/BasicCounter.java.
0002  // Root class of the Counters hierarchy providing the
0003  // essential counting functionality.
0004  //
0005  // Written for JOF book Chapter 3.
0006  // Fintan Culwin, v0.1, August 1997.
0007
0008  package Counters;
0009
0010  abstract class BasicCounter {
0011
0012  private int counted        =0;
0013  private int theInitialCount =0;
0014
0015     protected BasicCounter( int initialCount) {
0016        counted          = initialCount;
0017        theInitialCount = initialCount;
0018     } // End alternative constructor.
0019
0020     protected BasicCounter() {
0021        this( 0);
0022     } // End default constructor.
0023
0024     protected void count() {
0025        counted++;
```

```
0026      } // End count.
0027
0028      protected void unCount() {
0029         counted--;
0030      } // End unCount.
0031
0032      protected void setCountTo( int setTo) {
0033         counted = setTo;
0034      } // End setCountTo.
0035
0036      public void reset() {
0037         counted = theInitialCount;
0038      } // End numberCountedIs.
0039
0040      public int numberCountedIs() {
0041         return counted;
0042      } // End numberCountedIs.
0043
0044 } // End BasicCounter
```

Lines 0001 to 0007 contain the expected header comments and line 0008 identifies this class as belonging to the **package** of classes collectively known as *Counters*. This is the reason for the filename being stated as *Counters/BasicCounter.java*; all the files containing the class definitions of the *Counters* package have to be collected together in a subdirectory of a default directory called *Counters*. The default directory is usually the current working directory, although it might sometimes be a different directory depending upon the configuration of the development environment.

Lines 0010 to 0044 encompass the declaration of the *BasicCounter* class. It is declared as an **abstract class** as the class hierarchy diagram shows it in a dotted lined box, indicating that it will only be used as the parent of an extended class and will never be used directly by a client. It is not declared as a **public** class to ensure that it is fully hidden within the package and is thus totally invisible to clients of the package but visible to its child classes.

The first declaration of the class is of the data attribute *counted*. The value of this attribute will always indicate the number of occurrences which have been counted and, as only a whole number of occurrences can be counted, it is declared as an **int**eger. It is declared as having **private** visibility so that it can only be seen and used within the limits of the class definition. Thus clients can only obtain or change its value by use of the supplied actions. The *theInitialCount* attribute, declared on line 0013, is likewise **private** and **int**. Both of these attributes are initialized to 0 upon declaration, which would be their default value if no initial value was specified, for reasons explained in the previous chapter.

The constructor is declared on lines 0015 to 0018 and is declared with **protected** visibility to allow it only to be used by the child classes of *BasicCounter* in accord with its class diagram. It is implemented as a sequence of two assignment statements which takes the value passed in its argument, *initialCount*, and assigns it to the two hidden data attributes *counted* and *theInitialCount*. The reasons for this will be explained below.

Lines 0020 to 0022 declare a constructor which requires no arguments and because of this it is known as the *default constructor*, as it will be called automatically by default if no explicit constructor is specified when an instance is created. It is implemented as a call of the previously declared constructor, which requires a single argument. This constructor is known as an alternative constructor, to distinguish it from the default constructor. The keyword **this** in the default constructor indicates the class instance currently being constructed and the single supplied argument indicates that the alternative constructor should be used. This is known as an *indirecting* call of the alternative constructor. It is possible for more than one alternative constructor to be supplied by a class, as will be illustrated below.

The *count()* and *unCount()* actions are implemented in similar ways. Both are declared **protected**, allowing only *BasicCounter*'s child classes to see and use them, and both are declared as actions of type **void**, which indicates that they will not return any information to the client which calls them. Line 0025 is interpreted to mean *increment* (++) the value of the variable *counted* by 1, thus counting an occurrence. Similarly line 0029 means *decrement* (−−) the value of *counted* by 1, thus uncounting an occurrence.

The last **protected** action, *setCountTo()*, is likewise declared **protected** and **void**. It is implemented in a similar manner to the alternative constructor, assigning the value of its argument, *setTo*, to the private variable *counted*. The effect is to set the number of occurrences counted to whatever is the value of the argument supplied.

The **public** *reset()* action, declared on lines 0036 to 0038, restores the counter to its initial state by assigning the value of the *theInitialCount()* attribute to the *counted* attribute. Thus the number of occurrences counted will be changed to the initial value which was specified when the instance was constructed.

The final action, *numberCountedIs()*, will return information to the client which makes use of it. As it is returning the number of occurrences counted, which is an integer value it is declared as an action which returns an **int** value. It does this by **return**ing the value of the private *counted* variable. This action will be inherited as a **public** action by all the descendant classes of this class, and so all non-abstract *Counters* will offer this action to their clients.

A summary of all these actions is illustrated in Figure 3.3. The illustration shows the data attributes totally enclosed within the boundaries of the *BasicCounter* class and the value of *counted* being accessed and changed by the actions which are provided by the class definition. The dotted line connecting the default constructor, *BasicCounter()*, at the top left of the diagram with the alternative constructor, *BasicCounter()*, at the top right indicates that the default constructor is implemented within the class as a call of the alternative constructor. The *reset()* action, on the left of the diagram, accesses the value of *theInitialCount* attribute passing its value into the counted attribute.

3.5 ▨ Demonstrating the *BasicCounter* class

It is important to demonstrate that the *BasicCounter* class appears to be working correctly at this stage, before it is extended into the *LimitedCounter* class. (Actually this is not sufficient; it is vital to *test* the implementation formally rather than merely demonstrate it. The processes involved in *testing* rather than merely *demonstrating* will be introduced in Chapter 11.) However, as this is a non-public **abstract** class it is not possible for a client to declare an instance of the class in order to subject it to demonstration. The solution to this problem is temporarily to make the class **public** and *non*-**abstract**, demonstrate it, and then change it back to an **abstract** implementation.

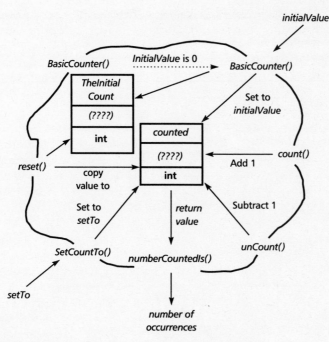

Figure 3.3   An illustration of the *BasicCounter* class.

To accomplish this the declaration of the class should be changed from:

```
0010 abstract class BasicCounter {
```

to:

```
0010 public class BasicCounter {
```

All the **protected** actions will also have to be declared **public** in order that the demonstration client can access them. For example, the first line of the *count()* action will have to be changed from:

```
0024 protected void count() {
```

to:

```
0024 public void count() {
```

The demonstration client will have to ensure that all actions declared in the class are used at least once. An initial design for the demonstration client might be as follows:

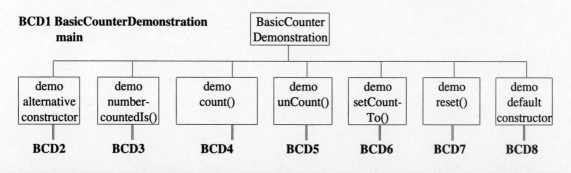

The detailed design of the component *Demo alternative constructor* might be as follows:

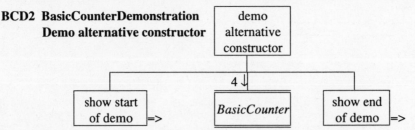

**BCD2 BasicCounterDemonstration
          Demo alternative constructor**

The implementation of this part of the design, and the preceding declarations, might be as follows:

```
0001 // Filename BasicCounterDemonstration.java.
0002 // Demonstration harness for the (temporarily)
0003 // amended BasicCounter class.
0004 //
0005 // Written for JOF book Chapter 3.
0006 // Fintan Culwin, v0.1, August 1997.
0007
0008 import Counters.BasicCounter;
0009
0010 class BasicCounterDemonstration {
0011
0012    public static void main( String argv[]) {
0013
0014    BasicCounter  aCounter;
0015
0016       System.out.println( "\n\n\t Basic Counter Demonstration");
0017
0018       System.out.print( "\n\nConstructing an instance with ");
0019       System.out.println( "the inital value 4.");
0020       aCounter = new BasicCounter( 4);
0021       System.out.print( "Instance created ... ");
```

Lines 0001 to 0006 contain the header comments; the filename does not contain a path component indicating that this file could be located in the parent directory of the *Counters* subdirectory although it would probably be more convenient to store it in the *Counters* directory. Line 0008 imports the *BasicCounters* class from the *Counters* package, and line 0010 declares the client program class, *BasicCounterDemonstration*, which contains a single *main()* action with the required signature, declared on line 0012.

Line 0014 declares a variable reference for an instance of the *BasicCounter* class called *aCounter*. This declaration does not create an instance of the class, merely a variable which can be initialized to **denote** an instance when it is subsequently created with a call of a constructor. If any attempt is made to use this variable as if it already denoted an instance, before the instance is constructed, a run-time exception will be raised.

Line 0016 outputs a title for the program and lines 0018 to 0021 implement the design fragment given above. The *BasicCounter* instance is created on line 0020 using the **new** keyword combined with a call of the alternative constructor, and the value of the variable *aCounter* is initialized to denote it. The argument to the call of the constructor indicates to Java that the alternative constructor should be used, not the default constructor which does not require an argument. The output of this part of the program should be as follows:

```
Basic Counter Demonstration

Constructing an instance with the initial value 4.
Instance created ...
```

This seems to demonstrate that the alternative constructor is working; if there were any major problems then a run-time error would have been reported. The real demonstration that it has worked correctly would be to retrieve the value of the *aCounter* object and show that it has been correctly initialized to 4. The next part of the demonstration does this:

BCD3 BasicCounterDemonstration
Demonstrate Number Counted Is

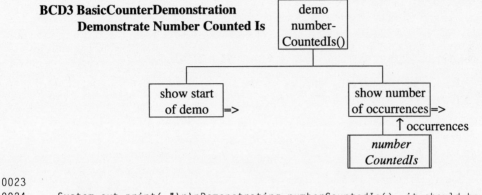

```
0023
0024        System.out.print( "\n\nDemonstrating numberCountedIs(), it should be 4 ... ");
0025        System.out.println( aCounter.numberCountedIs());
0026
```

The implementation of this design fragment involves the use of the System.out.println() action, outputting the value which is returned from the *aCounter* object when its *numberCountedIs()* action is used. The output from this fragment should be:

```
Demonstrating numberCountedIs(), it should be 4 ... 4
```

The next two demonstrations involve the *count()* and *unCount()* actions; their design, implementation and output are similar to that of the *numberCountedIs()* action:

BCD4 BasicCounterDemonstration   **BCD5 BasicCounterDemonstration**
Demonstrate Count   **Demonstrate unCount**

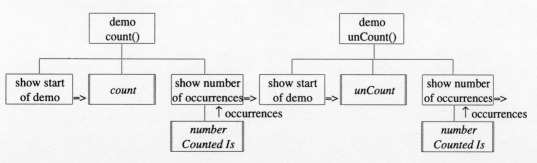

```
0028          System.out.println( "\n\nDemonstrating count().");
0029          aCounter.count();
0030          System.out.print( "Showing the changed value, it should be 5 ... ");
0031          System.out.println( aCounter.numberCountedIs());
0032
0033          System.out.println( "\n\nDemonstrating unCount(). ");
0034          aCounter.unCount();
0035          System.out.print( "Showing the changed value, it should be 4 ... ");
0036          System.out.println( aCounter.numberCountedIs());
```

```
Demonstrating count().
Showing the changed value, it should be 5 ... 5


Demonstrating unCount().
Showing the changed value, it should be 4 ... 4
```

The next part of the demonstration illustrates the *setCountTo()* action:

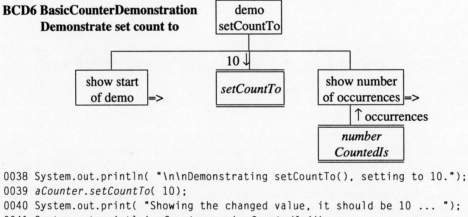

BCD6 BasicCounterDemonstration
     Demonstrate set count to

```
0038 System.out.println( "\n\nDemonstrating setCountTo(), setting to 10.");
0039 aCounter.setCountTo( 10);
0040 System.out.print( "Showing the changed value, it should be 10 ... ");
0041 System.out.println( aCounter.numberCountedIs());
```

```
Demonstrating setCountTo(), setting to 10.
Showing the changed value, it should be 10 ... 10
```

The next demonstration is of the *reset()* action; the design, implementation and output of this part is as follows:

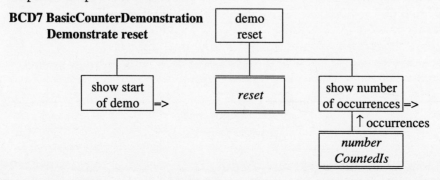

BCD7 BasicCounterDemonstration
     Demonstrate reset

```
0043          System.out.println( "\n\nDemonstrating reset().");
0044          aCounter.reset();
0045          System.out.print( "Showing the reset value, it should be 4 ... ");
0046          System.out.println( aCounter.numberCountedIs());
```

```
Demonstrating reset().
Showing the reset value, it should be 4 ... 4
```

As the instance was constructed with an initial value of 4 resetting the value restores this value, as shown. The final part of the demonstration involves the use of the default constructor, inherited from the **Object** class, which requires a second instance of the *BasicCounter* to be created:

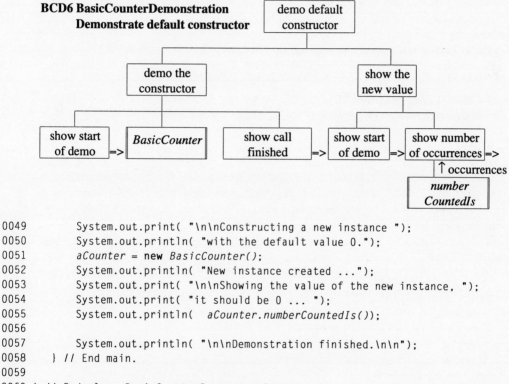

BCD6 BasicCounterDemonstration
Demonstrate default constructor

```
0049          System.out.print( "\n\nConstructing a new instance ");
0050          System.out.println( "with the default value 0.");
0051          aCounter = new BasicCounter();
0052          System.out.println( "New instance created ...");
0053          System.out.print( "\n\nShowing the value of the new instance, ");
0054          System.out.print( "it should be 0 ... ");
0055          System.out.println( aCounter.numberCountedIs());
0056
0057          System.out.println( "\n\nDemonstration finished.\n\n");
0058    } // End main.
0059
0060 } // End class BasicCounterDemonstration.
```

In this code fragment the absence of an argument to the call of the constructor, *BasicCounter*, on line 0051, indicates to Java that the default constructor, which does not reset the number of occurrences counted from its default value of 0, should be used and not the alternative constructor which requires an argument.

```
Constructing a new instance with the default value 0.
New instance created ...
Showing the value of the new instance, it should be 0 ... 0


Demonstration finished.
```

When the new instance is constructed on line 0051, the existing instance is known by Java to be no longer required and will be destroyed in due course, a process known as *garbage collection*. Having completed the demonstration the source code of the *BasicCounter* should be changed back to make the actions **protected** and the class **abstract**.

3.6 ■ The design of the *LimitedCounter* class

The process of producing the *LimitedCounter* class follows that used for the *BasicCounter* class. The first stage is to produce a class diagram, from which its implementation can be derived, and then a demonstration harness used to verify that it operates correctly. The *LimitedCounter* class introduces into the hierarchy limits upon the range of values which the counter can count between, although it does not enforce these limits.

The class diagram for the *LimitedCounter* class is shown in Figure 3.4. This diagram indicates that the class will contain four data attributes. The first two of these, *DEFAULT_MINIMUM* and *DEFAULT_MAXIMUM*, are shown in bold boxes and the capitalization indicates that they are class constants. The next two data attributes, *minimumCount* and *maximumCount* are shown in normal boxes indicating that they are instance variables.

If the first constructor, without any arguments, is used then the range which the *LimitedCounter* will count through will be the range of values between *DEFAULT_MINIMUM* and *DEFAULT_MAXIMUM*. However, if the second constructor is used then the client must supply values for the limits of the range. In all situations the range of values which a particular counter instance will count between are stored in its instance variables *minimumCount* and *maximumCount*.

The two constructor actions are **protected** and are only intended to be used by this class's children. The remaining actions are **public** and will be inherited by all the child classes developed by extension. The first two **public** actions are **boolean** enquiry

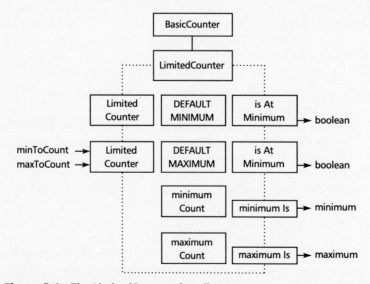

Figure 3.4   The *LimitedCounter* class diagram.

actions which will return **true** if the number of occurrences counted is at the minimum or maximum of its range respectively. If the counter is not at the minimum or maximum of its range then the actions will respectively return **false**. The last two actions will inform a client of the value of the minimum and maximum of the range respectively.

3.7 ▨ The implementation of the *LimitedCounter* class

The first part of the implementation, as far as the end of the constructors, is as follows:

```
0001 // Filename Counters/LimitedCounter.java.
0002 // First extension of the Counters hierarchy defining
0003 // limits upon the range of values which can be counted.
0004 //
0005 // Written for JOF book Chapter 3.
0006 // Fintan Culwin, v0.1, August 1997.
0007
0008 package Counters;
0009
0010 abstract class LimitedCounter extends BasicCounter {
0011
0012 static private final int DEFAULT_MINIMUM = 0;
0013 static private final int DEFAULT_MAXIMUM = 999;
0014
0015 private int minimumCount;
0016 private int maximumCount;
0017
0018
0019    protected LimitedCounter( int minToCount, int  maxToCount){
0020        super( minToCount);
0021        minimumCount = minToCount;
0022        maximumCount = maxToCount;
0023    }  // End alternative Constructor.
0024
0025    protected LimitedCounter(){
0026        this( DEFAULT_MINIMUM, DEFAULT_MAXIMUM);
0027    } //  End Default Constructor.
```

Following the header comments, line 0008 indicates that this class is a member of the *Counters* package of classes, and line 0010 that this file contains an extension of the *BasicCounter* class called *LimitedCounter*. As an extension of the *BasicCounter* class this class has access to all the **public** and **protected** resources of that class. However, it has no direct access to the **private** resources of its parent class.

Lines 0012 and 0013 declare the two class constants *DEFAULT_MINIMUM* and *DEFAULT_MAXIMUM*. The modifier **static** indicates that they are class wide, **private** hides them entirely within this class, **final** that they are constants and **int** that they store a primitive integer value. As they are declared as **final** it is essential that a value is assigned to them as they are declared, and once assigned this value can never be changed.

Lines 0015 and 0016 declare the two instance variables *minimumCount* and *maximumCount* in a manner which is directly comparable with the declaration of the instance variables *counted* and *theInitialCount* in the *BasicCounter* class above. An instance of the *LimitedCounter* class will contain its own *counted*, *theInitialCount*, *minimumCount* and *maximumCount* data attributes. However, as the *counted* and *theInitialCount* variables are **private** to the *BasicCounter* class, the *counted* attribute can only be accessed from the implementation of the *LimitedCounter* class via the **public** and **protected** actions of the *BasicCounter* class. The *theInitialCount* attribute cannot be accessed by any action, but can be used indirectly by calling the *reset()* action which transfers its value to the *counted* attribute.

An alternative constructor is declared on lines 0019 to 0023; it takes two arguments *minToCount* which defines the lower limit of the range which it will count and *maxToCount* which defines the upper limit. Its first action is to call the alternative constructor of its parent class, passing the *minToCount* value as the argument. In order to access the constructor of its parent the **super** reserved word is used. Just as the **this** keyword always indicates the current instance which is being declared, the **super** reserved word indicates the instance of the parent class which is considered a component part of the current instance being extended.

Having called the *BasicCounter* constructor it then completes the initialization of the *LimitedCounter* instance by storing the value of its *minToCount* argument in the *minimumCount* attribute and the *maxToCount* argument in the *maximumCount* attribute. The default constructor takes no arguments and is implemented as a call of the alternative constructor passing the values of the class variables *DEFAULT_MINIMUM* and *DEFAULT_MAXIMUM* as the arguments. The effect is to construct an instance which will count between the values of the class constants, 0 and 999.

The implementation of the two **boolean** enquiry actions is as follows:

```
0032      public boolean isAtMinimum() {
0033          return this.numberCountedIs() == minimumCount;
0034      } // End isAtMinimum.
0035
0036      public boolean isAtMaximum() {
0037          return this.numberCountedIs() == maximumCount;
0038      } // End isAtMaximum.
```

The implementation of the *isAtMinimum()* action on line 0033 uses the *BasicCounter* *numberCountedIs()* action to determine the number of occurrences counted. It is not possible for this implementation to access the value of the instance variable *counted* directly as it is totally **private** to the *BasicCounter* class. As an instance of the *LimitedCounter* class *is a*n extended instance of the *BasicCounter* class it can access the *numberCountedIs()* action using **this** rather than **super**. The value obtained from the *numberCountedIs()* action is compared with the value of the *minimumCount* instance variable using the *is equal to* operator (==). This comparison can only be **true** or **false**; if the number of occurrences counted is equal to the limit of the range then the comparison will be **true** and **false** in all other cases. The value of this comparison is **return**ed as the value of the action. Objects of type **boolean** can only have the value **true** or **false**, as will be fully explained in the following chapters and summarized in Appendix A3.

The *isAtMaximum()* action is implemented in an almost identical manner. The implementation of the two enquiry actions, *minimumIs()* and *maximumIs()*, is as follows:

```
0041      public int minimumIs() {
0042          return minimumCount;
0043      } // End minimumIs .
```

```
0044
0045    public int maximumIs() {
0046       return maximumCount;
0047    } // End maximumIs.
0048
0049 } End LimitedCounter.
```

These actions are implemented in a similar manner to the *BasicCounter numberCountedIs()* actions, returning the value of the **private** attributes to the client. A visualization of the implementation of this class is given in Figure 3.5.

This diagram shows both constructors and only the *minimumIs()* and *isAtMinimum()* actions. The *maximumIs()* and *isAtMaximum* actions are essentially identical and have been omitted for the sake of clarity.

The dotted lines in this diagram indicate that an action in the same class is being used. For example, the default constructor at the top left of the diagram calls the alternative constructor, passing the values of the class constants *DEFAULT_MINIMUM* and *DEFAULT_MAXIMUM* as arguments.

A dotted box within the diagram indicates a call of an action supplied by the *BasicCounter* class. For example, the *isAtMinimum()* action makes use of the *numberCounterIs()* action, comparing the value returned from this action with the value of the *minimumIs()* action

3.8 ▒ Demonstrating the *LimitedCounter* class

As with the demonstration of the *BasicCounter* class, the *LimitedCounter* class will have to be temporarily implemented as a **public** non-**abstract** class with **public** methods. Only a partial demonstration of the *LimitedCounter* class, without a design,

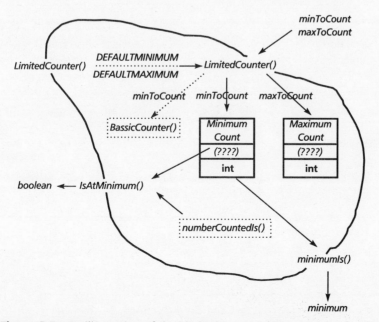

Figure 3.5   An illustration of the *LimitedCounter* class.

will be presented here. A full demonstration, and the production of designs for it, will be left as an end-of-chapter exercise.

The first part of the demonstration client, as far as the output of the title and the creation of a *LimitedCounter* instance, might be as follows:

```
0001 // Filename LimitedCounterDemonstration.java.
0002 // Demonstration harness for the (temporarily)
0003 // amended LimitedCounter class.
0004 //
0005 // Written for JOF book Chapter 3.
0006 // Fintan Culwin, v0.1, August 1997.
0007
0008 import Counters.LimitedCounter;
0009
0010 class LimitedCounterDemonstration {
0011
0012    public static void main( String argv[]) {
0013
0014    LimitedCounter aCounter;
0015
0016       System.out.println( "\n\n\t Limited Counter Demonstration");
0017
0018       System.out.print( "\n\nConstructing an instance with the");
0019       System.out.println( "range 10 to 12.");
0020       aCounter = new LimitedCounter( 10, 12);
0021       System.out.print( "Instance created ...");
```

This fragment is directly comparable with the first part of the *BasicCounterDemonstration* client. The **import** clause on line 0008 need only import the *LimitedCounter* class as it is an extension of the *BasicCounter* class and this allows access to the **public** aspects of the *BasicCounter* class, without the necessity of having to **import** it explicitly. The call of the alternative constructor on line 0020 has to specify the lower and upper limits of the range and in order to simplify the demonstration these delineate a very small range between 10 and 12. The output of this part of the client should be as follows:

```
          Limited Counter Demonstration


Constructing an instance with the range 10 to 12.
Instance created ...
```

The next part of the client demonstrates the *minimumIs()* action. Its implementation and output are as follows:

```
0023          System.out.print( "\nDemonstrating minimumIs(), ");
0024          System.out.print( "it should be 10 ... ");
0025          System.out.println( aCounter.minimumIs());
```

```
Demonstrating minimumIs(), it should be 10 ... 10
```

The implementation of this fragment and the output should be familiar from the previous demonstration. The next part of the client demonstrates the *numberCountedIs()* and *isAtMinimum()* actions:

```
0027          System.out.print( "\n\nDemonstrating numberCountedIs(), ");
0028          System.out.print( "it should be 10 ... ");
0029          System.out.println( aCounter.numberCountedIs());
0030
0031          System.out.print( "\n\nDemonstrating isAtMinimum(), ");
0032          System.out.print( "it should be true ... ");
0033          System.out.println( aCounter.isAtMinimum());
```

```
Demonstrating numberCountedIs(), it should be 10 ... 10


Demonstrating isAtMinimum(), it should be true ... true
```

The call on line 0029 of the *BasicCounter numberCountedIs()* action is permissible as the *LimitedCounter* instance denoted by *aCounter is a*n extended instance of the *BasicCounter* class and thus inherits all of its **public** actions as **actions**.

The call of the *LimitedCounter isAtMinimum()* action on line 0033 returns a value of type **boolean**. This value is immediately output by the System.out.println() action which will output "true" if the value is **true** and "false" if it is **false**. As shown on the output the value at this stage of the demonstration is true. This is the expected output as the previous call of *numberCountedIs()* indicates that 10 occurrences have been counted and the call of *minimumIs()* indicates that 10 is the minimum value of the range.

Summary

- *Class hierarchies* are used to construct a complex object in a number of simpler stages.

- Class hierarchies make construction, debugging and maintenance easier and encourage reuse.

- Every class in a hierarchy has only one *parent class*, but a class can have any number of *child classes*.

- A child class is an extension of its parent and inherits all of its parent's resources.

- Classes in a hierarchy can be abstract or non-abstract; clients of the hierarchy can only instantiate objects from non-abstract classes. Abstract classes are only used as the foundation of non-abstract classes.

- All the classes in a hierarchy should be collected together in a package of classes.

- Classes have **public**, **private** and **protected** resources: **private** resources are totally invisible outside the class, **protected** resources are only visible to child classes and **public** resources are totally visible.

- Classes are designed using a class diagram which shows the **public** resources on the right, the **protected** resources on the left and may show its **private** resources in the middle.

- Classes themselves can be **protected** or **public**; only **public** classes are visible outside the package.

- A child class can only access the **private** resources of its parent by using the **protected** or **private** actions.

- A class hierarchy should be constructed in stages by building a class and demonstrating that it seems to work before continuing with the next class in the hierarchy.

Exercises

3.1 Produce the design of the partial *LimitedCounterDemonstration* client.

3.2 Complete the design and implementation of the *LimitedCounter* demonstration.

3.3 Design a class hierarchy for Noah, whose click counter as he counted the animals into the ark incremented by 2 every time he pressed it.

3.4 A specialized vehicle counter is required which counts 1 for every motorcycle which passes, 2 for every car, 5 for every bus and 10 for every van. Include this class, called *GreenVehicleCounter*, into the class hierarchy.

3.5 Revisit the *Friend* class in Chapter 2 and implement it as a *Friends* hierarchy by isolating the two data attributes into two classes. Use the same demonstration client from the chapter to demonstrate the equivalence of the two implementations.

3.6 Extend the hierarchy from Exercise 3.5 by adding two sibling classes, one which contains a phone number to contact the friend and one which contains their e-mail address. Extend the demonstration client to demonstrate each of these classes.

Chapter four

The completion of the *Counters* hierarchy

In this chapter the class hierarchy which was introduced in Chapter 3 will be completed. Each of the three non-abstract classes, the *RollOverCounter*, *StoppingCounter* and *WarningCounter* classes, will be designed, implemented, described and demonstrated.

In order to implement actions in all three of these classes a mechanism for a Java program to make a decision will have to be introduced. For example, in the *RollOverCounter* class the *count()* action will have to decide between simply counting an occurrence, if the counter is not at the maximum of its range, or resetting it to the minimum of its range, if it is at its maximum. This ability of a program fragment to make a decision is known as a *selection* and is fundamental to constructing programs with seemingly intelligent behaviour.

This also implies that the *RollOver()* class will have to declare its own *count()* action which will replace the *count()* action inherited from the *BasicCounter* class. This is known as action *overriding* and is an essential part of development by extension.

The brief description of the *WarningClass* in Chapter 3 stated that it would issue a warning if an attempt were made to count above or below its range. The mechanism to issue such a warning is known as *throwing an exception*, and is a necessary technique to the production of very robust software artefacts.

4.1 ▧ The design and implementation of the *RollOverCounter* class

The object diagram for the *RollOverCounter* class is given in Figure 4.1.

The diagram shows that the *RollOverCounter* class is an extension of the *LimitedCounter* class, that it has two public constructors which are comparable with the protected constructors of the *LimitedCounter* class and that it has two actions called *count()* and *unCount()*. The implementation of this design as far as the end of the two constructors is as follows:

```
0001 // Filename Counters/RollOverCounter.java.
0002 // Providing a non-abstract counter class with
0003 // roll over behaviour.
0004 //
0005 // Written for JOF book Chapter 4 see text.
0006 // Fintan Culwin, v0.1, August 1997.
0007
0008 package Counters;
```

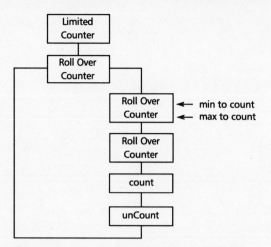

Figure 4.1   The *RollOverCounter* class diagram.

```
0009
0010 public class RollOverCounter extends LimitedCounter {
0011
0012     public RollOverCounter() {
0013         super();
0014     } // End default Constructor.
0015
0016     public RollOverCounter( int minToCount, int maxToCount) {
0017         super( minToCount, maxToCount);
0018     } // End principal Constructor.
0019
```

The header comments, package statement and start of the declaration of the *RollOverCounter* class on lines 0001 to 0010 are directly comparable with the start of previous class declaration files.

The two constructors, between lines 0012 to 0018, are implemented as dispatching calls to the protected *LimitedCounter* constructors by making use of the **super** reserved word. Just as the reserved word **this** always refers to the class which is currently being declared, the reserved word **super** refers to its parent class. The *RollOverCounter* class adds no additional data attributes and so it does not need to perform any additional initialization upon construction and can dispatch immediately to its parent constructors. As was explained in Chapter 3, the effect of the *LimitedCounter* constructors is to establish the range of values which an instance can count between, either the default range for the default constructor or the range defined by the arguments of the alternative constructor.

The implementation of the *count()* action will require a design which introduces a new design technique. A **protected** *count()* action without any arguments has already been introduced into the hierarchy by the *BasicCounter* class. This action cannot be used directly as it has no knowledge of the limits introduced by the *LimitedCounter* class. The *count()* action in the *RollOverCounter* class must only call the *BasicCounter count()* action if it is appropriate to do so, i.e. when the current value is not at the upper limit of its range. If the counter is at the upper limit of its range then the **protected** *setCountTo()* action of the *BasicCounter* class should be used to reset the counter to the start of its range, using the **protected** *minimumIs()* action of the *LimitedCounter* class to provide the value to set the counter to. This can be expressed on a JSP design as follows:

RollOverCounter count() action

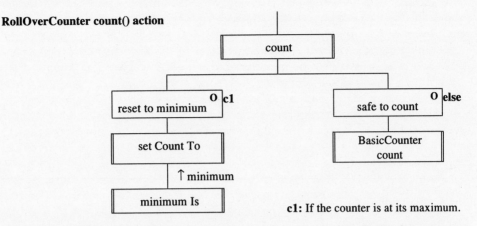

c1: If the counter is at its maximum.

The interpretation of this design is that the action *count()* is a *selection* between two possibilities: *reset to minimum* and *safe to count*. Any design step with an **o** in the top right hand corner is taken to be an *o*ptional part of a selection and the step must be accompanied by a *c*ondition key to explain how the decision between the options will be made. In this design the decision is made by evaluating condition 1 (**c1**) and if it is true then the actions associated with its option, i.e. calling the actions *setCountTo()* making use of the *minimum Is()* action, will be performed. Otherwise if condition 1 is not true the actions associated with the **else** option, i.e. calling the *BasicCounter count()* action, will be performed. The implementation of this design is as follows:

```
0021        public void count(){
0022            if ( this.isAtMaximum()) {
0023               this.setCountTo( this.minimumIs());
0024            } else {
0025               super.count();
0026            } // End if.
0027        } // End count.
```

The implementation of the selection is in the form of an *if else* control structure, the general form of which is as follows:

```
if ( condition) {
     first actions;
} else {
     second actions;
} // End if.
```

When Java meets a structure like this the first thing it does is evaluate the *condition*, which must be written so that it will only work out to be either **true** or **false**. If it is **true** the actions identified as *first actions* will be performed and *second actions* will be ignored. Otherwise the condition must be **false** and the *second actions* will be performed whilst the *first actions* are ignored.

Returning to the implementation of the *count()* action, the condition part of the **if** structure is a call of the *isAtMaximum()* action. This was introduced into the hierarchy as a protected action of the *LimitedCounter* class which returned a **boolean** value. It was explained in Chapter 3 that a **boolean** value can be either **true** or **false**, and that this action would be **true** if the counter was at the maximum of its range and **false** otherwise. As the *RollOverCounter* class *is a*n extended instance of the *LimitedCounter* class it inherits the *isAtMaximum()* action as a protected action and thus can call it using **this**.

Assuming that the counter is at the maximum of its range the condition on line 0022 will evaluate **true** so the statement on line 0023 will be performed and the statement on line 0025 will be ignored. The effect of the statement on line 0023 is to reset the counter using the *setCounterTo()* action inherited from *BasicCounter*, specifying the value obtained from the *minimumIs()* action inherited from *LimitedCounter*. As these actions are inherited, and thus actions of the current instance, the **this** designator is used. The effect is to reset the counter to the minimum of its range.

Assuming that the counter is not at the maximum of its range the condition on line 0022 will evaluate **false** so the statement on line 0025 will be performed and the statement on line 0023 will be ignored. The statement on line 0025 calls the *BasicCounter count()* action to record an occurrence. If this statement were written as **this**.*count()*, there would be a potential ambiguity. There are two possible meanings for the *count()* action: either the one in the *RollOverCounter* class or the one inherited from the *BasicCounter* class via the *LimitedCounter* class.

However, the statement **this**.*count()* is not ambiguous to Java which would interpret it to mean the *count()* action in the class currently being declared. (It does not matter to Java that it is already in the middle of executing this action; an action can call itself! This possibility, known as *recursion*, is a very powerful technique and will be introduced in Chapter 15.)

In order for the developer to indicate to Java that the *BasicCounter count()* action is intended the **super** reserved word has to be used. This will cause Java to use the *count()* action inherited from its parent class, not the *count()* action declared in the current class. In this circumstance the *count()* action is actually introduced into the class hierarchy by the *RollOverCounter*'s grandparent class, *BasicCounter*, but is inherited by the *LimitedCounter* class which is the **super** class of the *RollOverCounter* class.

When an action with the same return type, name and arguments is implemented in two places in a hierarchy it is known as *overriding*. It is used to allow a class to specialize an action to its own requirements. For example, in this case the *count()* action of the *RollOverCounter* class behaves in a different way to the *count()* action of the *BasicCounter* class, and also in a different way to the *count()* actions of the *StoppingCounter* and *WarningCounter* classes, as will be shown below. Within a class declaration the overriding action can be explicitly specified by the developer with the **this** keyword and the overridden action with the **super** keyword.

The implementation of the *RollOverCounter unCount()* action is essentially identical to the implementation of the *count()* action, though with a reversal of its logic. Its declaration completes the declaration of the *RollOverCounter* class:

```
0030    public void unCount(){
0031       if ( this.isAtMinimum()) {
0032         this.setCountTo( this.maximumIs());
0033       } else {
0034         super.unCount();
0035       } // End if.
```

```
0036     } // End unCount.
0037
0038 } // End RollOverCounter
```

4.2 ▧ The *RollOverCounterDemonstration* client program

As with the two classes in Chapter 3 a client program containing a single *main()* action will be provided, whose only purpose is to demonstrate that the *RollOverCounter* class appears to be working correctly. In order to facilitate this demonstration the *RollOverCounter* instance will be constructed to count between a very small (10 to 12) range of values. The high level design for this demonstration is as follows:

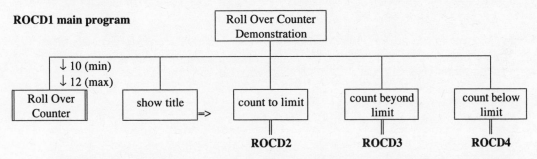

ROCD1 main program

This design indicates that the demonstration will create a *RollOverCounter* instance with a minimum of 10 and a maximum of 12, output a title and count up to the limit before first counting beyond the limit and then counting back below the limit in order to demonstrate the roll over behaviour from both directions. The implementation of this design as far as the *show title* step is as follows:

```
0001 // Filename RollOverCounterDemonstration.java.
0002 // demonstration client program for the
0003 // RollOverCounter class.
0004 //
0005 // Written for JOF book Chapter 4 see text.
0006 // Fintan Culwin, v0.1, August 1997.
0007
0008
0009 import Counters.RollOverCounter;
0010
0011 public class RollOverDemonstration {
0012
0013 public static void main( String argv[]) {
0014
0015     RollOverCounter  demoCounter = new RollOverCounter( 10, 12);
0016
0017     System.out.println( "\n\t\t Roll Over Counter demonstration \n");
```

The filename indicates that this demonstration program is not necessarily stored in the *Counters* directory and the **import** statement on line 0009 has to specify the package name and the class name to obtain access to the *RollOverCounter* class. Apart from this, this part of the listing is essentially identical to the two demonstration clients from Chapter 3. The design of the next step *count to limit* is as follows:

ROCD2 count to limit

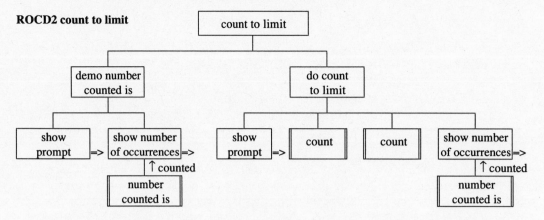

This stage consists of two steps, the first of which demonstrates the *numberCountedIs()* action which this class inherits as a **public** action from the *BasicCounters* class. This will also demonstrate that the constructor has operated correctly as the value output should be 10. The second step of the stage calls the *count()* action twice which should cause the counter to have the value 12, and the *numberCountedIs()* action is used to confirm this. The implementation of this design is as follows:

```
0023        System.out.println( "\n Demonstrating numberCountedIs()");
0024        System.out.print( "The value should be 10 ... ");
0025        System.out.print( demoCounter.numberCountedIs());
0026        System.out.println( "." );
0027
0028        System.out.println( "\n Counting two occurrences with count()");
0029        demoCounter.count();
0030        demoCounter.count();
0031        System.out.print( "Its value should now be 12 ... ");
0032        System.out.print( demoCounter.numberCountedIs());
0033        System.out.println( "." );
```

The output expected from the program up to this point is as follows:

```
                Roll Over Counter demonstration

The counter has been created with a
range of 10 to 12 and an initial value of 10.

Demonstrating numberCountedIs()
The value should be 10 ... 10.

Counting two occurrences with count()
Its value should now be 12 ... 12.
```

At this point a further call of the *count()* action should cause the counter to roll over to its minimum value, 10. The next part of the design is intended to demonstrate this behaviour:

ROCD3 count beyond limit

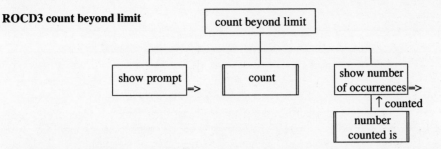

If the class is working correctly the counter should now be at the minimum of its range and uncounting an occurrence should cause it to roll over back to the maximum of its range. The final part of the design is intended to demonstrate this behaviour:

ROCD3 count below limit

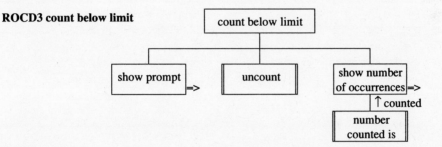

The implementation of these two design fragments is as follows:

```
0035    System.out.println( "\nCounting another occurrence with count()");
0036    demoCounter.count();
0037    System.out.print( "Its value should now be 10 ...");
0038    System.out.print( demoCounter.numberCountedIs());
0039    System.out.println( "." );
0040
0041    System.out.println( "\n Uncounting an occurrence with unCount()");
0042    demoCounter.unCount();
0043    System.out.print( "Its value should now be 12 ... ");
0044    System.out.print( demoCounter.numberCountedIs());
0045    System.out.println( "." );
0046    } // End main.
0047
0048 } // End RollOverDemonstration.
```

The expected output from this part of the program is as follows:

```
Counting another occurrence with count()
Its value should now be 10 ... 10.

Uncounting another occurrence with unCount()
Its value should now be 12 ... 12.
```

4.3 ▓ The design, implementation and demonstration of the *StoppingCounter* class

The object diagram of the *StoppingCounter* class is essentially identical to that of the *RollOverCounter* class, and is given in Figure 4.2 for the sake of completeness.

The difference between a *RollOverCounter* and a *StoppingCounter* is that if a request is made to *count()* an occurrence when the counter is at the maximum limit of its range, it will do nothing. Likewise if a request is made to *unCount()* an occurrence when the counter is at its minimum, it will do nothing.

The implementation of the two constructors does not differ significantly from the *RollOverCounter* constructors and will not be presented. A possible design for the *StoppingCounter count()* action, following the *RollOverCounter count()* design, might be as follows:

StoppingCounter count() action

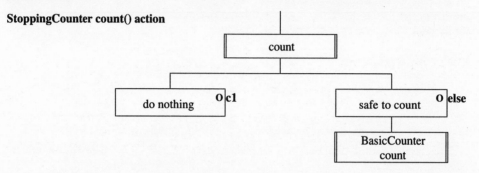

c1: If the counter is at its maximum.

This design indicates that if the counter is at the maximum limit of its range then the *count()* action will do nothing, otherwise it will count the occurrence using the *BasicCounters count()* action. This design could be implemented. However, there is a more straightforward design, and consequent implementation, possible:

StoppingCounter count() action

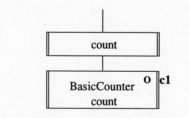

c1: If the counter is **not** at its maximum.

By reversing the logic of the decision a one way, as opposed to a two way, selection can be designed and implemented as follows:

```
0021          public void count() {
0022              if ( ! this.isAtMaximum()) {
0023                  super.count();
0024              } // End if.
0025          } // End count.
```

The *!* operator on line 0022 is read as *not* and it negates the meaning of the following term. So the condition can be read as *'if the counter is **not** at the maximum of its range'*.

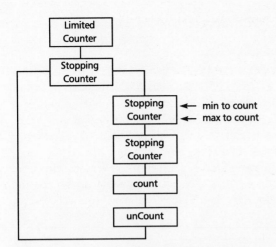

Figure 4.2 The *StoppingCounter* class diagram.

More formally, if the *isAtMaximum()* action returns **true** the not operator will negate it to **false**, and if it returns **false** it will be negated to **true**. The effect of this fragment is that the *BasicCounter count()* action will only be called if the counter is not at the maximum of its range. If it is at the maximum of its range then nothing will happen as the **else** clause has been omitted from this **if** structure.

The design and implementation of the *StoppingCounter unCount()* action are essentially identical:

StoppingCounter unCount() action

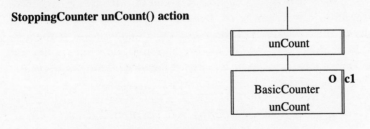

c1: If the counter is **not** at its minimum.

```
0028    public void unCount(){
0029      if ( ! this.isAtMinimum()) {
0030        super.unCount();
0031      } // End if.
0032    } // End unCount.
```

The demonstration client program for this class would follow the design and implementation of the *RollOverDemonstration* client as far as the *count beyond limit* step. The *count below limit* step will be left as an end-of-chapter exercise. The design of the *count beyond limit* step would not differ, but the prediction made by the program would be that after the *count()* action had been called, the value of the counter would still be 12. The implementation of this step and the expected output of the entire program would be as follows:

```
0035    System.out.println( "\nCounting another occurrence with count()");
0036    demoCounter.count();
0037    System.out.print( "Its value should still be 12 ... ");
```

```
0038        System.out.print( demoCounter.numberCountedIs());
0039        System.out.println( "." );
```

```
              Stopping Counter demonstration

  The counter has been created with a
  range of 10 to 12 and an initial value of 10.

  Demonstrating numberCountedIs()
  The value should be 10 ... 10.

  Counting two occurrences with count()
  Its value should now be 12 ... 12.

  Counting another occurrence with count()
  Its value should still be 12 ... 12.
```

4.4 ▓ The design and implementation of the *WarningCounter* class

The behaviour of the *RollOverCounter* and *StoppingCounter* classes is potentially very dangerous. For example, a Geiger counter could be used to monitor the amount of radiation being used to treat a cancer. If the software controlling the treatment machine made use of either of these classes, with its maximum limit set to the maximum safe dose, then there is no guarantee that it would stop the treatment before a dangerous dose of radiation was administered. The *WarningCounter* class is intended to increase the security of the software implementation by arranging for a warning to be issued if any attempt is made to count beyond the maximum limit, or to uncount below the minimum. This is accomplished in Java by the ***throwing*** of an ***exception***, the details of which will be explained below.

The class diagram for the *WarningCounter* class is given in Figure 4.3. It differs from the previous two classes in that the *count()* and *unCount()* actions have an

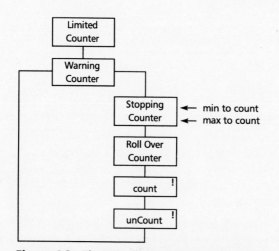

Figure 4.3 The *WarningCounter* class diagram.

exclamation mark (!) in the top right hand corner to indicate that an exception might be thrown when they are used.

The exception which will be thrown is a developer supplied extension of the Java supplied *RuntimeException* class, called *CounterException*. Its object diagram is given in Figure 4.4.

The actions of this class consist of a single constructor. As this class will be used by the *WarningCounter* class its class declaration will be presented first:

```
0001 // Filename Counters/CounterException.java.
0002 // Provides an extension of the RuntimeException class
0003 // for use with the Counters hierarchy.
0004 //
0005 // Written for JOF book Chapter 4 see text.
0006 // Fintan Culwin, v0.1, August 1997.
0007
0008 package Counters;
0009
0010 class CounterException extends RuntimeException {
0011
0012     public CounterException( String reason) {
0013         super( reason);
0014     } // End CounterException constructor.
0015
0016 } // End CounterException
```

The implementation of the class is very straightforward: it is implemented as a non-**public** class as it is only required by the classes in the *Counters* hierarchy and, as its filename indicates, should be stored in the same directory. The constructor is implemented by a call to the equivalent *RuntimeException* constructor using **super**; the use which is made of the *reason* argument will be explained below.

With the *CounterException* class implemented the *WarningCounter* class can be implemented. It differs significantly from the previous classes only in the design and implementation of the *count()* and *unCount()* actions. It differs insignificantly in having to import the *Counters.CounterException* class in its header. The design of the *count()* action is as follows:

WarningCounter count() action

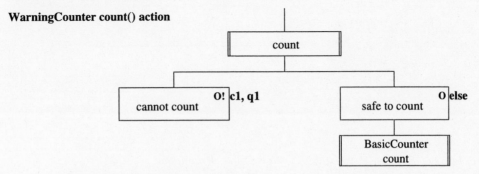

c1: If the counter is at its maximum.
q1: Throw counting beyond exception.

The structure of the decision, and its condition, is identical to the structure and condition of the *RollOverCounter count()* design. It differs only in the consequences of the counter being at the maximum of its range; this is the design step *cannot count*.

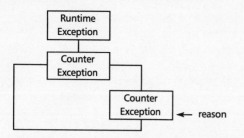

Figure 4.4   The *CounterException* class diagram.

This is annotated with an **o** in the top right hand corner to indicate that is it part of a selection and also has a **!** to indicate that an exception will be thrown. The exception is keyed at the bottom of the design with a **q**, for *q*uit, and the precise reason why the exception will be thrown. The implementation of this design is as follows:

```
0021    public void count() {
0022        if ( this.isAtMaximum()) {
0023            throw new CounterException( "Attempt to count beyond limit.");
0024        } else {
0025            super.count();
0026        } // End if.
0027    } // End count.
```

The design stage *cannot count* is implemented on line 0023 with a Java **throw** statement. The exception which is thrown is a *CounterException* constructed with the **new** statement and the *reason* argument set to the string shown. The condition on line 0022 indicates that this exception will only be thrown if the *count()* action is called when it is at the maximum limit of its range, otherwise the call of the *BasicCounter count()* action on line 0025 will count the occurrence. The consequences of throwing an exception will be described in the demonstration client below.

The design and implementation of the *WarningCounter unCount()* action are essentially identical:

WarningCounter unCount() action

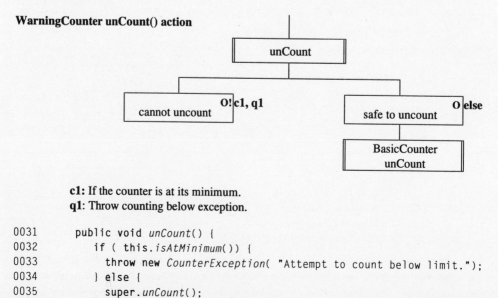

c1: If the counter is at its minimum.
q1: Throw counting below exception.

```
0031    public void unCount() {
0032        if ( this.isAtMinimum()) {
0033            throw new CounterException( "Attempt to count below limit.");
0034        } else {
0035            super.unCount();
```

```
0036          } // End if.
0037        } // End unCount.
```

4.5 ▓ The design and implementation of the *WarningDemonstration* client program

The first parts of the *WarningDemonstration* client, as far as the *count beyond limit* step, are essentially identical to the first parts of the two previous demonstration clients. The design of the *WarningDemonstration count beyond limit* step is as follows:

WD3 count beyond limit

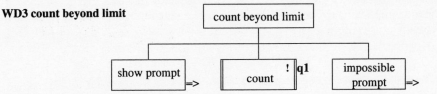

q1: Beyond limit exception will be raised.

As the counter is at the maximum limit of its range when this stage starts it is expected that the exception will be thrown when the *count()* action is attempted. This will interrupt the flow of control in the program, causing it immediately to finish and so the *impossible prompt* should never be issued. The implementation of this design is as follows:

```
0035        System.out.println( "\nCounting another occurrence with count()");
0036        System.out.println( " This should throw an exception ... ");
0037        demoCounter.count();
0038        System.out.print( "This message should never appear");
```

When this program was executed the following output was produced:

```
                   Warning Counter demonstration

    The counter has been created with a range of
    10 to 12 and an initial value of 10.

    Demonstrating numberCountedIs()
    The value should be 10 ... 10.

    Counting two occurrences with count()
    Its value should now be 12 ... 12.

    Counting another occurrence with count()
    This should throw an exception ...
    Counters.CounterException: Attempt to count beyond limit.
            at Counters.WarningCounter.count(WarningCounter.java:27)
            at WarningDemonstration.main(WarningDemonstration.java:31)
```

The exception was thrown as expected when the *count()* action was attempted with the counter having its maximum value of 12. This caused the *count()* action and subsequently the program to be immediately abandoned, with a message indicating that a *CounterException* was raised and outputting the reason "*Attempt to count beyond limit.*", as specified when the exception was constructed in the *WarningCounter* class. The message also indicates, using line numbers, exactly where in the *WarningCounter* class declaration the exception was raised, and exactly where in the *WarningCounter-Demonstration* declaration the action which caused the exception to be thrown was called. Seen from the other direction this shows the action calls through which the exception was ***propagated***.

The information provided when the exception is thrown is intended to assist the developer in locating, and subsequently correcting, the error which caused it to be thrown. In other circumstances it may be more appropriate for an exception which is ***thrown*** to be ***caught*** by another part of the program, allowing the program to attempt to recover from the error. The techniques for catching an exception will be introduced in Chapter 6

4.6 ▨ The *Counters* hierarchy in retrospect

The designs which have been presented for the *Counters* hierarchy are not the only set of designs which could have been presented. One possibility might have been not to implement a hierarchy at all but to have used three distinct classes. The problem with this design is that there would have been much duplication between the three classes. Also, if at some stage in the future a maintenance change is required this might mean a change in three different classes. With the hierarchy design a change in one of the common classes would be inherited by all three non-abstract classes. This makes maintenance easier and ensures that all three classes which might be used by a client are all changed simultaneously.

It would also have been more difficult to build three large classes than to build a total of five small classes. With the hierarchy design each class was relatively small and simple, and each was demonstrated to be operating correctly before additional complexity was added to it. This method of development, known as ***build, test, build, test . . .***, is hoped to allow functionality to be developed in stages with any errors being located and corrected as early as possible. The consequences of not detecting and correcting an error at an early stage might be an extensive redesign and reimplementation of a large amount of code.

Assuming that the arguments for the construction of a hierarchy have been accepted, this is not the only hierarchy which could have been constructed. One possibility might have been to make the *WarningCounter* a child class of the *StoppingCounter*, as a *WarningCounter* not only refuses to count beyond the limits of its range but also throws an exception if any attempt is made to do so. Thus a *WarningCounter* can be thought of, and implemented as, an extended *StoppingCounter*.

For any specification there is always a large number of possible designs, many of which will be acceptable and each of which will have its advantages and disadvantages. The skill of design is to recognize these possibilities and to make the trade-offs which minimize the complexity of the design whilst maximizing its potential for reuse. Like any skill it is only by practising these decisions that competence will emerge.

In the design as implemented an instance of any of the three non-abstract classes will offer to a client the following actions: *count()*, *unCount()*, *numberCountedIs()*, *reset()*, *minimumIs()*, *maximumIs()*, *isAtMaximum()* and *isAtMinimum()*.

Summary

- A child class can *override* an action in its parent class by declaring an action with the same name, return type and arguments, but with a differing visibility.

- The **this** keyword refers to the current class declaration and the **super** keyword to the parent class.

- The **super** keyword can be used in an overriding action declaration to indicate that an overridden action should be used.

- JSP designs can include optional steps which are shown with an **o** in the top right hand corner and keyed with a **c** for *c*ondition.

- Selections in a design can be one way or two way (or multi-way).

- Selections can be implemented in Java by use of an **if** structure.

- A condition in a selection can be negated with a not (**!**) operator.

- The pre-supplied *RuntimeException* class can be extended and an instance of the extended exception thrown by an action to indicate an error.

- An action in a class diagram which can throw an exception is shown with an exclamation mark (**!**) in the top right hand corner.

- JSP design steps which throw an exception are shown with an exclamation mark (**!**) in the top right hand corner and keyed with a **q** for *q*uit.

- If an exception is not caught it will *propagate* and halt a program with a reason and a trace of the actions which have been abandoned.

Exercises

4.1 Complete the design and implementation of the *StoppingCounter* and *WarningCounter* demonstration clients.

4.2 Produce a diagram similar to that given in Figure 3.5 to describe the actions of one of the *Counter* classes in this chapter.

4.3 Redesign, reimplement and redemonstrate the class hierarchy with the *WarningCounter* as a child class of the *StoppingCounter*.

4.5 Implement and demonstrate the specialized counters from Exercises 3.3 and 3.4.

4.6 To control pollution a limit is to be placed on the number of vehicles which enter a road. Extend the *GreenVehicleCounter* class from Exercise 3.4 to provide a *RoadClosureCounter* class which will throw a *CloseRoad* exception as a particular number of vehicle units, determined by an argument to its constructor, is counted.

Chapter five

The *RoomMonitor* class and *MoneyRegisters* hierarchy

This chapter will continue the consideration of development by extension by introducing new classes which further extend the *Counters* hierarchy. There are relatively few additional concepts introduced in this chapter and it is intended to provide an opportunity for the many concepts which have been presented in the previous chapters to be consolidated. Accordingly there are a larger number of end-of-chapter exercises for the skills to be practised and consolidated.

The first class which will be presented in this chapter is called the *RoomMonitor* class, although this name is somewhat misleading. It is intended to provide a class which can monitor the number of people who are entering and leaving a building, although it could just as easily be used for monitoring the number of vehicles entering and leaving a stretch of road, or other similar patterns of occurrences. In order to allow for some design considerations to be explained it will be implemented in two different ways and the advantages and disadvantages of each design approach will be discussed.

A separate extension to the *Counters* hierarchy will start by introducing a simple *MoneyRegister* class which in addition to counting the number of transactions will also record the amount of money taken into the register. This class will be extended to provide a *MultipleRegister*, which will be able to maintain separate totals for the amount taken by cash, by cheque, by debit card and by credit card. The chapter will end with a review of the process of development by extension.

5.1 ■ The *RoomMonitor* design and first implementation

The *RoomMonitor* class is intended to provide facilities to monitor the number of people entering and leaving a room. To accomplish this it will need to be able to report to its clients the total number of people currently in the room, the total number of people who have ever entered the room and the maximum number of people ever in the room, and in order to do this it will have to provide actions for entering and leaving a room. The class diagram for the *RoomMonitor* class is given in Figure 5.1.

The fundamental nature of this class is concerned with counting entry and exit occurrences and as such it has much in common with the *Counters* classes which have already been introduced. As the diagram shows it is implemented as an extension to the *WarningCounters* class.

The diagram indicates that the class will supply a default constructor, *enterRoom()* and *exitRoom()* actions and three enquiry actions: *numberCurrentlyInRoomIs()*, *maximumEverInRoom()* and *totalNumberEnteredIs()*. The *enterRoom()* and

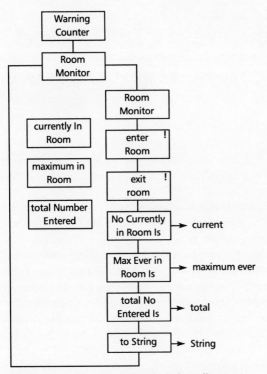

Figure 5.1   The *RoomMonitor* class diagram.

exitRoom() actions may throw exceptions and this is noted on the diagram. The meaning and use of the final public action, *toString()*, will be explained below. The class diagram also suggests that there are three data attributes corresponding to the three enquiry functions. However, as has been mentioned before, this information is provided only to assist the understanding of a developer using the client, and the class need not actually be implemented in this manner.

The basis of the first implementation is to extend the *WarningCounters* class mapping the *enterRoom()* action onto the *count()* action and the *exitRoom()* onto the *unCount()* action. Thus the current value returned by the *BasicCounter numberCountedIs()* action will indicate the number of people currently in the room. The remaining two data attributes, *maximumEverInRoom* and *totalNumberEntered*, will have to be provided as data attributes. The first part of this implementation, as far as the end of the constructor, is as follows:

```
0001 // Filename Counters/RoomMonitor.java.
0002 // Providing a non-abstract class which monitors
0003 // entry and exit occurrences, first implementation.
0004 //
0005 // Written for JOF book Chapter 5 see text.
0006 // Fintan Culwin, v0.1, August 1997.
0007
0008 package Counters;
0009
0010 public class RoomMonitor extends WarningCounter {
0011
```

```
0012 private int maxEverInRoom      = 0;
0013 private int totalNumberEntered  = 0;
0014
0015
0016    public RoomMonitor() {
0017       super(0, Integer.MAX_VALUE);
0018       maxEverInRoom      = 0;
0019       totalNumberEntered = 0;
0020    } // End default constructor.
```

The class declaration file starts with the expected header comments. The detailed design considerations decided that the counter should be able to count from zero to the largest possible positive integer value.

The implementation commences with the declaration of the two data attributes on lines 0012 and 0013. The declaration of the default constructor is on lines 0016 to 0020. It starts with a call of the parent (*WarningCounter*) constructor specifying a range of 0 to the value of the class constant *Integer.MAX_VALUE*. The Java Integer class supplies two constants, MIN_VALUE and MAX_VALUE, which delineate the range of values which the an **int** can represent. Thus the default constructor ensures that a *RoomMonitor* instance can count all positive **int** values. The constructor concludes by explicitly specifying the values of the two data attributes. The explicit values for the data attributes in the constructor do not differ from their default values, but it is regarded as good style to set all values in a constructor explicitly.

The design of the *enterRoom()* action has to consider counting the occurrence as a *Counter* object and of updating the values of the two data attributes. The design of this action is as follows:

RoomMonitor
   enterRoom() action

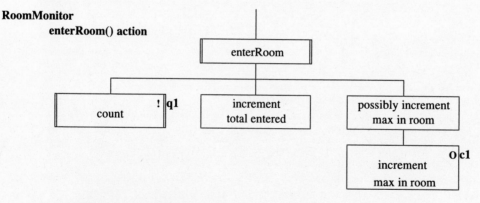

c1: If the current number in the room is greater than the maximum ever in the room.
q1: Possible counting beyond exception.

The design indicates that the first step is to count the entry as an occurrence, possibly throwing an exception, and then to increment the number of people recorded as having ever entered the room. The final step is to increment the maximum number of people ever in the room only if the current value of the number of people in the room is greater than the maximum ever recorded in the room so far. The implementation of this design is as follows:

```
0023    public void enterRoom() {
0024       this.count();
```

```
0025        totalNumberEntered++;
0026        if ( this.numberCurrentlyInRoomIs() > this.maxEverInRoomIs()) {
0027          maxEverInRoom++;
0028        } // End if.
0029      } // End enterRoom.
```

The implementation follows directly from the design with the first step, on line 0024, a call of the inherited *count()* action which might raise the *CounterException*, as explained in the previous chapter. The second step, on line 0025, is the incrementation of the data attribute *totalNumberEntered*. The final step is implemented as an **if** structure on lines 0026 to 0038. The condition makes use of the *numberCurrentlyInRoom()* and *maxEverInRoomIs()* enquiry actions whose implementation will be described below. The value returned from these enquiry action calls are then tested against each other using the *is greater than* (>) relational operator. This will evaluate **true** if the value on its left is greater than the value on its right and **false** if the value on the right is equal to or less than the right hand value. If this condition evaluates **true** it indicates that there are more people currently in the room than the maximum ever recorded and so the value of the *maxEverInRoom* data attribute is incremented to allow for this.

The design and implementation of the *exitRoom()* action is much simpler:

RoomMonitor
    exitRoom() action

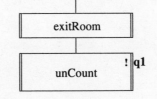

q1: Possible count below exception.

```
0032   public void exitRoom() {
0033      this.unCount();
0034   } // End exitRoom.
```

Just as entering a room is regarded as counting an occurrence, leaving a room is regarded as uncounting an occurrence and may result in an exception being thrown. The three enquiry functions have equally straightforward implementations:

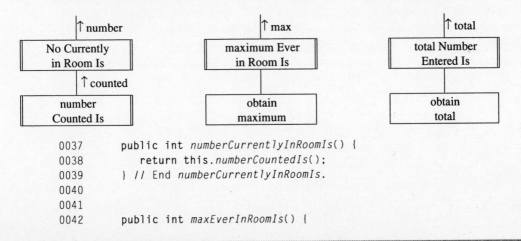

```
0037        public int numberCurrentlyInRoomIs() {
0038          return this.numberCountedIs();
0039        } // End numberCurrentlyInRoomIs.
0040
0041
0042        public int maxEverInRoomIs() {
```

```
0043            return maxEverInRoom;
0044        } // End maxEverInRoomIs.
0045
0046
0047    public int totalNumberEnteredIs() {
0048        return totalNumberEntered;
0049    } // End totalNumberEnteredIs.
```

The implementation of these three actions is straightforward and requires minimal explanation. The *totalNumberEnteredIs()* action and *maxEverInRoomIs()* action return the value of their respective data attributes and the *numberCurrentlyInRoomIs()* action indirects to the inherited *BasicCounter numberCountedIs()* action.

The final action of this implementation, *toString()*, constructs and returns a string which contains details of the current status of the class instance. Its implementation is as follows, and an example of the string which would be returned might be "Now in room : 3 Max in room 4 : Total entered 5". This string is constructed by adding together (+) a series of messages and values returned from enquiry actions, a process known as the *catenation* of strings:

```
0052    public String toString() {
0053        return "Now in room : "    + this.numberCurrentlyInRoomIs() +
0054                " Max in room : "    + this.maxEverInRoomIs()          +
0055                " Total entered : " + this.totalNumberEnteredIs();
0056    } // End toString.
0057
0058 } // End RoomMonitor.
```

The use to which this action is put will be described in the demonstration client below.

5.2 ■ The *RoomMonitorDemonstration* client

The design and construction of the *RoomMonitorDemonstration* client does not differ significantly from the design and construction of the previous clients. Its purpose is to demonstrate that the class appears to be working correctly. In the interests of brevity the design will be omitted. It would indicate that following the construction of a *RoomMonitor* instance, four people enter the room, two leave and then one more enters. This should indicate that the current number of people in the room is three, the total number of people who have ever entered is five and the maximum ever in the room is four – which is attempted to be demonstrated with the output from the three enquiry functions. The implementation of this client is as follows:

```
0001 // Filename Counters/RoomMonitorDemonstration.java.
0002 // Demonstration client for the RoomMonitor class.
0003 //
0004 // Written for JOF book Chapter 5 see text.
0005 // Fintan Culwin, v0.1, August 1997.
0006
0007 import Counters.RoomMonitor;
0008
0009 public class RoomMonitorDemonstration {
0010
0011    public static void main( String argv[]) {
```

```
0012
0013        RoomMonitor   demoMonitor = new RoomMonitor();
0014
0015          System.out.println( "\n\t\t Room Monitor demonstration \n");
0016
0017          System.out.println( "The monitor has been created ...");
0018
0019          System.out.println( "\n Four people enter the room ... ");
0020          demoMonitor.enterRoom();
0021          demoMonitor.enterRoom();
0022          demoMonitor.enterRoom();
0023          demoMonitor.enterRoom();
0024
0025          System.out.println( "\n Two people leave the room ... ");
0026          demoMonitor.exitRoom();
0027          demoMonitor.exitRoom();
0028
0029          System.out.println( "\n One person enters the room ... ");
0030          demoMonitor.enterRoom();
0031
0032          System.out.print( "The value of numberCurrentlyInRoomIs() should be 3 ...");
0033          System.out.print( demoMonitor.numberCurrentlyInRoomIs());
0034          System.out.println( "." );
0035
0036          System.out.print( "The value of maxEverInRoomIs() should be 4 ... ");
0037          System.out.print( demoMonitor.maxEverInRoomIs());
0038          System.out.println( "." );
0039
0040          System.out.print( "The value of totalNumberEnteredIs() should be 5 ... ");
0041          System.out.print( demoMonitor.totalNumberEnteredIs());
0042          System.out.println( "." );
0043
0044          System.out.println( "\n Demonstrating the toString() action ...");
0045          System.out.println( demoMonitor);
0046      } // End main
0047
0048 } // End RoomMonitorDemonstration
```

```
Room Monitor demonstration

The monitor has been created

Four people enter the room ...
Two people leave the room ...
One person enters the room ...

The value of numberCurrentlyInRoomIs() should be 3 ... 3.
The value of maxEverInRoomIs() should be 4 ... 4.
The value of totalNumberEnteredIs() should be 5 ... 5.

Demonstrating the toString() action
Now in room : 3 Max in room : 4 Total entered : 5.
```

The first part of this demonstration client and the output which it produces should be comprehensible from the previous demonstration clients. A new concept is introduced on line 0045 where the *RoomMonitor* instance is passed as an argument to the *System.out.println()* action. The effect of this is for Java to call the instance's *toString()* action and to output the *String* which is returned. Thus the last line of output shown is produced by this mechanism on line 0045 of the listing. The *toString()* action is introduced into the Java class hierarchy by the *Object* class, from which all other Java classes are derived, so it can be guaranteed that all objects will have a *toString()* action.

5.3 ■ A second implementation of the *RoomMonitor* class

The first implementation of the *RoomMonitor* class has been demonstrated to appear to work correctly. However, it does have a problem: because a *RoomMonitor* is an extended *WarningCounter* it inherits publicly all *WarningCounter* public actions. This means that in addition to the *enterRoom()* and *exitRoom()* actions it also inherits the *count()* and *unCount()* actions, as well as the other actions listed at the end of the previous chapter.

This means that there is a danger that a client can use the *count()* action of the *RoomMonitors* class and bypass the *enterRoom()* action. This would mean that the *numberCurrentlyInRoomIs()* action would report one too many people in the room and the *maximumInRoomIs()* action might also report an inaccurate figure.

Thus there is a potential insecurity in the implementation of the *RoomMonitor* class which cannot be corrected by removing the *count* action as an extension to a class can add new actions or change an action by overriding it, but cannot remove an action. There are a number of possible solutions to this. One might be to override the *count()* action in the *RoomMonitor* class and have it either do nothing or raise an exception. Or the *RoomMonitor* class might be introduced into the hierarchy as a child of the *LimitedCounter* class. The final possible solution is to implement a *RoomMonitor* *count()* action which indirects to the *enterRoom()* action. None of these solutions is particularly elegant; either technique which overrides the *count()* action is making the best of a bad job, and implementing it as a child of the *LimitedCounter()* class would imply that the warning behaviour would have to be reimplemented.

The problem is caused by the *RoomMonitor* being considered as an extended *WarningCounter*, i.e. that a *RoomMonitor is a WarningCounter* with extra bits added. One other way of thinking about the relationship between the two classes is that a *RoomMonitor has a WarningCounter* contained within itself. The only change which this would make to the class diagram is that the *RoomMonitor* class would be considered an extension of the Java pre-supplied **Object** class. The revised diagram is shown in Figure 5.2.

The first part of the implementation of this revised implementation, as far as the end of the constructor, is as follows:

```
0001 // Filename Counters/RoomMonitor.java.
0002 // Providing a non-abstract class which monitors
0003 // entry and exit occurrences, second implementation.
0004 //
0005 // Written for JOF book Chapter 5 see text.
0006 // Fintan Culwin, v0.1, August 1997.
0007
```

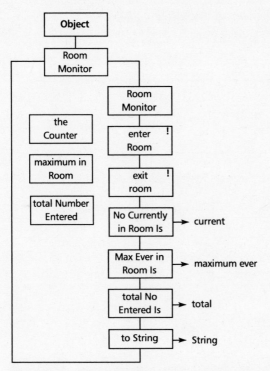

Figure 5.2   The revised *RoomMonitor* class diagram.

```
0008 package Counters;
0009
0010 import Counters.WarningCounter;
0011
0012 public class RoomMonitor extends Object {
0013
0014 private WarningCounter theCounter;
0015
0016 private int maxEverInRoom       = 0;
0017 private int totalNumberEntered  = 0;
0018
0019
0020     public RoomMonitor() {
0021       theCounter = new WarningCounter( 0, Integer.MAX_VALUE);
0022       maxEverInRoom       = 0;
0023       totalNumberEntered  = 0;
0024     } // End default constructor.
```

This implementation differs by importing the *Counters.WarningCounter* class and by the declaration of a **private** data attribute which is an instance of the *WarningCounter* class called *theCounter*. The remaining parts of the file should replace any references to the *count()*, *unCount()* and *numberCounterIs()* actions actions which were accessed via **this** to be accessed via *theCounter*. Any references to *RoomMonitor* actions should remain being accessed via **this**. The existence of the *theCounter* data attribute does not need to be indicated on the class diagram as it contributes little to the understanding of what the class does. The revised implementation is as follows:

```
0027    public void enterRoom() {
0028        theCounter.count();
0029        totalNumberEntered++;
0030        if ( this.numberCurrentlyInRoomIs() > this.maxEverInRoomIs()) {
0031            maxEverInRoom++;
0032        } // End if.
0033    } // End enterRoom.
0034
0035
0036    public void exitRoom() {
0037        theCounter.unCount();
0038    } // End exitRoom.
0039        _
0040
0041    public int numberCurrentlyInRoomIs() {
0042        return theCounter.numberCountedIs();
0043    } // End numberCurrentlyInRoomIs.
0044
0045
0046    public int maxEverInRoomIs() {
0047        return maxEverInRoom;
0048    } // End maxEverInRoomIs.
0049
0050
0051    public int totalNumberEnteredIs() {
0052        return totalNumberEntered;
0053    } // End totalNumberEnteredIs.
0054
0055
0056    public String toString() {
0057        return "Now in room : "    + this.numberCurrentlyInRoomIs() +
0058            " Max in Room : "   + this.maxEverInRoomIs()          +
0059            " Total entered : " + this.totalNumberEnteredIs();
0060    } // End toString.
0061
0062 } // End RoomMonitor.
```

The *RoomMonitorDemonstration* client will require no changes and can be simply re-executed after the revised version of the *RoomMonitor* class has been compiled. It should indicate that the behaviour of the two implementations is identical.

5.4 ■ The *MoneyRegisters* hierarchy and the *MoneyRegister* implementation

The second part of this chapter will introduce an extension to the *Counters* hierarchy which implements a series of increasingly sophisticated cash registers. The revised class hierarchy diagram, including the second implementation of the *RoomMonitor* class, is given in Figure 5.3.

The *MoneyRegister* class supplies the basic functionality including: knowing how much cash is in the register when it is started, known as the ***initial float***, the amount of cash in the register and, by inheritance, the number of deposits which have been

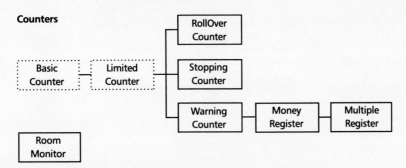

Figure 5.3   The extended *Counters* class hierarchy diagram.

made. The *MultipleRegister* keeps separate accounts for the amount of payments made by cash, by cheque, by debit card and by credit card. The class diagram of the *MoneyRegister* class is given in Figure 5.4.

The diagram indicates that the *MoneyRegister* is an extension of the *WarningCounter* class whose constructor requires the initial amount of cash (*initialFloat*) in the register to be specified. The *deposit()* action will allow an *amount* of money to be deposited into the register and the *numberOfDepositsIs()* action will indicate the number of *deposits* which have been made. The *takingsAre()* action will return the total amount of money deposited into the register and the *totalInRegisterIs()* action the total amount, including the *initialFloat*. The final action, *toString()*, returns a string indicating the state of the register.

The first part of the implementation of this class, as far as the end of the constructor, is as follows:

```
0001 // Filename Counters/MoneyRegister.java.
0002 // Providing an initial Cash Register model.
0003 //
```

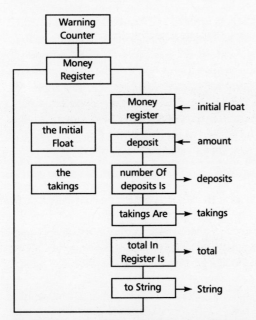

Figure 5.4   The *MoneyRegister* class diagram.

```
0004 // Written for JOF book Chapter 5 see text.
0005 // Fintan Culwin, v0.1, August 1997.
0006
0007 package Counters;
0008
0009 public class MoneyRegister extends WarningCounter {
0010
0011
0012 private double theCashFloat = 0.0;
0013 private double theTakings   = 0.0;
0014
0015     public MoneyRegister( double initialFloat) {
0016         super( 0, Integer.MAX_VALUE);
0017         theCashFloat = initialFloat;
0018         theTakings  = 0.0;
0019     } // End MoneyRegister Constructor.
```

This cash register assumes a currency like British pounds or American dollars which has a fractional part (e.g. *£53.86* or *$18.32*), unlike currencies like the Italian lira which have no fractional part (e.g. *7345* lire). A solution to this problem will be suggested in an exercise at the end of Chapter 9. In order to allow for the fractional parts a ***floating point*** data type will have to be used for the data attributes and used where appropriate as the return type, or argument type, of the class's actions.

Thus the two data attributes, *theCashFloat* and *theTakings*, on lines 0014 and 0015, are declared as being of type **double**, which is the preferred Java floating point type. Details of the Java floating point types are given in Appendix A2.

The declaration of the constructor follows on lines 0017 to 0020. Its first action is a call to the *WarningCounters* constructor using the **super** keyword, passing values as described in the *RoomMonitor* class above. The value of the argument, *initialFloat*, is then assigned to the data attribute *theCashFloat*, and the value of the other data attribute *theTakings* is confirmed as zero.

The *deposit()* has to *count()* a transaction occurrence and then add the value of its argument indicating the *amount* deposited to *theTakings*. The first enquiry action, *numberOfDepositsIs()*, is implemented as a call of the *Counters numberCountedIs()* action. The *takingsAre()* enquiry action returns the value of the data attribute *theTakings*. The final enquiry action, *totalInRegisterIs()*, uses the *takingsAre()* enquiry action to determine the value of the takings and adds the value of the data attribute *initialCashFloat* to obtain the value of the total amount of money in the register, as follows:

```
0023     public void deposit( double amount) {
0024         this.count();
0025         theTakings += amount;
0026     } // End deposit.
0027
0028
0029     public int numberOfDepositsIs() {
0030         return this.numberCountedIs();
0031     } // End numberOfDepositsIs.
0032
0033
0034     public double takingsAre() {
```

```
0035            return theTakings;
0036        } // End takingsAre.
0037
0038
0039    public double totalInRegisterIs() {
0040            return this.takingsAre() + theCashFloat;
0041        } // End totalInRegisterIs.
```

It would be possible to implement line 0040 as **return** *theTakings + theCashFloat*; but if at some stage in the future the data attribute *theTakings* is changed in some way this implementation might not then return the correct amount. For example, *theTakings* might be refined into two data attributes, one which records the amount of sales tax and one the net amount. The *takingsAre()* action would now return the combined value of the two attributes and thus it will still be correct, but the alternative implementation would be broken. If an enquiry action has been declared to obtain a value from a class then it should be used in preference to accessing the value of the data attribute directly. For this reason the *toString()* action makes use of the appropriate enquiry actions, as follows:

```
0042
0043    public String toString() {
0044        return "Initial float      : " + theCashFloat              + "\n" +
0045               "Number of deposits : " + this.numberOfDepositsIs() + "\n" +
0046               "Total takings      : " + this.takingsAre()         + "\n" +
0047               "Total in register  : " + this.totalInRegisterIs();
0048    } // End toString.
0049
0050 } // End WarningCounter
```

The output produced by this action will be illustrated in the demonstration client which follows.

5.5 The *MoneyRegisterDemonstration* program client

The *MoneyRegisterDemonstration* client follows the design of previous demonstration clients. It constructs a *MoneyRegister* instance called *demoRegister* with an initial cash float of £100.00, then makes three deposits into the register, using the *deposit()* action, and finally shows the state of the register with *toString()* via *System.out.println()*, as described above. The implementation and output from this program are as follows:

```
0001 // Filename MoneyRegisterDemonstration.java.
0002 // Demonstration client for the MoneyRegister class.
0003 //
0004 // Written for JOF book Chapter 5 see text.
0005 // Fintan Culwin, v0.1, August 1997.
0006
0007 import Counters.MoneyRegister;
0008
0009 public class MoneyRegisterDemonstration {
0010
0011    public static void main( String argv[]) {
0012
```

```
0013    MoneyRegister demoRegister = new MoneyRegister( 100.00);
0014
0015       System.out.println( "\n\t\t Money Register demonstration \n");
0016
0017       System.out.print(    "The Money Register has been created ");
0018       System.out.println( "with a cash float of 100.00");
0019
0020       System.out.println( "\nDepositing 5:00, 4.56 and 8.93.");
0021       demoRegister.deposit( 5.00);
0022       demoRegister.deposit( 4.56);
0023       demoRegister.deposit( 8.93);
0024
0025       System.out.println( "\nThe state of the register is ...");
0026       System.out.println( demoRegister);
0027    } // End main
0028
0029 } // End MoneyRegisterDemonstration
```

```
        Money Register demonstration

The Money Register has been created with a cash float of 100.00

Depositing 5:00, 4.56 and 8.93.

The state of the register is ...
Initial float     : 100
Number of deposits : 3
Total takings      : 18.49
Total in register  : 118.49
```

A little arithmetic indicates that the class appears to be operating correctly, although the formatting of the output leaves a little to be desired. The demonstration program does not need to demonstrate explicitly the correct operation of the three enquiry actions as these are used in the implementation of the *toString()* action. Thus, as the output of the *System.out.println()* appears correct, it can be assumed that the enquiry actions are also correct. Thus an additional reason for making use of enquiry actions, instead of accessing data attributes directly within the implementation of a class, is to allow them to be indirectly demonstrated via the class's *toString()* action.

5.6 ▓ The *MultipleRegister* design and implementation

The *MultipleRegister* extends the *MoneyRegister* to allow it to record both the total amount in the register and the separate amounts deposited by cash, by cheque, by debit card and by credit card. The class diagram is shown in Figure 5.5.

This diagram indicates that the *MultipleRegister* class is an extension of the *MoneyRegister* class. The first thing shown as being exported are *DEPOSIT_METHODS* which will define the names of four methods which can be used to deposit into an instance of this class. The capitalization of the exported component suggests that these will be implemented as class wide constants and can be regarded as a selection between

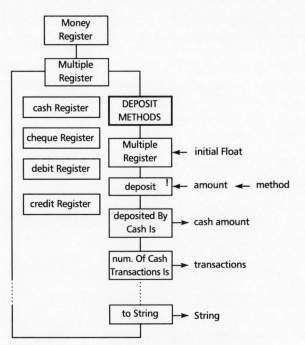

Figure 5.5 The *MultipleRegister* class diagram.

four possibilities. This can be shown on a JSP schematic as follows:

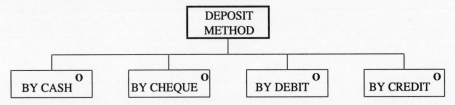

This diagram differs from the previous JSP schematics as it is describing the structure of a data object, not the structure of an action. Thus it contains nouns rather than verbs and the selections do not have to be keyed. The diagram states that a *DEPOSIT_METHOD* has to be one of *BY_CASH*, *BY_CHEQUE*, *BY_DEBIT*(card) or *BY_CREDIT*(card).

The single constructor requires an *initialFloat* for the same reasons as were given for the *MoneyRegister* constructor above. The *deposit()* action in this class requires both the amount to deposit and also the method of deposit. Two enquiry actions, *depositedByCashIs()* and *numberOfCashTransactionsIs()*, which will return the total amount of cash deposited and the number of cash transactions, are shown. The dotted lines below these actions indicate that other methods, equivalent to these two enquiry methods but relating to the other deposit methods, have been omitted from the diagram. The final action shown is a *toString()* action.

The inside of the class diagram suggests that there are four totally private data attributes, each of which is a *MoneyRegister*. In order for this class to implement its specification it will have to count the total amount of money deposited in cash and the number of cash transactions. This is exactly the specification that the *MoneyRegister* class was implemented to satisfy and so the most elegant way of implementing this class is to provide it with a *MoneyRegister* data attribute for the amount of cash deposited, and one for each of the other methods also. This can be illustrated on an context diagram, as shown in Figure 5.6.

The diagram shows that the *MultipleRegister* class *is a MoneyRegister* (and so *is a WarningCounter* etc.), and that it also *has a* number of *MoneyRegister* instances contained within it. The intention is that the total amount of money recorded in all of the four *has a* registers will always be equal to the amount of money recorded in the data attributes inherited by the *MultipleRegister* from the *MoneyRegister* class. The implementation of this class as far as the end of the constructor is as follows:

```
0001 // Filename Counters/MultipleRegister.java.
0002 // Providing a MoneyRegister able to take cash,
0003 // cheque, debit card and credit card deposits.
0004 //
0005 // Written for JOF book Chapter 5 see text.
0006 // Fintan Culwin, v0.1, August 1997.
0007
0008 package Counters;
0009
0010 public class MultipleRegister extends MoneyRegister {
0011
0012 public static final int BY_CASH   = 1;
0013 public static final int BY_CHEQUE = 2;
0014 public static final int BY_DEBIT  = 3;
0015 public static final int BY_CREDIT = 4;
0016
0017 private MoneyRegister cashRegister   = new MoneyRegister( 0.0);
0018 private MoneyRegister chequeRegister = new MoneyRegister( 0.0);
0019 private MoneyRegister debitRegister  = new MoneyRegister( 0.0);
0020 private MoneyRegister creditRegister = new MoneyRegister( 0.0);
0021
0022    public MultipleMoneyRegister( double initialCashFloat) {
0023       super( initialCashFloat);
0024    } // End MultipleMoneyRegister Constructor.
```

The four manifest values are declared as **public** class wide constants on lines 0012 to 0015. The four encapsulated *MoneyRegister* instances are declared and constructed, with an initial cash float of zero, on lines 0017 to 0020. The only required action of

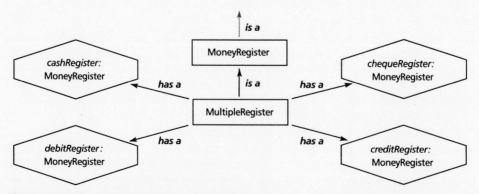

Figure 5.6 The *MultipleRegister* context diagram.

the constructor is to call its parent *MoneyRegister* constructor passing on the value of its argument. The design of the *deposit()* action is as follows:

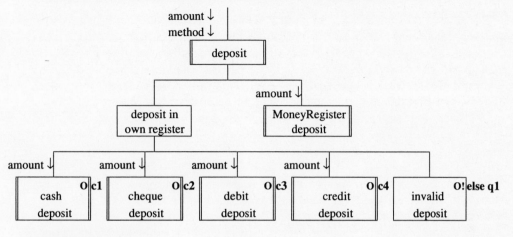

c1: If payment by cash.
c2: If payment by cheque.   **q1**: Throw some exception.
c3: If payment by debit card
c4: If payment by credit card.

The design indicates the first step is to make a deposit into one of the encapsulated *MoneyRegister*s depending upon what method of payment is indicated. This is a five way selection with the fifth option indicating that an invalid method of payment has been specified and throwing an exception to indicate this. Only if the exception is not thrown is the second step of the design, depositing into the actual *MultipleRegister* instance, performed. If these two steps were reversed then an invalid deposit might be made into the *MultipleRegister* instance which would subsequently have to be undone in some way in order for the amounts to tally. The implementation of this design is as follows:

```
0027    public void deposit( double amount,
0028                         int    method) {
0029
0030        switch ( method) {
0031          case BY_CASH:
0032            moneyRegister.deposit( amount);
0033            break;
0034          case BY_CHEQUE:
0035            chequeRegister.deposit( amount);
0036            break;
0037          case BY_DEBIT:
0038            debitRegister.deposit( amount);
0039            break;
0040          case BY_CREDIT:
0041            creditRegister.deposit( amount);
0042            break;
0043          default:
0044            // Unknown deposit method - throw exception!
0045        } // End switch.
0046        this.deposit( amount);
0047    } // End deposit.
```

The five way selection has been implemented using a **switch** structure whose general form is as follows:

```
switch ( selector) {
   case value1:
      first branch
      [break]
   case value2:
   case value3:
      second branch
      [break]
[  default:
      default branch]
} // End switch
```

The decision is controlled by the value of the *selector*; if it matches one of the **case values** then the actions associated with that **case** branch are executed. As soon as one **case** *value* is matched than all actions in all the following branches are also executed. To avoid this and cause all remaining actions to be ignored the **break** keyword can be used at the end of a branch. The last branch can be a **default** section which will be performed if none of the other branches are performed.

In the general example above, if the *selector* matches *value1* then the *first branch* will be performed and, if the **break** is not included, the *second branch* and the *default branch*. If the **break** keyword is used then only the *first branch* will be performed. If the *selector* matches either *value2* or *value3* then the *second branch*, and possibly the *default branch* depending upon the inclusion of a **break**, will be performed. If the *selector* does not match any of *value1*, *value2* or *value3* then the default *branch* will be performed.

In the *deposit()* action above the following complex **if/else if** structure could have been used:

```
0030          if ( method = BY_CASH) {
0031              moneyRegister.deposit( amount);
0032          } else if ( method == BY_CHEQUE) {
0033              chequeRegister.deposit( amount);
0034          } else if ( method == BY_DEBIT) {
0035              debitRegister.deposit( amount);
0036          } else if ( method == BY_CREDIT) {
0037              creditRegister.deposit( amount);
0038          } else {
0039              // Unknown deposit method – throw exception!
0040          } // End if.
```

It should be apparent that the **switch** structure is clearer in its intention and easier to maintain and debug than the equivalent **if/else if** structure and should be favoured for multi-way decisions when it is possible to use it. The major restriction on the use of a **switch** statement is that the selector must be a simple value, e.g. an integer, and not a complex value, e.g. a **double**. The **throw**ing of the exception will be left as an end-of-chapter exercise.

The implementation of the two enquiry actions shown on the class diagram is relatively straightforward, making use of the *MoneyRegister* actions of the appropriate instance:

```
0050    public double depositedByCashIs() {
0051        return moneyRegister.takingsAre();
```

```
0052    } // End depositedByCashIs.
0053
0054    public int numberOfCashTransactionsIs() {
0055        return moneyRegister.numberOfDepositsIs();
0056    } // End numberOfCashTransactionsIs.
```

The implementation of the six other enquiry actions is directly comparable with these two. Finally the *toString()* action constructs its string by catenating the output from all eight enquiry actions to the string returned by the *MoneyRegister toString()* action.

```
0059    public String toString(){
0060        return super.toString() + "\n" +
0061                    this.numberOfCashTransactionsIs()      +
0062                    " cash          transactions totalling " +
0063                    this.depositedByCashIs() + ".\n"      +
0064                    this.numberOfChequeTransactionsIs()   +
0065                    " cheque        transactions totalling " +
0066                    this.depositedByChequeIs() + ".\n"    +
0067                    this.numberOfDebitTransactionsIs()    +
0068                    " debit card transactions totalling " +
0069                    this.depositedByDebitIs() + ".\n"     +
0070                    this.numberOfCreditTransactionsIs()   +
0071                    " credit card transactions totalling " +
0072                    this.depositedByCreditIs() + ".";
0073    } // End toString.
0074
0075 } // End MultipleRegister.
```

The output produced by this action will be illustrated in the demonstration client below.

5.7 ▪ The *MultipleRegisterDemonstration* program client

The demonstration client for this class constructs a *MultipleRegister* instance and makes a number of deposits by all four methods before using System.out.println() to show the action of the *toString()* action. The implementation and output are as follows:

```
0001 // Filename MultipleRegisterDemonstration.java.
0002 // Demonstration of the MultipleRegister class.
0003 //
0004 // Written for JOF book Chapter 5 see text.
0005 // Fintan Culwin, v0.1, August 1997.
0006
0007 import Counters.MultipleRegister;
0008
0009 public class MultipleRegisterDemonstration {
0010
0011    public static void main( String argv[]) {
0012
0013    MultipleRegister  demoRegister = new MultipleRegister( 100.00);
0014
```

```
0015        System.out.println( "\n\t\t Multiple Register demonstration \n");
0016
0017        System.out.print( "The Multiple Register has been created ");
0018        System.out.println( "with a float of 100.00.");
0019
0020
0021        System.out.println( "\nDepositing 5.00, 4.56 and 8.93 by cash.");
0022        demoRegister.deposit( 5.00, MultipleMoneyRegister.BY_CASH);
0023        demoRegister.deposit( 4.56, MultipleMoneyRegister.BY_CASH);
0024        demoRegister.deposit( 8.93, MultipleMoneyRegister.BY_CASH);
0025
0026        System.out.println( "\nDepositing 3.22 by cheque.");
0027        demoRegister.deposit( 3.22, MultipleMoneyRegister.BY_CHEQUE);
0028
0029        System.out.println( "\nDepositing 9.75, 0.56 by debit card.");
0030        demoRegister.deposit( 9.75, MultipleMoneyRegister.BY_DEBIT);
0031        demoRegister.deposit( 0.56, MultipleMoneyRegister.BY_DEBIT);
0032
0033        System.out.println( "\nDepositing 34.67 by credit card.");
0034        demoRegister.deposit( 34.67, MultipleMoneyRegister.BY_CREDIT);
0035
0036        System.out.println("\nThe state of the register is ...\n");
0037        System.out.println( demoRegister);
0038    } // End main.
0039
0040 } // End MultipleRegisterDemonstration.
```

```
              Multiple Register demonstration

   The Multiple Register has been created with a float of 100.00.

   Depositing 5.00, 4.56 and 8.93 by cash.

   Depositing 3.22 by cheque.

   Depositing 9.75, 0.56 by debit card.

   Depositing 34.67 by credit card.

   The state of the register is ...

   Initial float    : 100
   Number of deposits : 7
   Total takings     : 66.69
   Total in register : 166.69
   3 cash        transactions totalling 18.49.
   1 cheque      transactions totalling 3.22.
   2 debit card  transactions totalling 10.31.
   1 credit card transactions totalling 34.67
```

Again a little arithmetic will indicate that the *MultipleRegister* appears to be working correctly and that, as the output from the *toString()* action appears to be correct, it can be assumed that the eight enquiry actions are also correct.

5.8 ▦ Development by extension

Chapters 3, 4 and 5 have introduced the design and implementation of a class hierarchy using a build, test, build, test ... technique. These classes will be (re)used in the following chapters to illustrate other aspects of Java and software development. It would thus be very appropriate at this point to review and revisit the contents of all five initial chapters, before proceeding.

A whistle stop summary of the important points from these chapters might be that in order to deal with the complexity of software artefacts they are built up a stage at a time, each stage adding a small amount of functionality. In order to provide the functionality a class can extend an existing class, in which case it has an *is a* relationship with it. Alternatively it can encapsulate an instance of the class, in which case it has a *has a* relationship with it. The remaining possibility is that it has neither an *is a* nor a *has a* relationship, in which case it merely *uses* an instance of the other class. For example, the program clients do not extend or encapsulate an existing class but declare an instance of them for their own use.

In a Java class hierarchy a class can have only one parent class, although a parent class can have any number of child classes. Within the hierarchy a class can be either **public** or, by default, implicitly **private** and can be **abstract** or non-**abstract**. Each action or data attribute in the class can be **private**, **protected** or **public** and additionally can be class wide or associated with an instance. Data attributes may also be declared as constants but only in a class wide manner.

A class can extend its parent class by the addition of new actions or the overriding of existing actions to make them more specialized. However, it cannot remove actions which, should it be necessary, would suggest a *has a* rather than an *is a* relationship. Finally, a consideration which has not been introduced so far, two classes can declare actions which have identical signatures and comparable effects. Such actions are known as *polymorphic* (from the Greek for many forms). One example of a polymorphic action is the *toString()* action introduced in the three sibling *Counters* classes.

Summary

▦ A child class extending its parent establishes an *is a* relationship.

▦ As a child class cannot remove actions from a parent, which may cause the child to have inappropriate or dangerous actions, this would suggest a *has a* relationship.

▦ A class can override the *toString()* action in order to define what output will be produced when it is passed as an argument to the System.out.println() action.

▦ Attribute enquiry actions should be used in the implementation of the class, rather than using direct access to the attributes, to assist with maintenance and demonstration.

Exercises

5.1 The *RoomMonitor* class as implemented at the start of this chapter *is a WarningMonitor* class, but did not have its warning behaviour demonstrated. Adapt the demonstration client to allow this aspect of its behaviour to be demonstrated.

5.2 Using the first implementation of the *RoomMonitor* class presented in this chapter, adapt the demonstration harness to show that the _count()_ action can be used and results in the monitor having an incorrect set of attribute values.

5.3 Correct the fault in the _RoomMonitor_ class shown in Exercise 5.2 by overriding the _count()_ action in the _RoomMonitor_ declaration to indirect to the _enterRoom()_ action.

5.4 Implement, and demonstrate, the _RoomMonitor_ class as a child class of the _LimitedCounter_ class.

5.5 Review the results of Exercises 5.3 and 5.4 against the second implementation of the _RoomMonitor_ class given in the chapter. Which implementation do you favour? Why?

5.6 Design, implement and demonstrate a _LimitedRoomMonitor_ class which places a limit upon the number of people who can be in the room. It will have to provide a **boolean** _isRoomFull_ action and raise a suitable exception if an attempt is made to enter an room which is full.

5.7 Revisit one of the demonstration clients from a previous chapter and pass an instance of one of the classes to the System.out.println() action in order to discover what is output by the Object toString() action.

5.8 Refer to Chapter 4 and implement a suitable exception class, an instance of which should be thrown in the _MultipleRegister deposit()_ action if an invalid deposit method is specified. Extend the demonstration client to illustrate the throwing of the exception.

5.9 Reimplement the _deposit()_ action in Exercise 5.6 to make use of an **if** structure instead of a **switch** structure. Use the same demonstration client to show the equivalence of the two implementations.

5.10 The _MultipleRegister_ class, as presented in this chapter, could have been implemented without an encapsulated _cashRegister MoneyRegister_ instance, and would store the amount of cash deposits in its inherited attributes. Adapt the implementation to this design consideration and demonstrate its equivalence to the original implementation. Which implementation do you favour? Why?

5.11 Extend the _MoneyRegister_ class to implement a _SalesTaxRegister_ class. Every deposit into the register can be _TAX_FREE_ or _TAX_DUE_ at 17½%. A _TAX_DUE_ deposit should be assumed already to contain the tax which should be removed and an account of the amount of tax kept separate from the amount of takings. Design, implement and demonstrate this class.

5.12 Extend the _SalesTaxRegister_ class to implement a _ChangeGivingTaxRegister_ class. A deposit into this class should specify the amount of the purchase and the amount tendered, and the action should return the change due.

Chapter six

The *BasicMenu* class

All the programs which have been used so far have only produced *output* on the screen and have not required the user to *input* any information from the keyboard. Inputting information is much more complex than outputting information as it cannot be assumed that the user will always respond as expected to any instructions which they are given.

This chapter will introduce a *BasicMenu* class, instances of which can be constructed to offer a number of options and obtain a validated response from the user. In order to do this techniques for representing and manipulating single characters, and sequences of characters known as Strings, will have to be introduced. Each option presented to the user on the menu is represented as a string and, as a number of options have to be presented, the techniques for representing an *iteration* of strings will also have to be introduced. *Iteration* is the technical term for a *repetition*, either of data objects or of actions. The term iteration is preferred as an iteration can represent zero occurrences whereas a repetition implies at least one occurrence.

When the user is presented with the opportunity to respond to the menu it cannot be assumed that they will provide a valid input. Should this happen they will have to be informed that their input is not acceptable and be allowed to respond again. Thus the program will have to iterate a sequence of actions and the techniques for implementing this will also be introduced.

The *BasicMenu* demonstration harness will present a standard *menu/dispatch* design which can be used as a basic design in other applications. The following chapter will illustrate such an application and extend the *BasicMenu* to produce a menu which can dynamically change the options which it offers.

6.1 ▓ The *BasicMenu* user interface

The starting point for the design of any program, or program component, which will interact with the user is to specify the pattern of communication which will happen between the program and the user. This can be thought of as a conversation between the interface designer and the end user, and will be most satisfying to the user if the computer's side of the conversation is conducted with a maximum degree of respect and support. For example, when the user does not respond as expected it should not be regarded or reported as an error or an illegal occurrence, but as a misunderstanding. The reason why the response is unacceptable should be explained and the range and/or format of acceptable responses should be described. The design of the user interface for the *BasicMenu* is as follows:

```
        This is a title for the menu

A. This is the first option.
B. This is the second option.
C. This is the third option.

This is the prompt Z

   Please enter a response between A and C.

This is the prompt a
```

The menu starts with a *title*, which can be specified by the developer, and is followed by a sequence of *options* each of which is labelled with an upper case character. There is no limit on the number of options which the *BasicMenu* can present, but good user interface designs do not have more than about seven options, so as not to overload the user with choices. The list of options is followed by a *prompt*, which can be specified by the developer, and the menu will then wait for the user to type in a response terminated with the ⟨ENTER⟩ key. Only the first character that the user types will be regarded as their response; any other characters will be ignored.

If the user types in a character which does not correspond to one of the menu options a message indicating which responses are acceptable, as shown, will be output and the user will be asked to input a response again. There is no limit on the number of attempts which the user can have to supply a valid response. Once the user has supplied an acceptable character, either in upper or lower case, the menu will terminate.

The example above illustrates a menu with three options and shows the user first inputting an upper case *Z* character. The message 'Please enter a response between A and C' is output to guide the user before the prompt is repeated. The second response from the user is a lower case *a* character, which is acceptable, and the menu terminates.

6.2 ▨ The *BasicMenu* class diagram

The class diagram for the *BasicMenu* class is given in Figure 6.1.

The constructor requires as arguments the *title* for the menu, the *prompt* to be used and the *options* which are to be offered. The square brackets of the *options* argument indicate that this is an iteration which can contain a number of individual options.

Two public actions are exported, *offerMenuAsChar()* and *offerMenuAsInt()*, each of which offers the menu to the user and then conducts a conversation with the user to obtain a valid response. The *offerMenuAsChar()* action will return the user's response as an upper case character identifying which option was selected. The *offerMenuAsInt()* action returns the user's response as an integer value with 1 identifying the first option, 2 the second and so on. The reasons for this second action will be explained when the demonstration harnesses are introduced. The class diagram also indicates a private action, called *showMenu()*, which will actually offer the menu to the user. This is known to be a private action, as opposed to a data attribute, as it contains a verb phrase and has doubled vertical lines.

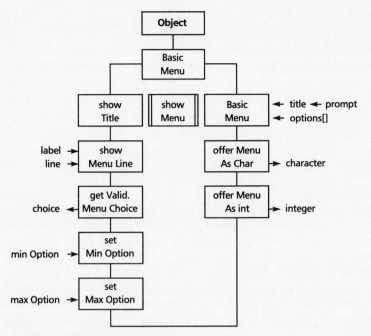

Figure 6.1 *BasicMenu* class diagram.

Additionally a number of protected actions are shown on the left of the diagram. These have been provided in order to make it easier to extend this class; their meaning and use will be described below.

6.3 ▓ The *BasicMenu* data attributes

There are five private data attributes which are required to represent the structure of the menu within the class. These are declared on lines 0011 to 0015 of the following listing:

```
0001 // Filename Menus/BasicMenu.java.
0002 // Providing an initial Interactive Menu.
0003 //
0004 // Written for JOF book Chapter 6 see text.
0005 // Fintan Culwin, v0.1, August 1997.
0006
0007 package Menus;
0008
0009 public class BasicMenu extends Object {
0010
0011 private String theTitle  = null;
0012 private String thePrompt = "Please enter your choice :";
0013 private String theOptions[];
0014 private char   minimumOption;
0015 private char   maximumOption;
```

The first two attributes *theTitle* and *thePrompt* are the title which will be displayed at the top of the menu and the prompt which will invite the user to respond to the menu. Only *thePrompt* is given a default value for reasons which will be explained below.

The default value of *theTitle*, or any other *String*, would be **null**, but this has been made explicit in this listing. On line 0013 *theOptions* are declared, the square brackets indicating to Java that this attribute can contain a number of Strings. It does not actually specify at this stage the number of *String*s which will be stored in it, merely that it is an iteration. An iterative structure such as this is known as an *array*. The final two variables, *minimumOption* and *maximumOption*, identify the range of acceptable responses. The declaration of private attributes concludes with lines 0017 and 0018:

```
0017 private java.io.DataInputStream keyboard =
0018               new java.io.DataInputStream( System.in);
```

In previous programs output has been produced on the screen by using the System.out *stream* object. Streams are places where data can be sent out of, or received into, a program. The destination, or origin, of the data can include disk files, modems, network connections or, for System.out, the screen, and, for System.in, the keyboard. When information is sent to the screen no special processing of the data is required and so the System.out stream, which is a *raw stream*, can be used. When information is obtained from the keyboard raw data would not be especially useful. The raw data stream from the keyboard only knows about characters and not about integers, strings or floating point values. The declaration of the *keyboard* java.io.DataInputStream object, on lines 0017 and 0018, provides a stream which knows about the formatting of data. The *keyboard* stream is constructed from the pre-supplied raw System.in stream. Streams will be introduced in more detail in Chapter 12.

6.4 ▓ The *BasicMenu* constructor

The design of the constructor is as follows:

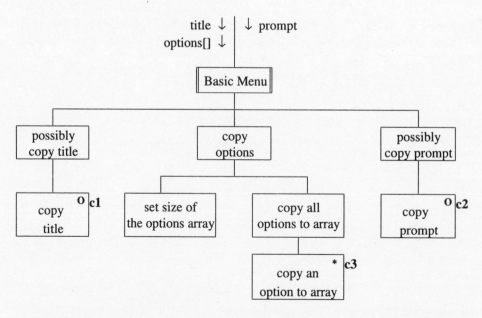

c1: If the title argument is not empty.   c3: For all strings in the options[] argument.
c2: If the prompt argument is not empty.

The first and third steps of the design are concerned with the menu's title and prompt and will be considered after the middle step, *copy options*. The declaration of the private array data attribute, *theOptions[]*, emphasized that it can store an iteration of Strings, but that it did not specify the actual number of *Strings*. The number of Strings which will have to be stored in each instance of this structure depends upon the number of options in the menu and this cannot be known until the menu is constructed.

Thus the first action of this step is to set the size of *theOptions[]* instance attribute array from the size of the *options[]* argument array. Once this has been done each option in turn can be copied from the argument array, *options[]*, to the instance array, *theOptions[]*. To accomplish this a *definite iteration* is indicated on the design. An iterated step is indicated with an asterisk (*) in the top right hand corner of its box and is accompanied by a condition key which states the number of times which it has to be repeated. So, the *copy all options to array* step is implemented as an iteration of the *copy an option to array* step, with the iterated step being repeated as many times as there are strings in the argument array. The condition key identifies this as a definite iteration by using the word *for*.

The implementation of this design, with the *copy options* step between lines 0031 and 0036, is as follows:

```
0021    public BasicMenu( String title,
0022                      String options[],
0023                      String prompt) {
0024
0025    int thisOption;
0026
0027      if ( title.length() > 0 ) {
0028         theTitle = new String( title);
0029      } // End if.
0030
0031      theOptions = new String[ options.length];
0032      for ( thisString = 0;
0033            thisString < options.length;
0034            thisString++              ){
0035         theOptions[ thisString] = new String( options[ thisString]);
0036      } // End for.
0037
0038      if ( prompt.length() > 0) {
0039         thePrompt = new String( prompt);
0040      } // End if.
0041    } // End BasicMenu.
```

Line 0031 implements the design step *set size of the options array*. It does this by using an array constructor (**new** []) to construct a new array of strings (String[]) and causes *theOptions* private array attribute to reference it. The number of Strings is determined by the argument to the constructor and uses the length attribute of the *options[]* argument array. The effect is that *theOptions[]* array is now ready to contain as many Strings as there are Strings in *options[]*, but does not yet contain them.

Each String in *theOptions[]* array is created in turn, on line 0035, using the String constructor specifying as its argument the corresponding String from *options[]*, using *thisOption* as the array index. This is accomplished by enclosing line 0035 within a **for** loop structure, whose general form is as follows:

```
for( Initial Actions;
     Termination Condition;
     Loop End Actions      ){
   // Loop Body.
} // End for loop.
```

The behaviour of this structure is first to execute the _Initial Actions_ and to evaluate immediately the _Termination Condition_. If the _Termination Condition_ evaluates **false** at this stage the loop structure will terminate without the body of the loop being performed even once. Otherwise the _Loop Body_ actions will be executed, following which the _Loop End Actions_ will be performed. At this stage the _Termination Condition_ is evaluated for a second time and will cause the loop structure to terminate if it is now **false**. If not, the pattern of executing the _Loop Body_ and the _Loop End Actions_ before re-evaluating the _Termination Condition_ will continue until at some stage the condition will (hopefully) evaluate **false** and terminate the loop.

This should become clearer if this part of the constructor is traced using a menu consisting of three options, "_First option_", "_Second option_" and "_Third option_". The state of the program objects just before line 0031 is executed can be visualized as shown in Figure 6.2.

The diagram shows the _options_ array of type String[] at the left containing an array of three strings indexed by the values 0, 1 and 2. In the middle is the local variable _thisOption_ of type **int** with its default value 0 and on the right is _theOptions_ of type String[] which does not yet reference an array.

The execution of line 0031 will cause Java to determine the number of strings in the _options_ array (_options.length_) and use this value to construct a new array of strings with the same number of elements (**new** String[_options_.length]) and cause _theOptions_ to reference it. The situation is now as shown in Figure 6.3.

The array _theOptions_ is now capable of storing three strings, but does not at this stage actually contain any strings. The first action of the **for** loop on line 0032 is to assign the value 0 to _thisOption_ and then test the termination condition,

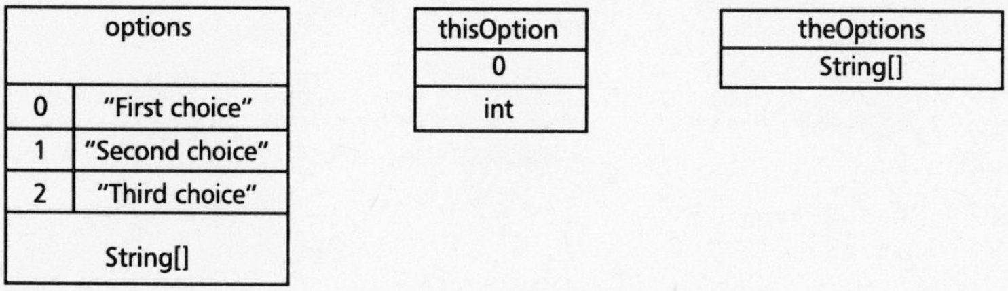

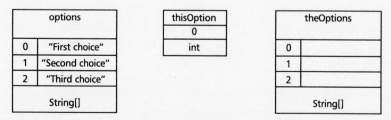

Figure 6.2   _BasicMenu_ constructor before array sizing.

Figure 6.3   _BasicMenu_ constructor after array sizing.

thisOption < *options*.length. This is effectively 0 < 3 which is **true** and causes the body of the loop on line 0035 to be performed. This line causes the *theOptions* array element indexed by the value of *thisOption* to refer to a newly created String object with a value initialized from the *options* array element indexed by the same value. Or, put more simply, if a little less accurately, it copies the string from position 0 in the *options* array to the same position in *theOptions* array. As this is the end of the loop body the *Loop End Actions* of the **for** structure, on line 0034, are performed, incrementing the value of *thisOption* to 1. The situation is now as shown in Figure 6.4.

At this point the *Termination Condition* will be evaluated for a second time, effectively 1 < 3, which is still **true**. The loop body will iterate for a second time making a copy of the string indexed by 1 in *theOptions* array and incrementing the value of *thisOption* to 2. The condition will still evaluate **true** causing a third iteration to copy the string at index position 2 before incrementing *thisOption* to 3. The situation at this stage is shown in Figure 6.5.

At this stage the *Termination Condition* will be effectively 3 < 3, which is **false**, and the loop will terminate.

The remaining parts of the constructor are concerned with initializing *theTitle* and *thePrompt* data attributes from their corresponding arguments. *TheTitle* is declared on line 0011 with no default value and *thePrompt* on line 0012 with the default value "Please enter your choice :". The call to the constructor need not specify a *Title* argument in which case no *theTitle* string is constructed on lines 0027 to 0029, and, as will be shown, no title will be displayed before the menu is shown. Likewise the constructor need not be provided with a *Prompt* argument, in which case the default prompt is not changed on lines 0038 to 0040.

Before finishing the consideration of the *BasicMenu* constructor one potential insecurity ought to be noted. If the call of the constructor does not specify any strings in the *options[]* argument, or even if it specifies only a single string, this implementation will not notice and will present a menu with no choices or a single choice. This insecurity will be addressed in an end-of-chapter exercise.

options	
0	"First choice"
1	"Second choice"
2	"Third choice"
String[]	

thisOption	
1	
int	

theOptions	
0	"First choice"
1	
2	
String[]	

Figure 6.4   *BasicMenu* constructor after first iteration of the loop.

options	
0	"First choice"
1	"Second choice"
2	"Third choice"
String[]	

thisOption	
3	
int	

theOptions	
0	"First choice"
1	"Second choice"
2	"Third choice"
String[]	

Figure 6.5   *BasicMenu* constructor after third iteration of the loop.

6.5 ▨ The *BasicMenu showMenu()* action and its supporting actions

The class diagram at the start of this chapter suggested that there is a private action called *showMenu()* whose detailed considerations would indicate that it has to display the menu and set the values of the two instance data attributes, *minimumValidChoice* and *maximumValidChoice*, appropriately. It does this by making use of some of the semipublic actions shown on the left of the class diagram:

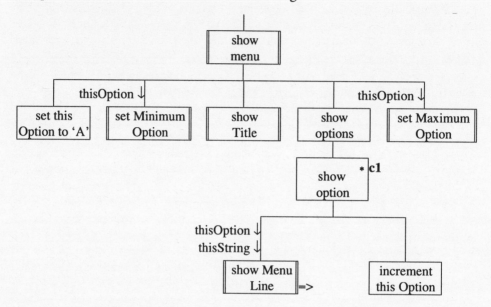

c1: For all menu options.

The basis of the design is to set the value of a local **char**acter variable, called *thisOption*, to 'A', and initialize the value of *minimumOption* to this value using the *setMinimumOption()* action. Then, after calling the *showTitle()* action, each menu option is iteratively output by using the *showMenuLine()* action before the value of *thisOption* is incremented. Outside the loop the *setMaximumOption()* is called passing the value of *thisOption* as its argument. The implementation of this design is as follows:

```
0062    private void showMenu() {
0063
0064    int   thisString;
0065    char thisOption = 'A';
0066
0067      setMinimumOption( thisOption);
0068
0069      showTitle();
0070
0071      for ( thisString = 0;
0072           thisString < theOptions.length;
0073           thisString++ ){
0074        showMenuLine( thisOption, thisString);
0075        thisOption++;
0076      } // End for.
```

```
0077        setMaximumOption( --thisOption);
0078    } // End showMenu.
```

On line 0064 a local variable of type **int** called *thisString* is declared and will be used to count through the **for** loop when the menu is output in exactly the same way as in the constructor above. On line 0065 a second local variable of type **char** called *thisOption* is declared and initialized to 'A'. This variable will be used to record the key for the current menu option. The *setMinimumOption()* is then called on line 0067 to set the value of the *minimumOption* attribute to the value of *thisOption*, effectively 'A'. The value of the *minimumOption* attribute delineates the minimum acceptable choice which the user can select from the menu.

On line 0069 the *showTitle()* action is called before the **for** loop starts on line 0071. The construction of this loop is essentially identical to that used in the constructor above. Within the body of the loop a call of *showMenuLine()* is made passing as arguments the values of *thisOption* and of the loop index *thisString*. The effect of *showMenuLine()*, as will be explained below, is to output its first argument as the menu key and use the second argument to indicate which option is to be output as the menu element text. The effect of this call is to output 'A' as the key and "First choice" as the text.

Before the loop body finishes the value *thisOption* is incremented; just as the incrementation of an integer variable caused it to take the next integer value in sequence, the incrementation of a character variable causes it to take the next character value in sequence. So, as *thisOption* had the value 'A' at the start of the first iteration it would have the value 'B' after the first execution of line 0075. The state of the instance attributes following the first iteration of the loop including the end of the loop actions of the **for** statement, based upon the visualizations given above, is as shown in Figure 6.6.

The diagram shows the two local variables on the left and three of the five instance variables on the right. The value of *maximumOption* is shown as a null character (") which is its known default value. As the **for** loop termination condition will evaluate **true** (1 < 3) the body of the loop will iterate for a second time calling *showMenuLine()* which will output the key 'B' and the "Second choice" string before incrementing the value of the two local variables to 2 and 'C' respectively.

As the condition is still **true** (2 < 3) the loop will iterate for a third time outputting 'C' and "Third choice" before incrementing the two variables to 3 and 'D'. At this point the **for** loop will terminate as 3 < 3 is **false**.

The next action on the design is a call of *setMaximumOption()* which, if it were

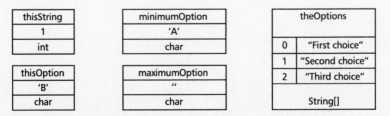

Figure 6.6 Variables and attributes during *ShowMenu* iteration.

simply passed the value of *thisOption*, would result in the upper limit of the range of valid options being set to 'D', which is incorrect. Accordingly line 0077 passes the decremented value as the argument. The effect of this operation (*--thisOption*) is first to decrement the value of *thisOption*, from 'D' to 'C', and then pass the resulting value to *setMaximumOption()*. If it were mis-implemented as *setMaximumOption (thisOption--)*, the effect would be first to pass the value 'D' and then decrement the value to 'C'. The first of these possibilities, *--thisOption*, is known as a pre-decrement operation; the second, *thisOption--*, as a post-decrement operation.

The implementation of the *showMenu()* action relies upon the implementation of the four actions: *showTitle()*, *showMenuLine()*, *setMinimumOption()* and *setMaximumOption*. The implementation of these actions is as follows:

```
0081    private void showTitle() {
0082       if ( theTitle != null) {
0083           System.out.println( "\t" + theTitle + "\n");
0084       } // End if.
0085    } // End showTitle.
0086
0087
0088    protected void showMenuLine( char menulabel, int menuText) {
0089       System.out.println( menulabel + ".    " + theOptions[ menuText]);
0090    } // End showMenuLine.
0091
0092
0093    protected void setMinimumOption( char setTo) {
0094       minimumOption = setTo;
0095    } // End setMinimumOption.
0096
0097
0098    protected void setMaximumOption( char setTo){
0099       maximumOption = setTo;
0100    } // End setMinimumOption.
```

The *showTitle()* action will only output a title for the menu if one has been set by the constructor, otherwise it outputs nothing. The implementation of *setMinimumOption()* and *setMaximumOption()* is straightforward, setting the value of the appropriate attribute from their single argument. The *showMenuLine()* action has two arguments: the first is a **char**acter called *menuLabel* which is output directly as the label for the menu line; the second argument, an **int**eger called *menuText*, is used to index into *theOptions* array to obtain the text which is to be output on the line.

6.6 ■ The *BasicMenu getValidatedMenuChoice()* action

The purpose of the *getValidatedMenuChoice()* action is to engage the user in a dialog, asking them to input a choice from the menu and deciding if it is, or is not, an acceptable choice. If the user does not supply an acceptable choice they should be given advice concerning what responses are acceptable and invited to try again. The action will not finish until the user has supplied a validated choice from the menu:

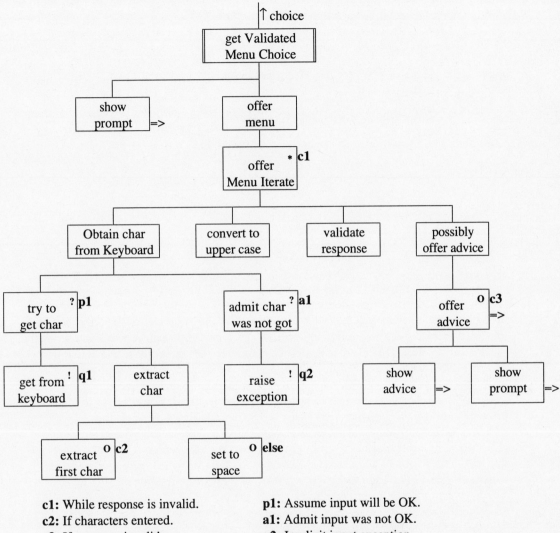

c1: While response is invalid.
c2: If characters entered.
c3: If response invalid.

p1: Assume input will be OK.
a1: Admit input was not OK.
q2: Implicit input exception.
q1: Raise explicit exception.

Obtaining input from the keyboard is one of the most potentially dangerous parts of a program, as it cannot be known exactly what the user might actually do. Java recognizes this and guards any input actions with exceptions which the developer must handle. This is shown on this design as the step *obtain char from keyboard* and is implemented as a *posit/admit* design structure. The *posit* part of the design assumes that everything will occur without an exception being thrown, while the *admit* recognizes that something did go wrong. Both of these are shown on the design with a ? in the top right hand corner of their boxes; the posit is keyed with a **p** and the admit with an **a**. Precise details of posit/admit design structures will be introduced in Chapter 9. For the time being the implementation of this action as far as the end of the posit/admit structure is as follows:

```
0103    protected char getValidatedMenuChoice(){
0104
0105    String   fromKeyboard      = new String( "");
0106    char     possibleResponse  = ' ';
0107    boolean  isNotGoodResponse = true;
0108
0109       System.out.print( "\n"+ thePrompt + " ");
0110       System.out.flush();
0111
0112       while ( isNotGoodResponse) {
0113          try {
0114             fromKeyboard =  new String( keyboard.readLine());
0115             if ( fromKeyboard.length() > 0) {
0116                possibleResponse  = fromKeyboard.charAt( 0);
0117             } else {
0118                possibleResponse  = ' ';
0119             } // End if.
0120          } catch( java.io.IOException exception) {
0121             // do something
0122          } // end try/catch.
0123
```

The first part of the action is to output the prompt, accomplished on lines 0109 to 0110. As the user interface design indicates that the response is expected to be obtained from the same screen line a *print()*, not a println(), action has been used to output the prompt. However, this will not guarantee that the prompt will actually be visible to the user at the end of this action, as it is very common for lines of output not to be *flushed* to the screen until a new line is required. To ensure that the prompt is certainly visible a call to the System.out flush() action is used. The effect of this call is to make sure that all characters sent to the screen have definitely been output.

The posit/admit design structure is implemented in Java as a **try/catch** structure. The **try** part corresponds to the posit and the **catch** to the admit. The first action of the try part is to obtain whatever the user types in at the keyboard using the readLine() action on line 0114. The readLine() action is in some ways the inverse of a println() action, accepting characters typed at the keyboard until an ⟨ENTER⟩ keypress is made. The user's response from readLine() is used as the argument of a String constructor and the resulting string is referenced by the local variable *fromKeyboard*.

Assuming that the readLine() action does not throw an exception, the next action is to examine the input provided by the user. It is possible that the user has just pressed the ⟨ENTER⟩ key without providing a response, in which case *fromKeyboard* will be empty and its length will be zero. If this is the case the value of the local character variable *possibleResponse* is set to a space on line 0118. If the user did supply a response then the first character, at location 0, is extracted from it using the String charAt() action on line 0116 and stored in *possibleResponse*. If no exception is thrown the **catch** part of the **try/catch** structure is skipped and execution of the action continues with the statements following the **catch**, from line 0123 onwards.

However, the readLine() action may throw a java.io.IOException at line 0114 in which case lines 0115 to 0119 are skipped and the exception is caught by the **catch** statement at line 0120. The statements in the **catch** part of the structure should attempt to deal with the problem which has been detected; the techniques for doing this will be introduced in Chapter 9. The remaining parts of the implementation of this action are as follows:

```
0124        possibleResponse = Character.toUpperCase( possibleResponse);
0125
0126        isNotGoodResponse = ( (possibleResponse < minimumValidOption) ||
0127                              (possibleResponse > maximumValidOption) );
0128
0129      if ( isNotGoodResponse ) {
0130          System.out.println( "\n Please enter a response between " +
0131                                      minimumOption + " and " +
0132                                      maximumOption + ".");
0133          System.out.print( "\n"+ thePrompt + " ");
0134          System.out.flush();
0135      } // End if
0136    } // End while.
0137    return possibleResponse;
0138 } // End getValidatedMenuChoice.
```

The first step in the design is *convert to upper case* and this is accomplished on line 0124 with a call to the class wide **Character** action toUppercase(). This action takes a character as an argument and returns the character unchanged if it is already an upper case character or does not have an upper case equivalent, otherwise the upper case equivalent of the character is returned. The effect of line 0124 is to make sure that, if an alphabetic character is obtained from the user, it is an upper case character before it is validated.

The character is validated on lines 0126 and 0127 where the result of a complex boolean expression is assigned to the local **boolean** variable *isNotGoodResponse*. The expression can be read as "(if) the value of *possibleResponse* is less than (<) the value of *minimumOption* or (||) the value of *possibleResponse* is greater than (>) the value of *maximumOption*". The evaluation of this expression makes use of the ***boolean or rule*** which combines two boolean values to produce a single boolean value as shown in Table 6.1.

The or rule can be summarized by saying that the resulting expression is true if either or both the subexpressions are true. Further details of the use of the **boolean** primitive type can be found in Appendix A3. The or rule can be investigated in the context of this action by considering the effects when the user enters '@', 'A', 'C' or 'D' when *minimumOption* and *maximumOption* have the values 'A' and 'C' respectively. The value '@' was chosen as it is the character whose value is immediately less than that of 'A', and 'D' as it is the character whose value is immediately greater than that of

Table 6.1 The boolean or rule.

	or	
Left	**Right**	**Result**
false	false	false
true	false	true
false	true	true
true	true	true

'C'. These relations can be confirmed from the character table in Table A4.1. The evaluation of the combined expression is shown in Table 6.2.

This table shows that the combined expression is false only when the user enters 'A' or 'C', and by implication 'B'; the expression is true in all other circumstances. The resulting **boolean** value is assigned to the local **boolean** variable *isNotGoodResponse* and is used in the next step of the design to decide if a helpful message should be output.

The implementation of the *possibly offer advice* step is on lines 0129 to 0135 and uses the value of *isNotGoodResponse* as the condition of an **if** structure. Thus if the user entered an acceptable response the value of *isNotGoodResponse* will be **false** and the message will not be output. Otherwise *isNotGoodResponse* will be **true** and the advice will be given. The advice is constructed by catenating together various messages with the values of *minimumOption* and *maximumOption* to produce an output something like this:

```
Please enter a response between A and C.
```

Following the output of the advice the prompt is again issued and flushed to the screen ready for the next response from the user.

Line 0136, immediately following the End if on line 0135, is commented as the end of the **while** loop structure which started on line 0112. When the menu options were being output Java was able to decide from the array length attribute how many times the loop would have to iterate. However, in this action there is no way that Java can know how many times the loop is to iterate until an acceptable response is obtained from the user. The difference between these two situations is the difference between a definite (**for**) loop and an indefinite (**while**) loop. The general form of a **while** loop is as follows:

```
while ( Condition) {
    // Loop body.
} // End loop.
```

The effect of this structure, when it is executed, is that the *Condition* is first evaluated and if it is **true** the loop terminates without the *Loop Body* actions ever being executed. Otherwise the *Loop Body* actions are executed and then the condition is evaluated again. Should the condition again evaluate **true** this pattern will repeat indefinitely until (hopefully) at some stage the condition will evaluate **false**, causing the loop to terminate.

Table 6.2 The or rule in the *offerMenuAsChar()* action.

possibleResponse	possibleResponse < minimumOption ('A')	possibleResponse > maximumOption ('C')	Result
'@'	true	false	true
'A'	false	false	false
'C'	false	false	false
'D'	false	true	true

In the context of this action, the local **boolean** variable *isNotGoodResponse* is declared with the initial value **true**, which causes the **while** condition on line 0112 to evaluate **true** when it is encountered for the first time. This will ensure that at least one response is obtained from the user and assuming that it is not acceptable the value of *isNotGoodResponse* will be set **true** again, on lines 0126 and 0127, causing the advice to be output and the **while** condition to be re-evaluated.

As the re-evaluation will still be **true**, the loop will iterate for a second time obtaining another response from the user. This could again be an unacceptable response which will cause exactly the same pattern of events to occur, leading to a third response being obtained from the user. This process will continue indefinitely until the user eventually provides an acceptable response. This will cause the value of *isNotGoodResponse* to be set **false** on lines 0126 and 0127, causing the advice not to be output and the **while** condition to evaluate **false**, terminating the loop.

When the **while** loop terminates the final part of this action is, on line 0137, to **return** the value of *possibleResponse*, which is now known to be a valid choice from the menu, as the result of the action.

6.7 ▦ The *BasicMenu offerMenuAsChar()* and *offerMenuAsInt()* actions

The *offerMenuAsChar()* action makes use of the **private** and **protected** actions which have already been described. It commences by calling the *showMenu()* action to present the menu and then the *getValidatedMenuChoice()* action to obtain a valid response. The validated menu response is stored in a local character variable, called *validatedResponse*, before being returned to the client as the result of the function:

```
0044    public char offerMenuAsChar() {
0045
0046    char validatedResponse;
0047
0048       this.showMenu();
0049       validatedResponse = getValidatedMenuChoice();
0050       return validatedResponse;
0051    } // End offerMenuAsChar.
```

The final action of the *BasicMenu* class is *offerMenuAsInt()* which is implemented as a call of *offerMenuAsChar()*, followed by the conversion of the **char**acter value to an **int**eger value. The implementation of this action is as follows:

```
0054    public int offerMenuAsInt() {
0055
0056    char responseAsChar = offerMenuAsChar();
0057
0058       return ( ((int) responseAsChar) - ((int) 'A') ) + 1;
0059    } // End offerMenuAsInt.
```

Line 0056 obtains the user's response as a **char**acter and on line 0058 it is converted to an **int**eger value. This is accomplished by obtaining the difference between the **int**eger value of *responseAsChar* and the **int**eger value of character 'A', and then adding 1. For example, if the user entered 'B' then 'B' − 'A' would be 1, which with 1 added would be 2. Thus, using the three option menu as illustrated throughout this chapter, if the user entered 'A', 1 would be returned by this action, 'B' would return 2 and 'C' would return 3. The use of this action will be illustrated in the second demonstration client below.

6.8 ▦ The *BasicMenuDemonstration* clients

In order to demonstrate the *BasicMenu* class two demonstration clients, one using the *offerMenuAsChar()* action and one illustrating the use of the *offerMenuAsInt()* action, will be presented. The implementation of the first version is as follows:

```
0001 // Filename BasicMenuDemonstration.java.
0002 // Providing a demonstration of the initial Interactive Menu.
0003 //
0004 // Written for JOF book Chapter 6 see text.
0005 // Fintan Culwin, v0.1, August 1997.
0006
0007 import Menus.BasicMenu;
0008
0009 public class BasicMenuDemonstration {
0010
0011     public static void main( String argv[]) {
0012
0013     String demoOptions[] = { "This is the first option",
0014                              "This is the second option",
0015                              "This is the third option"};
0016
0017     char demoCharChoice;
0018
0019     BasicMenu demoMenu = new BasicMenu( "This is the title",
0020                                         demoOptions,
0021                                         "This is the prompt");
0022
0023         System.out.println( "\n\t\t Basic Menu demonstration ");
0024
0025         System.out.println( "\n\n Testing the offerMenuAsChar() action ... \n\n");
0026         demoCharChoice = demoMenu.offerMenuAsChar();
0027         System.out.println( "\n\You chose " + demoCharChoice + " from the menu.");
0028     } // End main.
0029 } // End BasicMenuDemonstration.
```

On line 0013 an array of Strings called *demoOptions[]* is declared and implicitly sized as it is initialized to contain the prompts for three menu options. A *BasicMenu* called *demoMenu* is constructed on lines 0019 to 0021 specifying a title, the options from *demoOptions[]* and a prompt. On line 0026 the menu is offered using the *demoMenu offerMenuAsChar()* action and the character obtained stored in the character variable *demoCharChoice*, before being output as a confirmation of the correct implementation of the action. The behaviour of this harness when it was executed and interacted with was as follows, with the user's input shown highlighted.

```
                    Basic Menu demonstration


        Testing the offerMenuAsChar() action ...


                This is the title

        A.    This is the first option
        B.    This is the second option
        C.    This is the third option

        This is the prompt D
        Please enter a response between A and C.

        This is the prompt @
        Please enter a response between A and C.

        This is the prompt b

        You chose B from the menu.
```

The second demonstration harness, known as *MenuDispatchDemonstration*, illustrates the intended use of the *obtainMenuAsInt()* action. The implementation of this harness is as follows:

```
0001 // Filename MenuDispatchDemonstration.java.
0002 // Providing a demonstration of the initial Interactive Menu,
0003 // showing its use with manifest values.
0004 //
0005 // Written for JOF book Chapter 6 see text.
0006 // Fintan Culwin, v0.1, August 1997.
0007
0008 import Menus.BasicMenu;
0009
0010 public class MenuDispatchDemonstration {
0011
0012 private static final int FIRST_OPTION  = 1;
0013 private static final int SECOND_OPTION = 2;
0014 private static final int THIRD_OPTION  = 3;
0015
0016    public static void main( String argv[]) {
0017
0018    String demoOptions[] = {"This is the first option",
0019                            "This is the second option",
0020                            "This is the third option"};
0021
0022    int   demoIntChoice;
0023
```

```
0024    BasicMenu demoMenu = new BasicMenu( "",
0025                                        demoOptions,
0026                                        "");
0027
0028       System.out.println( "\n\t\t Basic Menu demonstration ");
0029
0030       System.out.println( "\n\n Testing the offerMenuAsInt() action ... \n\n");
0031       demoIntChoice = demoMenu.offerMenuAsInt();
0032
0033       switch ( demoIntChoice) {
0034          case FIRST_OPTION:
0035             System.out.println( "\n\n You chose the first option.");
0036             break;
0037          case SECOND_OPTION:
0038             System.out.println( "\n\n You chose the second option.");
0039             break;
0040          case THIRD_OPTION:
0041             System.out.println( "\n\n You chose the third option.");
0042       } // End switch.
0043    } // End main.
0044 } // End   MenuDispatchDemonstrations.
```

The harness illustrates, on lines 0024 to 0026, the calling of the *BasicMenu* constructor with empty *Title* and *Prompt* arguments, which should cause the menu to be presented without a title and with the default prompt. However, the major difference is the use of manifest values to identify which option has been chosen from the menu, and to dispatch to an appropriate **case** branch within a **switch** structure. In order to do this the *offerMenuAsInt()* action has to be used as manifest values are, by convention, **int**eger. An outline general design for this harness, which can be easily adapted for more realistic clients, would be as follows:

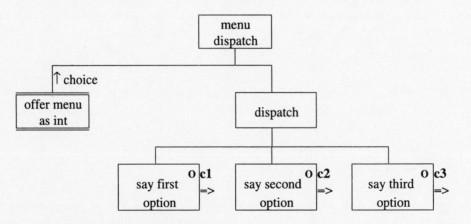

c1: If first menu option chosen.
c2: If second menu option chosen.
c3: If third menu option chosen.

A sample output from this program is as follows:

```
          Basic Menu demonstration


Testing the offerMenuAsInt() action ...



A.    This is the first option
B.    This is the second option
C.    This is the third option

Please enter your choice : k
Please enter a response between A and C.

Please enter your choice : d
Please enter a response between A and C.

Please enter your choice : B

You chose the second option.
```

As expected this demonstration presents the menu with no title and with the default prompt.

Summary

- A user interface is a conversation between the computer and the user designed by the developer.

- An iterative data structure is known as an *array* and is shown as an iterated component on a data structure diagram.

- Arrays can be sized implicitly as they are declared or explicitly when they are constructed.

- The length attribute of an array indicates the number of elements which it contains.

- System.in can be used as a raw input stream, but is more useful if it is used to construct a DataInputStream.

- The number of times a *definite iteration* will iterate can be known by the time Java reaches the loop and is implemented by a **for** loop.

- The number of times an *indefinite iteration* will iterate cannot be known until the loop is reached and is implemented in Java by a **while** loop.

- A *pre-increment* operation, e.g. ++variable, increments the value and then references it. A *post-increment* operation, e.g. variable++, references the value before incrementing it.

- Exception handling can be designed with a posit/admit approach and implemented in Java as a **try/catch** structure.

- Two **boolean** values can be combined with an or (||) operator.

Exercises

6.1   Extend the demonstration harnesses so that they provide a more comprehensive demonstration that the *BasicMenu* class operates correctly. For example, it has only been demonstrated with three options.

6.2   Reimplement the *BasicMenu* constructor so that it throws a suitable exception, which should not be caught, if it is called with zero or one options. Demonstrate that the exception is thrown when appropriate.

6.3   The **catch** part of the exception handler in the *offerMenuAsInt()* action should propagate the exception by raising its own specific exception. Reimplement the action to accomplish this and then demonstrate it by generating an end-of-file character from the keyboard. (Under MS-DOS an end of file is a ⟨CONTROL⟩C keypress, under Unix a ⟨CONTROL⟩D and on some other systems ⟨CONTROL⟩Z.)

6.4   Implement and demonstrate, using *offerMenuAsInt()*, a menu which offers choices for payment by cash, cheque, debit card and credit card, as introduced in the *MultipleRegister* class from Chapter 5.

Chapter seven

The *AdaptingMenu* class

This chapter will extend the *BasicMenu* class, presented in the previous chapter, to produce the *AdaptingMenu* class. An adapting menu introduces the possibility of parts of the menu being made unavailable to the user under certain conditions, a frequent requirement in user interface design.

For example, a menu to control an application which makes use of the *RoomMonitor* class may contain options to record a person entering the room, record a person leaving the room, to show the state of the monitor and to exit from the program. All four of these options may be present on a menu, but the option to record a person leaving the room should not be made available until at least one person has entered the room. Likewise the option to exit from the program should not be available unless there are no people in the room.

The reason for introducing this class at this stage in the book is to consolidate the understanding of iterative data structures which were introduced in the previous chapter. Consequently there are no major new concepts introduced.

7.1 ▓ The *AdaptingMenu* class diagram, data attributes and constructor

The *AdaptingMenu* class diagram is presented in Figure 7.1.

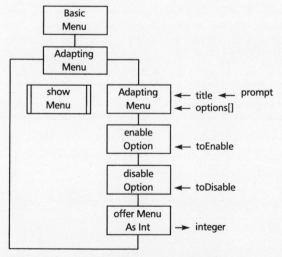

Figure 7.1 *AdaptingMenu* class diagram.

The diagram shows that, in addition to the constructor, the class supplies new actions to enable and to disable a menu option, as well as an overriding *offerMenuAsInt()* action. It also suggests that it provides its own private *showMenu()* action. The implementation of this design as far as the end of the constructor is as follows:

```
0001 // Filename Menus/AdaptingMenu.java.
0002 // Providing an extended menu which can change
0003 // the options which it presents.
0004 //
0005 // Written for JOF book Chapter 7 see text.
0006 // Fintan Culwin, v0.1, August 1997.
0007
0008 package Menus;
0009
0010 public class AdaptingMenu extends Menus.BasicMenu {
0011
0012 boolean inUse[];
0013 char    optionKey[];
0014
0015    public AdaptingMenu( String title,
0016                         String options[],
0017                         String prompt) {
0018
0019
0020       super( title, options, prompt);
0021       inUse     = new boolean[ options.length];
0022       optionKey = new    char[ options.length];
0023    } // End AdaptingMenu constructor.
```

This class introduces two additional iterative data attributes: a **boolean** array called *inUse* which indicates which options are currently in use, and a **char**acter array called *optionKey* which indicates which menu key is associated with each option. The use made of these arrays will be described below.

The three arguments of the constructor are used in exactly the same way as the three arguments of the *BasicMenu* constructor. The first step of the *AdaptingMenu* constructor is to call the *BasicMenu* constructor passing on the three arguments. The remaining actions of the constructor are to create the two arrays, *inUse[]* and *optionKey[]*, with sizes determined by the number of elements in the *options[]* argument array. The state of the data attributes of an instance of the *AdaptingMenu* class, using the same example values as were used for the *BasicMenu* class immediately after it has been constructed, is shown in Figure 7.2.

The default value of a **boolean** variable is **false** and so all values in the *inUse[]* array are shown to be false. This will be interpreted to mean that upon construction none of the menu options are active. The default value of a character variable is the null character, shown as °. The use of the *optionKey[]* array will be described below.

7.2 ■ The *enableMenuOption()*, *disableMenuOption()* and *showMenu()* actions

The implementation of the *enableMenuOption()* and *disableMenuOption()* actions is straightforward, setting the corresponding value of the *inUse[]* array to **true** or **false**

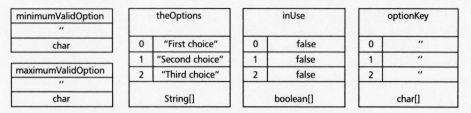

Figure 7.2   Default state of the attributes of an *AdaptingMenu* instance.

respectively. The implementation of these two actions is as follows:

```
0025    public void enableMenuOption( int toEnable){
0026      inUse[ toEnable] = true;
0027    } // End enableMenuOption.
0028
0029    public void disableMenuOption( int toDisable){
0030      inUse[ toDisable] = false;
0031    } // End enableMenuOption.
```

The *showMenu()* action has to display only the active menu options, each preceded by a consecutive menu key. For example, if an instance of the *AdaptingMenu* class has the state as shown in Figure 7.3, the menu presented to the user should be as follows:

```
    Adapting Menu Demonstration

 A First choice.
 B Third choice.

 Please enter your choice :
```

Figure 7.3 also illustrates the required state of the *optionKey[]* array and the *minimumOption* and *maximumOption* attributes after the *showMenu()* action has completed. The *optionKey[]* array indicates which character is currently associated with each menu option, or a space if the option is not in use. As with the *BasicMenu* class the *minimumValidOption* and *maximumValidOption* attributes delineate the range of acceptable responses to the menu. It is the responsibility of the *showMenu()* action to ensure that these attributes are placed into this well defined state. The design of the

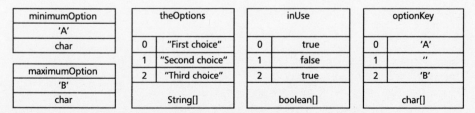

Figure 7.3   Example state of the attributes of an *AdaptingMenu* instance.

showMenu() action is as follows:

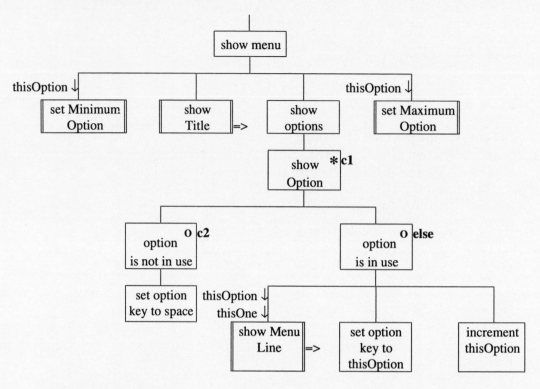

c1: For all menu options.
c2: If this option is not in use.

The basis of the design is first to set the *minimumOption* to the value of a local variable called *thisOption* and to call the *showTitle()* action. Each menu option is then considered in turn and if it is not currently in use the corresponding entry in the *optionKey[]* array is set to a space. Otherwise the option must be in use and it is output with a call to *showMenuLine()* passing the value of *thisOption* and the loop index *thisOne* as arguments. The *optionKey* entry is then set to the value of *thisOption* before the value of *thisOption* is incremented. The final action of *showMenu()* is to set the *maximumOption*. The implementation of this design is as follows:

```
0054    private void showMenu() {
0055
0056    int  thisOne;
0057    char thisOption = 'A';
0058
0059        setMinimumOption( thisOption);
0060
0061        showTitle();
0062
0063        System.out.println();
0064        for (thisOne = 0;
0065            thisOne < optionKey.length;
0066            thisOne ++ ) {
0067            if ( ! inUse[thisOne]) {
```

```
0068                     optionKey[ thisOne] = ' ';
0069             } else {
0070                 showMenuLine( thisOption, thisOne);
0071                 optionKey[ thisOne] = thisOption;
0072                 thisOption++;
0073             } // End if.
0074         } // End for.
0075         setMaximumOption( --thisOption);
0076     } // End showMenu.
```

The clue to understanding this design is the relationship between *thisOption* and *thisOne*: *thisOption* is only incremented whenever an option is output and so the menu is presented with a continuous range of menu keys ('A', 'B', 'C', etc.). The variable *thisOne* is the loop index and so it is incremented on every iteration. Thus the values of *thisOption* and *thisOne* will not always both be incremented on every iteration.

7.3 ▨ The *offerMenuAsInt()* action

The final action of the *AdaptingMenu* class is the *offerMenuAsInt()* action. The design for this action is as follows:

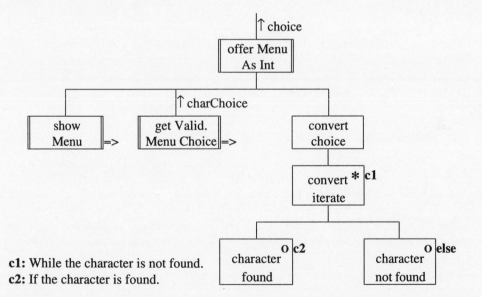

c1: While the character is not found.
c2: If the character is found.

The basis of this design is to show the menu, using *showMenu()*, and obtain a validated character choice, using *getValidatedMenuChoice()* inherited from *BasicMenu*. The character obtained from the user is then converted into the appropriate integer value by searching through the *optionKey[]* array until the character entered by the user is located. The index of this location is then used as the value to be returned by the action.

Using the visualization shown in Figure 7.3 and assuming that the user entered 'B', the search would locate 'B' in the *optionKey[]* array at location 2 and return this as the user's choice from the menu options. Thus it is always the manifest value of the option which is returned by this action, not the position which the option might occupy on the menu. The implementation of this design is as follows:

```
0034    public int offerMenuAsInt() {
0035
0036    char    responseAsChar;
0037    int     thisOne      = 0;
0038    boolean isNotFound   = true;
0039
0040        showMenu();
0041        responseAsChar = getValidatedMenuChoice();
0042
0043        while ( isNotFound) {
0044            if ( optionKey[ thisOne] == responseAsChar) {
0045                isNotFound = false;
0046            } else {
0047                thisOne++;
0048            } // End if.
0049        } // End while.
0050        return thisOne;
0051    } // End offerMenuAsInt.
```

The indefinite loop controlling the search of the *optionKey[]* array is controlled by a **boolean** variable called *isNotFound* in a similar way to the control of the loop in *getValidatedMenuChoice()*, as described in the previous chapter. This action trusts the *showMenu()* action to make sure that the values of *minimumOption* and *maximumOption* and the *optionKey[]* array are set as specified above. Thus the value obtained by *getValidatedMenuChoice()* must be one of the values stored in the *optionKey[]* array and this guarantees that the loop in this action will terminate without attempting to access a value outside the range of the array.

7.4 ■ The *AdaptingMenuDemonstration* client

The basis of this demonstration client is to construct an *AdaptingMenu* instance and enable all of its options, before offering it to the user for the first time. One option is then disabled and the menu is offered to the user for a second time. Each time the menu is offered the value of the response returned from the *offerMenuAsInt()* action is displayed in order to confirm the correct implementation of the class. The implementation of the *AdaptingMenuDemonstration* client is as follows:

```
0001 // Filename AdaptingMenuDemonstration.java.
0002 // Providing a demonstration of the AdaptingMenu class.
0003 //
0004 // Written for JOF book Chapter 7 see text.
0005 // Fintan Culwin, v0.1, August 1997.
0006
0007 import Menus.AdaptingMenu;
0008
0009 public class AdaptingMenuDemonstration {
0010
0011    public static void main( String argv[]) {
0012
0013    String demoOptions[] = { "This is the first option",
0014                             "This is the second option",
```

```
0015                              "This is the third option"};
0016
0017
0018     int demoIntChoice;                                 '
0019     int index;
0020
0021     AdaptingMenu demoMenu = new AdaptingMenu( "Adapting Menu Demonstration",
0022                                               demoOptions,
0023                                               "");
0024        for ( index =0; index < 3; index++){
0025          demoMenu.enableMenuOption( index);
0026        } // End for.
0027
0028
0029        demoIntChoice = demoMenu.offerMenuAsInt();
0030        System.out.println( "\nYou chose " + demoIntChoice + " from the menu.");
0031
0032        System.out.println( "\n\t Disabling second option and offering again \n");
0033
0034        demoMenu.disableMenuOption( 1);
0035        demoIntChoice = demoMenu.offerMenuAsInt();
0036        System.out.println( "\nYou chose " + demoIntChoice + " from the menu.");
0037     } // End main.
0038 } // End BasicMenuDemonstration.
```

The purpose of lines 0024 to 0026 is to enable all menu options, which are disabled by default upon construction. On line 0034, after the menu has been offered for the first time on line 0029, the second menu option, at index location1, is disabled before the menu is offered for the second time on line 0035. An example interaction with this client might be as follows:

```
                 Adapting Menu Demonstration

    A.    This is the first option
    B.    This is the second option
    C.    This is the third option

    Please enter your choice : c
    You chose 2 from the menu.

           Disabling second option and offering again

           Adapting Menu Demonstration

    A.    This is the first option
    B.    This is the third option

    Please enter your choice : b
    You chose 2 from the menu.
```

This demonstration indicates that the manifest value of the third option (2) is returned whenever the option labelled 'This is the third option' is selected, no matter where it might appear on the menu.

7.5 ▓ The *RoomMonitorMenuDemonstration* client

In order to illustrate how an *AdaptingMenu* can be used in a more realistic situation a client which can be used to interact with a *RoomMonitor* instance will be presented. The menu to control this client will contain four options: one to record a person entering the room, one to record a person leaving the room, one to show the state of the monitor and one to exit from the application.

Of these options the option to enter a room should be unavailable when the room is full and the option to leave the room should be unavailable when it is empty. Additionally the exit option should only be available when the room is empty; the option to show the state of the monitor should always be available.

The context diagram for this application is given in Figure 7.4. The diagram indicates that the client program is an instance of the *RoomMonitorMenuDemonstration* class and uses an instance of the *AdaptingMenu* class called *roomMenu* as well as an instance of the *RoomMonitor* class called *roomMonitor*. The context diagram also indicates the hierarchies from which the classes which are used are extended.

The high level design of this client program is as follows:

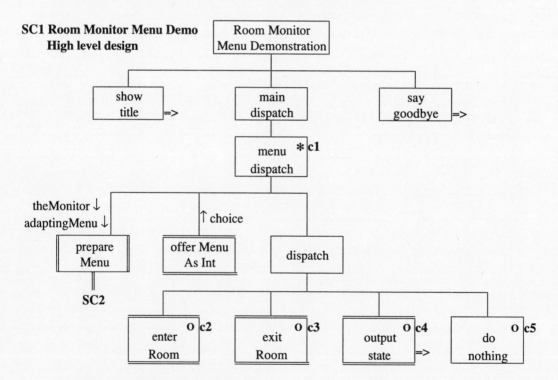

c1: While the user does not want to finish.
c2: If option to enter the room chosen.
c3: If option to leave the room chosen.
c4: If option to show the room's status chosen.
c5: If option to exit chosen.

The essence of this design is based upon the standard menu/dispatch design given in the previous chapter. It differs in having the options of the dispatch replaced with calls

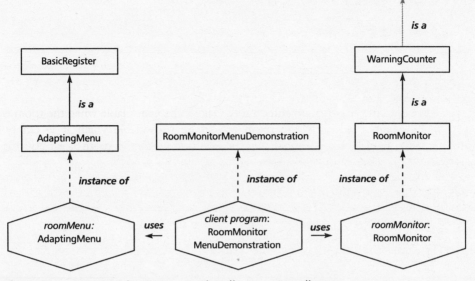

Figure 7.4 *RoomMonitorDemonstration* client, context diagram.

of the appropriate action of the *RoomMonitor* instance, and by being enclosed within an iterative structure which ensures that the menu is repeatedly presented to the user until they indicate that they wish to exit. The remaining change from the standard design is the call of the local action *prepareMenu()* at the start of each iteration. The design of this action is as follows:

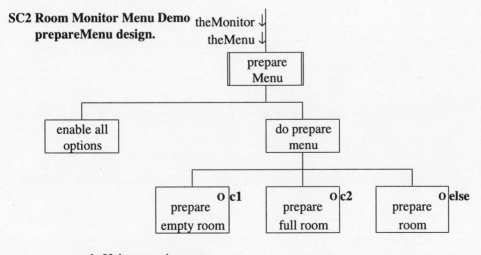

SC2 Room Monitor Menu Demo prepareMenu design.

c1: If the room is empty.
c2: if the room is full.

Each of the steps *prepare empty room*, *prepare full room* and *prepare room* are implemented by disabling the options which are not to be offered in each of the circumstances identified. The implementation of this design is as follows:

```
0001  // Filename RoomMonitorMenuDemonstration.java.
0002  // Providing a second demonstration of the AdaptingMenu class.
0003  //
0004  // Written for JOF book Chapter 7 see text.
0005  // Fintan Culwin, v0.1, August 1997.
0006
0007  import Menus.AdaptingMenu;
0008  import Counters.RoomMonitor;
0009
0010  public class RoomMonitorMenuDemonstration {
0011
0012  private static final int INVALID_OPTION = -1;
0013  private static final int ENTER_OPTION   = 0;
0014  private static final int LEAVE_OPTION   = 1;
0015  private static final int STATUS_OPTION  = 2;
0016  private static final int EXIT_OPTION    = 3;
0017
0018  private static final int ROOM_LIMIT     = 3;
0019
0020
0021     public static void main( String argv[]) {
0022
0023     String roomMenuOptions[] = { "Enter the room",
0024                                  "Leave the room",
0025                                  "Show room status",
0026                                  "Exit program"};
0027
0028
0029     AdaptingMenu roomMenu     = new AdaptingMenu( "Room Monitor menu",
0030                                                   roomMenuOptions,
0031                                                   "");
0032     RoomMonitor roomMonitor = new RoomMonitor( ROOM_LIMIT);
0033
0034
0035     int  usersChoice = INVALID_OPTION;
0036
0037        System.out.println( "\t Room menu demonstration client \n");
0038
0039        while ( usersChoice != EXIT_OPTION ) {
0040
0041           prepareMenu( roomMenu, roomMonitor);
0042
0043           usersChoice = roomMenu.offerMenuAsInt();
0044
0045           switch ( usersChoice){
0046
0047              case ENTER_OPTION :
0048                 roomMonitor.enterRoom();
0049                 break;
0050
```

```
0051                case LEAVE_OPTION :
0052                    roomMonitor.exitRoom();
0053                    break;
0054
0055                case STATUS_OPTION :
0056                    System.out.println( roomMonitor);
0057                    break;
0058
0059                case EXIT_OPTION :
0060                    break;
0061
0062            } // End switch.
0063        } // End while.
0064
0065
0066        System.out.println( "\n\t Have a nice day! \n");
0067    } // End main.
0068
0069
0070    private static void prepareMenu( AdaptingMenu theMenu,
0071                                     RoomMonitor  theMonitor) {
0072
0073        theMenu.enableMenuOption( ENTER_OPTION);
0074        theMenu.enableMenuOption( LEAVE_OPTION);
0075        theMenu.enableMenuOption( STATUS_OPTION);
0076        theMenu.enableMenuOption( EXIT_OPTION);
0077
0078
0079        if ( theMonitor.numberCurrentlyInRoomIs() == 0) {
0080            theMenu.disableMenuOption( LEAVE_OPTION);
0081        } else if ( theMonitor.numberCurrentlyInRoomIs() == ROOM_LIMIT) {
0082            theMenu.disableMenuOption( EXIT_OPTION);
0083            theMenu.disableMenuOption( ENTER_OPTION);
0084        } else {
0085            theMenu.disableMenuOption( EXIT_OPTION);
0086        } // End if.
0087    } // End prepareMenu.
0088
0089 } // RoomMonitorMenuDemonstration.
```

A complete set of manifest values to represent the four possible menu choices is declared on lines 0012 to 0016. The manifest values include an *INVALID_OPTION* in order to allow the value of the *usersChoice* variable to be given a safe value which will ensure the loop starts iterating on line 0039.

The other manifest value *ROOM_LIMIT* is declared on line 0018 with the value 3 and is used on line 0032 to delimit the maximum number of people in the room as the *RoomMonitor* constructor is called. The value 3 was chosen to allow the actions to be readily demonstrated but a higher limit might be required for a more realistic client. Apart from this the implementation follows the designs presented very closely, and should be comprehensible from previous clients. An annotated interaction with this client might be as follows.

When the menu is presented for the first time, it is not possible for anyone to leave the room and it is possible to exit the program:

```
Room menu demonstration client

        Room Monitor menu

A.    Enter the room
B.    Show room status
C.    Exit program

Please enter your choice : a
```

Selecting option *a* from the opening menu admits one person into the room. This should enable the leave room option and disable the exit program option:

```
          Room Monitor menu

A.    Enter the room
B.    Leave the room
C.    Show room status

Please enter your choice : a

          Room Monitor menu


A.    Enter the room
B.    Leave the room
C.    Show room status

Please enter your choice : a
```

Having admitted three people the room should now be full and only the leave room and show status options should be presented:

```
          Room Monitor menu


A.    Leave the room
B.    Show room status

Please enter your choice : a
```

As the room is no longer full the enter room option should be re-enabled:

```
          Room Monitor menu

A.    Enter the room
B.    Leave the room
C.    Show room status

Please enter your choice : b
```

```
        Room Monitor menu


A.    Enter the room
B.    Leave the room
C.    Show room status

Please enter your choice : b
```

With all three people now having left the room the same options as in the opening menu should be available, and selecting the exit option will allow the program to terminate:

```
        Room Monitor menu


A.    Enter the room
B.    Show room status
C.    Exit program

Please enter your choice : c

        Have a nice day!
```

7.6 ▓ Menu driven user interfaces

The adapting menu driven user interface as presented in the previous section is not the only interface which could have been provided for this application and is capable of some improvements. The first point to note is that it does not implement the user interface design principle of *closure*. Whenever the user indicates that a person has entered or left the room there is no confirmation from the system that the action has been effected. This problem could be solved by including a confirmation message inside each of the relevant dispatch options. Providing closure in this manner is essential for novice users and does not impact too much upon the experience of more skilled users.

One other problem with this interface is that when admitting people into the room the user will be repeatedly selecting option *a* from the menu, until the room becomes full. At this point pressing *a* will indicate that a person has left the room. It is predictable that some users, under some circumstances, will not notice that the menu options have changed and continue pressing *a* in the belief that they are recording people entering the room. What will actually be happening is that pressing *a* will be alternatively indicating that a person has entered the room and that a person has left the room.

One solution to this problem might be not to use an adapting menu at all and to offer all four options at all times. However, this would then require an error dialog when the room becomes full and the user attempts to admit another person. For example:

```
Please enter your choice : a
As the room is full, no more people can be admitted.
 {menu re-presented}
```

It is predictable that this solution would cause exactly the same problem to occur under the same circumstances. The user might not attend to the dialog and continue pressing *a* in the belief that they are admitting people into the room, whereas they are actually causing the error dialog to be continually represented. A similar pattern of error dialogs would be required for the other menu options, apart from the show status option which is always available.

There are no simple and obvious solutions to user interface problems such as this. Each individual developer will favour one or other of the two possibilities presented above. The only way to decide which interface is 'better' is to construct both interfaces and investigate the behaviour of a representative sample of the people who will actually use the application. Deciding which interface is 'better' on the basis of objective measurements, such as the number of errors made, and subjective measurements such as the sample users' comments, is preferable to relying upon the developer's idiosyncratic judgement.

Summary

▓ Standard designs can be adapted to facilitate the construction of software artefacts.

▓ User interfaces should employ the principle of *closure* to provide an explicit confirmation that the requested action has been performed.

▓ User interfaces should be validated by measuring the behaviour of users rather than relying upon the developer's judgement.

Exercises

7.1 Using diagrams similar to those in Figures 7.2 and 7.3 trace the operation of the *AdaptingMenuDemonstration* client as presented in the chapter.

7.2 Extend the *RoomMonitorMenuDemonstration* client to include two new options to show the number of people currently in the room and the maximum number of people ever in the room.

7.3 Implement the alternative version of the *RoomMonitorMenuDemonstration* client using error dialogs as described in section 7.5. Attempt to demonstrate objectively which of the implementations is preferred by observing a sample of users.

7.4 Reimplement the error dialogs from Exercise 7.3 to require an explicit keypress (for example 'Z') to dismiss them, before the menu is re-presented. Does this ease or exacerbate the usability problems?

7.5 The *Menus* class hierarchy is flawed; for example, the *AdaptingMenu* inherits an *offerMenuAsChar()* action, which is now dangerous and should not be called. Redesign the hierarchy to make the *BasicMenu* and *AdaptingMenu* classes child classes of an abstract *Menu* class.

7.6 Implement a menu/dispatch system for a *MultipleCashRegister*. In order to facilitate the construction you should assume that all purchases are for a fixed amount, e.g. £10.00. The menu should offer an option to clear the register when the amount of cash exceeds a fixed amount, e.g. £50.00. When this option is chosen it is assumed that all transactions are cleared from the register. This option can be effected by constructing a new register. Implement and demonstrate this client.

Chapter eight

Concurrent processes

All of the programs presented so far have had a single *thread* of control running through them. However, many applications require two or more threads of control to be used. Such programs give the impression that the computer is able to do more than one thing at a time. For example, a word processor might be responding to the users input on one thread, while printing on a second thread and checking the spelling on a third.

When more than one thread is being used in a program the threads are executing concurrently and are known as *concurrent processes*. Multi-threaded programs can allow more effective use of a computer's resources but require greater effort on the part of the developer to produce them. This chapter will provide an initial introduction to the design and implementation of concurrent programs, but will not attempt to provide a complete introduction to this very specialized topic.

8.1 ▓ An initial concurrent example

To introduce the development of concurrent programs a simple example involving a *RoomMonitor* will be developed. In the first version of the program there will be a total of four threads. The first thread is the main program thread whose task is to start the other three threads. Two other threads are used to simulate people entering the room and to simulate people leaving the room. The final thread is used occasionally to show the status of the *RoomMonitor*.

The program component which will be used to simulate the entry of people into the room will be an instance of the *RoomFiller* class whose class diagram is given in Figure 8.1.

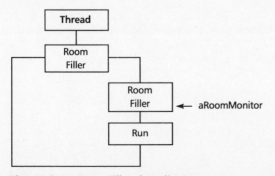

Figure 8.1 *RoomFiller* class diagram.

The class diagram indicates that the *RoomFiller* class is an extension of the Java pre-declared Thread class. Most of the complexity of establishing and controlling a thread is supplied by the Thread class and the minimum that needs to be done is to override its run() action. The *RoomFiller* constructor requires a *RoomMonitor* as an argument in order for it to know which room people are to be admitted into. The implementation of this design, as far as the end of the constructor, is as follows:

```
0001 // Filename RoomFiller.java.
0002 // Providing a thread to admit people into the room.
0003 //
0004 // Written for JOF book Chapter 8 see text.
0005 // Fintan Culwin, v0.1, August 1997.
0006
0007 import Counters.RoomMonitor;
0008 import java.util.Random;
0009
0010 public class RoomFiller extends Thread {
0011
0012 RoomMonitor   roomToFill;
0013 Random        generator = new Random();
0014
0015    public RoomFiller ( RoomMonitor aRoomMonitor) {
0016       roomToFill = aRoomMonitor;
0017    } // End RoomFiller Constructor.
0018
```

The context clause of this class imports the *Counters.RoomMonitor* class and the java.util.Random standard class. This latter class supplies a random number generator which is used to introduce a small degree of unpredictability into *RoomFiller*'s behaviour. A partial class diagram of the *java.util.Random* class is given in Figure 8.2.

The *nextDouble()* action will supply a random double value in the range 0.0 to 1.0 each time it is called. The *nextInt()* action will supply a random integer value between the lowest and highest integer value. An instance of the *Random* class called *generator* is constructed on line 0013.

The *RoomFiller* constructor does not construct its own *RoomMonitor* instance but requires an already constructed *RoomMonitor* instance to be supplied as a *RoomFiller* is constructed. The *RoomFiller* constructor is implemented by storing the identity of the *RoomMonitor* passed as an argument, in the instance attribute called *roomToFill*.

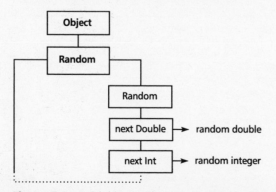

Figure 8.2   Partial java.util.Random class diagram.

The design of the *run()* action is as follows:

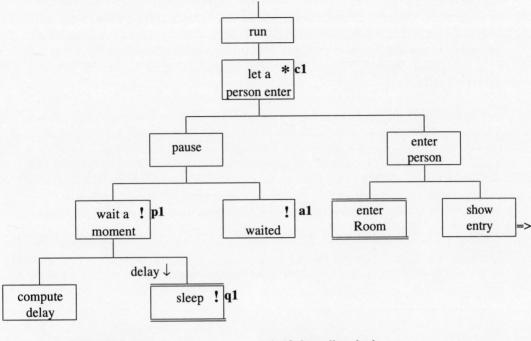

c1: For ever. **q1:** If sleep disturbed.
p1: Posit a delay. **a1:** Admit delay interrupted.

The basis of the design is to iterate for ever and on each iteration to pause for a random amount of time before admitting a person into the room and confirming this on the terminal screen. In order to implement the *pause* part of the design the thread has to be put to sleep, and this can only be done within a posit/admit structure which guards against the sleep being interrupted. The implementation of this design is as follows:

```
0019    public void run() {
0020
0021    int delay;
0022
0023        while ( true) {
0024          try {
0025            delay = (int) ( generator.nextDouble() * 200.0);
0026            this.sleep( delay);
0027          } catch ( InterruptedException exception ){
0028            // Do nothing.
0029          } // End try/catch.
0030          roomToFill.enterRoom();
0031          System.out.println( "Entered ...");
0032        } // End while.
0033    } // End run.
0034
0035 } // End RoomFiller.
```

On line 0023 the loop condition is expressed as the **boolean** value **true**, which can never be interpreted as **false** and so the loop will iterate for ever. In accord with the design the body of the iteration starts with a **try/catch** structure. Within the **try** part of the structure the value of the local **int**eger variable *delay* is given a value between 0 and 200. This is accomplished by obtaining a double value from the random number *generator* which will be between 0.0 and 1.0. This value is multiplied by 200.0 to produce a value between 0.0 and 200.0 which is subsequently cast to an **int**eger between 0 and 200.

On line 0026 the sleep() action of the *RoomFiller* instance, which is inherited from the Thread class, is called to suspend the thread for a delay specified by its argument. The value of the argument indicates the number of milliseconds which the thread should be suspended for. It is possible for the suspension to be interrupted and this has to be handled in the **catch** part of the **try/catch** structure on lines 0027 to 0028. In this case no action needs to be taken and so the **catch** is empty. The overall effect of the **try/catch** structure is to delay the thread for between 0.0 and 0.2 seconds. The necessity for enclosing a sleep() call within a **try/catch** structure will be explained in Chapter 9.

Following the pause a person is admitted to the room by calling the *enterRoom()* action of the *roomToFill RoomMonitor* instance which was supplied when the *RoomFiller* instance was constructed. Once a person has been admitted into the room a message is sent to the screen to indicate to the user that it has happened.

The second thread is responsible for removing people from the room and is implemented as an instance of the *RoomEmptyer* class whose class diagram does not differ significantly from that presented in Figure 8.2 for the *RoomFiller* class. The implementation of this class is as follows:

```
0001 // Filename RoomEmptyer.java.
0002 // Providing a thread to remove people from a room.
0003 //
0004 // Written for JOF book Chapter 8 see text.
0005 // Fintan Culwin, v0.1, August 1997.
0006
0007 import Counters.RoomMonitor;
0008 import java.util.Random;
0009
0010 public class RoomEmptyer extends Thread {
0011
0012 RoomMonitor   roomToEmpty;
0013 Random        generator = new Random();
0014
0015    public RoomEmptyer ( RoomMonitor theMonitor) {
0016       roomToEmpty = theMonitor;
0017    } // End RoomEmptyer Constructor.
0018
0019
0020    public void run() {
0021
0022    int    delay;
0023    double leaveRoom;
0024
0025       while ( true) {
```

```
0026            try {
0027                delay = (int) (generator.nextDouble() * 200.0);
0028                this.sleep( delay);
0029            } catch ( InterruptedException exception ){
0030                // Do nothing.
0031            } // End try/ catch
0032            leaveRoom = generator.nextDouble() *
0033                        (double) roomToEmpty.numberCurrentlyInRoomIs();
0034            if ( leaveRoom > 0.33) {
0035                roomToEmpty.exitRoom();
0036                System.out.println( "Exited ...");
0037            } // End if.
0038        } // End while.
0039    } // End run.
0040
0041 } // End RoomEmptyer.
```

The only significant difference in this class is that after the pause in the *run()* action the decision on leaving the room is based upon the generation of a second random number which is multiplied by the number of people currently in the room. Thus the chance of a person leaving the room on each iteration increases as the number of people in the room increases. This is in accord with a consideration of what would happen in the real world. Should the room be empty then the number of people reported to be in the room will be zero and so the *leaveRoom* variable will have the value 0, ensuring that no one can leave an empty room.

The third thread is responsible for reporting on the status of the room and is provided as an instance of the *RoomReporter* class whose object diagram and construction does not differ significantly from the previous two classes. The **while** loop of the *run()* action of this class is as follows:

```
0023        while ( true) {
0024            try {
0025                this.sleep( 2000);
0026            } catch ( InterruptedException exception ){
0027                // Do nothing.
0028            } // End try/ catch
0029            System.out.println( roomToReportOn);
0030        } // End while.
```

This indicates that the state of the room will be reported upon approximately every 2 seconds. The demonstration client for this example, called *ThreadDemo*, has the following design:

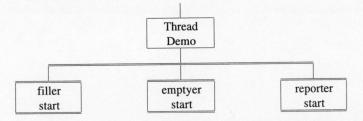

The significant difference in this design is the use of a double horizontal line to connect two or more components, which indicates that the components will execute concurrently. The implementation of this design is as follows:

```
0001 // Filename ThreadDemo.java.
0002 // Implements a concurrent process involving three subservient
0003 // threads, filling, emptying and reporting on a room.
0004 //
0005 // Written for JOF book Chapter 8 see text.
0006 // Fintan Culwin, v0.1, August 1997.
0007
0008 import Counters.RoomMonitor;
0009
0010 public class ThreadDemo {
0011
0012     public static void main( String argv[]) {
0013
0014     RoomMonitor  aMonitor  = new RoomMonitor();
0015     RoomFiller   aFiller   = new RoomFiller(   aMonitor);
0016     RoomEmptyer  anEmptyer = new RoomEmptyer(  aMonitor);
0017     RoomReporter aReporter = new RoomReporter( aMonitor);
0018
0019        aFiller.start();
0020        anEmptyer.start();
0021        aReporter.start();
0022     } // End main.
0023
0024 } // End ThreadDemo.
```

Within the *main()* action an instance of the *RoomMonitor* class is constructed and consequently used as the argument of the *RoomFiller*, *RoomEmptyer* and *RoomReporter* constructors. This causes each thread to use the same *RoomMonitor* instance. Once all three thread objects have been constructed the start() action of each of them is called. The start() action is supplied by the Thread class and inherited by each of the specialized classes implemented above. The effect of calling the start() action is for Java to arrange for the *run()* action of the instance being started to be executed in a concurrent manner. The first part of the output produced by this client when it was executed was as follows:

```
Entered ...
Exited ...
Entered ...
Exited ...
Entered ...
Entered ...
Exited ...
Entered ...
Entered ...
Entered ...
Entered ...
Entered ...
Exited ...
Entered ...
Exited ...
Exited ...
```

```
Entered ...
Entered ...
Exited ...
Entered ...
Exited ...
Entered ...
Now in room : 6 Max in room : 6 Total entered : 14
```

As the program has no way of stopping itself it had to be stopped by interrupting it from the keyboard. The precise patterns of entering and exiting and the output of the state of the monitor cannot be precisely predicted from a consideration of the code. Running the program for a second, or subsequent, time will produce a different pattern of events.

What is happening is that Java is dividing its time between all three active threads, the fourth thread concerned with the *main()* action having finished. It will allocate an amount of time, known as a *time slice*, to each thread and suspend it once its slice has expired. Flow of control will then be passed to one of the other threads and returned to the suspended thread in due course, allowing it to continue for another time slice.

8.2 ▓ Synchronization of data attributes

The simple example above appears to work, but contains a subtle and dangerous error. The interruption of a time slice can occur at any instant, possibly in the middle of an action, and this can result in the objects data attributes being left in an invalid state. To illustrate this possibility a class, called *Dangerous*, containing two data attributes will be produced. It also supplies three actions: one to write the same value to both data attributes and two actions to retrieve the value of each of the data attributes. The implementation of the *Dangerous* class, presented without a class diagram, is as follows:

```
0001 // Filename Dangerous.java.
0002 // Contains an updatable object without synchronization,
0003 // leading to the possibility of an invalid update.
0004 //
0005 // Written for JOF book Chapter 8 see text.
0006 // Fintan Culwin, v0.1, August 1997.
0007
0008 public class Dangerous extends Object {
0009
0010 private int anAttribute;
0011 private int anotherAttribute;
0012
0013     public void update( int updateTo) {
0014         anAttribute      = updateTo;
0015         anotherAttribute = updateTo;
0016     } // End update.
0017
0018
0019     public int getAnAttribute() {
0020         return anAttribute;
0021     } // End getAnAttribute.
```

```
0022
0023
0024     public int getAnotherAttribute() {
0025        return anotherAttribute;
0026     } // End getAnotherAttribute.
0027
0028 } // End Dangerous.
```

The implementation of this class should be comprehensible from a consideration of the many classes which have already been introduced. Two extended **Thread** classes called *DangerousWriter* and *DangerousReader*, constructed in a manner comparable with the *RoomFiller* and *RoomEmptyer* classes above, will also be required. The implementation of the *DangerousWriter* class is as follows:

```
0001 // Filename DangerousWriter.java.
0002 // Providing class to write the dangerous attributes.
0003 //
0004 // Written for JOF book Chapter 8 see text.
0005 // Fintan Culwin, v0.1, August 1997.
0006
0007 import Dangerous;
0008
0009 public class DangerousWriter extends Thread {
0010
0011 Dangerous writeThis;
0012
0013    public DangerousWriter ( Dangerous toWrite) {
0014        writeThis = toWrite;
0015    } // End DangerousWriter Constructor.
0016
0017
0018    public void run() {
0019
0020    int index = 0;
0021
0022       while ( true) {
0023          writeThis.update( index++);
0024       } // End while.
0025    } // End run.
0026
0027 } // End DangerousWriter.
```

The *run()* action will loop for ever continuously calling the *update()* action of the *writeThis Dangerous* object passed to the *DangerousWriter* instance when it was constructed. Should the value of *index* ever reach the maximum positive integer value(+2147483647), incrementing it will result in its taking the minimum negative value (−2147483648). The reasons for this are explained in Appendix A1. Another class, *DangerousReader*, is needed to monitor the running of *DangerousWriter*. The implementation of the *DangerousReader* class is as follows:

```
0001 // Filename DangerousReader.java.
0002 // Providing class to read the dangerous attributes.
0003 //
0004 // Written for JOF book Chapter 8 see text.
```

```
0005 // Fintan Culwin, v0.1, August 1997.
0006
0007 import Dangerous;
0008
0009 public class DangerousReader extends Thread {
0010
0011 Dangerous   readThis;
0012
0013    public DangerousReader( Dangerous toRead) {
0014       readThis = toRead;
0015    } // End DangerousReader Constructor;
0016
0017
0018    public void run() {
0019
0020    int firstAttribute;
0021    int secondAttribute;
0022
0023       while ( true) {
0024          firstAttribute = readThis.getAnAttribute();
0025          secondAttribute = readThis.getAnotherAttribute();
0026          if ( firstAttribute != secondAttribute) {
0027             System.out.println( "Danger proved ... "        +
0028                                  firstAttribute +  " and " +
0029                                  secondAttribute + ".");
0030          } // End if.
0031       } // End while.
0032    } // End run.
0033
0034 } // End DangerousReader.
```

As with the *DangerousWriter run()* action, the *DangerousReader run()* action is a
non-terminating loop which, in this case, continually reads the values of the two data
attributes. The calls of *getAnAttribute()* and *getAnotherAttribute()* on lines 0024 and
0025 should, in a secure implementation, never result in two different values being
returned. The remaining part of the *run()* loop tests the two values obtained and
outputs a message if they are ever different.

To demonstrate the insecurity of this implementation a demonstration client called
DangerousDemo, whose implementation is as follows, is required:

```
0001 // Filename DangerousDemo.java.
0002 // Providing a demonstration of the possibility of
0003 // an invalid update happening to a Dangerous object.
0004 //
0005 // Written for JOF book Chapter 8 see text.
0006 // Fintan Culwin, v0.1, August 1997.
0007
0008
0009 public class DangerousDemo {
0010
0011    public static void main( String argv[]) {
0012
0013    Dangerous         dangerous = new Dangerous();
0014    DangerousWriter   aWriter   = new DangerousWriter( dangerous);
```

```
0015    DangerousReader    aReader    = new DangerousReader( dangerous);
0016
0017       aWriter.start();
0018       aReader.start();
0019    } // End main.
0020 } // End DangerousDemo.
```

The construction of this client is directly comparable with the construction of the *ThreadDemo* client above. When executed this client produced the following output:

```
Danger proved ... 8156 and 8155.
Danger proved ... 15419 and 24246.
Danger proved ... 33086 and 37437.
Danger proved ... 37437 and 42018.
Danger proved ... 42018 and 51202.
Danger proved ... 51203 and 51202.
```

As with the *ThreadDemo* client the program had to be interrupted from the keyboard in order to stop it and if the client were executed for a second time the precise output produced would differ. The output indicates that the implementation is insecure, and thus dangerous, as the value of the two attributes read from the *Dangerous* object are shown to be different. This could be caused by a suspension happening between lines 0024 and 0025 of the *DangerousReader run()* action as the two values are read, or between lines 0014 and 0015 of the *Dangerous update()* action as the two values are written. Further investigation would indicate that both types of suspension were happening, as is suggested by the pattern of outputs involving values which are close together and others which are wildly apart.

This is regarded as a dangerous occurrence as the internal state of any object has to be maintained in a well defined consistent pattern at all times. For example, the *AdaptingMenu* class from the previous chapter emphasized that the state of its *inUse* and *optionKey* arrays was essential to its secure implementation. If an *AdaptingMenu* instance were to be used in a program containing independent threads then it is possible that the state of the arrays might become inconsistent, causing the program to operate incorrectly.

The solution to this problem is to indicate to Java which parts of the program code are essential to its correct operation in a threaded environment, so that it can be ensured that those parts will not be interrupted until they have completed. This is accomplished by use of the **synchronized** keyword.

Corresponding to the four source code files concerned with the *Dangerous* class, four corresponding files concerned with a *Safe* class, which illustrates the correct operation of the software when the tasks are synchronized, will be introduced.

To prevent the possibility of the *Safe update()* action being interrupted while the values are being written it can be declared with the modifier **synchronized**, as follows:

```
0013    // update action from the Safe class.
0014    public synchronized void update( int updateTo) {
0015      anAttribute     = updateTo;
0016      anotherAttribute = updateTo;
0017    } // End update.
```

The **synchronized** modifier ensures that the action will be executed without being suspended and that only one thread can run it at a time. In this example this will ensure that both attributes are always updated and so the object can never be left in an invalid state by being suspended between, or during, lines 0015 and 0016.

To prevent the other possibility of the *SafeReader run()* action being suspended between reading the first and second attributes, and during this suspension an update action changing the value of the attributes, a part of the *run()* action can be **synchronized**, as follows:

```
0023        // Loop from the SafeReader run() action.
0024        while ( true) {
0025          synchronized( readThis) {
0026            firstAttribute  = readThis.getAnAttribute();
0027            secondAttribute = readThis.getAnotherAttribute();
0028          } // End synchronize.
0029          if ( firstAttribute != secondAttribute) {
0030            System.out.println( "Danger proved ... " +
0031                      firstAttribute + " and "     +
0032                      secondAttribute + ".");
0033          } // End if.
0034        } // End while.
```

This use of the **synchronized** facility encloses a block of statements, delineated by its opening and closing braces, and has to indicate which object is being guarded. In this example the synchronization statement indicates that the *readThis* object is being guarded; it has a similar effect to the synchronization of an entire action above. Java will ensure that this thread is not suspended until the end of the synchronized block and will ensure that no other threads can use any of the actions associated with the object guarded by the **synchronized** statement.

When the *SafeDemo* client was executed no output was produced, indicating that the *SafeReader* task never obtained invalid information from the *Safe* object. As with the other tasking demonstration programs the program had to be interrupted from the keyboard to terminate it.

8.3 ▦ Synchronization of actions

The example above illustrated the synchronization of tasks by controlling access to shared objects and their data attributes. It is also possible, and in some cases essential, to synchronize two, or more, tasks by ensuring that an action in one task can only take place after an action in a separate task has completed.

For example, a simple software model of a road junction controlled by traffic lights may have one set of lights controlling the north–south flow of traffic and another set of lights controlling the east–west traffic flow. In order for the model to be an accurate representation of the junction it is essential that the operation of both lights is synchronized to ensure that both lights are never on green at the same time.

In this model the repeating pattern of traffic lights as used in the UK will be used. The repeating sequence of lights, from red back to red, is given in Table 8.1.

For the simple north–south/east–west junction the repeating sequence of lights given in Table 8.2 must be enforced.

Table 8.1 Repeating sequence of a single traffic light.

Light colour	Meaning to driver
red	wait
red amber	prepare to move
green	move
amber	stop
red	wait

Table 8.2 Repeating sequence of a pair of traffic lights.

North–south	East–west
red	red
red amber	red
green	red
amber	red
red	red amber
red	green
red	amber
red	red

The basis of this implementation is to model the activity of a single traffic light, following the sequence given in Table 8.1. When the change from *amber* to *red* is made the traffic light should suspend itself and send a message to the other light that it can resume its sequence. As this other light must have suspended itself when it changed to *red*, upon resumption, it will cycle through its *red amber*, *green* and *amber* states until it changes back to *red*. At this point the second light will suspend itself and send a message back to the original light that it can resume its sequence, whilst it waits on *red*, and so on.

This pattern of activity can be shown on a ***state diagram***, as shown in Figure 8.3. Each part of the diagram indicates the pattern of activity of one of the lights, labelled with the name of the light. Each consists of four states labelled with the colour of the lights which it will display whilst in that state and transitions which link each state to its next. Three of the transitions are not labelled and this indicates, in this diagram, that they will be taken after a period of time. The fourth transition, between the *red* and *red amber* states, is labelled with *switch* which indicates that it will be taken when its object receives a *switch* message. The transition between the *amber* and *red* states is shown as originating a *switch* message to the other *TrafficLight* object.

Taken together, the *north south* light will send a *switch* message to the *east west* light as it transits from the *amber* to the *red* state. The receipt of the *switch* message by the *east west* light will allow it to transit from the *red* to the *red amber* state and then, after a period of time, to the *green* and then to the *amber* state. Subsequently when it transits from the *amber* to the *red* state it will send a *switch* message to the *north south* light allowing it to transit from the *red* to the *red amber* state. The *north south* light will as a result transit through its *red*, *red amber* and *green* states and subsequently to its *red*

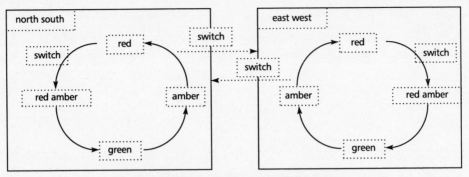

Figure 8.3 *TrafficDemo* state diagram.

state, sending a *switch* message to the *east west* light. This pattern of activity will continue indefinitely.

The *TrafficLight* class diagram, which implements this behaviour, is given in Figure 8.4.

Each *TrafficLight* instance is given a name upon construction in order that the output from the program can identify which light produced it. A *TrafficLight* instance has to know which light it has to send a message to when it has completed its cycle and is about to suspend itself. However, it cannot be informed of this upon construction as the light which it has to inform may not yet have been constructed. Accordingly an action to inform each *TrafficLight* instance of which light it is to send the message to is required. The remaining instance attribute is the *state* of the light which records its current light colour.

In addition to the *run()* action two private actions, *holdOn()* to provide a delay and *report()* to output the state of the light, are indicated on the class diagram. The implementation of this design as far as the end of the *setOtherLight()* action is as

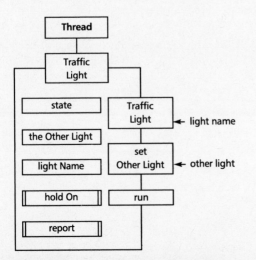

Figure 8.4 The *TrafficLight* class diagram.

follows:

```
0001 // Filename TrafficLight.java.
0002 // Providing a simple model of a traffic light.
0003 //
0004 // Written for JOF book Chapter 8 see text.
0005 // Fintan Culwin, v0.1, August 1997.
0006
0007
0008 public class TrafficLight extends Thread {
0009
0010 private static final int RED       = 0;
0011 private static final int RED_AMBER = 1;
0012 private static final int GREEN     = 2;
0013 private static final int AMBER     = 3;
0014 private int              state     = AMBER;
0015
0016 private String        lightName;
0017 private TrafficLight theOtherLight;
0018
0019    public TrafficLight( String name){
0020      lightName = new String( name);
0021    } // End TrafficLight constructor.
0022
0023
0024    public void setOtherLight(TrafficLight otherLight) {
0025      theOtherLight = otherLight;
0026    } // End setOtherLight.
```

The implementation declares four private manifest values to define the patterns of the lights and the *state* instance attribute is initialized to the value *AMBER*, for reasons which will be explained below. The constructor installs its argument as the name of the light into the *lightName* instance attribute, and the *setOtherLight()* action installs its argument into *theOtherLight* instance attribute. Before considering the design and implementation of the *run()* action the implementation of the two private actions will be presented:

```
0059       private void holdOn() {
0060         try {
0061            this.sleep( 500);
0062         } catch ( InterruptedException exception ){
0063            // Do nothing.
0064         } // End try/ catch.
0065       } // End holdOn.
0066
0067
0068
0069       private void report() {
0070
0071       String stateString = "";
0072
0073         switch ( state) {
0074           case RED :
0075              stateString = new String(" red.");
0076              break;
```

```
0077                case RED_AMBER :
0078                    stateString = new String(" red amber.");
0079                    break;
0080                case GREEN :
0081                    stateString = new String(" green.");
0082                    break;
0083                case AMBER :
0084                    stateString = new String(" amber.");
0085                    break;
0086            } // End switch
0087            System.out.println( "The " + lightName        +
0088                                " lights have changed to " +
0089                                stateString);
0090    } // End report.
```

The *holdOn()* action provides a half second delay every time it is called and is intended to be used to slow down the output in order to make the demonstration more watchable. The *report()* action outputs a message to the terminal and is intended to be called every time the colour of the light changes. The output indicates which light has changed and what colour it has changed to. The design of the *run()* action is as follows:

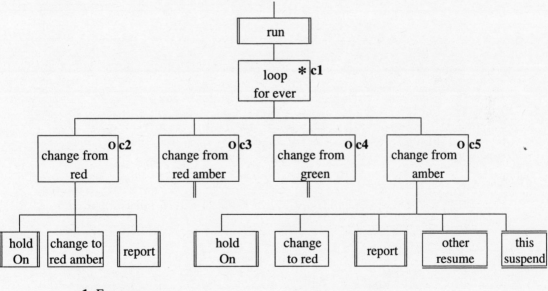

c1: For ever.
c2: If current state is red.   **c4:** If current state is green.
c3: If current state is red and amber.   **c5:** If current state is amber.

The steps performed within the loop when the lights are currently *red* are to *holdOn()*, change the state of the light to *red amber* and then to *report()* on the change. A similar pattern of events takes place when the lights are *red amber* or *green*, but these details have been omitted from the design in the interests of clarity.

When the lights are *amber* the first three steps are essentially identical to those of the other states. They are followed by a call of the *otherLight*'s *resume()* action before the current thread is *suspend*ed. The implementation of this design is as

follows:

```
0028    public void run() {
0029        while ( true) {
0030          switch ( state ) {
0031            case RED :
0032                this.holdOn();
0033                state = RED_AMBER;
0034                this.report();
0035                break;
0036            case RED_AMBER :
0037                this.holdOn();
0038                state = GREEN;
0039                this.report();
0040                break;
0041            case GREEN :
0042                this.holdOn();
0043                state = AMBER;
0044                this.report();
0045                break;
0046            case AMBER :
0047                this.holdOn();
0048                state = RED;
0049                this.report();
0050                theOtherLight.resume();
0051                this.suspend();
0052                break;
0053          } // End switch
0054        } // End while.
0055    } // End run.
```

The resume() and suspend() actions, which are called on lines 0050 and 0051, are inherited from the Thread class by the *TrafficLight* class. The effect of calling the suspend() action is to cause the thread to become inactive and it will not be scheduled for further execution until its resume() action is called.

The demonstration test harness is comparable with the other concurrent demonstrations which have already been presented in this chapter and its implementation is as follows:

```
0001 // Filename TrafficDemo.java.
0002 // Implementing a simple model of a road junction.
0003 //
0004 // Written for JOF book Chapter 8 see text.
0005 // Fintan Culwin, v0.1, August 1997.
0006
0007 import TrafficLight;
0008
0009 public class TrafficDemo {
0010
0011    public static void main( String argv[]) {
0012
0013    TrafficLight northSouth = new TrafficLight( "north south ");
0014    TrafficLight eastWest   = new TrafficLight( "east west   ");
0015
```

```
0016        northSouth.setOtherLight( eastWest);
0017        eastWest.setOtherLight(   northSouth);
0018
0019        northSouth.start();
0020        eastWest.start();
0021    } // End main.
0022
0023 } // End TrafficDemo.
```

On lines 0013 and 0014 two instances of the *TrafficLight* class, called *northSouth* and *eastWest*, are constructed with suitable names. Having created both *TrafficLights* each can be informed of the identity of the other by use of the *SetOtherLight()* actions. Finally the *start()* action of each *TrafficLight* is called. The output produced by this demonstration client is as follows:

```
The north south lights have changed to red.
The east west   lights have changed to red.
The north south lights have changed to red amber.
The north south lights have changed to green.
The north south lights have changed to amber.
The north south lights have changed to red.
The east west   lights have changed to red amber.
The east west   lights have changed to green.
The east west   lights have changed to amber.
The east west   lights have changed to red.
The north south lights have changed to red amber.
```

The output continued through the same pattern until interrupted from the keyboard. As each *TrafficLight* instance was created with a default state of *amber*, both lights will change immediately to *red*. The first light which changes to *red* will call the resume() action of the other light and then suspend() itself. Calling the resume() action of a Thread object which has not been suspended has no effect.

As the first light has suspended itself the second light can now change itself to *red*. It will then call the resume() action of the first light and suspend() itself. The first light is now active and the second suspended, so the first light will cycle through its changes until it returns to *red*. At this point it will resume() the other light and suspend() itself. This pattern will continue indefinitely with each light cycling through its sequence whilst the other light is suspended on *red* in compliance with the required pattern of lights shown in Table 8.2.

8.4 ■ Problems with concurrency

This chapter has necessarily only been an introduction to the design and implementation of concurrent processes, which are recognized as being one of the most specialized and difficult aspects of software development. Although it may not seem so at this stage the Thread facilities supplied by Java greatly ease the development of multi-threaded programs.

The commonest fault which will be encountered as more complex concurrent programs are developed is *mutual deadlock*. This occurs when two processes each synchronize, or *lock*, a resource which the other is waiting to obtain. For example, process *A* may have locked variable *one* and is not prepared to release the lock until it can have access to variable *two*. Meanwhile process *B* has locked variable *two* and is not prepared to release it until it has access to variable *one*. The effect is that each process cannot proceed as the other process is preventing it; this situation is commonly known as a *deadly embrace*.

The advice given to reduce the possibility of this situation arising includes making any **synchronized** actions as short and as simple as possible and designing and implementing concurrent software with a particular degree of care. Actions should be constructed so that if they find themselves blocked, after retrying a small number of times, they should release any locks and wait a random amount of time before trying again.

When implementing any class the possibility that the class might at some stage in the future be used in a concurrent program should be borne in mind. Any action which changes the state of an instance of the class should always leave the class in a well defined state and should be declared as a **synchronized** action. This may have a small penalty when the class is used by a non-concurrent program, but it will be of immense benefit if the class is ever used by a concurrent program as it will avoid introducing faults which are very difficult to detect and correct.

In the discussion in this chapter it has been implicitly suggested that the suspension of an action can only occur between two Java statements. This is quite simply not true! A single Java statement will be compiled into a number of Java virtual machine instructions and these in turn might be executed as a number of native processor instructions. An interruption can occur between any two native instructions and this is more likely to occur in the middle of a Java statement than between two Java statements. This was illustrated by the wildly differing values in the *DangerousDemo* client which suggested that the updating of one, or other, of the attributes was suspended before it had completed.

Summary

- Concurrent processes contain two, or more, independently executing threads.
- The Java Thread class can be extended to implement an application specific thread.
- When a Thread's start() action is called it causes the instance's run() action to be started in a concurrent manner.
- Actions, or parts of actions, can be made 'thread safe' by declaring them as **synchronized**.
- A running Thread can be temporarily stopped by calling its suspend() action and restarted by calling its resume() action.
- A Thread can be suspended for a period of time by calling its sleep() action.
- Two or more threads can co-ordinate their actions by suspending and resuming each other, and this can be designed using a *state diagram*.
- Concurrent programs require much more care in their design than non-concurrent programs and are subject to a number of very elusive bugs.

Exercises

8.1 It was asserted that the faults in the *Dangerous* client were caused by two different interruptions. Show that this is the case by implementing each synchronization in turn.

8.2 The correct operation of a *TrafficLight* instance depends upon its *setOtherLight()* action being called before its *run()* action, but it does not enforce this consideration. Reimplement the *run()* action to throw an exception if *theOtherLight* instance attribute has not been initialized. Adapt the *TrafficDemo* client to show that the *TrafficLight* class is now implemented in a secure manner.

8.3 Adapt the *holdOn()* action to give a different delay depending upon the colour of the light in order to make the simulation more realistic.

8.4 Attempt to demonstrate that a single Java statement can be interrupted. To do this implement a *DangerousWriter* class which either sets or clears all of its bits in a **long** attribute in a single action. The action can be shown to be dangerous if the value read from the class is not equal to the hexadecimal values 0x00000000 or 0xFFFFFFFF.

Hint: if the value of the integer attribute, called *dangerousInteger*, is 0 then all bits are currently clear and can be set by adding 0xFFFFFFFF; adding this value a second time will clear all bits. More details can be found in Appendix A1.

8.5 Design and implement a *TrafficMonitor* class which uses a random number generator to indicate if any traffic is waiting and if traffic is still flowing. Associate a *TrafficMonitor* instance with each *TrafficLight* instance. Adapt the *TrafficLight* class so that, when it is on *green*, it will continually ask its *TrafficMonitor* if traffic is still flowing and relinquish control as soon as none is flowing. Demonstrate the effectiveness of the revision using an unchanged *TrafficDemo* client.

8.6 Further extend the *TrafficLight* class from Exercise 8.5 so that whilst it is on *green* it asks its own *TrafficMonitor* for its traffic flow and asks the other *TrafficLight* for its traffic waiting. It should relinquish control as soon as its traffic flow is significantly lower than the traffic waiting at the other light. Demonstrate the effectiveness of the revision using an unchanged *TrafficDemo* client.

8.7 Design and develop a model of a pair of lifts (elevators) serving a multi-storey building. This should be approached in several stages. The initial stage should start with a single lift and two storeys, each of which has a call button. A call button can, at an indeterminate time, send a call for a lift if the lift is not currently at its level. The lift should respond by travelling to the level it was called from and then travel to the other level. The subsequent stages will require more complex considerations, designs and implementations.

Chapter nine

Keyboard input and formatted output

One of the most fundamental operations required by interactive programs is to obtain input from the user via the keyboard. This sounds a very simple operation, but in practice it can be fraught with problems. For example, whilst the program may be expecting the user to input a numeric value it must be prepared to accept and respond to anything which the user may type in. Java's standard classes do not supply any keyboard input routines for numeric values and the first part of this chapter will introduce a class hierarchy which provides this facility.

In order for this to happen the techniques by which exceptions can be thrown and caught will have to be introduced in greater detail than previously. Considering the example above, whilst the program is anticipating a number to be input the user may type in the word '*help*'. This will cause an exception to be thrown and, unless it is caught and handled, will cause the program to terminate prematurely. This is an unacceptable occurrence for production quality programs and can only be avoided by catching and handling the exception.

The System.out.printin() action has been used since the earliest chapters for the output of numeric values. However, the output produced by this action is determined entirely by Java and is consequently not always appropriate for the application's requirements. The latter part of this chapter will introduce a class which allows for numeric output to be precisely formatted. In order to do this the String and StringBuffer classes will have to be introduced and used in more detail than in previous chapters.

9.1 ▪ The *SimpleInput* and *ValidatedInput* class hierarchy

Input from the user was first obtained in Chapter 6 when the *BasicMenu* class was developed, but this input was limited to a single character. In order to accomplish the input an instance of the java.io.DataInputStream class was constructed from the pre-supplied System.in class. The reason for this was that the System.in class is a raw input stream which regards its input as a sequence of byte values and has no knowledge of its division into lines, each terminated by an <ENTER> keypress. The DataInputStream class is able to recognize the division of the user's input into lines and it will be instantiated again in this chapter to provide the basic input facility.

The abstract *SimpleInput* class will encapsulate the instantiation of the DataInput-Stream class within itself and supply two protected class wide actions, *getLong()* and *getDouble()*, both of which may throw an exception when they are called. These actions are provided to support the *ValidatedInput* class which supplies two

Figure 9.1 The *ValidatedInput* class hierarchy.

corresponding actions, *readLong()* and *readDouble()*. These actions implement an iterative dialog with the user and do not return until the user has provided a numeric value within limits supplied by their arguments. The class hierarchy diagram for these two classes is given in Figure 9.1.

9.2 ▤ The design and implementation of the *SimpleInput* class

The class diagram for the *SimpleInput* class is given in Figure 9.2.

The purpose of this class is to provide the *getLong()* and *getDouble()* actions to the *ValidatedInput* class, hiding the complexity of interacting directly with the input stream within itself. Consequently it is declared as an abstract class and its actions are protected, in order to prevent clients of the *ValidatedInput* class making any use of them. The diagram also indicates, by the bold boxes, that these actions are class wide, for reasons which will be explained when the *ValidatedInput* class is described. The implementation of this class as far as the start of the *getLong()* action is as follows:

```
0001 // Filename SimpleInput.java.
0002 // Provides simple input routines for primitive values.
0003 //
0004 // Produced for JOF book Chapter 9.
0005 // Fintan Culwin, v0.1, August 1997.
0006
0007 import java.io.DataInputStream;
0008 import java.io.IOException;
0009
0010 abstract class SimpleInput extends Object {
0011
```

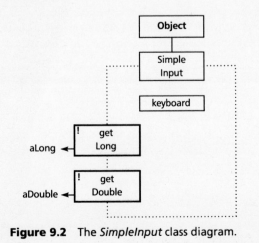

Figure 9.2 The *SimpleInput* class diagram.

```
0012 private static java.io.DataInputStream keyboard
0013                          = new java.io.DataInputStream( System.in);
0014
```

A static encapsulated instance of the **DataInputStream** class, called **keyboard**, is instantiated upon declaration. As this class contains only class wide actions it is unlikely that a constructor will ever be used, so the static variables have to be initialized into a usable state upon declaration. Java will ensure that the initialization takes place, preparing the **keyboard** instance, before it is required. The design of the **getLong()** action is as follows:

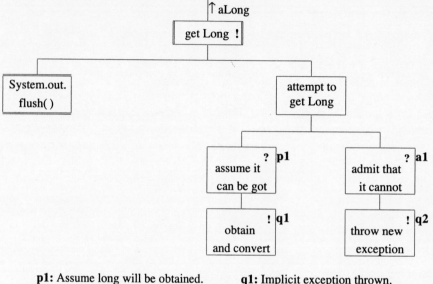

p1: Assume long will be obtained.   **q1:** Implicit exception thrown.
a1: Admit that long was not obtained.   **q2:** Explicit exception thrown.

The first action shown on the design is required to ensure that any characters waiting to be output to the screen are definitely visible to the user. The main part of the design is a posit/admit design, whose posit part assumes that the user's input will be obtained and converted without an ***implicit*** exception being thrown. The admit part recognizes that an error did occur and rethrows it as an ***explicit*** exception. The difference between an implicit and an explicit exception is that an implicit exception is thrown by a called action and thus is outside the control of the developer, whilst an explicit exception is thrown by the developer's code. The implementation of this design is as follows:

```
0015    protected static long getLong() throws IOException {
0016
0017    long    localLong = 0;
0018
0019        System.out.flush();
0020        try {
0021            localLong = Long.valueOf( keyboard.readLine().trim()
0022                                        ).longValue();
0023        } catch ( java.lang.Exception exception){
0024            throw new java.io.Exception();
0025        } // End try/ catch.
```

```
0026        return localLong;
0027   } // End getLong.
```

The central part of this action is the complex statement on lines 0021 and 0022 which can be understood by explaining the operation of its component phrases. The most central phrase, decided by the number of enclosing brackets, is *keyboard*.readLine().trim(). The readLine() action is supplied by the DataInputStream class and it accepts input from the *keyboard* until an <ENTER> keypress is provided. This input is used to create an anonymous String object, whose trim() action is immediately called. The trim() action removes any leading and trailing spaces from the String before it is passed to the class wide Long.valueOf action to be interpreted as an integer value and an anonymous instance of the Long class constructed from it. Finally, on line 0022, the longValue() action of the Long class is used to provide a long value which is assigned to the primitive variable *localLong*.

The two class instances constructed by this statement are described as anonymous as they are created by Java in order to execute, but are not otherwise required. The same effect could be obtained by performing each of the actions in a sequence of steps, using non-anonymous instances, as follows:

```
// Assuming tempString of class String &
// tempLong of class Long are declared.

tempString = keyboard.readLine();
tempString.trim();
tempLong = Long.valueOf( tempString);
localLong = tempLong.longValue();
```

The differences between the primitive **long** data type and the Long class, and the reasons for the difference, are explained in Appendix A1. Should all of this seem too complex, all that needs to be understood is that lines 0021 to 0022 will input a line supplied by the user from the keyboard and if it can be interpreted as an integer value the value of *localLong* will be set to the value. If it cannot be interpreted as an integer value a java.lang.NumberFormatException will be raised by the valueOf() action. In the unlikely event that an end of file is indicated from the keyboard a java.lang.io.Exception will be raised by the readLine() action. For reasons which will be explained shortly it is not possible to ignore these exceptions and the **try/ catch** structure which encloses this action is not optional. The **catch** clause on line 0023 states that it will handle exceptions of the java.lang.Exception class which, as it is the parent class of both possible exceptions, will allow the exception to be handled. The intention of the design is that the handler should propagate the exception from this action and to accomplish this it has to construct and throw a new exception. This is implemented on line 0024 where a java.io.IOException is created and thrown.

The declaration of the *getLong()* action on line 0015 indicates that a java.io.IOException may be thrown when this action is called. Any client which makes use of this action must indicate that it is aware of this by enclosing the call of the action within a **try/catch** structure. The declaration of the readLine() and valueOf() actions in the Java standard classes indicated in a similar manner that they might also throw an exception and so the use of these actions had to be guarded by a **try/catch** structure.

The implementation of the *getDouble()* action is essentially identical and is presented here for the sake of completeness:

```
0030    protected double getDouble() throws IOException {
0031
0032    double localDouble = 0.0;
0033
0034       System.out.flush();
0035       try {
0036          localDouble = Double.valueOf( keyboard.readLine().trim()
0037                                              ).doubleValue();
0038       } catch ( java.lang.Exception exception){
0039          throw new java.io.IOException();
0040       } // End try/ catch.
0041          return localDouble;
0042       } // End getDouble.
0043
0044 } // End SimpleInput.
```

It is not necessary to provide equivalent *getInt()* or *getFloat()* actions in this class as the **long** value returned from the *getLong()* action can be cast into an **int** (or **short** or **byte** value) and the value from *getDouble()* cast into a **float**. The possibility that the *getLong()* action might return a value which is outside the limits of the **int** type will be addressed when the *ValidatedInputDemonstration* client is described below.

In order to demonstrate this class it will have to be temporarily implemented as a non-**abstract** class with **public** actions; this will be left as an end-of-chapter exercise.

9.3 ▪ The design and implementation of the *ValidatedInput* class

The intention of the non-abstract *ValidatedInput* class is to supply clients with *readLong()* and *readDouble()* actions which will initiate a dialog with the user to obtain an integer or floating point value between two values supplied as arguments. The *ValidatedInput* class diagram is presented in Figure 9.3.

The class diagram indicates, by the use of bold boxes, that both actions supplied by *ValidatedInput* class are class wide actions, which means that a client using these facilities will not have to declare an instance of the *ValidatedInput* class. The design of

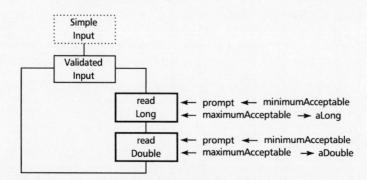

Figure 9.3 The *ValidatedInput* class diagram.

the *readLong ()* action is as follows:

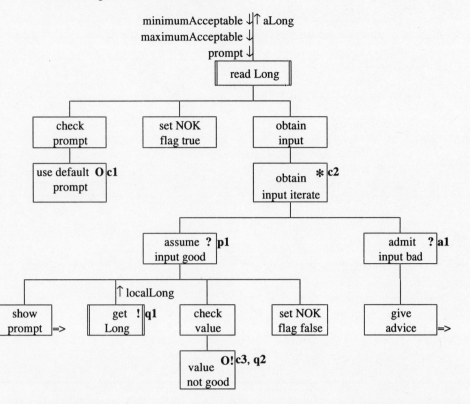

c1: If prompt supplied is empty.   **p1:** Assume input will be good.   **q1:** Implicit IO exception.
c2: While input is unacceptable.   **a1:** Admit input was not good.   **q2:** Explicit IO exception.
c3: If input outside range.

The essence of the design is to iterate until a valid input has been obtained from the user; so, because it can be guaranteed that this action will always return a valid numeric response, there is no need for the action to throw an exception. The main iteration consists of a posit/admit structure which assumes that the input supplied will be acceptable and provides advice if it turns out that it is not.

The posit part of the structure commences by outputting the prompt and continues by calling the *SimpleInput getLong ()* action which, as described above, may throw an exception. As the throwing of this exception is outside the control of this design it is shown on the key as an implicit exception. If *getLong ()* does not throw an exception then the value obtained from it, shown as *localLong*, is checked to make sure it is within the range specified by the arguments *minimumAcceptable* and *maximumAcceptable*. If it is not then an explicit exception is thrown. Finally, should neither of these exceptions be thrown the design component *set NOK flag false* is executed, which will cause the iteration to terminate and the value in *localLong* to be returned. The implementation of this design is as follows:

```
0012    public long readLong( String prompt,
0013                          long    minimumAcceptable,
0014                          long    maximumAcceptable){
0015
0016    long    localLong  = 0;
```

```
0017    boolean inputNotOK = true;
0018
0019     if ( prompt == null ) {
0020        prompt = new String( "Please enter an integer :");
0021     } // End if.
0022
0023     while ( inputNotOK) {
0024        System.out.print( prompt);
0025        try {
0026           localLong = getLong();
0027           if ( (localLong < minimumAcceptable) ||
0028               (localLong > maximumAcceptable) ){
0029              throw new java.io.IOException();
0030           } // End if.
0031           inputNotOK = false;
0032        } catch ( java.io.IOException exception) {
0033           System.out.println( "Please enter a value between" +
0034                          minimumAcceptable + " and "      +
0035                          maximumAcceptable + ".");
0036        } // End try/ catch.
0037     } // End while.
0038     return localLong;
0039 } // End readLong.
```

The **try/catch** structure is implemented within the **while** loop on lines 0025 to 0036. If either the call of the *SimpleInput getLong()* action on line 0026 throws an exception or the condition on lines 0027 and 0028 evaluates **true**, causing an exception to be thrown on line 0029, then flow of control is immediately passed to the **catch** part of the structure. Here, on lines 0033 to 0035, advice is given to the user.

Should this happen then the value of the **boolean** variable *inputNotOK* will still be **true** and the loop will iterate again. Only if no exception is thrown will line 0031 be executed, which will set the value of *inputNotOK* to **false** and cause the loop to terminate. Following this, on line 0038, the value of *localLong* will be returned as the result of the action.

The implementation of *getDouble()* is essentially identical and will be omitted from this chapter. Details of how it can be obtained are in Appendix B.

9.4 ■ The *ValidatedInputDemonstration* client

The implementation of the *ValidatedInputDemonstration* client is as follows:

```
0001 // Filename ValidatedInputDemonstration.java.
0002 // Demonstration harness for the ValidatedInput class.
0003 //
0004 // Produced for JOF book Chapter 9.
0005 // Fintan Culwin, v0.1, January 1997.
0006
0007 import ValidatedInput;
0008
0009 public class ValidatedInputDemonstration {
0010
```

```
0011     public static void main( String argv[]) {
0012
0013     long   demoLong;
0014     int    demoInt;
0015
0016        System.out.println( "\t Validated Input Demonstration \n\n");
0017
0018        System.out.println( "Inputting a long value between 200 and 300\n");
0019        demoLong = ValidatedInput.readLong(
0020                              "Please enter your value : ",
0021                              200, 300);
0022        System.out.println( "Thank you, you input " + demoLong);
0023
0024
0025        System.out.println( "\n\nInputting a positive int value \n");
0026        demoInt = (int) ValidatedInput.readLong(
0027                              "Please enter your value : ",
0028                              0, Integer.MAX_VALUE);
0029        System.out.println( "Thank you, you input " + demoInt);
0030     } // End main.
0031 } // End ValidatedInputDemonstration.
```

This demonstration harness makes two calls to *readLong()*. The first, on lines 0019 to 0021, is to obtain a **long** value between 200 and 300. The second call is on lines 0026 to 0028, where an **int** value between 0 and the maximum **int** value (Integer.MAX_VALUE) is requested. The cast on line 0026 shows how the *readLong()* action can be safely used to obtain an **int** value obviating the need for additional *readInt()* and, likewise, *readFloat()* actions.

The client does not declare any instances of the *ValidatedInput* class, as both of its actions are class wide, and so the calls of the actions are qualified with the class name. An example of an interaction with this program is as follows:

```
Validated Input Demonstration
Inputting a long value between 200 and 300
Please enter your value : 199
Please enter a value between 200 and 300.
Please enter your value : 301
Please enter a value between 200 and 300.
Please enter your value : 250
Thank you, you input 250

Inputting a positive int value

Please enter your value : -1
Please enter a value between 0 and 2147483647.
Please enter your value : 2147483648
Please enter a value between 0 and 2147483647.
Please enter your value : 2147483647
Thank you, you input 2147483647
```

which seems to demonstrate that the class hierarchy is working correctly.

9.5 ▇ The *OutputFormatter* class *formatLong()* action

The second part of this chapter will introduce a class called *OutputFormatter* which also contains only class wide actions; its class diagram is given in Figure 9.4.

The *formatLong()* action will format a **long** value, supplied in *toFormat*, to use as many characters as are expressed in *toWidth*, with leading zeros or blanks (*withZeros*) in a number base specified in *inBase*. For example, if it were asked to format the value 42 in base 16 with leading zeros to a width of 8, the string returned would be '0000002a'. If the width requested is less than the minimum number of characters required to express the value, it will be ignored and the minimum number of characters will be used. For example, if it were asked to format the value 12345 in decimal to a width of 4 it would return the five character string '12345'.

The *formatDouble()* action is similar, formatting the floating point value *toFormat* with *foreWidth* characters before the decimal point and *aftWidth* characters after the decimal point, using leading zeros or spaces before the decimal point and rounding the value after the decimal point as appropriate. For example, if it was asked to format the value 123.456 with leading zeros, five spaces before the decimal point and two after, it would return '00123.46'. At least one character will be used after the decimal point even though the call may ask for zero.

This version of the *formatDouble()* action is limited to formatting floating point values within the range of values which can be represented by the **long** data type. If it is asked to format a value outside this range it will throw an *OutputFormatException*. This exception will also be thrown if the number base requested is not possible. The *OutputFormatException* class is provided for use by this class and its class diagram is given in Figure 9.5.

The constructor for this exception requires a reason to be supplied which can subsequently be obtained using the *obtainReason()* action. The *toString()* action will provide a different *explanation* depending upon the reason supplied when the exception instance is created. The implementation of this class is as follows:

```
0001 // Filename OutputFormatException.java.
0002 // Providing specific exception for the
0003 // OutputFormatter class.
0004 //
0005 // Written for JOF book Chapter 9 see text.
0006 // Fintan Culwin, v0.1, August 1997.
0007
0008
```

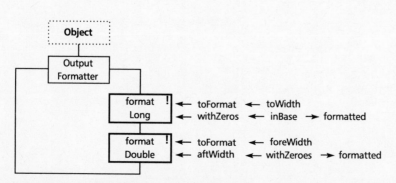

Figure 9.4   The *OutputFormatter* class diagram.

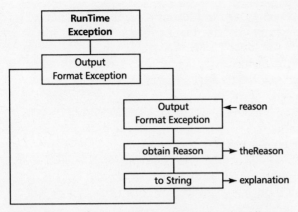

Figure 9.5   The *OutputFormatException* class diagram.

```
0009 class OutputFormatException extends RuntimeException {
0010
0011 public static final int UNKNOWN_REASON   = 0;
0012 public static final int INVALID_BASE     = 1;
0013 public static final int FP_TOO_LARGE     = 2;
0014
0015 private int theReason = UNKNOWN_REASON;
0016
0017    public OutputFormatException( int reason) {
0018       super();
0019       theReason = reason;
0020    } // End OutputFormatException constructor.
0021
0022
0023    public int obtainReason() {
0024       return theReason;
0025    } // End obtainReason.
0026
0027
0028    public String toString() {
0029
0030    String toReturn;
0031
0032       switch ( theReason) {
0033       case INVALID_BASE:
0034          toReturn = new String( "Output format exception : Invalid base.");
0035          break;
0036       case FP_TOO_LARGE:
0037          toReturn = new String( "Output format exception : Value too large.");
0038          break;
0039       default:
0040          toReturn = new String( "Output format exception : Unknown reason.");
0041       } // End switch.
0042       return toReturn;
0043    } // End toString.
0044
0045 } // End OutputFormatException.
```

The possible reasons why the exception may be thrown are publicly enumerated on lines 0011 to 0013, and when the instance variable *theReason* is declared on line 0015 it is given the value *UNKNOWN_REASON*. The remainder of the implementation should be comprehensible from the previous classes presented.

The design of the *OutputFormatter formatLong()* action is as follows:

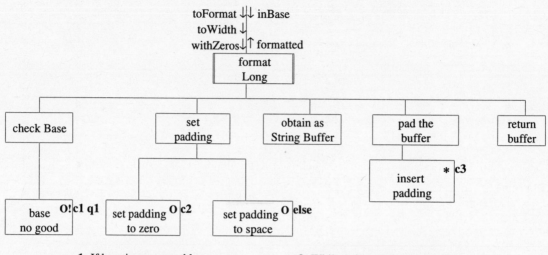

c1: If base is unacceptable.   **c3:** While string not long enough.
c2: If zero padding requested.   **q1:** Explicit Output Format Exception.

The maximal base which will be allowed is base 36. This is determined by the consideration that an additional alphabetic character has to be used for every base beyond 10 and as there are only 26 alphabetic characters this gives a total of 36 bases. The minimal base is base 2, and both of these values are supplied as manifest values in the Character class, as MIN_RADIX and MAX_RADIX. The implementation of the *OutputFormatter* class as far as the end of the *formatLong()* action is as follows:

```
0001 // Filename OutputFormatter.java.
0002 // Provides facilities for the formatting of numbers.
0003 //
0004 // Produced for JOF book Chapter 9.
0005 // Fintan Culwin, v0.1, August 1997.
0006
0007 import OutputFormatException;
0008
0009 public class OutputFormatter {
0010
0011 public static final int BINARY  = 2;
0012 public static final int OCTAL   = 8;
0013 public static final int DECIMAL = 10;
0014 public static final int HEX     = 16;
0015
0016 private static final char SPACE = ' ';
0017 private static final char ZERO  = '0';
0018
0019    public static String formatLong( long    toFormat,
0020                                     int     toWidth,
```

```
0021                                        boolean withZeros,
0022                                        int     inBase) {
0023
0024     StringBuffer formatString;
0025     char         padding;
0026
0027        if ( (inBase < Character.MIN_RADIX) ||
0028            (inBase > Character.MAX_RADIX) ){
0029          throw new OutputFormatException( OutputFormatException.INVALID_BASE);
0030        } // End if.
0031
0032        if ( withZeros) {
0033           padding = ZERO;
0034        } else {
0035           padding = SPACE;
0036        } // End if.
0037
0038        formatString = new StringBuffer( Long.toString( toFormat, inBase));
0039
0040        while ( formatString.length() < toWidth) {
0041           formatString.insert( 0, padding);
0042        } // End while.
0043
0044        return formatString.toString();
0045     } // End formatLong.
```

The public manifest values on lines 0011 to 0014 are supplied to assist clients in specifying a base for the *formatLong()* action. The private manifest values on lines 0016 and 0017 are supplied to make the implementation of *formatLong()* a little more readable.

The first action of the *formatLong()* action is to throw an *OutputFormatException* with the reason set to *INVALID_BASE* if the base requested is not within the limits supplied by the Character class. Following this a local character variable, called *padding*, is set as appropriate depending upon the value of the argument *withZeros*. The design component *obtain as String Buffer* is implemented on line 0038 where the class wide Long toString() action is used to obtain an anonymous String containing the value *toFormat* expressed in *inBase*. This String is immediately used to construct a StringBuffer called *formatString*. A StringBuffer is required instead of a String as a StringBuffer can be easily changed whilst a String is relatively unchangeable.

Having obtained the value in a StringBuffer the padding character is inserted at the front, using the StringBuffer insert() action, until it is as wide as requested in *toWide*. Should the StringBuffer already be as long, or longer, than *toWide* the loop will not iterate and no characters will be inserted. The final action of the *formatLong()* action is to convert the StringBuffer back into a String using the StringBuffer toString() action, and return this as the result of the action. Details of the StringBuffer class can be found in Appendix A5.

A fragment of a demonstration harness client for this action is as follows:

```
0012 // Assuming int demoInt = 255 has been declared.
0013 System.out.println( "\nOutputting " + demoInt + " in decimal with " +
0014                     "leading zeros and width 12 ... ");
0015 System.out.println( OutputFormatter.formatLong( (long) demoInt,
0016                                         12, true,
0017                                         OutputFormatter.DECIMAL));
```

```
0018
0019 System.out.println( "\nOutputting " + demoInt + " in hex with "  +
0020                      "leading spaces and width 12 ... ");
0021 System.out.println( OutputFormatter.formatLong( (long) demoInt,
0022                                      12, false,
0023                                      OutputFormatter.HEX));
```

The output from this fragment, which seems to indicate that the class is working correctly, was as follows:

```
Outputting 255 in decimal with leading zeros and width 12 ...
000000000255
Outputting 255 in hex with leading spaces and width 12 ...
          ff
```

9.6 ▦ The *OutputFormatter()* class *formatDouble()* action

The design of the *formatDouble()* action is as follows:

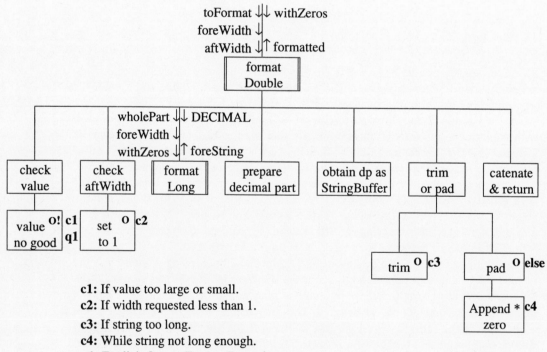

c1: If value too large or small.
c2: If width requested less than 1.
c3: If string too long.
c4: While string not long enough.
q1: Explicit Output Format Exception.

The basis of the design is to divide the floating point number into two parts: the whole number part before the decimal point and the decimal part after the decimal point. Each part can then be processed separately. In the design, after the value of *toFormat* is tested to make sure that it is within the limits of a **long** and *aftWith* has been checked to make sure that it is at least 1, the whole number part is formatted using a suitable call of the *formatLong()* action.

The formatting of the decimal part is in some respects very similar to the formatting of a **long** as described above. But, instead of adding padding characters to the front of the string until it is the correct length, zeros are added to the end of the string or, if the string is too long in the first place, it is truncated. The implementation of this design is as follows:

```
0049 public static String formatDouble( float    toFormat,
0050                                     int      foreWidth,
0051                                     int      aftWidth,
0052                                     boolean withZeros){
0053
0054 String       foreString;
0055 StringBuffer aftString;
0056 double       wholePart   = Math.floor( toFormat);
0057 double       decimalPart = toFormat - wholePart;
0058
0059    if ( ( ((long) toFormat) < Long.MIN_VALUE) ||
0060        ( ((long) toFormat) > Long.MAX_VALUE) ){
0061      throw new OutputFormatException( OutputFormatException.FP_TOO_LARGE);
0062    } // End if.
0063
0064    if ( aftWidth < 1) {
0065      aftWidth =1;
0066    } // End if.
0067
0068    foreString = formatLong( (long) wholePart, foreWidth, withZeros, DECIMAL);
0069
0070    decimalPart *= Math.pow( 10, aftWidth);
0071    decimalPart =  Math.round( decimalPart);
0072
0073    aftString = new StringBuffer( Long.toString( (long) decimalPart));
0074    if ( aftString.length() > aftWidth) {
0075      aftString.setLength( aftWidth);
0076    } else {
0077      while ( aftString.length() < aftWidth) {
0078        aftString.append( ZERO);
0079      } // End while.
0080    } // End if.
0081
0082    return foreString.toString() + "." + aftString.toString();
0083    } // End formatDouble.
0084 } // End NumberFormatter.
```

On lines 0056 and 0057 the floating point number is split into its whole number and decimal parts. This is accomplished by setting the *wholePart* variable to the floored part of the *toFormat* value. The **floor()** of a floating point value is the largest whole number which is smaller than or equal to the floating point value. So the floor of the value 123.456 would be 123.0 and the floor of the value 789.0 would be 789.0. Having obtained the *wholePart* of the number to format the *decimalPoint* can be obtained by subtraction. As the floor of 123.456 is 123.0 subtracting the floor from the original value leaves 0.456.

The implementation continues with lines 0059 to 0062 which implement the design component *check value* and which throw an *OutputFormatException* with the reason set to *FP_TOO_LARGE* if the value is not acceptable. The design component *check aftWidth* is implemented on lines 0064 to 0066 ensuring that the *aftWidth* argument is at least 1.

On line 0068 the fore part of the formatted string is prepared by calling the *formatLong()* action to prepare a suitable String. As a part of this the *wholePart* is cast to a **long** value, which is the primary reason for the restriction upon the range of values which this action can accept.

Having processed the fore part of the floating point value the remaining parts of the action are largely concerned with the aft part. The first action is to round the value correctly. For example, the value 0.456 formatted to two decimal places should be 0.46, not 0.45, and to one decimal place should be 0.5. To accomplish this the value is first multiplied by 10 to the power of however many decimal places are requested. For example, in formatting 0.456 to two decimal places this would be 10 to the power 2, which is 100, and when the value 0.456 is multiplied by 100 the result is 45.6. The Math.round() action is then used to obtain the correctly rounded whole number, in this case 46.0. The multiplication and subsequent rounding is implemented on lines 0069 to 0070.

The resulting value is then cast to a **long** value and its representation placed in a StringBuffer in an essentially identical manner to how the **long** value's representation was obtained in *formatLong()*. Continuing the example, the value 46.0 would be cast to 46 and obtained in a StringBuffer as '46'. The next part of the implementation either trims the length of this string to the number of characters required or pads it with trailing zeros up to the required length.

Having formatted the fore and the aft parts they are both converted to Strings using their toString() actions and catenated together with a decimal point in the middle; the resulting String is returned as the result of the action in line 0082. A fragment of a demonstration harness client for this action is as follows:

```
0026 // Assuming that float demoDouble = 123.456 has been declared.
0027 System.out.println( "\nOutputting " + demoDouble + " with leading zeros, " );
0028 System.out.println( "12 characters before and 2 after the decimal point ... ");
0029 System.out.println( OutputFormatter.formatFloat( demoDouble,
0030                                                  12, 2, true));
0031 System.out.println( "\nOutputting " + demoDouble + " with leading spaces, " );
0032 System.out.println( "12 characters before and 4 after the decimal point ... ");
0033 System.out.println( OutputFormatter.formatFloat( demoDouble,
0034                                                  12, 4, false));
0035 System.out.println( "\nOutputting " + demoDouble + " with leading spaces, ");
0036 System.out.println( "12 characters before and 0 after the decimal point ... ");
0037 System.out.println( OutputFormatter.formatFloat( demoDouble,
0038                                                  12, 0, false));
```

```
Outputting 123.456 with leading zeros,
12 characters before and 2 after the decimal point ...
000000000123.46
Outputting 123.456 with leading spaces,
12 characters before and 4 after the decimal point ...
      123.4560
Outputting 123.456 with leading spaces,
12 characters before and 0 after the decimal point ...
         123.5
```

which again appears to demonstrate that the action is working correctly.

9.7 ▨ Exceptions in Java

This chapter has introduced the throwing and catching of exceptions in Java in detail. These considerations, and some aspects which have not been brought out in the examples, will be summarized here.

The Java exception class hierarchy, whose root class is java.lang.Exception, is divided into two groups of classes which are treated differently by the Java language. First, there is the java.lang.RuntimeException class and all the classes which are derived from it; and second, all other classes descended from java.lang.Exception. To make the discussion which follows easier these will be referred to as the Runtime and non-Runtime exceptions. The essential difference between them is that a Runtime exception does not have to be caught, whilst a non-Runtime exception has to be caught.

Any action which throws an instance of a non-Runtime exception must do one of two things: either it must completely handle itself or it must indicate that the exception may be propagated from the action by including a **throws** clause in the signature of the action. For example, the declaration of the SimpleInput getLong() action from this chapter was as follows:

```
protected static long getLong() throws java.lang.IOException {
```

Any client of an action such as this, which indicates in its heading that it might throw a non-Runtime exception, <u>**must**</u> catch it. In practice this means that the call of the action must be enclosed within a **try/catch** structure or be contained within an action whose signature indicates that it might propagate the exception.

On the other hand, Runtime exceptions need not be handled within the action where they are thrown, nor need they indicate in their signature that they might propagate an exception. For example, the *WarningCounter count()* and *unCount()* actions both had the possibility of throwing a *CounterException*. However, as this exception was declared as an extended Runtime exception there was no requirement for these actions to include a **throws** clause in their header.

However, if a called action does throw a Runtime exception and the calling environment does not catch it, the exception will propagate to the place in the program where the calling environment was itself called from. If this part of the program does not provide a handler either, the exception will continue to propagate. Eventually the exception will be propagated to the *main()* action of the application where, if it is not handled, it will cause the program to finish early.

So Runtime exceptions are easier for the developer to throw, as they do not have to include a **throws** clause in the action's header, and are easier for the developer to work with as they do not have to provide a **try/catch** structure around the call. But precisely because of this they are more dangerous as an unhandled exception may crash the program.

The purpose of throwing an exception is to signal to the calling environment that something unexpected or unusual has happened. The information indicating exactly what has caused the exception to be thrown can be transmitted in the type of exception which is thrown. For example, the input routine in the **try** part of the *SimpleInput getLong()* action will throw a *NumberFormatException* if the user's input cannot be interpreted as an integer value or an *IOException* if an end-of-file condition occurs.

Alternatively the exception itself can encapsulate the reason why the exception was thrown and the exception's class can provide manifest values to support this. For example, the *OutputFormatException* thrown by the *OutputFormatter* actions has an *obtainedReason()* action which can be used to determine if the exception was thrown because the base is invalid (*INVALID_BASE*) or because the floating point number was too large or too small (*FP_TOO_LARGE*).

Using either of these two techniques the **catch** part of a **try/catch** structure can be divided into a number of different sections, each of which will attempt to deal with a different cause of the exception being thrown. For example, this fragment illustrates how to handle different errors with different exception types:

```
try {
    // Do something which might throw different exceptions
    // e.g. the input routine from SimpleInput getLong().
} catch ( java.io.IOException exception) {
    // Handle io errors here.
} catch ( java.io.NumberFormatException exception) {
    // Handle number format exception here.
} // End try/ catch.
```

whereas the next fragment illustrates how to handle different errors with the same type of exception:

```
try {
    // Do something which might throw an OutputFormatException.
} catch ( OutputFormatException exception) {
    switch (exception.obtainReason() ){
        case OutputFormatException.INVALID_BASE:
            // Handle invalid bases here.
            break;
        case OutputFormatException.FP_TOO_LARGE:
            // Handle invalid floating point value here.
            break;
    } // End switch.
} // End try/ catch.
```

In this second example the **catch** clause will only trap exceptions of the *OutputFormatException* class. Any exceptions of any other class which are thrown in the **try** part of the structure will not be handled and will be propagated upward to the next enclosing handler in the same or enclosing action.

To avoid this it is possible, though generally not advisable, to catch an exception in a general manner. For example, the following **catch** clause will catch all Runtime exceptions:

```
} catch ( java.lang.RuntimeException exception) {
```

and the following will catch all exceptions:

```
} catch ( java.lang.Exception exception) {
```

When a number of different exceptions are being handled with a sequence of **catch** statements the last of the sequence can be identified as **finally**, which will handle all remaining exception classes. For example:

```
try {
    // Do something which might throw various exceptions.
} catch ( java.lang.ArithmeticException exception) {
```

```
    // Handle arithmetic exception here.
} catch (java.io.IOException exception) {
    // Handle IO exception here.
} finally {
    // Handle all other exceptions here.
} // End try/ catch.
```

Sometimes an exception handler may only be able to deal with a part of the problem which has caused the exception to be thrown. In these situations the exception can be re-**throw**n, as follows.

```
try {
    // Do something which might throw an IOexception.
} catch (java.io.IOException exception) {
    // Handle part of the IO exceptions here ...
    // and then re-throw the exception.
    throw exception;
} // End try/ catch.
```

The rethrown exception will then propagate from this exception handler to be further handled as required. When exception handling is being used in the development of a program the details of its propagation route can be output with the *printStackTrace()* action. For example, the following outline could be put in place while the program was under development:

```
static void main( String args[]) {

// Declarations here.

    try {
        // Main's steps here.
    catch ( java.langException exception) {
        System.out.println( "Unhandled exception propagated to main.");
        System.out.println( exception);
        System.out.println( "\n propagated from ... ");
        exception.printStackTrace();
    } // End try/catch.
} // End main.
```

Any exceptions which are not handled, or are only partially handled, within *main()* or any actions called, directly or indirectly, by *main()* will be propagated to the exception handler at the end of *main()*. Here the details of the exception and the route through which it has been propagated will be displayed. The output will appear something like the following:

```
Unhandled exception propagated from main.
java.lang.ArithmeticException: / by zero

Propagated from ...
        at demo.main
        at class name/ action name
        ...
        at class name/ action name
```

The output from the *printStackTrace()* action indicates which actions, starting with the *main()* action, the exception has propagated through. This information can be very useful when debugging in order to locate the place where the error was originally noticed by Java, although this might not always be the location of the error. This technique should only be used during development and should be removed from production code as all possible eventualities which may cause an exception to be thrown should be handled.

There is thus a bewildering number of considerations and possibilities concerned with the throwing and catching of exceptions, of which this chapter can only be an introduction. For introductory programs, intended to produce initial confidence and competence in software development, the throwing and handling of exceptions can be largely ignored. However, for more realistic programs, and especially for production quality programs, these considerations are essential.

The design of any action should consider not only what it will do and how it will do it, but also what might go wrong and how it will be handled. As usual there are many more things that can cause a system to go wrong than help it to go right. The skills involved in recognizing these possibilities and in designing and implementing an appropriate strategy for dealing with them can only emerge from practical experience and considered reflection.

Summary

- Java does not supply numeric input facilities; the *ValidatedInput* class from this chapter is intended to be used for this requirement.

- The *FormattedOutput* class from this chapter is intended to be used for precise control over the output of numeric values.

- Complex string processing is essential to many applications.

- Exceptions can be divided into Runtime and non-Runtime classes.

- When a non-Runtime exception is thrown it must be caught within the action or stated in a **throws** clause in the action's header.

- Clients using an action whose header indicates that it might throw a non-Runtime exception must **catch** the exception.

- A Runtime exception need not be handled, nor need it be mentioned in a **throws** clause, but if it is not caught it may propagate and halt the program.

- The reasons why an exception is thrown may be communicated using the type of exception thrown or by constructing an exception class which encapsulates a reason.

Exercises

9.1 This chapter has introduced the importance of Strings. Make sure you are fully conversant with these facilities by referring to Appendix A5.

9.2 Demonstrate the *BasicInput* class by temporarily making it non-abstract and implementing a suitable harness.

9.3 Complete the *ValidatedInputDemonstration* client so that it demonstrates all actions and possibilities supplied, including the throwing of exceptions where appropriate.

9.4 Complete the *FormattedOutputDemonstration* client so that it demonstrates all actions and possibilities supplied, including the throwing of exceptions where appropriate; include a stack trace of the exception in the demonstration client.

9.5 Reimplement the exception handling from Exercise 9.3 so that the different reasons why the exception is thrown are stated.

9.6 Extend the signature of the *formatLong()* action so that it takes an additional **boolean** argument called *inCaps*. If this argument is true then any non-digit characters in the output should be capitalized, otherwise they should remain in lower case. Demonstrate the correct implementation of this feature.

9.7 Revisit the program in Exercise 7.6 so that the cost of the purchase can be input from the keyboard.

9.8 Reimplement the *CashRegister* and *MultipleCashRegister* classes so that they take advantage of the *FormattedOutput* facilities and demonstrate the effectiveness of the reimplementation by recompiling and executing the program in Exercise 9.6.

9.9 Extend the classes in Exercise 9.8 so that the constructor is informed of the number of decimal places which are to be shown. This will allow the cash registers to be able to handle currencies such as the Italian lira which have no decimal parts.

Chapter ten

The *JulianDate* hierarchy

This chapter will describe the design and implementation of a class to illustrate and consolidate the processes of designing a class hierarchy for a complex requirement. The examples which have been used previously have been either very simple in their requirements or artificially specified in order to be straightforward. The intention here is to provide an opportunity to examine a class which has been produced to professional standards and as a part of this to consider internationalization issues. The hierarchy will be used extensively in the subsequent chapters.

Many areas of activity have a requirement to represent calendar dates and to manipulate them, e.g. to determine the number of days between two dates. This requirement was first articulated by a sixteenth century French scholar called Joseph Scaliger. Within astronomy it is necessary to be absolutely precise about the meaning of a date, the relationships between different dates and how many days there are between two given dates. Scaliger proposed a concept, which he called *Julian dates*, where days were numbered sequentially from day 1. Day 1 was arbitrarily defined as 1 January 4713 BCE[1], and subsequent days are numbered from then. Joseph Scaliger named the concept Julian days in honour of his father Julius Caeser Scaliger. It has no other connection with Julius Caesar, nor with the calendar reforms which he instituted.

The requirement can thus be loosely stated as a need to provide a *JulianDate* class which will store, represent and manipulate calendar dates in Julian dates format. In the interests of manageable simplicity this implementation will restrict the range of dates to 1 January 1900 to 31 December 2199 (109573 days), which should be sufficient for the life span of any programs which make use of the hierarchy. In order to be developed further this vague statement of requirements will have to be refined into a precise specification of which operations are to be provided. For any class one way to assist the precise definition of operations for the type is to consider possible operations from the following categories:

- Actions to construct an instance of the class.
- Actions to enquire of the instances' attributes.
- Actions to set the value of an instances' attributes.
- Relational, arithmetic or pseudo-arithmetic operations.
- Input and output actions.
- Other actions which are specific to the class.

[1] BCE is before common era, also known as before christ (BC). The current era is known as common era (CE), also known as anno domini {after christ} (AD). The designations BCE and CE are preferred to BC and AD as they have no religious or cultural connotation.

10.1 ■ The *JulianDates* class hierarchy

To make the process more manageable, and to increase the possibility of successful reuse, a class hierarchy can be produced at this stage which will allocate the categories above to different classes. The *JulianDates* class hierarchy is presented in Figure 10.1.

The class hierarchy diagram indicates that all of these classes will be contained within a package called *JulianDates*. It includes a specific *JulianDateException* class whose design and construction is essentially identical to that of the *OutputFormatException* class as presented in the previous chapter. It will allow an exception to be constructed with a specific manifest reason which can be queried by its *obtainReason()* action in order for the exception handler to respond appropriately. The implementation of this class will not be represented here; details of how to obtain it are contained in Appendix B. The various manifest reasons supplied by this class will be introduced as they are required.

The *JulianDates* hierarchy commences with an abstract *BasicJulianDate* class which is largely concerned with the construction of the *JulianDate* instances, enquiry actions and a fundamental output action. The *ArithmeticJulianDate* class adds the relational, arithmetic and pseudo-arithmetic actions and the non-abstract *JulianDate* class adds the specialized input and output operations.

10.2 ■ The *BasicJulianDate* class

The *BasicJulianDate* class is the most complex class which will be presented in this book. Consequently its design and implementation will be presented in two stages, starting with the partial class diagram in Figure 10.2.

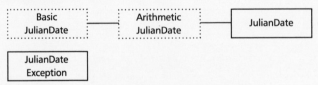

Figure 10.1   The *JulianDates* class hierarchy diagram.

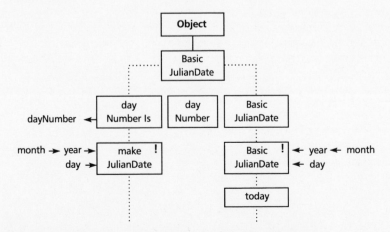

Figure 10.2   The start of the *BasicJulianDate* class diagram.

The first, default, constructor will construct a *JulianDate* instance which contains an invalid null date. The second constructor will attempt to construct an instance containing a representation of the date expressed in its arguments. It is possible that the arguments specify an invalid date, e.g. 31 June 1997, and so the action is shown as throwing an exception. The *today()* action will set the instance to the current date.

Both of these latter two actions will make use of a protected action called *makeJulianDate()* which may also throw an exception. It is theoretically possible that *today()* could cause an exception to be propagated from its call of the *makeJulian-Date()* action, but as it obtains its arguments from the system clock this is impossible and so it is not noted as throwing an exception. The diagram also indicates a single **private** data attribute called *dayNumber* and a **protected** action to obtain this value called *dayNumberIs()*.

The implementation of this class, as far as the end of the constructors, is as follows. The actions are preceded by a large number of manifest declarations whose use will be explained as they are used.

```
0001 // Filename BasicJulianDate.java.
0002 // Base of the JulianDate hierarchy providing the
0003 // essential functionality.
0004 //
0005 // Written for JOF Book Chapter 10.
0006 // Fintan Culwin, v0.1, August 1997.
0007
0008 package JulianDates;
0009
0010 import java.util.Date;
0011 import JulianDates.JulianDateException;
0012
0013 protected abstract class BasicJulianDate extends Object {
0014
0015 private int dayNumber;
0016
0017 private static final int DAYS_PER_YEAR      = 365;
0018 private static final int DAYS_PER_LEAP_YEAR = 366;
0019
0020
0021 private static final int MINIMUM_YEAR      = 1900;
0022 private static final int MAXIMUM_YEAR      = 2199;
0023 private static final int MINIMUM_MONTH     = 1;
0024 private static final int MAXIMUM_MONTH     = 12;
0025 private static final int MINIMUM_DAY       = 1;
0026
0027
0028 private static final String DAY_NAMES[]   = {
0029                                   "Sat", "Sun", "Mon", "Tue",
0030                                   "Wed", "Thu", "Fri" };
0031
0032 private static final String MONTH_NAMES[] = { "" ,
0033                                   "Jan", "Feb", "Mar", "Apr",
0034                                   "May", "Jun", "Jly", "Aug",
0035                                   "Sep", "Oct", "Nov", "Dec" };
0036
0037 protected static final int NULL_JULIAN_DATE   = 0;
```

```
0038 protected static final int MINIMUM_JULIAN_DATE = 1;
0039 protected static final int MAXIMUM_JULIAN_DATE = 109573;
0040
0041    public BasicJulianDate(){
0042       dayNumber = NULL_JULIAN_DATE;
0043    } // End JulianDate default constructor.
0044
0045
0046    public BasicJulianDate( int year, int month, int day )
0047                                        throws JulianDateException {
0048       dayNumber = makeJulianDate( year, month, day);
0049    } // End JulianDate alternative constructor.
```

The design of the *makeJulianDate()* action is as follows:

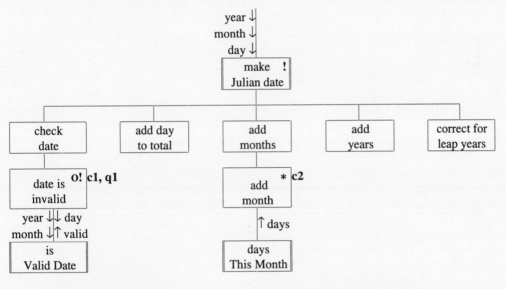

c1: If the date is invalid.   **q1:** Explicit JulianDateException.
c2: For each month elapsed.

The basis of this design, after ensuring that the arguments represent a valid date and throwing an exception if not, is to count the number of days since 1 January 1900 to the date represented by the arguments. It starts by adding the number of days in the current month and then iteratively adding the number of days in each month elapsed before adding the number of days in each elapsed year. This last stage makes no allowance for leap years and the final stage is to make a correction for this. The implementation of this design is as follows:

```
0062    protected int makeJulianDate( int year, int month, int day )
0063                                        throws JulianDateException {
0064
0065    int localDayNumber = 0;
0066    int thisMonth;
0067
0068       if ( ! isValidDate( year, month, day)) {
0069          throw new JulianDateException(
```

```
0070                              JulianDateException.DATE_CONSTRUCTION_ERROR);
0071        } // End if.
0072
0073        // Start with the day of the month
0074        localDayNumber = day;
0075
0076        // Add the number of days for the month.
0077        for ( thisMonth = 1; thisMonth < month; thisMonth++) {
0078            localDayNumber += daysThisMonth( year, thisMonth);
0079        } // End for.
0080
0081        // Add the number of days for the year (ignoring leap years).
0082        localDayNumber += (year - MINIMUM_YEAR) * DAYS_PER_YEAR;
0083
0084        // Correct for the number of leap years passed.
0085        localDayNumber += ((year - MINIMUM_YEAR) /4)   -
0086                          ((year - MINIMUM_YEAR) /100);
0087        if ( year > 2000) {
0088            localDayNumber++;
0089        } // End if.
0090
0091        return localDayNumber;
0092    } // End MakeJulianDate.
```

Omitting the validation of the arguments, line 0074 starts computing the number of days by assigning the day of the month to a local variable called *localDayNumber*. It then adds the number of days in each month elapsed, using a private action called *daysThisMonth()* to obtain a value for the number of days in the month. The number of days in the years elapsed since 1900 is then added on line 0082, without considering leap years. Finally, using the rule that every fourth year is a leap year, apart from every 100th year unless it is a 400th year, the number of leap years is added. The expression on lines 0085 to 0086 will allow for 1900 not being a leap year but will not recognize that 2000 is a leap year. Consequently a correction for this has to be included on lines 0087 to 0089. The implementation of the *isValidDate()* action is as follows.

```
0254    private static final boolean isValidDate( int year, int month, int day ) {
0255
0256    boolean isGoodYear  = (year >= MINIMUM_YEAR) &&
0257                          (year  <= MAXIMUM_YEAR);
0258    boolean isGoodMonth = (month >= MINIMUM_MONTH) &&
0259                          (month <= MAXIMUM_MONTH);
0260    boolean isGoodDay    = false;
0261
0262        if ( isGoodYear && isGoodMonth) {
0263            isGoodDay = (day >= MINIMUM_DAY) &&
0264                        (day <= daysThisMonth( year, month));
0265        } // End if.
0266        return isGoodYear && isGoodMonth && isGoodDay;
0267    } // End isValidDate
```

This action is declared **static** as it makes use only of the arguments passed to it and no use of any instance attributes. It is declared **final** as it is considered highly unlikely that it will ever have to be overridden and a **final** action cannot be extended. The validation of the *year* and *month* arguments is accomplished on lines 0256 to 0259. Only if they are validated is the *day* validated by comparing its value against the minimum and maximum days of the specified month. The result of the function is the **and**ed combination of the three **boolean** flags containing the validations of the three arguments. The action will only return **true** if all three of these flags are **true**, as shown in the and rule table in Appendix A3. This action also relies upon the *daysThisMonth()* action whose implementation is as follows:

```
0223    private static final int daysThisMonth( int thisYear, int thisMonth) {
0224
0225    int localDays;
0226
0227       switch ( thisMonth) {
0228          case 4:
0229          case 6:
0230          case 9:
0231          case 11:
0232             localDays = 30;
0233             break;
0234          case 2:
0235             if ( isLeapYear( thisYear)) {
0236                localDays = 29;
0237             } else {
0238                localDays = 28;
0239             } // end if
0240             break;
0241          default:
0242             localDays = 31;
0243       } // End switch.
0244       return localDays;
0245    } // End daysThisMonth.
0256
0257
0258    private static boolean isLeapYear( int thisYear) {
0259
0260       return (  (thisYear % 400) == 0) ||
0261             ( ((thisYear % 4)   == 0) &&
0262               ((thisYear % 100) != 0) );
0263    } // End isLeapYear.
```

The implementation of *days ThisMonth()* is based upon the rhyme:

> Thirty days hath September,
> April, June and November.
> All the rest have 31; save February alone
> which has 28 in each year clear,
> and 29 in each leap year.

This is the basis of the **switch** structure between lines 0227 and 0243, with February considered between lines 0235 and 0239. This option is supported by the **boolean** action *isLeapYear()* whose implementation is also presented and is based upon the same rules for leap years as stated above.

The actions shown so far have explained how the alternative constructor is implemented by a call of *makeJulianDate()* which relies upon *isValidDate()*, which itself is dependent upon *daysThisMonth()* and through it *isLeapYear()*. The implementation of *today()*, as follows, also relies upon the default constructor:

```
0092    public void today(){
0093
0094    Date theSystemDate = new java.util.Date();
0095    int theYear  = theSystemDate.getYear()  + MINIMUM_YEAR;
0096    int theMonth = theSystemDate.getMonth() +1;
0097    int theDay   = theSystemDate.getDate();
0098
0099      dayNumber = makeJulianDate( theYear, theMonth, theDay);
0100    } // End today.
```

The standard class *java.util.Date* supplies facilities to obtain the date from the system clock. An instance of this class is declared and automatically initialized upon construction to the current date and time. Three enquiry actions are then used to obtain the year, month and day components. The year value returned by **getYear()** starts with a value of 0 indicating the year 1900 and has the value of *MINIMUM_YEAR* (1900) added to it to make it compatible with the *makeJulianDate* requirements. Likewise the **getMonth()** action will return 0 to represent January and 11 to represent December and has to have 1 added to it to make it compliant. Having obtained the year, month and day in formats which are compatible with *JulianDates* conventions the *makeJulianDate()* action can be called.

The *BasicJulianDate* class supplies a *toString()* action which provides a basic output facility which can be used until the *JulianDate* class is completed. It will output the date in the format "ddd nn mmm yyyy", e.g. "Sun 1 Jan 1900". The implementation of the *toString()* action will require access to a number of other actions which are shown on the completion of the class diagram in Figure 10.3.

The implementation of the *toString()* action is as follows:

```
0277 public String toString(){
0278   if ( this.dayNumber == NULL_JULIAN_DATE ) {
0279     return "Date not yet set.";
0280   } else {
0281       return   this.dayNameIs() + " " + this.dayIs() + " " +
0282                this.MONTH_NAMES[ monthIs()] + " " + this.yearIs();
```

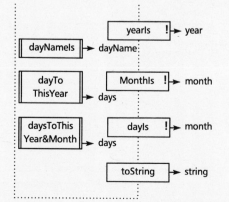

Figure 10.3 Completion of the *BasicJulianDate* class diagram.

```
0283    } // End if.
0284 } // End toString.
```

This implementation makes use of the three enquiry actions which precede it on the class diagram. The first of these, *yearIs()*, is implemented by iteratively subtracting the number of days in each year from a copy of the instance attribute *dayNumber*, called *daysRemaining*, whilst incrementing the number of years elapsed, until the number of days remaining is less than the number of days in the next year. The design and implementation of this action are as follows:

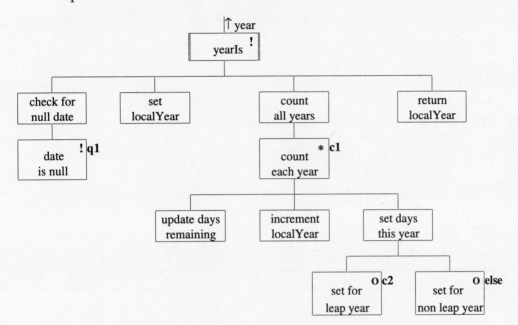

c1: While the days remaining are greater   **c2:** If this year is a leap year.
than the number of days in this year.   **q1:** Explicit JulianDateException.

```
0107    public int yearIs() throws JulianDateException {
0108
0109    int daysThisYear  = DAYS_PER_YEAR; // 1900 is not a leap year!
0110    int daysRemaining = dayNumber;
0111    int localYear     = MINIMUM_YEAR;
0112
0113       if ( this.dayNumber == NULL_JULIAN_DATE) {
0114          throw new JulianDateException( JulianDateException.NULL_DATE);
0115       } // End if.
0116
0117       while ( daysRemaining > daysThisYear) {
0118          daysRemaining -= daysThisYear;
0119          localYear++;
0120          if ( isLeapYear( localYear)){
0121             daysThisYear = DAYS_PER_LEAP_YEAR;
0122          } else {
0123             daysThisYear = DAYS_PER_YEAR;
0124          } // End if.
0125       } // End while.
```

```
0126        return localYear;
0127     } // End yearIs.
```

The *monthIs()* action is somewhat similar, starting by initializing a local variable, called *daysRemaining*, to the value of the instance attribute *dayNumber* minus the number of days up to this year, obtained by calling the private action *daysToThisYear()*. The design and implementation of *monthIs()* are as follows:

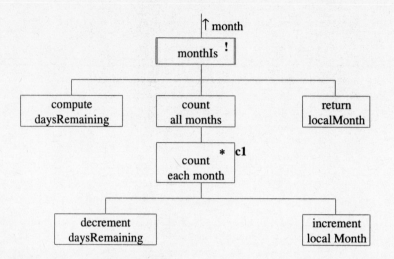

c1: While the days remaining are greater
than the number of days in this month.

```
0129     public int monthIs() throws JulianDateException {
0130
0131     int daysRemaining = dayNumber - daysToThisYear();
0132     int localYear     = yearIs();
0133     int localMonth    = 1;
0134
0135        if ( this.dayNumber == NULL_JULIAN_DATE) {
0136           throw new JulianDateException( JulianDateException.NULL_DATE);
0137        } // End if.
0138        while ( daysRemaining > daysThisMonth( localYear, localMonth)) {
0139           daysRemaining -= daysThisMonth( localYear, localMonth);
0140           localMonth++;
0141        } // End while.
0142        return localMonth;
0143     } // End monthIs.
```

This implementation depends upon the implementation of the private action *daysToThisYear()* whose design considerations are similar to those required for the *makeJulianDate()* action described above. The implementation of this action is as follows:

```
0160     private int daysToThisYear() {
0161
0162     int localYears   = yearIs() - MINIMUM_YEAR;
0163     int daysElapsed  = 0;
0164
```

```
0165        daysElapsed = ( (localYears * DAYS_PER_YEAR) +
0166                        (localYears /4)           -
0167                        (localYears /100)              );
0168        if ( localYears > 100) {
0169           daysElapsed++;
0170        } // End if.
0171        return daysElapsed;
0172     } // End daysToThisYear.
```

The value returned from the *monthIs()* action is an integer indicating the month number, with January having the value 1. Within the *toString()* action this value is used as an index into the *MONTH_NAMES* array to obtain the name of the month. As arrays in Java must start from index 0 the first (zeroth) element of this array is a null string, as shown on line 0032 of the declarations above.

The implementation of the *dayIs()* action subtracts from the instance attribute the number of days up to this year and month, obtained from the private *daysToThisYear-AndMonth()* action; the resulting value is the day number in the current month. The implementation of these two actions is as follows:

```
0145    public int dayIs() throws JulianDateException {
0146        if ( this.dayNumber == NULL_JULIAN_DATE) {
0147           throw new JulianDateException( JulianDateException.NULL_DATE);
0148        } // End if.
0149        return dayNumber - daysToThisYearAndMonth();
0150    } // End dayIs.
```

```
0173    private int daysToThisYearAndMonth() {
0174
0175    int daysElapsed   = daysToThisYear();
0176    int daysRemaining = dayNumber - daysElapsed;
0177    int localYear     = yearIs();
0178    int localMonth    = 1;
0179
0180        while ( daysRemaining > daysThisMonth( localYear, localMonth)) {
0181           daysRemaining -= daysThisMonth( localYear, localMonth);
0182           daysElapsed   += daysThisMonth( localYear, localMonth);
0183           localMonth++;
0184        } // End while.
0185        return daysElapsed;
0186    } // End daysToThisYearAndMonth.
```

The construction of the *daysToThisYearAndMonth()* action is similar to the *monthIs()* action described above. The final action used by the *toString()* action is *dayNameIs()* whose implementation is as follows:

```
0144    public String dayNameIs(){
0145        return DAY_NAMES[ dayNumber % 7];
0146    } // End dayNameIs.
```

The modular division results in a value between 0 and 6 and as 1 January 1900 happened to be a Sunday and has the *JulianDay* number 1, "Sun" has to be in the second (index value 1) location of the *DAY_NAMES* array. This determines the location of the other day names as shown on lines 0028 to 0030 of the listing above.

The only remaining action of the *BasicJulianDate* class is the protected *dayNumberIs()* enquiry action whose implementation is as follows:

```
0152    protected int dayNumberIs() {
0153      return this.dayNumber;
0154    } // End dayNumberIs.
```

The demonstration of this class will be considered in the next chapter.

10.3 ▩ The *ArithmeticJulianDate* class

The *ArithmeticJulianDate* class introduces actions which allow dates to be calculated, and actions which allow two dates to be compared, returning a **boolean** value. The object diagram for this class is given in Figure 10.4.

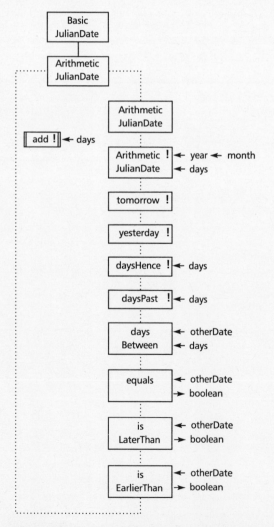

Figure 10.4 The *ArithmeticJulianDate* class diagram.

The diagram indicates that two constructors, comparable with the *BasicJulianDate* constructors, will be supplied. The *tomorrow()* and *yesterday()* actions will increment or decrement the date by 1 day. This may cause the date to attempt to go beyond the maximum date or below the minimum date and so each might throw an exception. Likewise the *daysHence()* and *daysPast()* actions will increment or decrement the date by the number of *days* specified in the argument. The implementation of this design as far as the end of the *daysPast()* action is as follows:

```
0001 // Filename ArithmeticJulianDate.java.
0002 // First extension of the JulianDate hierarchy
0003 // to provide (pseudo)-arithmetic operations.
0004 //
0005 // Written for JOF Book Chapter 10.
0006 // Fintan Culwin, v0.1, August 1997.
0007
0008 package JulianDates;
0009
0010 import JulianDates.JulianDateException;
0011
0012 public abstract class ArithmeticJulianDate extends BasicJulianDate {
0013
0014     public ArithmeticJulianDate() {
0015        super();
0016     } // End ArithmeticJulianDate default constructor.
0017
0018     public ArithmeticJulianDate( int year, int month, int day) {
0019                                       throws JulianDateException;
0020        super( year, month, day);
0021     } // End ArithmeticJulianDate alternative constructor.
0022
0023
0024     public final void tomorrow() throws JulianDateException {
0025        this.add( 1);
0026     } // End tomorrow.
0027
0028     public final void yesterday() throws JulianDateException {
0029        this.add( -1);
0030     } // End yesterday.
0031
0032     public final void daysHence( int toElapse) throws JulianDateException {
0033        this.add( toElapse);
0034     } // End daysHence.
0035
0036     public final void daysPast( int hasPassed) throws JulianDateException {
0037        this.add( -hasPassed);
0038     } // End daysPast.
```

The two constructors are implemented by calling the appropriate super, *BasicJulianDate* constructor, passing on the arguments, if any. The four actions are all implemented as a call to the **private** *add()* action whose implementation follows.

The signatures of these actions also include the modifier **final** the effect of which is to prevent the action from being overridden when the class is extended. This modifier should be used when the implementation of the action is so fundamental to the correct operation of the class that any change to it may invalidate the class. It also has the effect of making the calls of this action more efficient. This modifier should only be used very sparingly and if there is any doubt regarding its appropriateness it should not be used.

```
0041    private final void add( int toAdd) throws JulianDateException {
0042       if ( (this.dayNumberIs() + toAdd >  MAXIMUM_JULIAN_DATE)  ||
0043          (this.dayNumberIs() + toAdd <  MINIMUM_JULIAN_DATE)    ) {
0044       throw new JulianDateException(
0045                       JulianDateException.ARITHMETIC_ERROR);
0046       } // End if.
0047       this.dayNumber += toAdd;
0048    } // End add.
```

The action is guarded by a test which attempts to make sure that the result of the addition would not result in a value which was too large or too small and if so throws a suitable *JulianDateException*, otherwise the addition is performed. So, for example, the calculation of yesterday is implemented by adding -1 to the current *dayNumber*, which will throw an exception if the current date is the minimum date. The *daysBetween()* action will return the number of dates between this date and the *otherDate* passed to it; its implementation is as follows:

```
0051    public final long daysBetween( ArithmeticJulianDate since) {
0052       return this.dayNumberIs() - since.dayNumberIs();
0053    } // End daysBetween.
```

It returns the result of subtracting the *dayNumber* of the argument *since* from the current *dayNumber*. This will result in a negative number of days if *since* is in the future compared with the instance date. The implementations of the remaining actions are somewhat similar:

```
0056    public final boolean equals( ArithmeticJulianDate toCompare) {
0057       return this.dayNumberIs() == toCompare.dayNumberIs();
0058    } // End equals.
0059
0060
0061    public final boolean isLaterThan( ArithmeticJulianDate toCompare) {
0062       return this.dayNumberIs() > toCompare.dayNumberIs();
0063    } // End isLaterThan.
0064
0065
0066    public final boolean isEarlierThan( ArithmeticJulianDate toCompare) {
0067       return this.dayNumberIs() < toCompare.dayNumberIs();
0068    } // End isEarlierThan.
```

The first of these actions, *equals()*, overloads the default *equals()* action supplied by the Object class. This action is used by a number of the pre-supplied utility classes and should always be implemented in a developer supplied class. All three actions are implemented as relational comparisons of the *dayNumber* values contained in the two instances being compared. There is no need to supply actions equivalent to *notEquals()*, *isEarlierThanOrEqualTo()* or *isLaterThanOrEqualTo()* as these actions can be obtained by a negation of the supplied actions if required. That is, *notEquals()* is the same as not *equals()*, *isEarlierThanOrEqualTo()* is equivalent to not *isLaterThan()* and *isLaterThanOrEqualTo()* is equivalent to not *isEarlierThan()*. The demonstration of these actions will be considered in the next chapter.

10.4 ▨ The *JulianDate* class

The non-abstract *JulianDate* class adds input and output actions to the *ArithmeticJulianDate* class making the type suitable for general purpose interactive use. The *BasicJulianDate toString()* action provided a fundamental output operation which would output dates in the format "ddd nn mmm yyyy", e.g. "Sun 1 Jan 1900". That is, an abbreviated day name, the month day number as either one or two digits, an abbreviated name of the month and a four digit year number. Assuming that the user can read English this output format is always unambiguous.

This format can be a little verbose and there are two conventions for a more compact and fixed size representation. In most of Europe a date is conventionally expressed as dd/mm/yyyy, e.g. 01/01/1900 or 31/12/2199; however, the American convention is mm/dd/yyyy, e.g. 01/01/1900 or 12/31/2199. This class will provide additional output operations allowing this more sparse format to be used and will provide a simple input routine which allows for the input of dates in the appropriate national format. The class diagram for the *JulianDate* class is given in Figure 10.5.

This implementation provides two manifest *LOCALE*s: the default locale specifies a European convention with an alternative for the American one. The second constructor allows the locale to be set explicitly without specifying particular date and the third allows a particular date to be constructed with the specified locale. The implementation of this design, as far as the end of the constructors, is as follows:

```
0001 // Filename JulianDate.java.
0002 // Second extension of the JulianDate hierarchy
0003 // to provide internationalized i/o operations.
0004 //
```

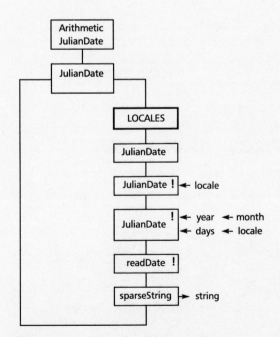

Figure 10.5 The *JulianDate* class diagram.

```
0005 // Written for JOF Book Chapter 10.
0006 // Fintan Culwin, v0.1, August 1997.
0007
0008 package JulianDates;
0009
0010 import java.io.DataInputStream;
0011 import java.io.IOException;
0012 import JulianDates.JulianDateException;
0013 import OutputFormatter;
0014 import OutputFormatException;
0015
0016
0017 public class JulianDate extends ArithmeticJulianDate {
0018
0019 public static final int EUROPEAN = 0;
0020 public static final int AMERICAN = 1;
0021
0022 private int theLocale = EUROPEAN;
0023
0024 private static java.io.DataInputStream keyboard =
0025                     new java.io.DataInputStream( System.in);
0026
0027     public JulianDate(){
0028        super();
0029     } // End JulianDate default constructor.
0030
0031     public JulianDate( int locale){
0032        super();
0033        theLocale = locale;
0034     } // End JulianDate alternative default constructor.
0035
0036     public JulianDate( int year, int month, int day,
0037                        int locale) throws JulianDateException {
0038        super( year, month, day);
0039        theLocale = locale;
0040     } // End JulianDate alternative constructor.
```

The context clause imports a number of other classes whose use will be explained as they are used. The design and implementation of the *sparseString()* action are as follows:

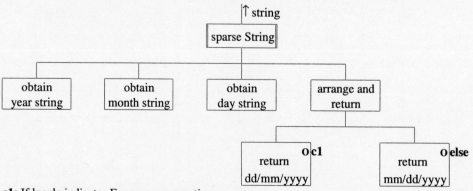

c1: If locale indicates European conventions.

```
0095    public String sparseString() {
0096
0097    String theYear  = OutputFormatter.formatLong(
0098                                 this.yearIs(), 4, true,
0099                                 OutputFormatter.DECIMAL );
0100    String theMonth = OutputFormatter.formatLong(
0101                                 this.monthIs(), 2, true,
0102                                 OutputFormatter.DECIMAL );
0103    String theDay   = OutputFormatter.formatLong(
0104                                 this.dayIs(), 2, true,
0105                                 OutputFormatter.DECIMAL );
0106
0107      if ( theLocale == EUROPEAN){
0108        return theDay + "/" + theMonth + "/" + theYear;
0109      } else {
0110        return theMonth + "/" + theDay + "/" + theYear;
0111      } // End if.
0112    } // End sparseString.
```

Each component of the **String**, the year, the month and the day, is obtained using the appropriate *BasicJulianDate* enquiry action and formatted with leading zeros using the *OutputFormatter formatLong* action. These strings are then catenated together in the sequence appropriate to the locale and the resulting string returned from the action.

The input action, *readDate()*, is much more complicated; its design and implementation are as follows:

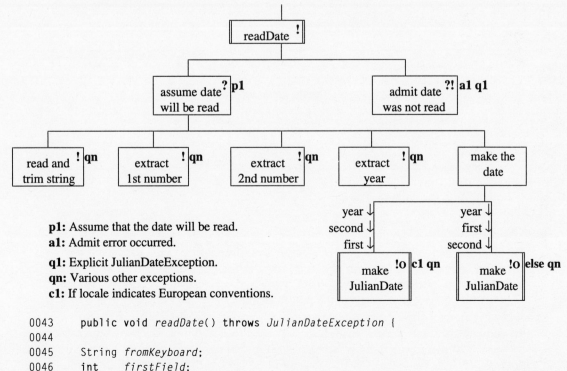

p1: Assume that the date will be read.
a1: Admit error occurred.

q1: Explicit JulianDateException.
qn: Various other exceptions.
c1: If locale indicates European conventions.

```
0043    public void readDate() throws JulianDateException {
0044
0045    String fromKeyboard;
0046    int    firstField;
0047    int    secondField;
```

```
0048    int    yearField;
0049    int    startOfField;
0050    int    endOfField;
0051    char   separator = '/';
0052
0053
0054       System.out.flush();
0055       try {
0056          fromKeyboard = keyboard.readLine().trim();
0057          endOfField = fromKeyboard.indexOf( separator);
0058          if ( endOfField != -1) {
0059             firstField = Integer.valueOf( fromKeyboard.
0060                                 substring( 0, endOfField)).intValue();
0061          } else {
0062             throw new java.lang.Exception();
0063          } // End if.
0064
0065          startOfField = endOfField + 1;
0066          endOfField   = fromKeyboard.lastIndexOf( separator);
0067          if ( endOfField != -1) {
0068             secondField = Integer.valueOf( fromKeyboard.
0069                                 substring( startOfField,
0070                                          endOfField)).intValue();
0071          } else {
0072             throw new java.lang.Exception();
0073          } // End if.
0074
0075          startOfField = endOfField + 1;
0076          yearField    = Integer.valueOf( fromKeyboard.
0077                                 substring( startOfField,
0078                                          fromKeyboard.length())).intValue();
0079
0080          if ( theLocale == EUROPEAN) {
0081             makeJulianDate( yearField, secondField, firstField);
0082          } else {
0083             makeJulianDate( yearField, firstField, secondField);
0084          } // End if.
0085       } catch ( java.lang.Exception exception ) {
0086          throw new  JulianDateException(
0087                      JulianDateException.DATE_INPUT_ERROR);
0088       } // End try/ catch.
0089
0090    } // End readDate.
```

The implementation commences by flushing any waiting output to the screen and then obtaining a line of input from the user in a String via an instantiation of the java.io.DataInputStream called *keyboard*, in a manner essentially identical to the *SimpleInput getLong()* action from the previous chapter.

Having obtained the user's input in a String, called *fromKeyboard*, it has to be divided into the three numeric fields hopefully contained within it which are separated by slash (/) characters. This is accomplished by using the String *indexOf()*, or *lastIndexOf()*, action to locate the position of the slashes, if they can be found. Having located the slashes the String *substring()* action can be used to isolate the characters between the slashes and these are converted to integer values using the same technique as was used in the ValidatedInput *getLong()* action in the previous chapter.

Having obtained the three integers supplied by the user they are passed to the protected *BasicJulianDate makeJulianDate()* action in a pattern appropriate to the locale. Practically all of these actions may cause a variety of different exceptions to be thrown and these are all caught and processed in the same way, throwing a new instance of the *JulianDateException* with the reason set to *DATE_INPUT_ERROR*. The design has avoided becoming too complex by indicating with a single quit key the locations where exceptions might be thrown as the String is parsed. The demonstration of this class will be considered in the next chapter.

Summary

▨ Julian dates represent calendar dates as sequential integer values, allowing arithmetical calculations to be easily made.

▨ The starting point for the design of any class hierarchy can be the consideration of a standard list of action categories.

▨ The six possible relational operations (=, ! =, >, <, > =, < =) can be supplied as three actions (=, >, <) and their corresponding negations (! =, < =, > =).

▨ Software should be designed from the outset for international use.

Exercises

10.1   Despite the promise to consider the demonstration of this hierarchy in the next chapter, prepare for this by constructing and executing a demonstration client.

10.2   Produce an application which asks for your date of birth and informs you of how many days you have lived.

10.3   Produce an application which automatically tells you the number of days to the millennium (1 Jan 2000). Or, if you are reading this after the millennium, how many days since the millennium.

10.4   Extend the *JulianDate* class to supply a *readValidDate()* action which will conduct a dialog, with suitable internationalized advice, and not return until a valid date has been entered.

10.5   Extend the *JulianDate* class to support a third locale, called *ORDERED*, which outputs the date in the format yyyy/mm/dd. This format is useful as a sort of the dates will place them into ascending date order.

10.6   Design, implement and demonstrate a *TwentyFourHourClock* hierarchy which supports the representation of a time in the hh:mm:ss (hours, minutes and seconds) format.

10.7   Combine the *JulianDates* hierarchy with the *TwentyFourHourClock* hierarchy to produce a combined *DateAndTime* hierarchy.

10.8   Extend the *JulianDates* hierarchy to provide an international date class whose *toString()* action will output the month names and day names in a language other than English.

Chapter eleven

Testing software

In previous chapters client programs have been provided to *demonstrate* that the artefacts produced appear to be working correctly. This is not altogether satisfactory and this chapter will introduce techniques by which artefacts can be *tested* to improve the confidence that they are implemented correctly. However, techniques to provide an absolute *proof* that an artefact has been implemented correctly are beyond the scope of this book, and are very difficult and expensive to apply in practice.

One way of obtaining such a proof is to use exhaustive testing; however, this approach is impossible in all but the simplest situations. Taking the *tomorrow()* action from the *JulianDate()* package as an example, in order to test this exhaustively all possible dates between 1 January 1900 and the 31 December 1999 would have to be demonstrated to be working correctly. This would involve applying a total of 109573 trials, all of which would have to be checked to make sure that they were not faulty. Even though this might just be possible, this is only one of 25 actions in the *JulianDates* hierarchy, all of which would require a similar approach.

As exhaustive testing is clearly impractical all that can be done is to demonstrate that the artefact appears to be correct on a set of trials and supply an argument that the set chosen is sufficiently representative of all possibilities for the confidence in the correct operation of the artefact to be acceptable. The argument to support the contention that the set is representative is known as a *test rationale*.

There are two fundamental approaches to producing a test rational. One relies only upon the specification of the artefact and is known as *black box* testing. The second approach relies upon an understanding of the implementation and is known as *glass box* testing. This chapter will introduce the techniques of black box testing in detail and conclude with a brief consideration of glass box testing.

11.1 ▓ Testing the *BasicJulianDate* default constructor

The most fundamental test to perform is of the *JulianDate* default constructor. However, there has to be some way by which the correct operation of the constructor can be shown to be correct, and the most obvious way to do this is to test the fundamental output routine *toString()* at the same time. There is an obvious problem here: a fault in the output may be caused by a fault in the constructor or a fault in the output action and there would be no simple method to determine which one is faulty. However, testing has to start somewhere and there is no way of avoiding this dilemma.

The specification of the default constructor indicates that its correct operation is to set the date to a null value and the output action is to report that the date has not yet been set. A black box diagram of a combined test of the default constructor and the *toString()* action is given in Figure 11.1.

The diagram indicates that this routine has no inputs and has two possible outputs. The exception output can be refined into a ***range diagram*** showing that the exception might or might not be thrown. The range diagram for the message output can be refined into three conditions showing that a suitable message will be produced, that anything else will be shown on the terminal or that nothing will be shown on the terminal. The range diagrams are shown in Figure 11.2.

The range diagrams contain a key which shows the significant points on the ranges. These points are collected together to produce a list of ***test cases***, as shown in Table 11.1.

The final stage in the planning of the trials for this test is to plan a number of ***test runs*** which will, as a minimum, ensure that all possible cases from the list of test cases have been considered. In this test there is a single trial shown in Table 11.2.

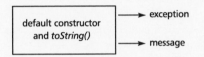

Figure 11.1   *JulianDate* default constructor and *toString()* black box diagram.

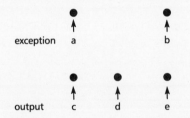

Figure 11.2   *JulianDate* default constructor and *toString()* range diagrams.

Table 11.1 *JulianDate* default constructor and *toString()* test cases.

Case	Value
a	exception raised
b	exception not raised
c	suitable message output
d	other message output
e	no output produced

Table 11.2 *JulianDate* default constructor and *toString()* test run.

Trial	Input	Cases
1	none	b c

This shows that a single trial will require no inputs and should result in no exception being thrown and a suitable message being output on the terminal. A test harness client program can be constructed to apply this test, as follows:

```
0001  // Filename JulianDateTestHarness.java.
0002  // Client test harness for the JulianDate hierarchy.
0003  //
0004  // Written for JOF Book Chapter 11.
0005  // Fintan Culwin, v0.1, August 1997.
0006
0007
0008  import JulianDates.JulianDate;
0009  import JulianDates.JulianDateException;
0010
0011  class JulianDateTestHarness {
0012
0013     public static void main(String args[]) {
0014
0015     JulianDate testDate;
0016
0017        System.out.println( "\t Julian Date Test Harness \n");
0018
0019        System.out.println( "Test run 1 - default constructor");
0020        try {
0021           testDate = new JulianDate();
0022           System.out.println( "Date constructed without throwing exception.");
0023           System.out.println( testDate);
0024        } catch ( JulianDateException exception) {
0025           System.out.println( "Exception thrown ... test failed");
0026        } // End try/ catch.
```

If the software is working correctly the output should be as follows:

```
Date constructed without throwing exception.
Date not yet set.
```

11.2 ■ Testing the *BasicJulianDate* alternative constructor

The testing of the default constructor above followed a complete black box process which seemed far too complex for the facility being tested. However, the value of the process will become apparent in this example which is significantly more complex. The black box diagram for this test is shown in Figure 11.3.

The three arguments to the alternative constructor are now shown as inputs to the black box and will have to appear on the range diagram, which is shown in Figure 11.4.

The year, month and day inputs are shown on this diagram as continuous ranges with the limits indicating the minimum and maximum valid values for the argument and with other significant points marked. The terminal output and exception outputs are shown as discrete ranges with the significant points marked.

Taking the year input as an example, point *a* is the value 1899 which was chosen as the largest invalid value below the acceptable range and is taken as indicative of all

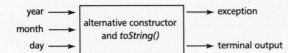

Figure 11.3 *JulianDate* alternative constructor and *toString()* black box diagram.

values between the minimum integer value and 1899. A prediction will be made that this value will cause an exception to be thrown whenever it is used and, by extension, all other values below it will also cause an exception. Point *b* is the value 1900 and is the minimum valid year which should not cause the exception to be thrown, nor should any value as far as point *f* which is 2199. Point *g* is the value 2200 and is the smallest invalid value above the acceptable range and is taken as representative of all values between it and the largest integer value. This value should cause an exception to be thrown and, by extension, so should all others above it.

Taking these four predictions together, it is assumed that any year value between 1900 and 2199 should not cause an exception to be thrown, given that their year and month components are acceptable, and any value outside this range will cause the exception to be thrown. Thus exhaustive testing which would have required 2^{32} (the full integer range) separate trials has reduced this figure to 4.

Point *c* is the value 1904 and has been arbitrarily chosen as representative of all common leap years. Point *d* is 1905 and is arbitrarily representative of all non-leap years. Finally point *e* is 2000 and is the special case of a year which is divisible by 4 but is not a leap year. These reasons, and the reasons for selecting all the other points, are summarized in Table 11.3. The possibility of the *toString()* action not producing any output has been discounted following the previous test and the two possibilities are now to produce the correct output or the wrong output.

These cases are then combined to produce the minimum number of trials which can be used to ensure that every case, and significant combinations of cases, is demonstrated at least once. The list of trials for this requirement is given in Table 11.4.

The trials cover all cases with the exception of case *w* whose omission is an implicit predication that it should never happen. The test harness program can be extended to allow these trials to be applied. Only trials 1 and 2 are shown; the rest can be

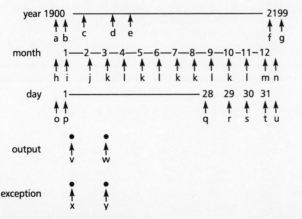

Figure 11.4 *JulianDate* alternative constructor and *toString()* range diagrams.

Table 11.3 *JulianDate* alternative constructor and *toString()* test cases.

Case	Value	Notes
a	year 1899	largest invalid value below 1900
b	year 1900	smallest valid value
c	year 1904	common leap years
d	year 1905	non-leap years
e	year 2000	special case – not a leap year
f	year 2199	largest valid value
g	year 2200	smallest invalid value above 2199
h	month 0	largest invalid value below 1
i	month 1	smallest valid value
j	months 1, 3, 5, 7, 8, 10, 11, 12	months with 31 days
k	months 4, 6, 9, 11	30 days hath September ...
l	month 2	February
m	month 12	largest valid value
n	month 13	smallest invalid value above 12
o	day 0	largest invalid value below 1
p	day 1	smallest valid value
q	day 28	largest always valid day
r	day 29	invalid for month 2 apart from leap years
s	day 30	invalid for month 2
t	day 31	invalid for months 2, 4, 6, 9, 11
u	day 32	smallest invalid value above 31
v	output correct	
w	output not correct	
x	exception thrown	
y	exception not thrown	

Table 11.4 *JulianDate* default constructor and *toString()* test run.

Trail	Day	Month	Year	Outcome	Cases
1	31	12	1899	exception	a, x
2	1	1	1900	1 Jan 1900	b, p, v, y
3	31	12	2199	31 Dec 1900	f, m, t, v, y
4	1	1	2200	exception	g, x
5	1	0	1900	exception	h, x
6	1	13	1900	exception	n, x
7	0	1	1900	exception	o, x
8	32	1	1900	exception	u, x
9	31	1	1900	31 Jan 1900	j, i, v, y
10	31	4	1900	exception	t, x
11	30	4	1900	30 Apr 1900	k, v, y
12	30	2	1904	exception	s, l, x
13	29	2	1904	29 Feb 1904	r, c, v, y
14	29	2	1905	exception	r, d, x
15	28	2	1905	28 Feb 1905	q, l, d, v, y
16	29	2	2000	29 Feb 2000	r, c, e, v, y

implemented in a similar manner:

```
0028      System.out.println( "\t Test run 2 - alternative constructor \n");
0029
0030      System.out.println( "\n Trial 1 - attempt to construct 31/12/1899 \n");
0031      try {
0032         testDate = new JulianDate( 1899, 12, 31, JulianDate.EUROPEAN);
0033         System.out.println( "No exception thrown,  ... trial failed.");
0034      } catch ( ) {
0035         System.out.println( "Exception thrown ... trial passed.");
0036      } // End try/ catch.
0037
0038      System.out.println( "\n Trial 2 - attempt to construct 1/1/1900 \n");
0039      try {
0040         testDate = new JulianDate( 1900, 1, 1, JulianDate.EUROPEAN );
0041         System.out.println( "No exception thrown,  ... trial passed.");
0042         System.out.println( "Date is " + testDate + ".");
0043      } catch ( ) {
0044         System.out.println( "Exception thrown ... trial failed.");
0045      } // End try/ catch.
```

The *JulianDate.EUROPEAN* argument has to be included to satisfy the calling requirements of the constructor and is not part of the test. The output from this fragment is as follows:

```
     Test run 2 - alternative constructor

Trial 1 - attempt to construct 31/12/1899.
Exception thrown ... trial passed.

Trial 2 - attempt to construct 1/1/1900.
No exception thrown, ... trial passed.
Date is Sun Jan 1 1900.
```

The 109573 valid days which this implementation of the Julian date concept is able to represent have been adequately tested with only 16 trials. This output does not prove, for example, that 12 March 1986 will not throw an exception nor that the 43rd day of the 19th month in 2699 will not. However, it is more convincing than a mere demonstration that some randomly selected possible dates do, or do not, throw exceptions or produce the anticipated output. It has increased the confidence that the constructor is operating correctly and the quality of the rationale expresses the degree of confidence obtained.

Should the output indicate that any of the trials had failed the first step is to double-check the test harness to make sure that it is not faulty. For example, an argument of the constructor might have been typed incorrectly causing an exception to be thrown in a trial which should not throw one. Otherwise the cause of the fault will have to be determined and corrected, a process known as *debugging*. Having located and corrected the fault, testing should recommence from the first test run, as the correction of the fault may cause the artefact now to fail a trial which it had previously passed. This process can be facilitated by the use of automated test harnesses, as are being constructed here.

11.3 ■ Relational and inverse testing of the *ArithmeticJulianDate* actions

The testing method in the examples above relied upon a *parallel* predictive method. This method relies upon the tester being able to predict the actual output of the program and this is indicated in the predicted output column in the test plan. There are two possible problems with parallel methods, the first being that for a complex specification predicting the actual output may rely upon a long and complicated computation, which may itself only be feasible by the use of a computer program. The second possible problem is that the software developer and the test designer, who may be the same person, may share the same misconception regarding how the specification is to be interpreted and thus how the result is to be computed. In this case both the results produced by the program and the results predicted by the test designer will be identical, but incorrect. Consequently the program will appear to pass a test which it should have failed.

As it is not always advisable, easy or convenient to predict the actual output there are other possible methods which can be used in the design of a black box test plan. The first of these is *inverse* testing, which is suitable when a software component can be 'driven in reverse' causing it to negate the effects of 'driving it forwards'. For example, using the *today()* action today's date can be obtained; the *tomorrow()* action can then be used to obtain tomorrow's date and the *yesterday()* action to obtain tomorrow's yesterday. If all this has operated correctly then the date which has been amended should be equal to today's date.

The second possibility is *relational* testing, where the effects of using a software artefact are constant over a range of inputs. Thus if the effect can be measured, it should be equal whatever value is used. Thus whatever date is used, the *tomorrow()* action should result in a date which is one day in the future, which can be proved by use of the *daysBetween()* action.

In order for these actions to be tested using relational and inverse testing the confidence of the *today()* action must be increased. The only way to do this is to use a parallel method. A suitable test run is presented in Table 11.5.

These series of tests are contained, for convenience, in a second test harness file called *ArithmeticJulianDateTestHarness*, whose implementation as far as the end of trial 2 is as follows:

```
0012 public static void main(String args[]) {
0013
0014 JulianDate aDate       = new JulianDate();
0015 JulianDate anotherDate = new JulianDate();
0016
0017    System.out.println( "\t Arithmentic Julian Date Test Harness \n");
0018
0019    System.out.println( "\t Test run 3 - today and equals");
0020
```

Table 11.5 *JulianDate today()* and *equals()* test run.

Trial	Input	Cases	Notes
1	none	a	today's date obtained and output
2	today() and today()	b	today's date compared with today's date

```
0021    System.out.println( "\nTrial 1 - today ");
0022    try {
0023       aDate.today();
0024       System.out.println( "Todays date obtained without exception.");
0025       System.out.println( "Todays date is " + aDate);
0026    } catch ( JulianDateException exception) {
0027       System.out.println( "Exception thrown ... test failed");
0028    } // End try/ catch.
0029
0030    System.out.println( "\nTrial 2 - equals ");
0031    try {
0032       anotherDate.today();
0033       System.out.println( "Today's date obtained again without exception.");
0034    } catch ( JulianDateException exception) {
0035       // Do nothing!
0036    } // End try/ catch.
0037    System.out.print( aDate);
0038    if ( aDate.equals( anotherDate)) {
0039       System.out.println( " is equal to " + anotherDate);
0040       System.out.println( "which is correct ... trial passed.");
0041    } else {
0042       System.out.println( "is not equal to " + anotherDate);
0043       System.out.println( "which is not correct ... trial failed.");
0044    } // end if.
```

The output produced by this part of the program when it was executed was as follows:

```
        Arithmentic Julian Date Test Harness

        Test run 3 - today and equals

  Trial 1 - today
  Today's date obtained without throwing exception.
  Todays date is Sat 1 Jan 2000

  Trial 2 - equals
  Today's date obtained again without throwing exception.
  Sat 1 Jan 2000 is equal to Sat 1 Jan 2000
  which is correct ... trial passed.
```

which seems to indicates that *today()* and *equals()* are correct. An inverse test plan for the *today()*, *yesterday()*, *daysHence()* and *daysPast()* actions is given in Table 11.6. Strictly speaking trials 7 and 8 are parallel, not inverse, tests but seem necessary to conclude with a high confidence that the artefact is correct.

The implementations of trials 1, 6 and 7 are as follows:

```
0048    System.out.println( "\n\t Test run 4 - inverse testing of " +
0049                        " ArithmeticJulianDate actions.\n");
0050
0051    System.out.println( "\nTrial 1 tomorrow's yesterday should be today ...");
0052    aDate.today();
0053    anotherDate.today();
0054    anotherDate.tomorrow();
```

Table 11.6 *ArithmeticJulianDate*, inverse test plan.

Trial	Note
1	today() tomorrow() yesterday() = today()
2	today() daysPast(1) daysHence(1) = today()
3	today() yesterday() tomorrow() = today()
4	today() daysHence(1) daysPast(1) = today()
5	01/01/1900 daysHence(109572) daysPast(109572) = 01/01/1900
6	31/12/2199 daysPast(109572) daysHence(109572) = 31/12/2199
7	01/01/1900 yesterday → JulianDateException
8	31/12/1900 tomorrow() → JulianDateException

```
0055     anotherDate.yesterday();
0056     if ( aDate.equals( anotherDate)) {
0057        System.out.println( "it is trial passed.");
0058     } else {
0059        System.out.println( "it isn't trial failed.");
0060     } // end if.


0107     System.out.println( "\nTrial 6 - 109572 days after 109572 before " +
0108                         " 31/12/2199 should be 31/12/2199 ...");
0109     aDate       = new JulianDate( 2199, 12, 31, JulianDate.EUROPEAN);
0110     anotherDate = new JulianDate( 2199, 12, 31, JulianDate.EUROPEAN);
0111     anotherDate.daysPast( 109572);
0112     anotherDate.daysHence( 109572);
0113     if ( aDate.equals( anotherDate)) {
0114        System.out.println( "it is trial passed.");
0115     } else {
0116        System.out.println( "it isn't trial failed.");
0117     } // end if.
0118
0119     System.out.println( "\nTrial 7 - yesterday of 01/01/1900 " +
0120                         " should throw an exception ...");
0121     aDate       = new JulianDate( 1900, 1, 1, JulianDate.EUROPEAN);
0122     try {
0123        aDate.yesterday();
0124        System.out.println( "it doesn't trial failed.");
0125     } catch ( JulianDateException exception) {
0126        System.out.println( "it does trial passed.");
0127     } // end if.
```

The output of the program for trials 1 to 8 was as follows:

```
      Test run 4 - inverse testing of ArithmeticJulianDate actions.


 Trial 1 - tomorrow's yesterday should be today ...
 it is trial passed.


 Trial 2 - 1 day before 1 day after today should be today ...
 it is trial passed.
```

```
Trial 3 - yesterday's tomorrow should be today ...
it is trial passed.

Trial 4 - 1 day after 1 day before today should be today ...
it is trial passed.

Trial 5 - 109572 days before 109572 days after
          01/01/1900 should be 01/01/1900 ...
it is trial passed.

Trial 6 - 109572 days after 109572 before
          31/12/2199 should be 31/12/2199 ...
it is trial passed.

Trial 7 - yesterday of 01/01/1900 should throw an exception ...
it does trial passed.

Trial 8 - tomorrow of 31/12/2199 should throw an exception ...
it does trial passed.
```

which seems to indicate that all is well despite not having made an actual prediction concerning the dates. The remaining actions can be tested using a relational test plan, as given in Table 11.7.

Strictly speaking this is in part relational and in part parallel as the prediction of a 1 day difference indicates. The implementation, and the output produced by the first trial confirming the correct operation of the actions, are as follows:

```
0140 System.out.println( "\n\t Test run 5 - relational testing of " +
0141                     " ArithmeticJulianDate actions.\n");
0142
0143 System.out.println( "\nTrial 1 - tomorrow should be later than today," +
0144                     " by 1 day ... ");
0145 aDate.today();
0146 anotherDate.today();
0147 aDate.tomorrow();
0148 if ( aDate.isLaterThan( anotherDate)) {
0149    System.out.print( "it is " );
0150    if ( aDate.daysBetween( anotherDate) == 1) {
0151      System.out.println( "by 1 day, trial passed.");
0152    } else {
0153      System.out.println( "by " + aDate.daysBetween( anotherDate) +
0154                          " days, trial failed.");
0155    } // End if.
0156 } else {
0157    System.out.println( "it isn't, trial failed.");
0158 } // End if.
```

Table 11.7 *ArithmeticJulianDate*, relational test plan.

Trial	Note
1	tomorrow() is greater than today() by 1 day
2	yesterday() is less than today() by 1 day

```
Trial 1 - tomorrow should be later than today, by 1 day ...
it is by 1 day, trial passed.
```

11.4 ▨ Composite and interactive testing of the remaining facilities

In addition to parallel, inverse and relational testing, black box test plans can be constructed using a *composite* technique. This technique is based upon breaking an instance down into its component parts and then reconstructing another instance from them. A test plan for the *BasicJulianDate yearIs()*, *monthIs()* and *dayIs()* actions using this technique is presented in Table 11.8.

This test run can be added to the *ArithmeticJulianDateTestHarness* as follows:

```
0162 System.out.println( "\n\t Test run 6 - composite testing of " +
0163                     " ArithmeticJulianDate actions.\n");
0164
0165 System.out.println( "\nTrial 1 - A date constructed from the component" +
0166                     " parts of another date );
0167 System.out.print(   "           should be equal to it ... ");
0168
0169 aDate.today();
0170 anotherDate = new JulianDate( aDate.yearIs(), aDate.monthIs(),
0171                               aDate.dayIs(),  JulianDate.EUROPEAN);
0172 if ( aDate.equals( anotherDate)) {
0173    System.out.println( "it is, trial passed.");
0174 } else {
0175    System.out.println( "it isn't, trial failed.");
0176 } // End if.
```

which, when executed, produced the expected output as follows:

```
Test run 6 - composite testing of BasicicJulianDate actions.

Trial 1 - A date constructed from the component parts of another date
          should be equal to it ... it is, trial passed.
```

The major remaining facilities to be tested are the input–output facilities contained within the *JulianDate* class. The testing of the output facilities can be accomplished with a non-interactive automated test harness and a test plan which uses a parallel technique. The plan would have to include outputs in *EUROPEAN* and *AMERICAN* formats and ensure that the correct fields widths were obtained with days and months whose representation contained a single digit.

Table 11.8 *ArithmeticJulianDate*, relational test plan.

Trial	Note
1	A *JulianDate* constructed from *getYear()*, *getMonth()* and *getDay()* should be equal to itself

The testing of the *JulianDate readDate()* action is a little more complex, requiring the tester to type in the test cases from the keyboard. A parallel test plan would have to duplicate all the trials from the alternative constructor test plan presented in section 11.2 above, using a selection of *EUROPEAN* and *AMERICAN* input formats. The start of a suitable test harness might be as follows:

```
0001 // Filename InteractiveJulianDateTestHarness.java.
0002 // Interactive client test harness for the JulianDate hierarchy.
0003 //
0004 // Written for JOF Book Chapter 11.
0005 // Fintan Culwin, v0.1, August 1997.
0006
0007
0008 import JulianDates.JulianDate;
0009 import JulianDates.JulianDateException;
0010
0011 class InteractiveJulianDateTestHarness {
0012
0013    public static void main(String args[]) {
0014
0015    JulianDate europeanDate = new JulianDate( JulianDate.EUROPEAN);
0016    JulianDate americanDate = new JulianDate( JulianDate.AMERICAN);
0017
0018       System.out.println( "\t Interactive Julian Date Test Harness \n");
0019
0020       System.out.println( "\n Trial 1 - attempt to construct 31st Dec 2199.");
0021       try {
0022          System.out.print( "\nPlease enter 31st Jan 2199 as 31/12/2199 ");
0023          europeanDate.readDate();
0024          System.out.println( "No exception thrown, ... test passed.");
0025          System.out.println( "The date is " + europeanDate + ".");
0026       } catch ( JulianDateException exception) {
0027          System.out.println( "Exception thrown ... test failed.");
0028       } // End try/ catch.
0029
0030       try {
0031          System.out.print( "\nPlease enter 31st Jan 2199 as 12/31/2199 ");
0032          americanDate.readDate();
0033          System.out.println( "No exception thrown, ... test passed.");
0034          System.out.println( "The date is' + americanDate + ".");
0035       } catch ( JulianDateException exception) {
0036          System.out.println( "Exception thrown ... test failed.");
0037       } // End try/ catch
```

whose interaction with the user might be as follows:

```
            Interactive Julian Date Test Harness

   Trial 1 - attempt to construct 31st Dec 2199.

   Please enter 31st Jan 2199 as 31/12/2199 31/12/2199
   No exception thrown, ... test passed.
   The date is Mon 31 Dec 2199.
```

```
Please enter 31st Jan 2199 as 12/31/2199 12/31/2199
No exception thrown, ... test passed.
The date is Mon 31 Dec 2199.
```

This adequately tests the input of a particular date in European and American formats and indicates that the input routine appears to be working correctly. The problem with this approach is that the typing in of the test date is laborious and error prone. All of the previous test harnesses have had the advantage of being non-interactive, which allowed them to be rapidly reapplied during development and debugging.

This problem can be solved by the operating system *redirection* facility. Redirection allows the output from a process to be sent to a disk file or for the input for a program to be taken from a disk file. To apply redirection to this program a file containing the expected input can be prepared. For example, the input required by this program would be:

```
12/31/2199↵
12/31/2199↵
```

The ↵ symbol indicates an end of line. If this file is stored on the disk in a file called "*InteractiveInput.data*" the test can be automatically applied (in MS-DOS and Unix) with the command line:

```
%java InteractiveJulianDateTestHarness < InteractiveInput.data
```

which would apply the tests using input from the file and produce the confirmation of the correct, or incorrect, actions on the screen.

11.5 ■ White box considerations

All of the testing presented so far in this chapter has employed *black box* techniques. The term black box indicates that the component under test has inputs and outputs and a specification which states the relationship between those inputs and outputs. The test rationale works on this knowledge only and does not take any account of the internal construction of the component. The alternative possibility should really be known as *glass box* testing as it is allowed to take account of the internal structure of the component, although it is conventionally known as *white box* testing.

One way in which this can be useful is to note that the black box testing implicitly tests some actions other than those which it is formally testing, and to take advantage of this in subsequent tests. For example, the implementation of the alternative *BasicJulianDate* constructor, as shown in section 10.2, is essentially a call of the **protected** *makeJulianDate()* action:

```
0047    // Alternative constructor from the BasicJulianDate class.
0048    public BasicJulianDate( int year, int month, int day)
0049                                           throws JulianDateException {
0050      dayNumber = makeJulianDate( year, month, day);
0051    } // End JulianDate alternative default constructor
```

The implementation of the *JulianDate getDate()* action also makes use of the *makeJulianDate()* action:

```
       // Extract from the JulianDate getDate() action.
0080   if ( theLocale == EUROPEAN) {
0081      makeJulianDate( yearField, secondField, firstField);
0082   } else {
0083      makeJulianDate( yearField, firstField, secondField);
0084   } // End if.
```

All of the other parts of the *getDate()* action are concerned with obtaining input from the user, extracting the various fields and preparing for this part of the action. Using this knowledge the testing of the *getDate()* action can be restricted to those tests designed to differentiate between the European and American formats and ensuring that incorrectly formatted inputs raise an exception. This will significantly reduce the number of trials required.

The second use of white box techniques is to make sure that all possible paths through and action have been exercised whilst the software is under test. To do this a *flowgraph* representing the actions structure has to be prepared and this can only be done once the source code for the action is available. A flowgraph is constructed from three basic constituent parts, representing sequence, selection and iteration. These components are shown in Figure 11.5.

The first of these flowgraphs shows a sequence of actions where flow of control will enter at point a and leave at point b. The second shows a selective structure where flow of control can move from point c to point d via the left or right hand path. This structure can be used to represent an **if** structure, a **case** structure and a **try/catch** structure; if required the number of paths can be increased beyond two. The final flowgraph shows an iterative structure where flow of control can enter at point d and leave immediately at point f without ever executing the body of the loop. Otherwise flow of control must enter at point d and follow the path to point f, representing the body of the loop, and then return to point d for the loop condition to be re-evaluated.

To illustrate how these components are used to construct a flowgraph for an action the *BasicDate makeJulianDate()* action will be considered: The implementation of this action is as follows:

```
0062 protected int makeJulianDate( int year, int month, int day)
0063                                        throws JulianDateException {
```

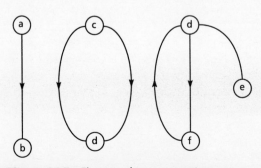

Figure 11.5 Flowgraph components.

```
0064
0065      int localDayNumber = 0;
0066      int thisMonth;
0067
0068        if ( ! isValidDate( year, month, day)) {
0069          throw new JulianDateException(
0070                      JulianDateException.DATE_CONSTRUCTION_ERROR);
0071        } // End if.
0072
0073        // Start with the day of the month
0074        localDayNumber = day;
0075
0076        // Add the number of days for the month.
0077        for ( thisMonth = 1; thisMonth < month; thisMonth ++) {
0078          localDate += daysThisMonth( year, thisMonth);
0079        }
0080
0081        // Add the number of days for the year (ignoring leap years).
0082        localDayNumber += (year - MINIMUM_YEAR) * DAYS_PER_YEAR;
0083
0084        // Correct for the number of leap years passed.
0085        localDayNumber = localDayNumber + ((year - MINIMUM_YEAR) /4)   -
0086                                          ((year - MINIMUM_YEAR) /100);
0087        if ( year > 2000) {
0088            localDayNumber++;
0089        } // End if.
0090
0091        return localDayNumber;
0092      } // End MakeJulianDate.
```

The flowgraph is derived in stages, starting with a simple flowgraph where a single path connects the two points where flow of control can enter the action and where it must eventually leave. This is shown as the left hand flowgraph in Figure 11.6. The first refinement of this is to divide it into the initialization part where the local variables are declared (lines 0063 to 0067), the main part of the action (lines 0068 to 0090) and the leaving of the action represented by lines 0091 to 0092. This is shown on the first refinement of the flowgraph.

The derivation continues by refining the actions in the main part of the action. The first of these is an **if** structure which might result in an exception being thrown. Should this happen then flow of control will pass immediately to the point where flow of control leaves the action. If the condition on the **if** structure is **false** flow of control will pass through the rest of the action. This is shown on the second refinement with the left hand path between *b* and *g* representing the throwing of the exception and the right hand path the rest of the steps in the action.

The next part of the actions is a single statement followed by a **for** structure. This can be accommodated into the flowgraph by replacing the right hand side of the path between *b* and *g* with an iterative flowgraph component, as shown on the third refinement. The path between *b* and *c* represents the action between the **if** and the **for** structure and the path between *e* and *g* the actions following the **for** structure.

The final refinement introduces the **if** structure on lines 0087 and 0089. With this in place the path between *c* and *e* represents the actions between the end of the **for**

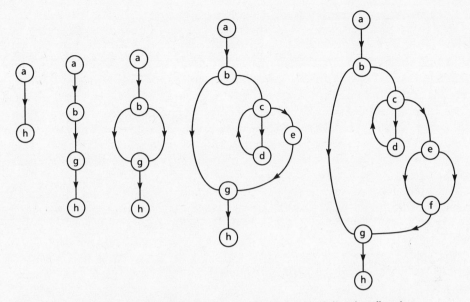

Figure 11.6 The derivation of the flowgraph for the *makeJuliandate()* action.

structure and the start of the **if** structure. The path between *f* and *g* represents the actions between the end of the **if** and the end of the action.

Having derived the flowgraph it can be used to calculate the number of possible paths which can be used to traverse it. This can be done by counting the number of regions on the graph, including the outside enclosing region, and adding 1. The final flowgraph in Figure 11.6 has a total of three regions giving a total of four possible paths. These paths are listed in Table 11.9.

The final part of this white box process is to review the black box trials to make sure that all of the possible paths obtained from the flowgraph are traversed. Should any of the paths not be traversed it could be because the path is not possible; for example, a **while** structure could be constructed so that the body of the loop must be executed at least once, preventing a traversal which does not execute the loop body. Otherwise the black box test plan has been shown to be inadequate and additional trials will be needed to make sure that the component is adequately tested.

Table 11.9 The possible paths through the last flowgraph in Figure 11.6.

makeJulianDate flowgraph possible paths
a b g h
a b c e^{left} f g h
a b c e^{right} f g h
a b c d e^{any} f g h

11.6 ▓ Comparison of methods and techniques

The contents of this chapter provide a partial test rationale and test plan for the testing of the *JulianDate* hierarchy. It should be clear from this that the testing of a software artefact is every bit as complex, if not more complex, than its production. What is perhaps not as clear from this chapter is that the processes of designing tests are not as clear cut as the processes of software design and testing. A good test is one which has a high probability of detecting a fault and a good test designer is one who can produce such tests. The techniques introduced in this chapter should be regarded as the starting points for the production of test plans; additional tests will be required in almost all cases.

The validity of the testing process is determined by the quality of the rationale. The rationale includes the black box diagrams, range diagrams, test cases, test plans, flowgraphs and lists of paths, but it should also contain a written commentary justifying why the successful passing of the tests provides sufficient confidence in the correctness of the software. A mechanistic application of the rationales is unlikely to produce sufficient confidence in the software and the imaginative application of testing principles is required in all cases.

The extent of the confidence required will depend upon the purpose of the software and upon the consequences of software failure. For a trivial program implementing a small, possibly temporary, part of a much larger software system where the consequences of failure are fairly negligible, the test rationale may be minimal. For a program which performs a 'mission critical' task, for the organization using it the rationale must be sufficiently thorough. Some software systems are so critical, particularly those involving a risk to human life, that testing of the program should consist of a validation process which attempts to use mathematical reasoning to provide an almost absolute proof of the programs correctness. Such proofs, known as *formal methods*, are at the moment not very well known and require such extensive, and thus expensive, skills that they are considered beyond the scope of this book.

Testing is essential to ensure the quality of the software product but in itself cannot introduce quality into the product. To ensure that the product has quality attributes, and thus has a high possibility of passing its tests with minimal effort, all stages of the production process are rigorously carried out. This implies that the developer must have a good understanding of the specification, produce a validated design and implement the design rigorously. Although testing is a time consuming and expensive process, the resulting quality assurance will pay off in the life span of the product. In the case of the *JulianDate* hierarchy, if the design, production and testing are carried out rigorously, then the class can subsequently be used by a large number of client programs with a high probability that no further development or maintenance will be required.

Of the four black box techniques – parallel, inverse, relational and composite – the only certainty is that the parallel method can always be applied to all programs. However, if there is a choice of methods, then the methods should be considered in the sequence:

```
most favoured   →  inverse
                   composite
                   relational
least favoured  →  parallel
```

The consideration should include not only the applicability of the method but also the ease and possibility of performing the composite or relational comparisons which will validate the outputs. Usually a combination of the methods will be used, as illustrated above.

The possibility of automated testing should always be considered, even in the case of interactive programs as described in section 11.4. The advantages of automated testing are that a larger number of tests can be applied in a shorter period of time with greater accuracy. It also allows the tests to be repeated either after the program has been amended when it has failed one of the tests, or when the program has been changed during maintenance. The disadvantage of automated testing is that a computer program to test the program under test has to be designed and implemented. This program itself will require testing before its result, which is increased confidence in the artefact under test, can be relied upon. This in itself is not an overwhelming problem as the effort of testing the test harness program will be repaid in the greater number of tests and the greater ease of testing the artefact and can be used to retest it after maintenance.

Finally the possibility of white box testing should always be borne in mind. White box methods are much more expensive and fragile than black box methods. A black box rationale can be derived from the artefact's specification and will not change unless the specification changes. White box rationales depend upon the structure of the source code which implements the artefact and so any changes to the code will require a new rationale to be prepared. Again a cost benefit analysis could be used to decide if white box testing is appropriate.

Summary

- Testing can only increase confidence in the correct implementation of the artefact; it cannot prove that the artefact is correct.
- Testing can be used to assure the quality of the artefact but, by itself, cannot introduce quality characteristics into the artefact.
- The quality of a test process depends upon the quality of the rationale.
- There are two approaches to testing, *black box* and *glass box*.
- Black box testing can use *inverse*, *composite*, *relational* and *parallel* techniques.
- Parallel techniques can always be used, but the techniques should be favoured in the sequence inverse, composite, relational and parallel.
- Automated test harnesses increase the costs of testing but pay off in an increased ease of (re)applying the tests.
- Testing is not a mechanistic process.

Exercises

11.1 Is the *JulianDate* hierarchy now adequately tested? If so do you have a greater confidence in it than in the hierarchies which have been previously introduced?

11.2 Choose one of the hierarchies which have been developed in the previous chapters and produce a black box rationale and test harness for it. Does this process increase your confidence in the quality of the implementation?

11.3 Produce flowgraphs for all the actions in the *JulianDate* hierarchy. Review all the flowgraphs and determine if there is a relationship between the complexity of the flowgraphs and your difficulty in understanding the implementation.

11.4 Produce flowgraphs for the hierarchy used in Exercise 11.2 and use them to review the black box test plans. Have the flowgraphs indicated any tests which were not covered by the black box plans?

11.5 If you decided that the *JulianDate* hierarchy was adequately tested in Exercise 11.1, run the interactive *JulianDateTestHarness* again and input the string 5/5/1900/1999. What does this tell you about the process of testing?

Chapter twelve

Streams

In the programs which have been presented so far all input to the program has come from the keyboard and all output has been sent to the screen. To be more useful an application may have to accept data from, and send data to, a wide variety of other sources and destinations. These might include disk files, printers, modems, fax machines, network connections and other processes running on the same, or a different, machine. Information is considered to flow from, or to, the device as a sequence of data items known as a *stream* of data.

The detailed consideration of the use of streams to connect with a variety of devices is beyond the scope of this book. Accordingly only the use of files on the local disk drive will be considered; the use of streams to connect with other devices is fundamentally very similar. The use of files will address another limitation of the programs which have been introduced so far; that is, any information which has been input has been lost as soon as the program finishes. This is rarely appropriate and most specifications require that information input during one run of a program is stored in a file in order that it can be made available to the same program when it is run again, or by another program in order to process the information further.

When considering the use of disk files a distinction needs to be made between files which are intended to be readable by humans and files which are intended only to be used by programs. Files which are readable by humans are known as *text files*; those intended only to be used by other programs are known as *binary files*. Binary files have the advantage of usually being smaller than the equivalent text files. However, the binary files produced by a particular compiler are not necessarily readable by a program produced by a different compiler and in these situations text files can be used to transfer information between programs.

One final aspect of communication with a program will also be introduced in this chapter: communication with the program from the command line. This facility is very often used with operating system command line programs. For example, when the command *copy this.file that.file* is issued at the system prompt, it can be thought of as starting a program called *copy* and passing to it the arguments *this.file* and *that.file*. Any additional information on the command line, following the name of the program, is made available to Java's *main()* action in the array of Strings, conventionally called *args[]*, which must form part of *main*'s signature.

12.1 ■ An initial example

To introduce the use of files a very simple application, equivalent to the operating system *type* command, will be developed. When this command is used it is usually followed by the name of a file on the disk, the contents of which are then displayed on the terminal screen. The first version of this program will always output the contents of a file called "*test.txt*", in order to allow the use of files to be introduced. The next section will introduce the use of *main ()*'s arguments which allow the name of any file to be specified on the command line. The design for this initial version is as follows:

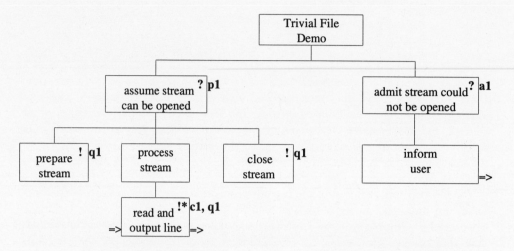

p1: Assume stream can be opened.   **q1:** Implicit input–output exception.
a1: Admit that the stream could not be opened.   **c1:** While data is available.

As was mentioned in Chapter 6 the input and output of information is always fraught with potential problems and so has to be associated with exception handlers. Thus the basis of this design is a posit/admit structure which guards against a file called *test.txt* not being available, or other possible errors, and informs the user if it could not be found or opened.

Assuming that the file can be opened, the processing of the file involves preparing an input stream, iteratively obtaining a line of information from it and outputting it to the screen before closing the file when no more lines remain in it. The implementation of this design is as follows:

```
0001 // Filename TrivialFileDemo.java.
0002 // Read a text file called "test.txt" and output
0003 // it to the screen.
0004 //
0005 // Written for JOF Book Chapter 12.
0006 // Fintan Culwin, v0.1, August 1997.
0007
0008 import java.io.*;
0009
0010 public class TrivialFileDemo extends Object {
0011
0012     public static void main(String args[]) {
0013
0014     DataInputStream inStream;
0015
```

```
0016        try {
0017            inStream = new DataInputStream(
0018                        new FileInputStream( "test.txt"));
0019
0020          while ( inStream.available() > 0 ) {
0021              System.out.println( inStream.readLine());
0022          } // End while.
0023
0024          inStream.close();
0025       } catch ( java.io.IOException exception)  {
0026        if ( exception instanceof FileNotFoundException) {
0027          System.out.println(
0028             "A file called test.txt could not be found, \n" +
0029             "or could not be opened.\n"                    +
0030             "Please investigate and try again.");
0031          } // End if.
0032       } // End try/ catch block.
0033    } // End main.
0034
0035 } // End TrivialFileDemo class.
```

In Chapter 6, when it was required to obtain data from the keyboard, the raw input stream from the keyboard, available to the program as System.in, was used to construct a DataInputStream called *keyboard* as follows:

```
java.io.DataInputStream keyboard =
        new java.io.DataInputStream( System.in);
```

The reason for this was that an instance of the DataInputStream class is able to interpret the raw data arriving in the stream, as individual characters, and convert them into strings, which can be obtained with the DataInputStream's *readLine()* action. On lines 0017 and 0018 a similar process is used to obtain a DataInputStream called *inStream* connected to the file called '*test.txt*'.

The phrase on line 0018, **new** FileInputStream("text.txt"), creates an anonymous instance of the FileInputStream class which provides a raw input stream from the file. In line 0017 this anonymous instance is used as an argument to the DataInputStream class constructor to provide a stream called *inStream*. Should the file not exist a FileNotFoundException will be thrown and caught on lines 0027 to 0030 where advice is given to the user before the program finishes.

Otherwise, if the file is opened and the stream is constructed, the available() action of the DataInputStream *inStream* instance can be used to determine if any more information is available from the stream. So long as information is known to be available the *inStream* readLine() action can be used to obtain a line of text from the stream which is immediately output to the screen using the System.out.println() action.

Once the available() action indicates that there is no more information available the *inStream* close() action is used to close the stream, and thus the file, before the program terminates.

This program can be demonstrated, or tested, by executing it within a directory which contains a text file called '*test.txt*'. The result should be that the contents of the file are displayed on the screen. However, if the file does not exist the advice on lines 0028 to 0030 should be given to the user.

12.2 ■ The *type* application

A small refinement to the *TrivialFileDemo* program will allow it to output the contents of any file specified on the command line. The changes to the design are as follows:

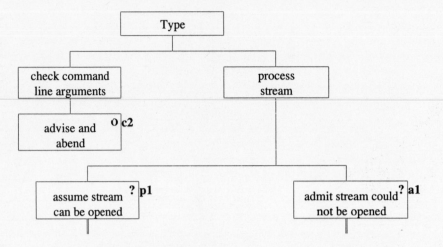

c2: If other than a single command line argument is given.

The parts of the design below the *process stream* stage are essentially identical to those of the *TrivialFileDemo* given above. Before this a check is made upon the number of command line arguments and, if other than a single argument is present, advice on the correct operation of the program is given before the program *abends*. An abend is an *ab*orted *end*ing of a program and is commonly used in situations like this where an initial check indicates that the program cannot continue. It should never be used in other situations, e.g. to abend in the middle of a program. The implementation of this design as far as the end of the stage *check command line arguments* is as follows:

```
0001 // Filename Type.java.
0002 // Read a text file named on the command line
0003 // and output to the screen.
0004 //
0005 // Written for JOF Book Chapter 12.
0006 // Fintan Culwin, v0.1, August 1997.
0007
0008
0009 import java.io.*;
0010
0011 public class Type extends Object{
0012
0013     public static void main(String args[]) {
0014
0015     DataInputStream inStream;
0016
0017         if ( args.length != 1) {
0018             System.out.println(
0019                 "To use this utility you must give the name\n" +
0020                 "of a single file which you want output.\n"    +
0021                 "You do not seem to have done this. \n\n");
```

```
0022                System.exit( -1);
0023        } // End if.
```

On line 0017 the **length** attribute of the *args[]* array is tested and if this indicates that a single argument has not been supplied, which might be no arguments or more than one argument, the advice on lines 0019 to 0021 is given to the user. On line 0022 the **System.exit()** action is used to abend the program. The -1 argument to the action indicates that the program finished owing to an error, and can be used by operating system batch scripts to take alternative actions depending upon the success or failure of the program.

The remaining parts of the implementation are essentially identical to that of the *TrivialFileDemo*, with all references to the file '*test.txt*' replaced with a reference to the first element in the *args[]* array. As was explained in Chapter 6, the first element in an array is located at the zeroth location, giving the following implementation:

```
0025        try {
0026            inStream = new DataInputStream(
0027                            new FileInputStream( args[ 0]));
0028
0029            while ( inStream.available() > 0 ) {
0030                System.out.println( inStream.readLine());
0031            } // end While.
0032
0033            inStream.close();
0034        } catch ( java.io.IOException exception) {
0035            if ( exception instanceof FileNotFoundException) {
0036                System.out.println(
0037                    "The file " + args[ 0] + " could not be found,\n" +
0038                    "or could not be opened.\n");
0039            } // End if.
0040        } // End try/ catch block.
0041    } // End main.
0042
0043 } // End class Type.
```

This program can be demonstrated by executing it from the command line with no arguments, with two arguments, with the name of a file which does exist and with the name of a file which does not exist.

12.3 ▓ An output file stream

In addition to input file streams, output file streams can also be used to place the output from a program directly into a file. In this section a developer supplied output stream class will be introduced which can be used to place formatted line numbers in front of every line. The demonstration client for this class can be used to prepare line numbered program listings as used in this book. The object diagram for this developer supplied class, called *NumberedPrintStream*, is given in Figure 12.1.

The *NumberedPrintStream* is an extension of the standard **PrintStream** class which is the class which implements the **System.out** instance. Its constructor action requires an existing **OutputStream** instance from which it creates a *NumberedPrintStream* instance. It maintains an encapsulated *lineNumber* data attribute which is initialized to

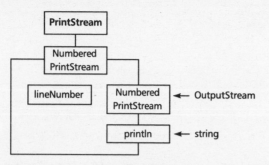

Figure 12.1 The *NumberedPrintStream* class diagram.

1 when the instance is created and is incremented by 1 every time a line is output via the overridden *println()* action. The implementation of this design is as follows:

```
0001 // Filename NumberedPrintStream.java.
0002 // Extension of the system PrintStream class to
0003 // provide a class which outputs formatted numbers
0004 // before every line.
0005 //
0006 // Written for JOF Book Chapter 12.
0007 // Fintan Culwin, v0.1, August 1997.
0008
0009 import java.io.*;
0010 import OutputFormatter;
0011
0012 public class NumberedPrintStream extends java.io.PrintStream {
0013
0014 private long lineNumber = 1;
0015
0016    public NumberedPrintStream( OutputStream out) {
0017       super( out);
0018       lineNumber = 1;
0019    } // End constructor.
0020
0021
0022    public void println( String anyString){
0023       super.println(
0024           OutputFormatter.formatLong( lineNumber, 4, true,
0025                                 OutputFormatter.DECIMAL)
0026           + " " + anyString);
0027       lineNumber++;
0028    } // End println.
0029
0030 } // end class NumberedPrintStream.
```

The constructor action on lines 0016 to 0019 first calls its parent, PrintStream, constructor passing on its argument before ensuring that the *lineNumber* attribute is set to 1.

The *NumberedPrintStream println()* action is implemented as a call of the PrintStream *println()* action passing its *anyString* parameter preceded by the String produced by the *OutputFormatter formatLong()* action, containing the *lineNumber* formatted in decimal to four digits with leading zeros. As a line has been output the *lineNumber* attribute is incremented so that the first call of *println()* will be labelled 0001, the second 0002 and so on.

To demonstrate the use of this class a utility program called *NumberList* will be developed. This program will take either one or two command line arguments. If only one command line argument is specified the program will attempt to open this file for input and output its contents onto the screen with line numbers. If two arguments are supplied the second argument will identify a file into which the output is to be placed. The design of this program is as follows:

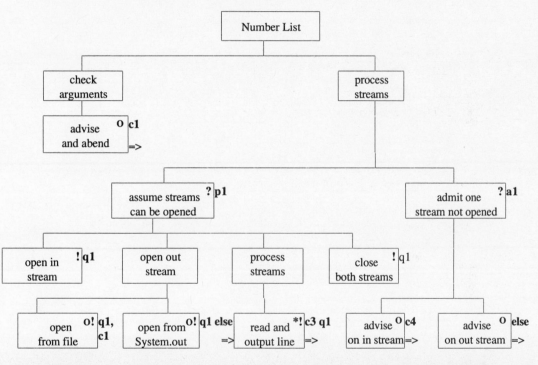

c1: If zero or more than two arguments supplied.
c2: If one argument supplied.
c3: While data is available.
c4: If input file could not be opened.

p1: Assume both streams can be opened.
a1: Admit a stream could not be opened.
q1: Implicit input–output exception.

The design commences with an abend component ensuring that only one or two command line arguments have been supplied. The posit part of the *process streams* stage commences by attempting to open the input stream. The output stream is then opened either by opening an output file and constructing a stream from it or by constructing a stream from the Standard.out stream. If this is accomplished without throwing an exception the streams are processed and then both streams are closed.

Should an exception be thrown as the streams are constructed a flag indicates if the input stream was successfully opened. This flag is used to determine if advice should be given to the user concerning the input file or the output file. The implementation of this design is as follows:

```
0001 // Filename NumberList.java.
0002 // Illustrates how to read command line arguments
```

```
0003 // and write to output files.
0004 //
0005 // Written for JOF Book Chapter 12.
0006 // Fintan Culwin, v0.1, August 1997.
0007
0008
0009 import java.io.*;
0010 import NumberedPrintStream;
0011
0012 public class NumberList extends Object {
0013
0014     public static void main(String args[]) {
0015
0016     DataInputStream        inStream;
0017     NumberedPrintStream  outStream;
0018     boolean                inStreamOpen = false;
0019
0020         if ( args.length == 0 || args.length > 2) {
0021             System.out.println(
0022                 "\nTo use this utility you must either give the name of a\n" +
0023                 "single file which you want line numbers put into and \n"    +
0024                 "sent to the screen.\n\n"                                    +
0025                 "Or give the names of two files and the contents of the \n" +
0026                 "first file will be sent with line numbers to the \n"        +
0027                 "second file.\n\n"                                          +
0028                 "You do not seem to have done this. \n\n");
0029             System.exit( -1);
0030         } // End if.
0031
0032         try {
0033             inStream = new DataInputStream(
0034                         new FileInputStream( args[ 0]));
0035             inStreamOpen = true;
0036
0037             if ( args.length == 2) {
0038                 outStream = new NumberedPrintStream(
0039                         new FileOutputStream( args[ 1]));
0040             } else {
0041                 outStream = new NumberedPrintStream( System.out);
0042             } // End if.
0043
0044             while ( inStream.available() > 0) {
0045                 outStream.println( inStream.readLine());
0046             } // End while.
0047
0048             inStream.close();
0049             outStream.close();
0050         } catch ( java.io.IOException exception) {
0051             if ( exception instanceof FileNotFoundException) {
0052                 if ( inStreamOpen) {
0053                     System.out.println(
0054                         "The file " + args[ 1] + " could not be opened.\n");
0055                 } else {
```

```
0056                    System.out.println(
0057                        "The file " + args[ 0] + " could not be found,\n" +
0058                        "or could not be opened.\n");
0059               } // End if.
0060            } // End if.
0061         } // End try/ catch block.
0062    } // End main.
0063
0064 } // End class NumberList.
```

The implementation of the abend component, on lines 0020 to 0030, is directly comparable with the abend component above. On lines 0033 to 0034 the *inStream* instance is created as described above. On lines 0037 to 0042 an instance of the *NumberedPrintStream* class, called *outStream*, is created, either from a file named in the second command line argument or from the System.out stream. Following this the processing of the streams involves inputting lines from the *inStream* and outputting them using the *outStream println()* action, before both files are closed. As the *outStream* is an instance of the *NumberedPrintStream* class this will cause the output to be preceded by line numbers.

The admit component of the design, on lines 0050 to 0061, tests the *inStreamOpen* flag which would have been set on line 0035 if the input stream had been successfully opened. This decision causes it to give advice to the user concerning which file could not be opened.

This program can be demonstrated by using it with a single argument identifying one file which does not exist and one which does exist. To demonstrate it with two arguments the first should again identify one file which does and one which does not, in combination with a second argument which identifies a file which can be written to and one which cannot. One way of specifying a file which cannot be opened for output is to specify a file which has its operating system read-only attribute set.

Examining the contents of the files after the program has executed should show that, when an existing file which can be written to is specified as the second argument, the existing contents of the file are lost and replaced with the new output.

12.4 ■ Homogeneous binary streams

This section will introduce the use of binary streams by developing a demonstration client which will write, and subsequently read, an array of objects to a stream. In this first example all of the objects will be of exactly the same class, and hence *homogeneous*. It is more useful, and more common, for a stream consisting of values of different classes to be written and read; such streams are described as *heterogeneous*. The handling of heterogeneous streams is more complex than the handling of homogeneous streams and will be considered in the next section.

The *WarningCounter* class, first introduced in Chapter 4, will be used, with minor modifications, for the instances to be stored in the stream. As the writing and reading of a single instance would not be a very convincing demonstration a data structure containing an iteration of *WarningCounters*, implemented in a class called *HomogeneousMonitors*, will be used. The reason why the collection of *Counters* is called a collection of *Monitors* will become clear in the next section. The object diagram of the *HomogeneousMonitors* class is given in Figure 12.2.

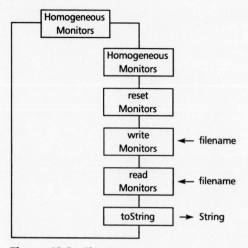

Figure 12.2   The *HomogeneousMonitors* class diagram.

The constructor will create an indeterminate number of *WarningCounter* instances (between 2 and 7) and will initialize each to an indeterminate state. This decision was made in order that the demonstration of the stream facility will be more convincing if a different number of items, with different values, are used each time the demonstration client is run. The design of the constructor is as follows:

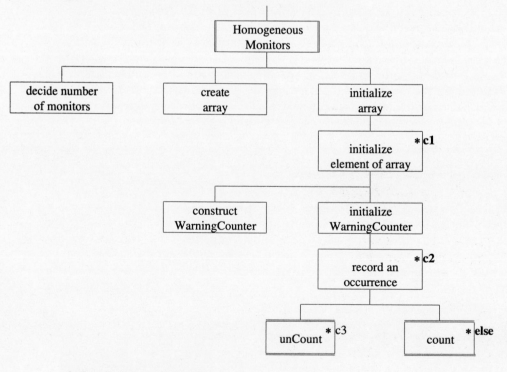

c1: For all elements in the array.
c2: A random number of times, between 10 and 30.
c3: On a 50/50 chance providing some occurrence has been counted.

The basis of this design is to decide randomly upon the number of counters and then to initialize an array of *WarningCounters* to this size. Each *WarningCounter* in turn is then constructed, with the default minimum and maximum limits, and is then initialized by randomly deciding upon the number of occurrences to *count()* and *unCount()*. An occurrence can only be uncounted if there is already an occurrence counted, otherwise there is an equal chance of an occurrence being counted or uncounted. The implementation of the constructor, and the context clause of the class, is as follows:

```
0001 // Filename HomogeneousMonitors.java.
0002 // Contains an indeterminate number of WarningCounter
0003 // instances with actions to write and then to read
0004 // them from a stream.
0005 //
0006 // Written for JOF Book Chapter 12.
0007 // Fintan Culwin, v0.1, August 1997.
0008
0009 import Counters.WarningCounter;
0010 import java.io.*;
0011 import java.util.Random;
0012 import java.util.Date;
0013
0014
0015 public class HomogeneousMonitors extends Object {
0016
0017 private Random generator = new Random();
0018 private WarningCounter theMonitors[];
0019
0020    public HomogeneousMonitors() {
0021
0022    int numberOfMonitors = 2 + (int) (generator.nextDouble() * 5.0);
0023    int index;
0024    int anotherIndex;
0025    int numberOfOccurrences;
0026
0027      theMonitors = new WarningCounter[ numberOfMonitors];
0028      for ( index =0; index < numberOfMonitors; index++) {
0029        theMonitors[ index] = new WarningCounter();
0030        numberOfOccurrences = 10 +
0031                  (int) (generator.nextDouble() * 20.0);
0032        for ( anotherIndex =0;
0033             anotherIndex < numberOfOccurrences;
0034             anotherIndex++) {
0035          if ( (generator.nextDouble() > 0.5)              &&
0036            (theMonitors[ index].numberCountedIs() > 0) ){
0037            theMonitors[ index].unCount();
0038          } else {
0039            theMonitors[ index].count();
0040          } // End if.
0041        } // End for anotherIndex.
0042      } // End for index.
0043    } // End HomogeneousMonitors constructor.
```

The local variable *numberOfMonitors* is initialized upon declaration using a random number on line 0022 and the value is subsequently used to determine the bounds of an array of *WarningCounters*, called *theMonitors*, on line 0027. A definite loop between lines 0028 and 0042 then considers each *WarningCounter* instance in turn. The *WarningCounter* is created, using the default constructor, on line 0029.

A second definite loop between 0032 and 0041, controlled by a random value obtained on lines 0030 and 0031, then calls either the *WarningCounters count()* or *unCount()* action on a 50/50 random basis. However, the *unCount()* action is only called if the *numberCountedIs()* enquiry action indicates that there is an occurrence to uncount.

The *resetMonitors()* action will reinitialize the monitors into their default state, where they have counted no occurrences, by *reset*ting each instance. The *toString()* action labels each counter as being associated with a room, and calls the *WarningCounter toString()* action to obtain a String representing the state of the counter to be appended to the label. The implementation of these two actions will be presented without a design, as follows:

```
0046        public void resetMonitors() {
0047
0048        int index;
0049
0050            for ( index =0; index < theMonitors.length; index++) {
0051                theMonitors[ index].reset();
0052            } // End for.
0053        } // End resetMonitors.



0099        public String toString(){
0100
0101        StringBuffer theString = new StringBuffer();
0102        int         index;
0103        char        theRoom = 'A';
0104
0105            for ( index =0; index < theMonitors.length; index++) {
0106                theString.append( "Room " + theRoom + "  " +
0107                                theMonitors[ index].toString() + "\n");
0108            ` theRoom++;
0109            } // End for.
0110            return theString.toString();
0111        } // End toString;
```

The first part of the demonstration harness for this class uses the constructor to create an instance of the *HomogeneousMonitors* class and then outputs it to the screen. The implementation of this part of the harness and the output which it might produce are as follows:

```
0001 // Filename HomoDemo.java.
0002 // Contains a demonstration harness for the
0003 // HomogeneousMonitors class.
0004 //
0005 // Written for JOF Book Chapter 12.
0006 // Fintan Culwin, v0.1, August 1997.
0007
```

```
0008 import HomogeneousMonitors;
0009
0010 public class HomoDemo extends Object {
0011
0012    public static void main(String args[]) {
0013
0014    HomogeneousMonitors demoMonitors;
0015
0016       System.out.println( "\tHomogeneous File Demonstration\n");
0017
0018       System.out.println( "\nPreparing and showing the monitors ... \n");
0019       demoMonitors = new HomogeneousMonitors();
0020       System.out.println( demoMonitors);
```

```
Homogeneous File Demonstration

Preparing and showing the monitors ...

Room A  Now in room : 5
Room B  Now in room : 0
Room C  Now in room : 2
```

On this run of the program three counters were created and placed into the states as shown. As aspects of the behaviour of this program are largely controlled by random numbers, a second, or subsequent, run of the program is unlikely to produce this precise output.

All of the actions which have been introduced so far have consolidated the use of arrays and random numbers which were first introduced in Chapter 6. The new aspects are introduced in the *writeMonitors()* and *readMonitors()* actions. The design of the *writeMonitors()* action is as follows:

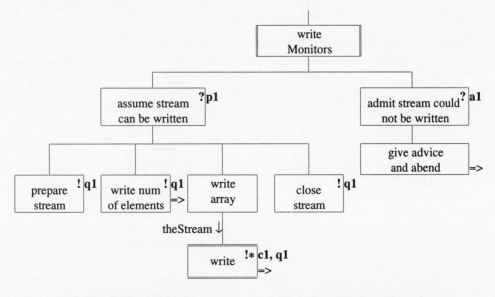

c1: For all elements in the array. **p1:** Assume stream can be written.
q1: Implicit input–output exception. **a1:** Admit stream could not be written.

The design indicates that the first action is to create the stream, using the filename supplied as an argument, and then to write the number of elements in the array. A definite loop then writes each element in the array to the stream, identified as *theStream*, making use of the *write()* action of the *WarningCounter* class. This action was not included in Chapter 4 and its implementation will be presented shortly. The implementation of the *writeMonitor()* action is as follows:

```
0056    public void writeMonitors( String filename) {
0057
0058    int index;
0059    DataOutputStream theStream;
0060
0061      try {
0062        theStream = new DataOutputStream(
0063                        new FileOutputStream( filename));
0064        theStream.writeInt( theMonitors.length);
0065        for ( index =0; index < theMonitors.length; index++) {
0066          theMonitors[ index].write( theStream);
0067        } // End for.
0068        theStream.close();
0069      } catch ( java.io.IOException exception) {
0070        System.out.println( "Exception thrown on writing ... abending");
0071        System.exit( -1);
0072      } // End try/catch.
0073    } // End writeMonitors.
```

The first part of the action, on lines 0062 to 0063, creates a **DataOutputStream** called *theStream* from a **FileOutputStream** associated with the filename supplied as an argument. This is exactly equivalent to the creation of **DataInputStreams** earlier in this chapter; the difference between a text stream and a binary stream is determined by the actions which are applied to the stream, not to the stream itself. The first of these actions is on line 0064 where the *writeInt()* action of *theStream* is used to output the (**int**eger) number of elements in the array to the stream.

This is followed by a definite iteration where each *WarningCounter* in the array has its *write()* action called, causing its state to be stored in the stream. The implementation of the *WarningCounter*'s write action is as follows:

```
0047 // Action to write state to a stream, added for Chapter 12.
0048 public void write( DataOutputStream writeTo) throws IOException {
0049    writeTo.writeInt( this.numberCountedIs());
0050 }  // End write.
```

This action is implemented using the *writeInt()* action of the stream passed as the *writeTo* argument. The only value which is written is the value of the *counted* data attribute of this class, obtained using its enquiry action. The limitations of this implementation will be considered in an end-of-chapter exercise.

Once all of the elements have been written the stream's *close()* action is called. All of the actions concerned with the stream in the *writeMonitors()* action may cause an **IOException** to be thrown and an exception handler is supplied which informs the user and abends the program.

The remaining action in the *HomogeneousMonitors* class is the *readMonitors()*

action whose design is as follows:

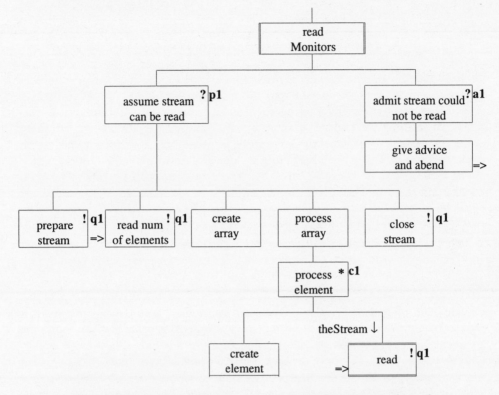

c1: For all elements in the array.   **p1:** Assume stream can be read.
q1: Implicit input–output exception.   **a1:** Admit stream could not be read.

In many ways this design is comparable with the *writeMonitors()* design above. It commences by preparing an input stream and then reads the number of elements from it. Having obtained this information it can recreate the array with this number of elements, before iterating through each element of the array creating a new *WarningCounter* instance and then using its *read()* action to restore its state from the stream. The implementation of this design is as follows:

```
0076        public void readMonitors( String filename) {
0077
0078        int index;
0079        int numberOfMonitors;
0080        DataInputStream theStream;
0081
0082          try {
0083            theStream = new DataInputStream(
0084                              new FileInputStream( filename));
0085            numberOfMonitors = theStream.readInt();
0086            theMonitors = new WarningCounter[ numberOfMonitors];
0087            for ( index =0; index < theMonitors.length; index++) {
0088              theMonitors[ index] = new WarningCounter();
0089              theMonitors[ index].read( theStream);
0090            } // End for.
```

```
0091        theStream.close();
0092     } catch ( java.io.IOException exception) {
0093        System.out.println( "Exception thrown on reading ... abending");
0094        System.exit( -1);
0095     } // End try/catch.
0096 } // End readMonitors.
```

On line 0085 the *readInt()* action of *theStream* is used to read the (**int**eger) number of elements back from the stream into the local variable *numberOfMonitors*. This value is then used on line 0086 to redetermine the bounds of *theMonitors* array. This action, of resetting the bounds of an array which already has bounds and contents, causes the existing contents of the array to be disposed of. Consequently there is no requirement that the new bounds of the array are equal to the old bounds of the array.

The definite loop on lines 0087 to 0090 then iterates through the array where, on line 0088, a new *WarningCounter* instance is created and its *read()* action is used on line 0089 to restore its state from the stream. The *read()* action of the *WarningCounter* class has also been added for this chapter. Its declaration is as follows:

```
0053        // Action to read the state from a stream, added for Chapter 12.
0054        public void read( DataInputStream readFrom) throws IOException {
0055             this.setCountTo( readFrom.readInt());
0056        } // End read.
```

On line 0055 the *readInt()* action of the *readFrom* stream, passed as an argument, is used to obtain an **int**eger value from the input stream. This value is then used as the argument of the **protected** *BasicCounter setCountTo()* action, which the *Warning-Counter* has inherited, to restore the state of its *Counted* data attribute.

The remaining parts of the *HomogeneousMonitor readMonitors()* action are concerned with closing the stream and handling any exceptions in a manner comparable with the *writeMonitors()* action. The remaining parts of the demonstration harness demonstrate the *writeMonitors()*, *resetMonitors()* and *readMonitors()* actions, as follows:

```
0022        System.out.println( "\nWriting the monitors ... ");
0023        demoMonitors.writeMonitors( "Homo.dat");
0024
0025        System.out.println( "\nResetting and showing the monitors ... ");
0026        demoMonitors.resetMonitors();
0027        System.out.println( demoMonitors);
0028
0029        System.out.println( "\nReading and showing the monitors ... ");
0030        demoMonitors.readMonitors( "Homo.dat");
0031        System.out.println( demoMonitors);
0032     } // End main.
0033 } // End HomoDemo.
```

The output from this part of the harness is as follows:

```
Writing the monitors ...

Resetting and showing the monitors ...
Room A   Now in room : 0
Room B   Now in room : 0
Room C   Now in room : 0
```

```
Reading and showing the monitors ...
Room A  Now in room : 5
Room B  Now in room : 0
Room C  Now in room : 2
```

which seems to show that the information in the *HomogeneousCounters* instance has been successfully written to and read back from a file. After this program has been executed a file called '*Homo.dat*' will exist in the file system. Unlike the text files produced earlier in this chapter this file is not intended to be read by humans; this can be verified by loading it into a text editor and attempting to examine its contents. The precise details of the contents of the file might differ from compiler to compiler and a detailed consideration of them is outside the scope of this book.

12.5 ■ Heterogeneous binary streams

The homogeneous data structure developed and demonstrated in the previous section was only capable of writing and reading instances of the *WarningCounters* class. This section will introduce the considerations concerned with the writing and reading of streams which can contain instances of different classes.

To accomplish this a comparable class called *HeterogeneousMonitors* will be developed which is capable of containing a mixture of *WarningCounter* and *RoomMonitor* instances. As with the version of the *WarningCounter* used above the *RoomMonitor* will require some additional actions, compared with the version presented in Chapter 4, for it to be suitable.

The first change is to add an overriding *count()* action as suggested in Exercise 5.3. This is essential in this implementation in order that an instance of the *RoomMonitor* class can respond appropriately to a *count()* action. Also, as with the *WarningCounter* class, a *write()* and a *read()* action will have to be supplied. The implementation of these three actions in the revised *RoomMonitor* class definition is as follows:

```
0069        // Action to ensure count() acts appropriately, added for Chapter 12.
0070        public void count() {
0071            this.enterRoom();
0072        } // End count.
0073
0074        // Action to write the state to a stream, added for Chapter 12.
0075        public void write( DataOutputStream writeTo) throws IOException {
0076            super.write( writeTo);
0077            writeTo.writeInt( maxEverInRoom);
0078            writeTo.writeInt( totalNumberEntered);
0079        } // End write.
0080
0081        // Action to read the state from a stream, added for Chapter 12.
0082        public void read( DataInputStream readFrom) throws IOException {
0083            super.read( readFrom);
0084            maxEverInRoom      = readFrom.readInt();
0085            totalNumberEntered = readFrom.readInt();
0086        } // End read.
```

The overriding *count()* declaration ensures that a call of the *count()* action has exactly the same effect as a call of the existing *enterRoom()* action by indirecting to it. The *write()* action commences by calling its parent's (*WarningCounter*) *write()* action, in order for it to write its data attribute, and then uses the *writeTo WriteInt()* action to write its own data attributes to the stream. The *read()* action is the inverse of this, first calling its parent's *read()* action and then reading, and restoring, its own two additional data attributes.

The class diagram for the *HeterogeneousMonitors* class does not differ significantly from that presented for the *HomogeneousMonitors* class, offering exactly the same actions. The design of the constructor differs only very slightly from the *HomogeneousMonitors* constructor, by randomly deciding between constructing an instance of a *WarningMonitor* and of a *RoomMonitor*. The implementation of the class as far as the end of the constructor is as follows:

```
0001 // Filename HeterogeneousMonitors.java.
0002 // Contains an indeterminate number of WarningCounter
0003 // or RoomMonitor instances with actions to write and
0004 // read them from a stream.
0005 //
0006 // Written for JOF Book Chapter 12.
0007 // Fintan Culwin, v0.1, August 1997.
0008
0009
0010 import Counters.WarningCounter;
0011 import Counters.RoomMonitor;
0012 import java.io.*;
0013 import java.util.Random;
0014
0015
0016 public class HeterogeneousMonitors extends Object{
0017
0018 private Random generator = new Random();
0019 private WarningCounter theMonitors[];
0020
0021
0022    public HeterogeneousMonitors() {
0023
0024    int numberOfMonitors = 2 + (int) (generator.nextDouble() * 5.0);
0025    int index;
0026    int anotherIndex;
0027    int numberOfOccurrences;
0028
0029    theMonitors = new WarningCounter[ numberOfMonitors];
0030    for ( index =0; index < numberOfMonitors; index++) {
0031       if (generator.nextDouble() > 0.5) {
0032          theMonitors[ index] = new WarningCounter();
0033       } else {
0034          theMonitors[ index] = new RoomMonitor();
0035       } // End if.
0036       numberOfOccurrences = 10 + (int) (generator.nextDouble() * 20.0);
0037       for ( anotherIndex =0;
0038             anotherIndex < numberOfOccurrences;
```

```
0039                anotherIndex++) {
0040          if ( (generator.nextDouble() > 0.5)              &&
0041             (theMonitors[ index].numberCountedIs() > 0) ){
0042             theMonitors[ index].unCount();
0043          } else {
0044             theMonitors[ index].count();
0045          } // End if.
0046       } // End for.
0047    } // End for.
0048 } // End HeterogeneousMonitors constructor.
```

This constructor differs significantly on lines 0032 to 0036 where there is a 50/50 chance of it constructing a *WarningCounter* or a *RoomMonitor*. The array *theMonitors* is declared, on line 0019, as an array of *WarningCounters*, yet on line 0035 a *RoomMonitor* instance might be stored in one of its elements. This is acceptable to Java as a *RoomMonitor* is an extended *WarningCounter*.

The implementation of the *toString()* action in the *heterogeneousMonitors* class is exactly identical to its implementation in the *HomogeneousMonitors* class and the implementation of the demonstration client is essentially identical to the previous demonstration client. The output produced by a run of the demonstration client, up to the point where an instance of the *HeterogeneousMonitors* has been created and output, might be as follows:

```
Heterogeneous File Demonstration


Preparing and showing the monitors ...

Room A   Now in room : 5
Room B   Now in room : 1 Max in room : 3 Total entered : 10
```

which indicates that a *WarningCounter* is stored in the first element of the array and a *RoomMonitor* in the second. It also indicates that the call of the *count()* action on line 0046 will **dynamically dispatch** to the appropriate *count()* action. That is, if the instance is a *WarningCounter* then Java will call the *WarningCounter count()* action; if it is a *RoomMonitor* it will call the *RoomMonitor count()* action. It is only able to make this decision when the program is running as the decision on whether an element in the array is a *RoomMonitor* or a *WarningCounter* is not made until the program is executing. Likewise the appropriate *toString()* action will be called to produce the representation of the state of each monitor. The *resetMonitor()* action has similar changes to the constructor, randomly deciding to create a random number of *RoomMonitor* or *WarningCounter* instances:

```
0053   public void resetMonitors() {
0054
0055   int index;
0056
0057      theMonitors = new WarningCounter[
0058                          2 + (int) (generator.nextDouble() * 5.0)];
0059      for ( index =0; index < theMonitors.length; index++) {
0060         if (generator.nextDouble() > 0.5) {
0061            theMonitors[ index] = new WarningCounter();
```

```
0062              } else {
0063                  theMonitors[ index] = new RoomMonitor();
0064              } // End if.
0065          } // End for.
0066      } // End resetMonitors.
```

Before considering the *writeMonitors()* and *readMonitors()* actions a small digression is essential. When the homogeneous data file was written in the previous section it consisted of an integer value indicating the number of items stored in the file followed by that many *WarningCounters*. The heterogeneous file which will be written by this class will also commence with an integer value indicating the number of items which follow it. However, each item in the file might be a *WarningCounter* or it might be a *RoomMonitor* and there has to be some way of deciding which is which.

One way to accomplish this might be to write a single character before each item in the file. If the character is a 'w' it might indicate that a *WarningCounter* is stored next, if it is an 'r' a *RoomMonitor*. This would work for this example, but if at some stage in the future an additional extended *WarningCounter* were to be stored in the file then the *write()* action and the *read()* action would require extensive modification. Development by extension is intended to avoid precisely this situation. If an additional class is added to a class hierarchy at some time in the future then all existing code, with the obvious exception of user interfaces, should not require any changes.

Java provides facilities for exactly this situation. The Object class from which all other classes in Java are directly or indirectly descended from supplies a **final** getClass() action which returns an instance of the Class class. An instance of the Class class provides a system descriptor of the class and the Class getName() action will return a String containing the name of the class. Thus for any instance of any class the term *anyInstance*.**get**Class().getName() will return a String containing the name of the class. This technique can be used in the *writeMonitors()* action to write a description of the class before each class is written, as follows:

```
0069      public void writeMonitors( String filename) {
0070
0071      int index;
0072      DataOutputStream theStream;
0073
0074          try {
0075              theStream = new DataOutputStream(
0076                              new FileOutputStream( filename));
0077              theStream.writeInt( theMonitors.length);
0078              for ( index =0; index < theMonitors.length; index++) {
0079                  theStream.writeUTF( theMonitors[ index].getClass().getName());
0080                  theMonitors[ index].write( theStream);
0081              } // End for.
0082              theStream.close();
0083          } catch ( java.io.IOException exception) {
0084              System.out.println('Exception thrown on writing ... abending');
0085              System.exit( -1);
0086          } // End try/catch.
0087      } // End writeMonitors.
```

On line 0079 the name of the class stored in each location in the array is obtained and written to the stream. The writeUTF()[1] action should be used when a String value is written to a binary stream, and subsequently read using *readUTF()* as will be shown below. The effect of this action is to write the number of items to the stream and then write each element stored in the array, preceded by a UTF encoded String describing its contents. Thus, if at some stage in the future an additional class is added to the hierarchy, no changes will be required to this action as the UTF description will be automatically written to the stream.

The *HeterogeneousMonitors readMonitors()* action must be able to read the UTF description of which class is stored next in the stream, create an instance of that particular class and then read the next item from the stream. This is accomplished within the *readMonitors()* action on lines 0107 to 0111.

```
0090 public void readMonitors( String filename) {
0091
0092 int   index;
0093 int   numberOfMonitors;
0094
0095 String className;
0096 Class  theClass;
0097 Object anObject;
0098
0099 DataInputStream theStream;
0100
0101    try {
0102       theStream = new DataInputStream(
0103                         new FileInputStream( filename));
0104       numberOfMonitors = theStream.readInt();
0105       theMonitors = new WarningCounter[ numberOfMonitors];
0106       for ( index =0; index < theMonitors.length; index++) {
0107          className = theStream.readUTF();
0108          theClass  = Class.forName( className);
0109          anObject  = theClass.newInstance();
0110          theMonitors[ index] = (WarningCounter) anObject;
0111          theMonitors[ index].read( theStream);
0112       } // End for.
0113       theStream.close();
0114    } catch ( Exception exception) {
0115       System.out.println( "Exception thrown on writing ... abending");
0116       System.exit( -1);
0117    } // End try/catch.
0118 } // End readMonitors.
```

On line 0107 the UTF string description of the class which follows is read from the stream and stored as a normal *String* in the local variable *className*. On line 0108 an instance of the Class class, which describes the class to the system, is created using the Class forName() action and passing the String *className* as an argument. On line 0109 having obtained a Class instance called *theClass*, which describes the class which is about to be read from the stream, its *newInstance()* action is used to create a new

[1]For the curious *UTF* is *UCS* (*Universal Character Set*) *Transformation Format*, which is a compact means of representing and storing strings which might contain 64 bit characters, but is expected to contain mostly 8 bit characters.

instance of the class described in *anObject*. On line 0110 this instance, of the appropriate type, is assigned, with type qualification, to an element of the *theMonitors* array. Having done all this, on line 0111 its *read()* action can be used to initialize itself from the stream.

It might appear that there is a fault in line 0111, if the instance being read is a *RoomMonitor*. However, as a *RoomMonitor is a*n extended *WarningCounter* instance this is acceptable to Java. The demonstration client below will show that even if the instance being read is a *RoomMonitor* is recovered from the stream and stored in the array.

The remaining output of the demonstration test harness again indicates that the *writeMonitor()* and *readMonitor* actions seem to be effective:

```
Writing the monitors ...

Resetting and showing the monitors ...
Room A  Now in room : 0 Max in room : 0 Total entered : 0
Room B  Now in room : 0 Max in room : 0 Total entered : 0
Room C  Now in room : 0

Reading and showing the monitors ...
Room A  Now in room : 5
Room B  Now in room : 1 Max in room : 3 Total entered : 10
```

In this run of the program the *resetMonitor()* action has, by chance, created an array of three elements, the first two of which are *RoomMonitors* and the third is a *WarningMonitor*. The *readMonitor()* action restores the state which was shown, before it was written, above.

Summary

- Streams are places where information can flow between a program and various devices.

- Text streams store information in a human readable format which can also be used to transfer information between different computer systems. However, a text stream is larger than its equivalent binary stream.

- The *args[]* argument to the *main()* action can be used to obtain the command line arguments, as Strings.

- Streams, and data structures, which contain items of exactly the same class are known as *homogeneous*. Those which contain items of different classes are known as *heterogeneous*.

- Data in text format is written to a stream with println() and read from the stream with readLine().

- Data in binary format is written to a stream with writeInt() (or writeDouble() etc.) and read with readInt() (or readDouble() etc.).

- Strings can be written to a binary stream with writeUTF() and read with readUTF().

- The Class class can be used to obtain a description of a class which can be used to write to and read from heterogeneous streams.

Exercises

12.1 Obtain the source code for the *TextFileDemo*, *Type* and *NumberList* programs, and then build and demonstrate them.

12.2 Adapt the *Type* program so that it takes an arbitrary number of arguments and iteratively outputs all of the files which they identify to the screen.

12.3 Adapt the *Type* program from Exercise 12.2 so that if it is not given any arguments it asks the user for the filename, with an iterative dialog, until they enter the name of a file which can be opened.

12.4 Implement a program which writes an indeterminate number of random integer values to a text file. Implement a second program which reads the integers from the file and outputs on the screen the number of integers in the file, the highest value, the lowest value and the floating point average value.

12.5 Extend the *NumberList* class to produce a *PageList* class. This class should encapsulate a page number attribute and its own line number attribute. Every 50 lines it should output three blank lines, a line containing the filename and page number and three more blank lines. The lines which form the page break should not be numbered.

12.6 The *WarningCounter write()* and *read()* actions, and thus the corresponding *RoomMonitor* actions, are only suitable for use when the default constructor is used. The *theInitialCount* attribute of the *BasicCounter* class and the *minimumCount* and *maximumCount* attributes of the *LimitedCounter* class have not been considered. This problem can be solved by implementing *read()* and *write()* actions in the *BasicCounter* and *LimitedCounter* class and removing them from the *WarningCounter* class. Reimplement both the *Monitors* class and the *Counters* hierarchy and demonstrate that they work correctly when a non-default constructor is used.

12.7 Extend the *RoomMonitor* class to produce an *ExtendedRoomMonitor* class. This class should not introduce any data attributes and need only supply a *toString()* action which clearly identifies it as an *ExtendedRoomMonitor*. Adapt the *HeterogeneousMonitors* class so that it can create instances of this class in the array and demonstrate that this is all that is needed for the class to be written and saved.

12.8 Design and implement a menu driven program which provides access to the *HeterogeneousMonitors* class. It should offer options to reinitialize, to show the structure on the screen, to write it to a file named by the user and to read the structure from a file named by the user. Use this client to demonstrate that a file produced by one run of the program can be used by a subsequent run of the program.

Chapter thirteen

Standard iterative data structures

The previous chapter introduced a class which contains a homogeneous iterative data structure. Prior to this the examples had, largely, concentrated upon the representation and manipulation of a single data item. Although single data items are fundamental to the production of software artefacts, most applications require that an iteration of data items is processed. The topic of iterative data structures is commonly known simply as *data structures* and is a large and complex part of software development. This book can only provide an initial introduction to this important topic.

The internal implementation of the iterative data structure in the previous chapter was by means of an *array*. This chapter will continue the introduction to arrays and will also introduce some other standard iterative data structures which are supplied by the Java environment. The two following chapters will continue with a consideration of some developer supplied iterative data structures.

13.1 Two-dimensional arrays

Arrays were first introduced in Chapter 6 and were revisited in the previous chapter. All array examples used so far have been *one-dimensional arrays*, i.e. they have been a single iteration of data elements. It is also possible, and for many requirements essential, to use arrays of two or more dimensions. For example, a commercial organisation may have three different offices and require each office to return its quarterly sales figures. This information would commonly be displayed as a table, as illustrated in Figure 13.1(a).

In order to represent this requirement elegantly an array of three offices, each element of which is itself an array of four elements, each of which is an integer value, would be appropriate. Such a structure is known as a *two-dimensional array* and consists of an array whose component elements are themselves arrays. The data structure diagram of the *SalesReturns* structure is shown in Figure 13.1(b). The

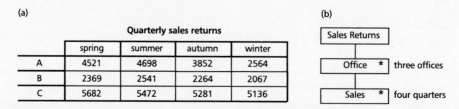

(a)

Quarterly sales returns

	spring	summer	autumn	winter
A	4521	4698	3852	2564
B	2369	2541	2264	2067
C	5682	5472	5281	5136

(b)

Sales Returns

| Office | * | three offices |

| Sales | * | four quarters |

Figure 13.1 (a) Quarterly sales table and (b) data structure diagram.

implementation of a class, called *Quarterly Sales*, to illustrate this example as far as the end of its constructor is as follows:

```
0001 // Filename QuarterlySales.java.
0002 // Illustrates the construction and use of a
0003 // two-dimensional array.
0004 //
0005 // Written for JOF Book Chapter 13.
0006 // Fintan Culwin, v0.1, August 1997.
0007
0008 import java.util.Random;
0009
0010 public class QuarterlySales extends Object {
0011
0012 private static int NUMBER_OF_OFFICES  = 3;
0013 private static int NUMBER_OF_QUARTERS = 4;
0014
0015 private int salesReturns[][] =
0016          new int [ NUMBER_OF_OFFICES] [ NUMBER_OF_QUARTERS];
0017
0018 private Random generator = new Random();
0019
0020
0021    public QuarterlySales() extends Object {
0022
0023    int thisOffice, thisQuarter;
0024
0025      for( thisOffice = 0;
0026           thisOffice < NUMBER_OF_OFFICES;
0027           thisOffice++) {
0028        for( thisQuarter = 0;
0029             thisQuarter < NUMBER_OF_QUARTERS;
0030             thisQuarter++) {
0031          salesReturns[ thisOffice] [ thisQuarter] = 2000 +
0032                          (int) (generator.nextDouble() * 5000.0);
0033        } // End for thisQuarter.
0034      } // End for thisOffice.
0035    } // End QuarterlySales default constructor.
```

On line 0015 The phrase **int** *salesReturns*[][] declares a two-dimensional array of **int**eger values. However, as with one-dimensional arrays, this merely states that it is a two-dimensional array; it does not actually construct the array. This is accomplished on line 0016 where the phrase **new int** [*NUMBER_OF_OFFICES*] [*NUMBER_OF_QUARTERS*]; constructs a new two-dimensional array with its bounds initialized as stated, effectively three and four. The constructor then, on lines 0025 to 0034, by means of a double definite iteration, places a random **int**eger value into each element of the array.

When this double loop iterates the outer loop index, *thisOffice*, will take the successive values 0, 1, 2. On each iteration of this loop the inner loop index, *thisQuarter*, will take the values 0, 1, 2, 3. The effect is that the body of the inner loop, on lines 0031 and 0032, will be executed 12 times with the two indexes having the pattern of values [0][0], [0][1], [0][2], [1][0], [1][1], ..., [2][2], [2][3]. As with one-dimensional arrays the first element of each dimension of the array is in the zeroth index location, so this pattern of indexes will ensure that each element is visited in turn.

This can be confirmed by the only other action of the package, a *toString()* action, which has a similar loop structure. The design of this action is as follows:

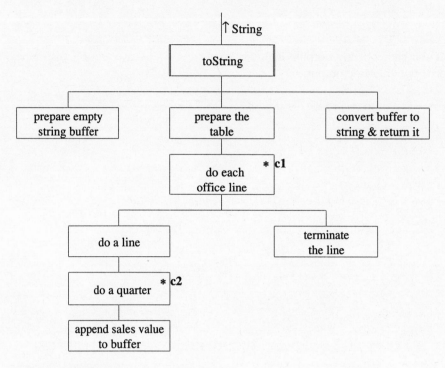

c1: For each office.
c2: For each quarter.

The sales figures from each office are to appear on its own line so the design indicates that each time an office is considered a line containing its sales figures is prepared. This is accomplished by appending each quarter's sales figure to a string buffer. Once a complete line has been added to the buffer it is terminated in order that the next line, if any, starts on a new line. The implementation of this design is as follows:

```
0038    public String toString() {
0039
0040    StringBuffer theBuffer = new StringBuffer();
0041    int thisOffice, thisQuarter;
0042
0043       for( thisOffice = 0;
0044           thisOffice < NUMBER_OF_OFFICES;
0045           thisOffice++) {
0046         for( thisQuarter = 0;
0047             thisQuarter < NUMBER_OF_QUARTERS;
0048             thisQuarter++) {
0049           theBuffer.append( Integer.toString(
0050                         sales[ thisOffice] [ thisQuarter]) +
0051                         "    ");
0052         } // End for thisQuarter.
```

```
0053          theBuffer.append("\n");
0054       } // End for thisOffice.
0055       return theBuffer.toString();
0056    } // End toString.
0057
0058 } // End class QuarterlySales;
```

The demonstration test harness for this class merely creates an instance of *Quarter-lySales* and subsequently outputs it to the screen. An illustrative run of this harness produced the following output:

```
Creating and outputting a QuarterlySales instance ...

6768 6318 6337 3525
4832 6942 6525 5248
5957 2689 3328 2217
```

The implementation of a suitable demonstration harness and the upgrading of the *toString()* action to produce table titles, as shown in Figure 13.1(a), will be left as an end-of-chapter exercise.

13.2 ▧ Ragged arrays

The two-dimensional array illustrated in the previous section was a regular array; that is, all of the component arrays which form its second dimension had exactly the same length. This is not always appropriate: for example, a salary structure may have two grades, A and B, with a different number of points on each grade. An example is given in Figure 13.2(a).

The data structure diagram for this table cannot indicate the size of a grade as the Lecturer A grade has four points but the Lecturer B grade has only two points. A class to implement this data structure is as follows:

```
0001 // Filename RaggedArray.java.
0002 // Illustrates the construction and use of a
0003 // two-dimensional ragged array.
0004 //
0005 // Written for JOF Book Chapter 13.
0006 // Fintan Culwin, v0.1, August 1997.
0007
0008 public class RaggedArray extends Object {
0009
```

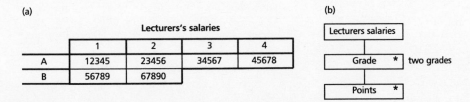

Figure 13.2   (a) Lecturers' salaries and (b) data structure diagram.

```
0010 private int salaries[][];
0011
0012    public RaggedArray() {
0013
0014       salaries = new int[ 2] [];
0015
0016       salaries[ 0] = new int[ 4];
0017       salaries[ 0] [ 0] = 12345; salaries[ 0] [ 1] = 23456;
0018       salaries[ 0] [ 2] = 34567; salaries[ 0] [ 3] = 45678;
0019
0020       salaries[ 1] = new int[ 2];
0021       salaries[ 1] [ 0] = 56789; salaries[ 1] [ 1] = 67890;
0022    } // End RaggedArray constructor.
0023
0024
0025    public String toString() {
0026
0027    StringBuffer    theBuffer = new StringBuffer();
0028    int thisIndex, anotherIndex;
0029
0030       for ( thisIndex = 0;
0031             thisIndex < salaries.length;
0032             thisIndex++) {
0033          for( anotherIndex = 0;
0034              anotherIndex < salaries[ thisIndex].length;
0035              anotherIndex++) {
0036            theBuffer.append( Integer.toString(
0037                         salaries[ thisIndex] [ anotherIndex]) +
0038                         "    ");
0039          } // End for anotherIndex.
0040          theBuffer.append("\n");
0041       } // End for thisIndex.
0042       return theBuffer.toString();
0043    } // End toString.
0044
0045 } // End class RaggedArray.
```

Line 0010 again declares a two-dimensional array of **int**eger values, this time called *salaries*, without actually intitializing the bounds of the dimensions. Within the constructor, on line 0014, the bounds of the first dimension are established. The phrase **new int**[2] [] states that there are two elements in the first dimension but does not initialize the bounds of either. This is accomplished on lines 0016 and 0020. For example, the phrase *salaries[0]*=**new int**[4] on line 0016 declares that the zeroth element of the first dimension of the array is itself a four element single-dimensional array of **int**s.

As the bounds of the array are not as clearly established in this example, the length attribute of the arrays is used on lines 0031 and 0034 to determine the number of times that each of the loops will iterate. The phrase on line 0031, *salaries*.length, determines the number of elements in the first dimension of the array, in this example two. On each iteration of this array the phrase on line 0034, *salaries[thisIndex]*.length, will determine the number of elements in each component array. In this example it will be evaluated twice, first with *thisIndex* having the value 0 and evaluating to 4, and second with *thisIndex* having the value 1 and evaluating to 2.

The output of a demonstration test harness is illustrated below. As with the *QuarterlySales* example above the implementation of the harness and the formatting of the table will be left as an end-of-chapter exercise.

```
           Creating and outputting a RaggedArray instance ...

    12345    23456    34567    45678
    56789    67890
```

13.3 ▧ Vectors

Arrays provide a convenient form of iterative storage for many applications but have one major limitation, which is that once the bounds of an array are declared there is no way in which they can be changed. To take an example, an application may want to store a list of e-mail addresses and names. If this were stored in an array then a decision would have to be made concerning how large the array should be and this will place a limit upon the number of names which could be stored.

One possible solution to this problem is to declare the array with an artificially large length, e.g. 1000 names. However, this would present two problems, the first being that it could not be guaranteed that a particular user would not want to store more than 1000 names. Second, for the vast majority of users this would be ridiculously large. Even if an average user were to store 250 names this would still imply that three quarters of the reserved storage space would never be used. Although the cost of computer memory is cheaper than it has ever been, and is expected to continue falling, the profligate waste of memory in this manner is very poor engineering.

What is required is an iterative data structure which can grow, and shrink, as and when required. A suitable data structure is provided by the java.util.Vector class; an instance of the Vector class can store an indeterminate number of heterogeneous elements. It actually has a limit upon the number of elements which can be stored at any instant but if, when it is full, an attempt is made to add another element it will automatically resize itself to provide more storage.

In order to illustrate the use of Vectors, and the other data structures in the rest of this and all of the next two chapters, a *Persons* class hierarchy will be used. The class hierarchy diagram for this class is given in Figure 13.3; the source for the hierarchy can be found in Appendix B.

The abstract *EmailPerson* class supports the most fundamental attribute of a person, so far as this hierarchy is concerned, their e-mail address; this is supplied as a distinct *EmailAddress* class. The two non-abstract classes *NamedPerson* and *PhonePerson* add the person's name and phone number respectively. Each class

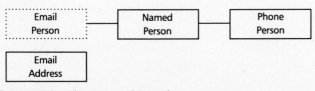

Figure 13.3 The *Persons* hierarchy.

supplies, in addition to a default and a suitable constructor, a *read()* action which allows its value to be input from the keyboard, an enquiry action to allow the value of its data attribute to be obtained and a *toString()* action to allow its value to be output.

To illustrate the use of the Vector class an application which maintains a list of personal contacts will be developed and presented. The main menu of this application will offer four options; to add a person's details to the list, to remove a person's details from the list, to show the contents of the list and to exit from the application. The first of these options, to add a person's details to the list, will offer a submenu which allows the user to indicate that they know the e-mail address and name only, or that they also know the phone number. The context clause and static declarations of this application, called *ContactList*, are as follows:

```
0001 // Filename ContactList.java.
0002 // Introduces the Vector class by storing
0003 // a list of people's details.
0004 //
0005 // Written for JOF book Chapter 13.
0006 // Fintan Culwin, v0.1, August 1997.
0007
0008 import Persons.*;
0009 import Menus.BasicMenu;
0010 import ValidatedInput;
0011
0012 import java.util.Vector;
0013 import java.io.*;
0014
0015 public class ContactList extends Object {
0016
0017 private static final char ADD_OPTION    = 'A';
0018 private static final char REMOVE_OPTION = 'B';
0019 private static final char SHOW_OPTION   = 'C';
0020 private static final char EXIT_OPTION   = 'D';
0021
0022 private static final char PART_OPTION   = 'A';
0023 private static final char FULL_OPTION   = 'B';
```

The implementation of this application makes use of the *BasicMenus* class which was introduced in Chapter 6. This class is imported in line 0009 and the manifest declarations on lines 0017 to 0023 are required to support the two menus which will be offered. The *Persons* package is imported on line 0008 to provide access to the objects which will be stored in the **Vector**. As this application will have to input a validated integer value from the keyboard the *ValidatedInput* class, introduced in Chapter 9, is imported on line 0010. The declarations of the *main()* action are as follows:

```
0029     public static void main(String args[]) {
0030
0031     String mainOptions[] = { "Add to contact list.",
0032                              "Remove from contact list",
0033                              "Show contact list.",
0034                              "Exit"};
0035
```

```
0036        String subOptions[]  = { "Add name and e-mail",
0037                                  "Add name, e-mail and phone number"};
0038
0039        BasicMenu mainMenu = new BasicMenu( "Contact list main menu",
0040                                            mainOptions,
0041                                            "");
0042
0043        BasicMenu subMenu = new BasicMenu( "Add contact sub menu",
0044                                           subOptions,
0045                                           "");
0046
0047        char   mainMenuChoice = ' ';
0048        Vector theList        = new Vector();
```

The two menus, the *mainMenu* and the *subMenu*, are constructed on lines 0031 to 0045 using the techniques which were introduced in Chapter 6, and a character variable to record the user's choice from the main menu is declared on line 0047. An instance of the Vector class, called *theList*, is constructed on line 0048. A newly constructed Vector contains no elements. The completion of the *main()* action is as follows:

```
0050            while ( mainMenuChoice != EXIT_OPTION ) {
0051               System.out.println( "\n\n");
0052               mainMenuChoice = mainMenu.offerMenuAsChar();
0053               System.out.println( "\n");
0054
0055               switch ( mainMenuChoice) {
0056
0057                  case ADD_OPTION:
0058                     addOption( theList, subMenu);
0059                     break;
0060
0061                  case REMOVE_OPTION:
0062                     removeOption( theList);
0063                     break;
0064
0065                  case SHOW_OPTION:
0066                     showOption( theList);
0067                     break;
0068
0069                  case EXIT_OPTION:
0070                     System.out.println( "Have a nice day");
0071                     break;
0072               } // End switch.
0073            } // End while.
0074         } // End main.
```

This is a menu/dispatch system corresponding to those first introduced in Chapter 6. Each **case** within the **switch** statement calls a local action passing on to it *theList* and in the case of the *addOption()* action the *subMenu* as well. The *addOption()*'s design requires it to offer the submenu and, depending upon the user's choice, construct an instance of the *NamedPerson* or *PhonePerson* class. Having constructed an instance its *read()* action can be called to input its details from the keyboard before it is added to the Vector. The implementation of this design is as follows:

```
0080        private void addOption( Vector       aList,
0081                                 BasicMenu theMenu) {
0082
0083        char        subMenuChoice;
0084        EmailPerson aPerson;
0085
0086           subMenuChoice = theMenu.offerMenuAsChar();
0087           if ( subMenuChoice == PART_OPTION) {
0088              aPerson = new NamedPerson();
0089           } else {
0090              aPerson = new PhonePerson();
0091           } // End if.
0092           aPerson.read();
0093           aList.addElement( aPerson);
0094        } // end addOption.
```

On line 0086 the submenu is offered to the user allowing them to indicate that they only have the person's e-mail address and name, or that they also have the person's phone number. If the user indicates that they only have partial details an instance of the *NamedPerson* class is constructed using its default constructor and assigned to the local *EmailPerson* variable *aPerson*, on line 0088. If the user indicates that they have a phone number then an instance of the *PhonePerson* class is constructed and assigned to *aPerson* on line 0090. As both the *namedPerson* and *PhonePerson* classes are extended instances of the *EmailPerson* class this is acceptable to Java as they both have an *is a* relationship with the *EmailPerson* class.

Having prepared a suitable instance in *aPerson* its *read()* action is called on line 0092. This is a dispatching call which will cause either the *NamedPerson* or *Phone-Person read()* action to be executed, as appropriate. Thus the user will be requested to input the details which they have indicated on the submenu. This completed instance is then added to the Vector by calling its *addElement()* action on line 0093. The *Vector addElement()* action will add a copy of the object supplied as an argument to the end of the existing list of objects. This can be confirmed when the *ContactList* application is executed by selecting the *Show contact list* option from the menu. The implementation of this action is as follows:

```
0116        static private void showOption( Vector aList) {
0117           System.out.println( aList);
0118        } // End showOption.
```

A sample interaction with the program, with the user's input emphasized, is as follows:

```
           Contact list main menu

A.   Add to contact list.
B.   Remove from contact list
C.   Show contact list.
D.   Exit

Please enter your choice : a
```

```
        Add contact sub menu

A.   Add name and e-mail
B.   Add name, e-mail and phone number

Please enter your choice : b
Please enter the email        : barney@bedrock.quarry.com
Please enter the name         : Barney Rubble
Please enter the phone number : 222-333-4444

        Contact list main menu

A.   Add to contact list.
B.   Remove from contact list
C.   Show contact list.
D.   Exit

Please enter your choice : c
[E-mail fred@bedrock.quarry.com Name : Fred Flintstone : Phone : 111-222-
3333, E-mail barney@bedrock.quarry.com Name : Barney Rubble : Phone 222-
333-4444]
```

The output indicates that Fred Flintstone's details were already stored in the structure before this fragment commenced. The output produced by this action is not very acceptable. The *toString()* action of the **Vector** class simply calls all the *toString()* actions of the objects which it contains and outputs them as a single string. This action will be upgraded below after the *removeOption()* action has been considered; the design of this action is as follows.

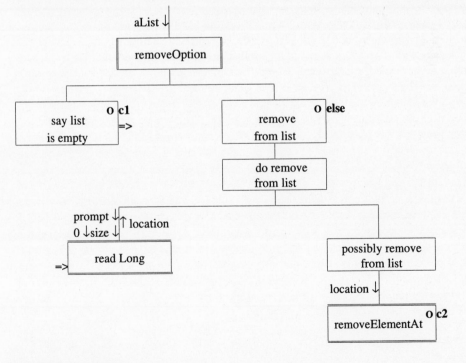

c1: If the list is empty.
c2: If the user did not abandon.

An overview of this design, assuming that the list is not empty, is that the user is invited to indicate the location in the list of the item to be removed, or to enter 0 to abandon the operation. Once a valid, non-zero, input is obtained the Vector *removeElementAt()* action is called passing the user's input as the location of the information to be removed from the list. The implementation of this design is as follows:

```
0098        private void removeOption( Vector aList) {
0099
0100          int toRemove = 0;
0101
0102            if ( aList.isEmpty()) {
0103              System.out.println( "The list is empty!" +
0104                    " So it is not possible to remove a person.");
0105            } else {
0106              toRemove = (int) ValidatedInput.readLong(
0107                              "Enter location of information to remove" +
0108                              "(Or 0 to abandon) : ",
0109                              0, aList.size());
0110              if ( toRemove != 0) {
0111                aList.removeElementAt( --toRemove);
0112              } // End if.
0113            } // End if.
0114        } // End removeOption.
```

On line 0102 the *aList isEmpty()* action is used to determine if the list contains any elements. On line 0109 the *aList size()* action is used to find out the number of elements in the list, which is then passed to the *readLong()* action as the upper limit which it can accept from the user. On line 0111 the *aList removeElementAt()* action is used to remove an element from the specified location in the list. As with arrays, the first location in a Vector is at index location 0, so the value *toRemove* has to be pre-decremented. So, if the user wants to remove the first name in the list they will input 1; this will be decremented to 0 before being passed to the action on line 0111, causing the zeroth element to be removed.

For the user, indicating which element is to be removed by specifying its location within the list is not particularly convenient. A more acceptable technique which allows the user to specify which entry to delete by using its e-mail address will be introduced in the next section.

This application has introduced the use of the Vector class and has introduced five of its actions: the default constructor, isEmpty(), addElement(), removeElementAt() and size(). A more complete list of the actions supplied by this class is given in Table 13.1.

The capacity and increment arguments, or defaults, for the constructors indicate the initial capacity of the Vector and the amount by which it is to grow when it becomes full. If no increment value is specified then the Vector's capacity will be doubled every time it becomes full. Details of the other actions of the Vector class can be found in the API documentation supplied with Java environments.

13.4 ▓ Iterator classes

The problem with the show list option, noted in the previous section, could be solved by a definite iteration which obtains each element in turn from the Vector

Table 13.1 Actions from the Vector class.

Action	Note
`public Vector();`	Default constructor, capacity 10 and increment 10
`public Vector( int initialCapacity);`	Alternative constructor specifying initial capacity
`public Vector( int initialCapacity,` `            int capacityIncrement);`	Alternative constructor specifying initial capacity and amount to increment by
`public final synchronized void` `        addElement( Object toAdd);`	Add a copy of the object supplied as an argument to the end of the vector, reallocating if required

`public final synchronized void`
`     insertElementAt( Object toAdd,`
`                 int    index)`
` throws ArrayIndexOutOfBoundsException;`
	Add a copy of the object supplied as an argument to the end of the vector at the location specified. Throws the exception if the location is beyond the current bounds (0 .. size())

`public final synchronized void`
`        setElementAt( Object toAdd,`
`                 int    index)`
` throws ArrayIndexOutOfBoundsException;`
	Replaces the object at the location specified with the object supplied. Throws the exception if the location is beyond the current bounds (0 .. size())

`public final synchronized Object`
`          elementAt( Object toAdd,`
`                 int    index)`
` throws ArrayIndexOutOfBoundsException;`
	Return a copy of the element at the location specified. Throws the exception if the location is beyond the current bounds (0 .. size())

`public final synchronized Object`
`       firstElement( Object toAdd,`
`                 int    index)`
`     throws NoSuchElementException;`
	Return a copy of the first element in the Vector. Throws the exception if the Vector is empty

`public final synchronized Object`
`        lastElement( Object toAdd,`
`                 int    index)`
`    thrown NoSuchElementException;`
	Return a copy of the last element in the Vector. Throws the exception if the Vector is empty

`public final synchronized void` `             removeAllElements()`	Empties the Vector by throwing away all elements

`public final synchronized void`
`       removeElementAt( int index)`
` throws ArrayIndexOutOfBoundsException;`
	Removes the element at the location specified, closing up the Vector. Throws the exception if the location is beyond the current bounds (0 .. size())

`public final int size();`	Returns the number of elements in the Vector
`public final boolean isEmpty();`	Returns true if the Vector is empty. false otherwise

using the *elementAt()* action and outputting it, preceded by its location. For example:

```
0116    private void showOption( Vector aList) {
0117
0118    int        thisElement;
0119    EmailPerson fromList;
0120
0121        for( thisElement = 0; thisElement < aList.size(); thisElement++){
```

```
0122              fromList = (EmailPerson) aList.elementAt( thisElement);
0123              System.out.println( (thisElement + 1) + "   " + fromList);
0124        } // End for.
0125    } // End showOption.
```

The elements within the **Vector** are indexed from location 0 but have to be presented to the user indexed from location 1. To accomplish this the value of the loop index is incremented, on line 0123, as it is output. Using the illustrative data above, this action would produce the following output:

```
1  E-mail fred@bedrock.quarry.com Name : Fred Flintstone Phone : 111-222-3333
2  E-mail barney@bedrock.quarry.com Name : Barney Rubble Phone : 222-333-4444
```

However, for some data structures, obtaining each element in sequence in this manner is not possible or appropriate, so Java supplies an iterator facility called **Enumeration** which can be used to traverse a structure. One advantage of using an iterator is that the precise data structure being used to implement the iterative storage becomes irrelevant so long as it can supply an **Enumeration** object. So, if the **Vector** in this example were at some time during maintenance replaced by some other type of storage, the *show-Option()* action above would be broken. However, by using an **Enumeration** object, as will be illustrated below, it will still work so long as the new data structure class supplies an action called **elements()** which returns an instance of an **Enumeration** class.

The **Enumeration** facility is defined as an *interface*, not as a *class*, a concept which will be fully explained in the next chapter. A class which complies with the **Enumeration** interface must supply two actions, a **boolean** hasMoreElements() action which returns **true** as long as there are more elements to iterate through, and a nextElement() action which returns the next **Object** in sequence from the structure. The first call of the **nextElements()** action of a newly constructed **Enumeration** object will return the first element from the structure, or throw a **NoSuchElementException** if the structure is empty. Each subsequent call will return the next element from the structure, or throw the exception if all elements have already been obtained.

The **Vector** class supplies an **elements()** action which returns an **Enumeration** object, allowing the *showOption* action of the *ContactList* application to be implemented for a third time, assuming that the java.util.Elements interface has been **import**ed as follows:

```
0116    private void showOption( Vector aList) {
0117
0118    int         thisElement = 1;
0119    EmailPerson fromList;
0120    Enumeration contacts     = aList.elements();
0121
0122       while( contacts.hasMoreElements()) {
0123          fromList = (EmailPerson) contacts.nextElement();
0124          System.out.println( thisElement + "   " + fromList);
0125       } // End while;
0126    } // End showOption.
```

The **Enumeration** object, called *contacts*, is obtained on line 0120 from the **Vector** *aList* using its **elements()** action. The *hasMoreElements()* action of this object is then used to control an indefinite iteration on lines 0122 to 0125 within which the *nextElement()* is obtained from the *contacts* object on line 0123 and output on line 0124. The Enumeration *nextElement()* action returns a value of the **Object** class which has to be cast, as shown on 0123, to its known actual class, *EmailPerson*, in order for Java to allow the assignment. The output from this action would be identical to that produced by the previous version.

13.5 ▩ Hashtables

The *ContactList* application developed in the previous section using a **Vector** will be redeveloped in this section by making use of a pre-supplied data structure called a **Hashtable**. As mentioned above, when using a **Vector** the remove name option is implemented in an inelegant manner, requiring the user to input the location of the element in the list which is to be removed.

It would be possible for this action to be replaced with one which requires the user to input the e-mail address of the person who is to be removed from the list. However, this would require a *sequential search*. Each element in turn would have to be obtained from the **Vector** and its e-mail attribute compared with the e-mail to be removed. If there was a match then the element could be removed, otherwise, once all elements in the **Vector** have been examined, the user could be informed that a person with that e-mail address is not present in the list.

This approach would be acceptable for small **Vector**s, but as the list which is being maintained becomes larger and larger it becomes increasingly inefficient. A more elegant and efficient solution would be to use a **Hashtable** instead of a **Vector** instance to store the list. In order for a **Hashtable** to be used, for any requirement, the data elements which are to be stored in it have to have a unique identifying *key*. The key value has to be specified when an element is stored in the **Hashtable** and can subsequently be used to identify which element is to be retrieved, or removed, from the table. In the example being considered the e-mail address of the personal details being stored in the list is a hopefully unique identifying key.

As the key value identifies each element uniquely it is not possible for two different elements in a table to have the same key. This consideration will correct a second fault in the previous version of the *ContactList* application. In that version it was possible for two entries in the list to have the same e-mail address. Again this could have been avoided by searching through the existing list before adding the new element, and again this would become increasingly unacceptable as the amount of information grows. When using a **Hashtable**, a request to store an element with a key which is already present will cause any existing element to be replaced by the new one.

The overall structure of the *ContactList* application will not change, but the context clause will have to **import** the java.util.Hashtable class and the declaration of *aList* will have to construct an empty **Hashtable** instance as follows:

```
0048 Hashtable aList = new Hashtable();
```

The design of the **Hashtable** version of the *removeOption()* action is as

follows:

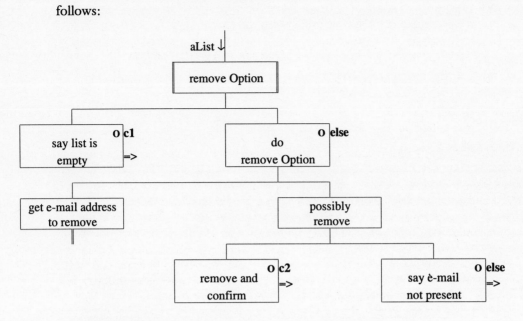

c1: If list is empty.
c2: If element with e-mail to remove is present.

The basis of the design, assuming the list is not empty, is to obtain the e-mail address of the person whose details are to be removed. If an element with this e-mail is present in the list the details can be removed, otherwise the user is informed that the requested details could not be found in the list. The implementation of this design is as follows:

```
0106 private void removeOption( Hashtable aList) {
0107
0108 String   toRemove = "";
0109 boolean emailOK = false;
0110
0111    if ( aList.isEmpty()) {
0112       System.out.println( "The list is empty! " +
0113            "So it is not possible to remove a person.");
0114    } else {
0115       while ( ! emailOK) {
0116          try {
0117             System.out.print(
0118               "Please enter the email address of the person to remove :");
0119             System.out.flush();
0120             toRemove = new String( theKeyboard.readLine()).trim();
0121             emailOK  = true;
0122          } catch ( IOException exception) {
0123             System.out.println(
0124                     "Sorry there seems to be a problem!\n" +
0125                     "Could you please try again?");
0126          } // End try/ catch.
0127       } // End while.
0128
```

```
0129        if ( aList.containsKey( toRemove)) {
0130            System.out.print( aList.get( toRemove));
0131            aList.remove( toRemove);
0132            System.out.println( " ... has been removed from the list.");
0133        } else {
0134            System.out.println( "That email address is not in the list.");
0135        } // End if.
0136    } // End if.
0137 } // End removeOption.
```

The *aList* isEmpty() action is used on line 0111 to make sure that the list contains at least one element before continuing. If the list is not empty the e-mail address *toRemove* is obtained, using a standard String input dialog, on lines 0115 to 0127. On line 0129 the e-mail address to be removed is used as the argument of the *aList* containsKey() action; this action will return **true** if an element in the list has the key specified and **false** otherwise. If it returns **true** then the details of the existing entry in the list are obtained on line 0130, using the *aList* get() action, and output before the new details are removed from the list using the *aList* remove() action on line 0131. Should the *containsKey()* action on line 0129 return **false** then a suitable message is output on line 0134. A sample interaction with this option is as follows:

```
        Contact list main menu

A.    Add to contact list.
B.    Remove from contact list
C.    Show contact list.
D.    Exit

Please enter your choice : c

1  E-mail fred@bedrock.quarry.com Name : Fred Flintstone Phone : 111-222-3333
2  E-mail barney@bedrock.quarry.com Name : Barney Rubble Phone : 222-333-4444

Contact list main menu

A.    Add to contact list.
B.    Remove from contact list
C.    Show contact list.
D.    Exit

Please enter your choice : b

Please enter the email address of the person to remove : fred@bedrock.quarry.com

E-mail fred@bedrock.quarry.com Name : Fred Flintstone Phone : 111-222-3333 ...
has been removed from the list.
```

The first option of the application, to add a person's details, will also require a redesign and reimplementation. The Hashtable put() action requires as arguments a key and an element; if the key is not already present in the table then the element is added. However, if the key is already present the existing contents of the identified element are replaced with the new contents. At a very minimum the user should be made aware of this and ideally should be asked to confirm the action before the details are replaced. This design will only inform the user; upgrading it to obtain a confirmation will be left as an end-of-chapter exercise.

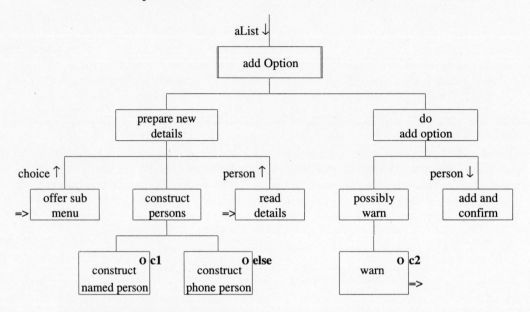

c1: If user indicates partial details.
c2: If the e-mail is already present in the list.

The basis of the design is to obtain a suitable new *EmailPerson* instance using exactly the same technique as was used in the previous version of the *addOption()*. However, before the details are added to the list a check is made and, if a person with the same e-mail address is already in the list, a warning is issued before the new details are added to the list. The implementation of this design is as follows:

```
0082        private void addOption( Hashtable aList,
0083                                BasicMenu theMenu) {
0084
0085        char        subMenuChoice;
0086        EmailPerson aPerson;
0087
0088            subMenuChoice = theMenu.offerMenuAsChar();
0089            if ( subMenuChoice == PART_OPTION) {
0090               aPerson = new NamedPerson();
0091            } else {
0092               aPerson = new PhonePerson();
0093            } // End if.
0094            aPerson.read();
0095
0096            if ( aList.containsKey( aPerson.eMailIs())) {
0097               System.out.println( aList.get( aPerson.eMailIs()) +
0098                            " ... has been removed.");
0099            } // End if.
0100
0101            aList.put( aPerson.eMailIs(), aPerson);
```

```
0102          System.out.println( aPerson + " ... has been added");
0103       } // end addOption.
```

The first part of this implementation, as far as line 0095, is identical with the previous version. On line 0096 the *aList* containsKey() action is used to find out if an element with the e-mail specified is already present in the list, *EmailPerson eMailIs()* enquiry action being used to obtain the key value for the new *Persons* instance. If the key is already present the details of the element which is about to be removed are output. Following this, in all cases, the new details are added using the *aList* put() action on line 0101. The put() action requires the key value and the element value to be supplied, as shown. Finally the action is closed by informing the user that the details have been added to the list. A possible interaction with this action, showing a new element replacing an existing element, might be as follows:

```
        Contact list main menu

A.    Add to contact list.
B.    Remove from contact list
C.    Show contact list.
D.    Exit

Please enter your choice : a

        Add contact sub menu

A.    Add name and e-mail
B.    Add name, e-mail and phone number

Please enter your choice : b

Please enter the email        : wilma@bedrock.quarry.com
Please enter the name         : Wilma Flintstone
Please enter the phone number : 555-666-7777

E-mail : wilma@bedrock.quarry.com Name : Wilma Flintstone ... has been
removed.

E-mail : wilma@bedrock.quarry.com Name : Wilma Flintstone  Phone: 555-
666-7777 ... has been added.
```

The implementation of the remaining *ContactList* action, *showOption()*, is identical to the third version of the *showOption()* action presented above. The Hashtable class supplies an elements() action returning an Enumeration instance, which can be used to iterate through the contents of the structure as before. As suggested by the illustrative output above there is no particular order in the sequence in which the elements are retrieved from the structure, a shortcoming which will be put right in the next chapter.

The *ContactList* implementation in this section has used a Hashtable constructor and its IsEmpty(), put(), get(), elements() actions. A summary of these actions, and of some of its other actions, is given in Table 13.2.

The capacity argument to the constructors indicates the initial capacity of the table and the load factor determines the point at which the table should reorganize itself.

Table 13.2 The actions of the Hashtable class.

Action	Note
`public Hashtable();`	Default constructor, capacity 101 and load factor 0.75
`public Hashtable( int initialCapacity);`	Alternative constructor specifying initial capacity and load factor 0.75
`public Hashtable( int initialCapacity,` `              int loadFactor;`	Alternative constructor specifying initial capacity and load factor.

`public final synchronized Object`
`            put( Object key,`
`                Object value);`
	Add a copy of the object supplied as value to the table using the key specified, replacing any existing element with the same key. Returns the old value of the object or null

`public final synchronized Object` `            get( Object key);`	Returns the Object stored with the key in the table, or null if no such object is stored.
`public synchronized Object` `            remove( Object key);`	Removes the element associated with the key, if any
`public synchronized boolean` `        containsKey( Object key);`	Returns **true** if an element in the table is associated with the key specified, or **false** otherwise
`public synchronized void clear();`	Empties the table of all elements
`public boolean IsEmpty();`	True if the table is empty
`public int size();`	Returns the number of elements in the table
`public synchronized Enumeration` `            elements();`	Returns an Enumeration instance which can be used to iterate through the table, in no defined sequence
`public synchronized Enumeration` `            keys();`	Returns an Enumeration which can be used to iterate through the table's keys. in no defined sequence

Once the load factor has been reached the table will allocate more space and reorganize its contents to maintain efficiency.

When using a Hashtable the class which is used to supply key values must have hashCode() and equals() actions defined. The Object class, from which all Java classes are implicitly extended, itself defines primitive versions of these actions, but in most cases they should be overloaded.

The characteristics of a suitable *hashCode()* action are beyond the scope of this book. The default is to base the code on the instance's memory address which is adequate, if inefficient, for most situations. An *equals()* action should be implemented for developer supplied classes which compares the appropriate attribute of the instances for equality. For example, if an *equals()* action were to be developed for the *Persons* hierarchy it should decide that two instances were equal if they both have the same e-mail address irrespective of the contents of the other attributes. The default would be to decide equality on the basis of the addresses of the objects so that two objects are considered equal only if they are the same object. Fortunately for the examples in this chapter the String class overloads the two actions with suitable implementations.

Summary

- Data structures contain an iteration of data elements; different structures have different techniques for storing, retrieving and removing elements.

- Arrays can be one dimensional, two dimensional or *n* dimensional. Multi-dimensional arrays can be ragged.

- A Vector is an unbounded data structure which can grow as required.

- An Enumeration class can be used to iterate through data structures.

- A Hashtable is a data structure where each element is associated with a unique key.

- A class which is to be used as a Hashtable key should overload the Object *hashCode()* and *equals()* actions.

Exercises

13.1   Obtain the source code of the two array example classes and reimplement the *toString()* actions to present the tables as illustrated in the chapter.

13.2   Extend the *Persons* hierarchy, e.g. by adding a class which encapsulates the person's snail mail address. Demonstrate the correct implementation of the extension and then upgrade one of the *ContactList* implementations to allow instances of this class to be stored.

13.3   Extend one of the *ContactList* implementations to allow the information to be stored in, and loaded from, a file.

13.4   Extend both *ContactList* implementations to offer a search facility. The user should be invited to input an e-mail address and the program should display the full details, or inform the user that a person with that e-mail is not in the list. Attempt to demonstrate that as the number of elements stored in the structure increases the Hashtable implementation outperforms the Vector implementation.

13.5   Reimplement the add option from the Hashtable *ContactList* implementation so that if an element with the specified e-mail address is already stored in the list it will only be replaced following an explicit confirmation from the user.

13.6   Reimplement one of the *ContactList* versions to take advantage of the *AdaptingMenu* class, so that, for example, the remove from list option is not available when the list is empty.

13.7   A library book has a unique *acquisition number* attribute and *class number*, *author* and *title* attributes. Design, implement and test a class hierarchy to model a library book. Then adapt the *ContactList* application to provide a *LibraryList* application.

Chapter fourteen

Developer supplied data structures

The data structures introduced in the previous chapter had two major problems which might limit their use, or make their use dangerous. First, it was possible for an object of any class to be stored in the structure at any time. For example, although the *ContactList* application was only supposed to store instances from the *Persons* package this was not enforced. It would be possible for a maintenance developer, or indeed the original developer, to avoid this limitation and store in the list instances of any class. This may not seem a sensible thing to do but the errors which creep into programs rarely have a sensible cause. Increased security can be enforced by ensuring that only instances of a specific class, which includes extended instances of the class, can be stored in a structure.

The second limitation concerns the pattern by which the instances are added to and retrieved from the structure. In the first version of the *ContactList* application, using a Vector, new elements were added to the end of the list and elements could be removed from any location in the list. In the second version, using a Hashtable, there was no consideration of ordering in the list; all that was important was the key value of the instance being added. Many applications require that the elements which are stored in a list are added, maintained and retrieved in a particular sequence. Examples include *queues* where elements can only be added to the end of the structure and removed from the front, *stacks* where elements can only be added and retrieved from the front, and *ordered lists* where the elements are maintained in a sequence determined by their keys.

These structures could be implemented by extending the pre-supplied Vector and Hashtable classes, as was done in the previous chapter. However, this would add a potential insecurity into the implementation. For example, if a Vector was extended to implement a queue it would be expected that a developer would only add elements at the end and remove elements from the front. However, as an extended Vector the queue structure would inherit all the other Vector operations which allow elements to be added or removed in the middle of the list. In order to provide a secure implementation of a queue, or stack, or ordered list, it is necessary to encapsulate an instance of a *Vector*, or array, or *Hashtable*, within the class and only export suitable operations from it.

The previous chapter also briefly introduced the use of Interfaces. An Interface is a mechanism which allows the statement of *what* actions a class supplies to be more clearly separated from the details of *how* the class implements those actions. The specification of what a class does is implicit in its class diagram and the action signatures from its implementation. The specification of how a class does what it does is contained within the implementation of its actions. It is possible, and in many cases desirable, for a number of different *how*s to be associated with a single *what*.

For example the Enumeration actions specify *what* actions can be used to iterate through the contents of a structure. The different implementations of the Enumeration actions in the Vector and Hashtable classes state *how* these actions are implemented in ways appropriate to the nature of the structure. For a user of an Enumerated class, details of *how* the actions are implemented are irrelevant; all that is necessary is to know *what* actions are supplied. In the next chapter this will be illustrated further when a set of Enumeration actions are introduced for a developer supplied data structure.

14.1 ▨ The abstract *UnorderedList* class

This section will introduce two abstract classes which will subsequently be used to implement the *Queue* and *Stack* classes. The class hierarchy diagram for this part of the hierarchy is given in Figure 14.1. The classes are contained within a package called *Generics*; a *generic* data structure is one whose instances are capable of containing only a specified class of objects. Should an attempt be made to add an instance of an inappropriate class to the structure, a *GenericException* will be thrown.

The abstract *GenericStructure* class is responsible, upon construction, to record the base class of the elements which are to be stored in the structure. It also provides an action which will determine if an element is, or is not, compatible with the nominated class.

The *UnorderedList* class encapsulates an instance of the Vector class and makes available a number of protected and public actions which the *Queue* and *Stack* classes use to implement their essential behaviour. The class diagram of the *GenericStructure* class is presented in Figure 14.2.

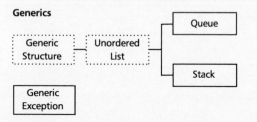

Figure 14.1   The *UnorderedList* class hierarchy diagram.

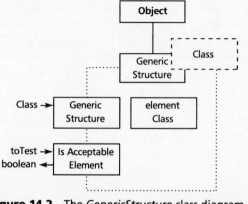

Figure 14.2   The *GenericStructure* class diagram.

This class diagram introduces a new convention to illustrate a generic structures. The dashed box at the top right of the *GenericStructure* component indicates that this class requires a type parameter upon construction which will determine which Class the structure will be able to store. The *GenericStructure* constructor requires an argument of the Class class which it subsequently uses to check that the *toTest* argument of the *IsAcceptableElement()* action is of a compatible class, returning **true** if so and **false** otherwise. The implementation of this class is as follows:

```
0001  // Filename GenericStructure.java.
0002  // Abstract base class for a collection of List
0003  // actions which will implement a number of
0004  // different data structures.
0005  //
0006  // Written for JOF book, chapter 14.
0007  // Fintan Culwin, v0.1, August 1997.
0008
0009  package Generics;
0010
0011  abstract class GenericStructure extends Object {
0012
0013  private Class elementClass;
0014
0015     protected GenericStructure( Class theElementClass) {
0016        super();
0017        elementClass = theElementClass;
0018     } // end GenericStructure constructor.
0019
0020
0021     protected boolean isAcceptableElement( Object toTest) {
0022        return elementClass.isInstance( toTest);
0023     } // End isAcceptableElement.
0024
0025  } // End GenericStructure.
```

The Class class was introduced in Chapter 12 as a Java system class which describes the nature of a class. Given an instance of any class, an instance of the Class class describing it can be obtained with its getClass() action. The constructor takes as an argument an instance of the Class class and stores this in the Class instance variable *elementClass*.

The only action of this class uses the **boolean** *isInstance()*[1] action of the encapsulated *elementClass*. This action will return **true** if the class of the argument supplied is the same as the class described by the *elementClass*, or any of its child classes, and **false** otherwise. The *isAcceptableElement()* action will be used by the *add()* action of the *UnorderedList* class whose class diagram is given in Figure 14.3.

The generic nature of the *GenericStructure* class is inherited by its child classes and if the *UnorderedList* class were not presented in the context of its parent it would require a generic qualification. The constructor action again requires a Class descriptor which will determine the nature of the elements which can be stored in non-abstract extensions of the class. To implement the list it contains an encapsulated Vector instance, called *theList*. The difference between an *obtain()* action and a *remove()*

---

[1] The *isInstance()* action is not present in the JDK 1.0 release. Appendix B2 contains an alternative implementation of this action which can be used with the JDK 1.0 release.

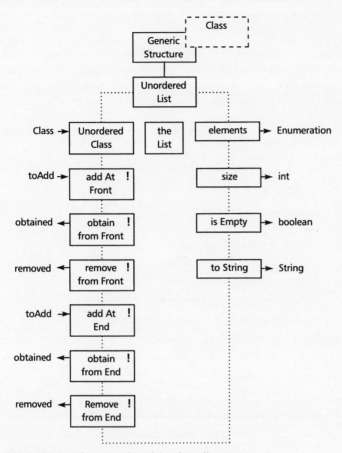

Figure 14.3   The *UnorderedList* class diagram.

action is that an obtain action will return an element from the structure without deleting it, whilst a remove action will return and delete it from the structure. The implementation of this design, as far as the end of the constructor, is as follows:

```
0001 // Filename UnorderedList.java.
0002 // Abstract class supplying the actions to
0003 // support the Stack and Queue classes.
0004 //
0005 // Written for JOF book, chapter 14.
0006 // Fintan Culwin, v0.1, August 1997.
0007
0008 package Generics;
0009
0010 import Generics.GenericException;
0011
0012 import java.util.Vector;
0013 import java.util.Enumeration;
0014 import java.util.NoSuchElementException;
0015 import java.lang.ArrayIndexOutOfBoundsException;
0016
0017
```

```
0018 abstract class UnorderedList extends GenericStructure {
0019
0020 private Vector theList = new Vector();
0021
0022    protected UnorderedList( Class theBaseClass) {
0023       super( theBaseClass);
0024    } // end UnorderedList constructor.
```

The implementation of the constructor, on lines 0022 to 0024, indicates that it dispatches immediately to its **super** (*GenericStructure*) constructor passing on its argument. The instance attribute *theList* of the Vector class is constructed on line 0020. The design of the *addAtFront()* action is as follows:

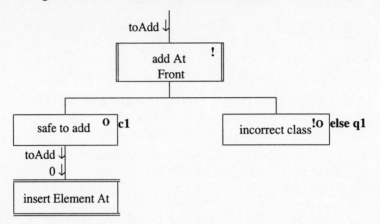

c1: If toAdd is of an acceptable class.
q1: Explicit GenericException.

The action will throw a *GenericException* if the class of the element *toAdd* is not acceptable, otherwise it calls *theList* insertElementAt() action to put the element at the front of the *theList* Vector. The implementation of this design is as follows:

```
0027        protected void addAtFront( Object toAdd) {
0028            if ( isAcceptableElement( toAdd)) {
0029                theList.insertElementAt( toAdd, 0);
0030            } else {
0031                throw new GenericException();
0032            } // End if.
0033        } // End addAtFront.
```

The design and implementation of the two remaining *front* actions are as follows:

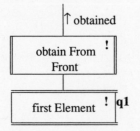

q1: Implicit NoSuchElement Exception.

```
0036          protected Object obtainFromFront() throws NoSuchElementException {
0037              return theList.firstElement();
0038          } // End removeFromFront.
```

p1: Assume element can be removed.   q1: Implicit ArrayIndex exception.
a1: Admit element could not be removed.   q2: Explicit NoSuchElement exception.

```
0043          protected Object removeFromFront() throws NoSuchElementException {
0044
0045          Object hold;
0046
0047              try {
0048                  hold = theList.firstElement();
0049                  theList.removeElementAt( 0);
0050                  return hold;
0051              } catch (ArrayIndexOutOfBoundsException exception) {
0052                  throw new NoSuchElementException();
0053              } // End try/catch.
0054          } // End removeFromFront.
```

The design and implementation of the *removeFromFront()* action has to *hold* the element obtained from the **Vector** with **firstElement()** whilst it is removed with **removeElementAt()**. It is possible for the index argument supplied to the **removeElementAt()** action to specify an element beyond the end of the list or any element in an empty list. This will cause an **ArrayIndexOutOfBoundsException** to be thrown which must be caught. In this implementation the exception will only be thrown if the list is empty and causes a **NoSuchElementException** to be thrown from the action.

The design and implementation of the *end* actions are essentially identical, using *theList* size() action to specify the element at the end of the **Vector** where appropriate. Their implementations are as follows:

```
0057          protected void addAtEnd( Object toAdd) {
0058              if ( isAcceptableElement( toAdd)) {
0059                  theList.addElement( toAdd);
0060              } else {
0061                  throw new GenericException();
0062              } // End if.
0063          } // End addAtEnd.
0064
0065
```

```
0066        protected Object obtainFromEnd() throws NoSuchElementException {
0067           return theList.lastElement();
0068        } // End removeFromFront.
0069
0070        protected Object removeFromEnd() throws NoSuchElementException {
0071
0072        Object hold;
0073
0074           try {
0075              hold = theList.lastElement();
0076              theList.removeElementAt( theList.size());
0077              return hold;
0078           } catch (ArrayIndexOutOfBoundsException exception) {
0079              throw new NoSuchElementException();
0080           } // End try/catch.
0081        } // End removeFromEnd.
```

The **public** actions make available the corresponding actions from the encapsulated *theList* instance, apart from the *toString()* action which uses an Enumeration to provide a numbered list of the contents. The implementation of these actions is as follows:

```
0088        public Enumeration elements() {
0089           return theList.elements();
0090        } // End elements.
0091
0092
0093        public int size() {
0094           return theList.size();
0095        } // End size.
0096
0097
0098        public boolean isEmpty() {
0099           return theList.isEmpty();
0100        } // End isEmpty.
0101
0102
0103        public String toString(){
0104
0105        int          thisElement = 0;
0106        Object       fromList;
0107        StringBuffer buffer      = new StringBuffer();
0108        Enumeration  contents     = theList.elements();
0109
0110           while( contents.hasMoreElements() ) {
0111              fromList = contents.nextElement();
0112              buffer.append( ++thisElement + "  " + fromList +"\n");
0113           } // End while.
0114           return buffer.toString();
0115        } // End toString.
```

14.2 ▓ The *Queue* class

The essential characteristic of a queue is that elements can only be *add*ed at the end of the queue and can only be *retrieve*d from the front. The actions are shown in the class diagram in Figure 14.4.

These actions are implemented by making the appropriate actions from the *UnorderedList* public, as follows:

```
0001 // Filename Queue.java.
0002 // A generic queue structure allowing elements of the
0003 // specified class to be removed from the front and
0004 // added to the end only.
0005 //
0006 // Written for JOF book, chapter 14.
0007 // Fintan Culwin, v0.1, August 1997.
0008
0009 package Generics;
0010
0011 import Generics.GenericException;
0012
0013 import java.util.NoSuchElementException;
0014
0015
0016 public class Queue extends UnorderedList {
0017
0018     public Queue( Class theBaseClass) {
0019         super( theBaseClass);
0020     } // end Queue constructor.
0021
0022     public void add( Object toAdd) throws GenericException {
0023         super.addAtEnd( toAdd);
0024     } // End add.
0025
0026     public Object retrieve() throws NoSuchElementException {
0027         return super.removeFromFront();
0028     } // End retrieve.
0029
0030 } // End Queue.
```

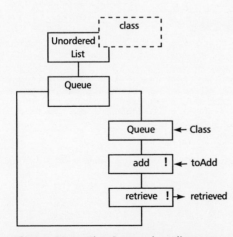

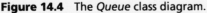

Figure 14.4 The *Queue* class diagram.

A context diagram for a demonstration harness for the *Queue* class, using a queue of *Persons* as introduced in the last chapter, is given in Figure 14.5. The diagram indicates that the client program contains a single *Queue* instance, called *demoQueue*, configured to contain *EmailPerson* instances. This is indicated by the angle brackets (<>) in its instance marker. The *demoQueue* contains an iteration of anonymous *EMailPerson* instances, indicated by the doubling of the hexagon marker and the absence of a name within it. The inversion of the *EmailPerson* hierarchy emphasizes that the queue contains instances of the *Persons* package, rather than specific instances of any of its classes.

The implementation of the *QueueDemo* harness is as follows:

```
0001 // Filename QueueDemo.java.
0002 // Demonstration harness of the Queue data
0003 // structure, using a queue of e-mail persons.
0004 //
0005 // Written for JOF book, chapter 14.
0006 // Fintan Culwin, v0.1, August 1997.
0007
0008
0009 import Generics.Queue;
0010 import Generics.GenericException;
0011 import Persons.*;
0012
0013 class QueueDemo {
0014
0015     public static void main(String args[]) {
0016
0017     NamedPerson demoNamedPerson= new NamedPerson();
```

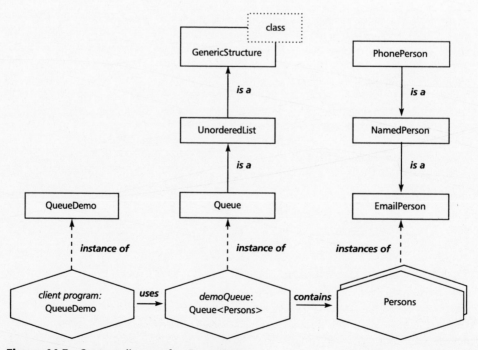

Figure 14.5 Context diagram for *QueueDemo*.

```
0018    PhonePerson demoPhonePerson;
0019    String      demoString;
0020
0021    Queue       demoQueue = new Queue( demoNamedPerson.getClass());
0022
0023
0024    System.out.println( "\tQueue Demonstration Program\n\n");
0025
0026    System.out.println( "Adding three instances to the queue ...");
0027
0028    demoNamedPerson = new NamedPerson( "anorak@boring.com",
0029                                      "Andy Anorak");
0030    demoQueue.add( demoNamedPerson);
0031
0032    demoPhonePerson = new PhonePerson( "geek@nowhere.edu",
0033                                      "Gary Geek",
0034                                      "111-2222");
0035    demoQueue.add( demoPhonePerson);
0036
0037
0038    demoNamedPerson = new NamedPerson( "sad@lost.org",
0039                                      "Suzie Sad");
0040    demoQueue.add( demoNamedPerson);
0041
0042    System.out.println( "\nShowing the queue ...\n");
0043    System.out.println( demoQueue);
0044
0045    System.out.println( "\n Retrieving and showing ...\n");
0046    System.out.println( demoQueue.retrieve());
0047    System.out.println( "\n The queue now contains " +
0048                    demoQueue.size() + " elements.");
0049
0050    System.out.println( "\nAttempting to add an element" +
0051                        "of an inappropriate class ...");
0052    try {
0053        demoString = new String( "Doesn't matter!");
0054        demoQueue.add( demoString);
0055        System.out.println( "No exception thrown ... " +
0056                            "which is incorrect.");
0057    } catch ( GenericException exception){
0058        System.out.println( "GenericException thrown ..." +
0059                            "which is correct.");
0060    } // End try/catch.
0061 } // End main.
0062
0063 } // End QueueDemo.
```

The *Queue* constructor, called on line 0021, needs to have an instance of the Class class passed to it in order that it can know which elements may be stored in the queue. This is accomplished by first constructing an instance of the *NamedPerson* class, using its default constructor on line 0017, and using its getClass() action to obtain its Class descriptor. The *namedPerson* class is the first non-abstract class in the *Persons* hierarchy. It would have been preferable to have used the abstract *EmailPerson* class, which is at the root of the hierarchy, but as it is not possible to construct an instance of an abstract class this is not possible.

Once constructed three instances of the *persons* Hierarchy, two *NamedPersons* and a *PhonePerson*, are added to the *demoQueue*, which is then output. Following this the first element from the queue is retrieved and output, with the *size()* action confirming that the queue now contains only two elements. Finally an attempt is made to add an inappropriate element to the queue in order to demonstrate that the *GenericException* will be thrown if this is attempted. The output of this harness, indicating that the queue appears to be working correctly, was as follows:

```
                     Queue Demonstration Program

    Adding three instances to the queue ...

    Showing the queue ...

    1  E-mail : anorak@boring.com Name : Andy Anorak
    2  E-mail : geek@nowhere.edu Name : Gary Geek Phone : 111-2222
    3  E-mail : sad@lost.org Name : Suzie Sad


     Retrieving and showing ...

    E-mail : anorak@boring.com Name : Andy Anorak

    The queue now contains 2 elements.

    Attempting to add an element of an inappropriate class ...
    GenericException thrown ... which is correct.
```

14.3 ▦ The *Stack* class

The essential characteristic of a stack is that elements can only be added to or removed from it at the front. Its behaviour can be described as *last in first out* (*lifo*) as opposed to a queue which would be *first in first out* (*fifo*). The action of adding an element to a stack is commonly known as *push*ing it onto the stack and the action of removing it *pop*ping. Stacks usually also allow the first element on the stack to be obtained without removing it, known as *peek*ing. These actions are shown on the class diagram in Figure 14.6.

As with the *Queue* class, the *Stack* class can be very simply implemented by making public a limited set of actions from the *UnorderedList* class, as follows:

```
0001 // Filename Stack.java.
0002 // A generic stack structure allowing elements of
0003 // the specified class to be added and removed at
0004 // the front only.
0005 //
0006 // Written for JOF book, chapter 14.
0007 // Fintan Culwin, v0.1, August 1997.
0008
```

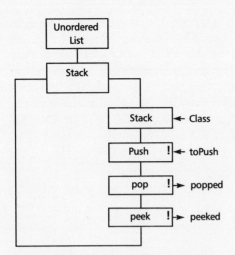

Figure 14.6   The *Stack* class diagram.

```
0009 package Generics;
0010
0011 import Generics.GenericException;
0012
0013 import java.util.NoSuchElementException;
0014
0015 public class Stack extends UnorderedList {
0016
0017    public Stack( Class theBaseClass) {
0018       super( theBaseClass);
0019    } // end Stack constructor.
0020
0021    public void push( Object toAdd) throws GenericException {
0022
0023       super.addAtFront( toAdd);
0024    } // End add.
0025
0026    public Object pop() throws NoSuchElementException {
0027
0028      return super.removeFromFront();
0029    } // End pop.
0030
0031    public Object peek() throws NoSuchElementException {
0032
0033      return super.obtainFromFront();
0034    } // End peek.
0035
0036 } // End Stack.
```

Possible applications of stacks are less common and tend to be more technical than those of queues. The demonstration harness will illustrate one possible use, converting a stream of digits into an integer value. When the user types an integer value at the keyboard the meaning of the first digit cannot be known until all the digits have been received. For example, if the user types the character '1', this might indicate 1 if it is the only digit, or it might indicate 10 if the full sequence is '10', or 100 if the sequence is '100', etc. To accomplish this all digit characters are pushed onto the stack as they are received, until the sequence is terminated with a non-digit character.

At this point it is known that the first digit popped from the stack will indicate the units, the next will indicate the tens, the next the hundreds, etc. A design to illustrate this is as follows:

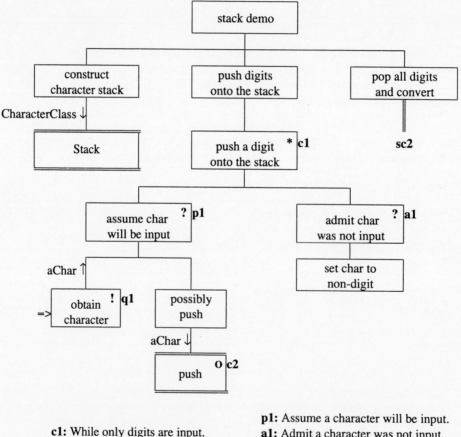

c1: While only digits are input.
c2: If current character is a digit.

p1: Assume a character will be input.
a1: Admit a character was not input.
q1: Implicit IO exception.

The first part of this design inputs characters from the system input stream until a non-digit character is input, or an input–output exception is thrown. As each character is obtained it is tested and, so long as it is a digit, pushed onto the stack. The implementation of this part of the design is as follows:

```
0001 // Filename StackDemo.java.
0002 // Demonstration harness for the Stack class,
0003 // pushing a sequence of digits onto a stack and
0004 // subsequently popping and converting them into
0005 // an integer value.
0006 //
```

```
0007 // Written for JOF book, chapter 14.
0008 // Fintan Culwin, v0.1, August 1997.
0009
0010 import Generics.Stack;
0011 import Generics.GenericException;
0012
0013 import java.lang.Character;
0014 import java.io.*;
0015
0016 public class StackDemo {
0017
0018    public static void main(String args[]) {
0019
0020    Character demoChar   = new Character( 'a');
0021    char      aCharacter = '0';
0022    Stack     demoStack = new Stack( demoChar.getClass());
0023    int place;
0024    int result;
0025
0026
0027       System.out.println( "\tStack Demonstration Program\n\n");
0028       System.out.print( "Please enter an integer value :");
0029       System.out.flush();
0030
0031       while ( Character.isDigit( aCharacter)) {
0032          try {
0033            aCharacter = (char) System.in.read();
0034            if ( Character.isDigit( aCharacter)) {
0035               demoChar = new Character( aCharacter);
0036               demoStack.push( demoChar);
0037            } // End if.
0038         } catch (IOException exception) {
0039            aCharacter = ' ';
0040         } // End try/ catch.
0041       } // End while.
```

A *Stack* called *demoStack* is constructed on line 0022 using an instance of the Character class to supply a Class description. A *Stack* can only contain classes which are, directly or indirectly, extended from the Object class. The primitive **char** type is not a class and so cannot be used. Instead an instance of the Character class, called *demoChar*, is constructed from a simple **char** literal on line 0020 and used in the call of the constructor.

The iteration between lines 0031 and 0041 obtains a character from the raw data input stream System.in on line 0033 using its read() action. This action returns an **int**eger value which is cast to a **char** and assigned to the **char** variable *aCharacter*. The class wide Character isDigit() enquiry action is then used to guard a call of the *demoStack push()* action on line 0036. Again a primitive **char** cannot be used so on line 0035 an instance of the Character class, called *demoChar*, is constructed from the value of the primitive *aCharacter* variable. It is possible, though unlikely, that the read() action may throw a non-Runtime IOException and so a **try/catch** structure is used to detect this and terminates the loop by setting the value of *aCharacter* to a space.

The design of the remaining part of the program is as follows:

SC2 pop and convert

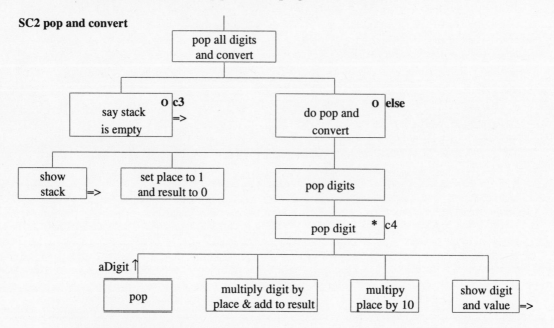

c3: If the stack is empty.
c4: While the stack is not empty.

Assuming that the *Stack* is not empty, the conversion commences by showing the contents of the *Stack* and setting the variables *place* to 1 and *result* to 0. The iteration then *pop*s each digit from the stack, converts it to its corresponding integer value, multiplies it by the value of *place* and adds it to *result*. On each iteration the value of *place* is multiplied by 10, so that the first digit popped is multiplied by 1, the second by 10, the third by 100, etc. The final action of the loop is to output the current digit and the current value of result. The implementation of this design is as follows:

```
0044    if ( demoStack.isEmpty()) {
0045        System.out.println( "The stack is empty!");
0046    } else {
0047        System.out.println( "Thank you, the stack contains");
0048        System.out.println( demoStack);
0049
0050        System.out.println( "\nConverting to integer and outputting");
0051        place   = 1;
0052        result  = 0;
0053        while ( !demoStack.isEmpty()){
0054            demoChar = (Character) demoStack.pop();
0055            result += (demoChar.charValue() - '0') * place;
0056            place *= 10;
0057            System.out.println( "Popped" + demoChar +
0058                            "value so far " + result + ".");
0059        } // End while.
0060    } // End if.
0061 } // End main.
```

On line 0054 the *pop()* action will return a value of the Object class which has to be cast to its known, Character, type and assigned to the *demoChar* variable. On line 0055 the charValue() action is used to obtain the value of *demoChar* as a **char** and this is converted to an **int**eger by subtracting the character '0' from it. Thus if the character is '0', '0' − '0' will be 0; if the character is '1', '1' − '0' will be 1; etc. The resulting **int**eger value is multiplied by the value of *place* and added to the current value of *result*.

The other lines from this fragment should be straightforward. A sample run of the program might produce the following interaction:

```
        Stack Demonstration Program

Please enter an integer value : 2468
Thank you, the stack contains
1   8
2   6
3   2
4   2


Converting to integer and outputting
Popped 8 value so far 8.
Popped 6 value so far 68.
Popped 4 value so far 468.
Popped 2 value so far 2468.
```

The output of the stack, after the value has been input, indicates that the first location contains the digit 8, the second 6, and so on. The instance diagram for this application would be similar to that presented for the *QueueDemo* application.

Before leaving the *UnorderedList* hierarchy it should be noted that several of the actions which the *UnorderedList* class introduces, e.g. *obtainFromEnd()*, have not been used by the *Queue* or *Stack* classes. The design and implementation of the *UnorderedList* class were made to maximize its potential for reuse. So, although these actions are not currently required, they may be required by other structures at some stage in the future and the costs of providing them at this stage are minimal compared with having to add them later.

14.4 ■ The *Generics* interfaces

A sibling class of the *UnorderedList* class, the *OrderedList* class, will be introduced in this part of the chapter. An ordered list maintains the elements in its structure according to some well defined key value. For example, using the *Persons* package the entries in the list might have to be held in an alphabetic ordering according to their e-mail addresses.

It would be possible to produce a specific *OrderedContactList* class which maintained a list of personal contacts ordered by their e-mail addresses, but this structure could not be reused to maintain, for example, a list of *LibraryBooks* ordered by their *AcquisitionNumbers* or a list of vehicles ordered by their *RegistrationNumbers*. This chapter is concerned with providing *generic* data structures rather than particular solutions and so a general approach will be presented.

In order for a generic *OrderedList* class to be produced there must be a limitation upon the classes which can be used to instantiate it. This limitation is that the class **must** supply two actions. The first, *keyValues()*, returns an Object which itself must have relational actions, and can be used to decide upon the ordering of the elements. The second required action is *copy()* which returns a copy of the instance.

The Java mechanism to guarantee that an action is supplied by a class is the use of *interfaces*. An Interface declaration states the signatures of the actions which a class declaring itself to be of that Interface **must** supply. In the example being developed the classes which are intended to be stored in an *OrderedList* must supply an action called *keyValues()* which returns an Object of the class *Orderable* and an action called *copy()* which must return an object of the class *Keyable*. This is stated in the *Keyable* interface declaration, as follows:

```
0001 // Filename Keyable.java.
0002 // Interface declaration for classes which are
0003 // intended to be used in OrderedStructures.
0004 //
0005 // Written for JOF book, chapter 14.
0006 // Fintan Culwin, v0.1, August 1997.
0007
0008 package Generics;
0009
0010 import Generics.Orderable;
0011
0012 public interface Keyable {
0013
0014     public Orderable keyValueIs();
0015
0016     public Keyable copy();
0017
0018 } // End interface Keyable.
```

The declaration of an **interface** is somewhat similar to the declaration of a class, but the action signatures only have to be stated and do not have to be defined. An **interface** can be designed and described in a *interface class diagram*; the interface class diagram for the *keyable* interface is given in Figure 14.7. An interface class diagram does not have a parent class which it extends and cannot have any private attributes, actions or any class wide actions, though it can have protected actions. It indicates that it is an interface and not a class by having the word interface in italics right justified below the name of the interface.

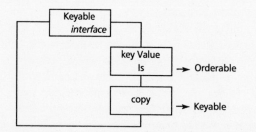

Figure 14.7   The *keyable* interface class diagram.

The *Persons EmailPerson* class declaration states that it implements the *Keyable interface* in its class declaration, as follows:

```
0011        import Generics.Orderable;
0012        import java.io.*;
0013
0014        abstract class EmailPerson extends    Object
0015                                    implements Keyable {
```

This would be also be shown in its context diagram, as given in Figure 14.8.

A class declaration can only **extend** a single parent class but can implement any number of Interfaces. In this example the class promises that it will declare suitable *keyValues()* and *copy()* actions and the Java compiler will make sure that it does. In return Java will allow an instance of the *EmailPerson* class, or of any class extended from it, to be used where the formal argument states that an instance of the *Keyable* class is expected.

The implementation of the *keyValueIs()* action in the definition of the *EmailPerson* class is as follows:

```
0050        public Orderable keyValueIs(){
0051            return this.theirEmail;
0052        } // End keyValueIs
```

The *theirEmail* data attribute of the *EmailPerson* class is of the *EmailAddress* class which itself implements the *Orderable* interface, whose definition is as follows:

```
0013 package Persons;
0014
0015 import Generics.Orderable;
0016 import java.io.*;
0017
0018 public class EmailAddress extends    Object
0019                                implements Orderable {
```

The *Orderable* interface promises that a class which implements its interface will supply actions which can be used to decide upon the ordering of instances of the class:

```
0001 // Filename Orderable.java.
0002 // Orderable interface definition, allowing
0003 // two objects to be compared for a defined relationship.
0004 // Required for the OrderedStructure generic class.
0005 //
0006 // Written for JOF book, chapter 14.
0007 // Fintan Culwin, v0.1, August 1997.
0008
0009 package Generics;
```

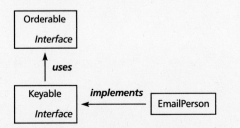

Figure 14.8 *EmailPerson*, context diagram.

```
0010
0011 public interface Orderable {
0012
0013    public boolean keyIsEqualTo( Orderable other);
0014
0015    public boolean keyIsGreaterThan( Orderable other);
0016
0017    public boolean keyIsLessThan( Orderable other);
0018
0019 } // End interface Orderable.
```

To summarize, a class which is intended to be used as the element type of an *OrderedList* must supply actions called *copy()* and *keyValuels()*. The *keyValuels()* action must return an instance of a class which itself must supply actions to determine the ordering of instances of this class. These requirements are enforced by the use of the *Keyable* and *Orderable* interface declarations.

The *OrderedList* class can now have its actions defined solely in terms of the *Orderable* and *Keyable* classes, which will ensure that, upon instantiation, it will be able to accept as elements any *Keyable* class. The most elegant way to do this is to declare an *OrderedStructure* interface and then declare the *OrderedList* class as implementing this interface. The *OrderedStructure* interface definition is as follows, its interface class diagram being given in Figure 14.9.

```
0001 // Filename OrderedStructure.java.
0002 // Interface for a set of ordered list actions,
0003 // to be implemented by a number of different data
0004 // structures.
0005 //
0006 // Written for JOF book, chapter 14.
0007 // Fintan Culwin, v0.1, August 1997.
0008
0009 package Generics;
0010
0011 import Generics.Orderable;
0012 import Generics.Keyable;
0013 import java.util.Enumeration;
```

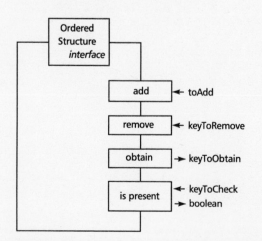

Figure 14.9 The *keyable* interface class diagram.

```
0014
0015 public interface OrderedStructure {
0016
0017     public void add( Keyable toAdd);
0018
0019     public Keyable remove( Orderable keyToRemove);
0020
0021     public Keyable obtain( Orderable keyToObtain);
0022
0023     public boolean isPresent( Orderable keyToCheck);
0024
0025     public boolean isEmpty();
0026
0027     public int size();
0028
0029     public Enumeration elements();
0030
0031 } // End interface OrderedStructure.
```

As this interface only states the types of the arguments to the actions as *Keyable* or *Orderable*, and the *OrderedList* class must implement these actions in order to implement this interface, an *OrderedList* list will then be capable of instantiation to store any *Keyable* elements.

Before considering the implementation and demonstration of the *OrderedList* class the nature of the *copy()* action needs to be clarified. From the earliest chapter use has been made of the **new** reserved word to create and construct an instance of a class. This is the only way in which an instance of a class can be created. However, the identifier which is used in conjunction with the new term merely *designates* the instance, it is not the instance itself.

The implication of this is that when the value of a *designator* is assigned to another identifier they both then designate the same instance. This can be illustrated in the following fragment:

```
WarningCounter aCounter        = new WarningCounter();
WarningCounter theSameCounter = aCounter;

aCounter.count();

System.out.println( "aCounter ... " +
                     aCounter.hashCode() +
                    " has counted " +
                    aCounter.numberCountedIs());

System.out.println( "theSameCounter ... " +
                     theSameCounter.hashCode() +
                    " has counted " +
                    theSameCounter.numberCountedIs());
```

Only one instance of the *WarningCounter* class is constructed but both *aCounter* and *theSameCounter* designate it. This is illustrated in the output produced by this fragment, which might be something like what follows:

```
aCounter & 4357648 has counted 1
theSameCounter & 4357648 has counted 1
```

The value output by the *hashCode()* action (4357648) indicates that both identifiers designate the same instance and so an action called by either of them may change the state of the instance and be reflected in the behaviour of the other.

The significance of this consideration is that the Vector and Hashtable structures from the previous chapters and the *Queue* and *Stack* structures above have only stored copies of the designators and not copies of the objects. So if an instance is stored within a structure it can be changed whilst it is within the structure if a designator still references it. So the state of the object retrieved from the structure may differ from its state when it was stored in the structure. This is sometimes the desired behaviour, but on other occasions the state of an object retrieved from a structure is required to be unchanged from that when it was stored. This behaviour will be accomplished in the following data structures by copying the instance into the structure when it is stored and copying it out again when it is retrieved.

A class instance continues to exist as long as there is something to designate it. When the last designator of an instance is reassigned to designate another instance or, if it is a local variable, is destroyed when the action terminates, the instance can no longer be accessed. Java will become aware of this and will ensure that, in due course, it is destroyed and its resources reclaimed for use, a process known as *garbage collection*. It is possible for the Object *finalize()* action to be overridden in a class declaration if there are any steps which should be taken before an instance is destroyed.

14.5 ■ The *OrderedList* constructor and *add()* actions

The class diagram for the *orderedList* class is given in Figure 14.10.

The *OrderedList* constructor is implemented as a call of its parent, *GenericStructure*, constructor. The implementation of the class, as far as the end of the constructor, is as follows:

```
0001 // Filename OrderedList.java.
0002 // Class to implement the OrderedStructure interface
0003 // making use of a Vector.
0004 //
0005 // Written for JOF book, chapter 14.
0006 // Fintan Culwin, v0.1, August 1997.
0007
0008
0009 package Generics;
0010
0011 import Generics.GenericException;
0012 import Generics.OrderedStructure;
0013 import Generics.AlreadyPresentException;
0014
0015 import java.util.Vector;
0016 import java.util.Enumeration;
0017 import java.util.NoSuchElementException;
0018 import java.lang.ArrayIndexOutOfBoundsException;
0019
0020
```

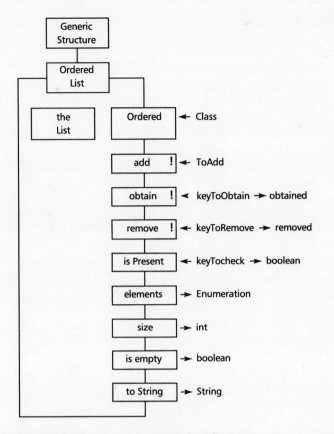

Figure 14.10   The *OrderedList* class diagram.

```
0021 public class OrderedList extends    GenericStructure
0022                         implements OrderedStructure{
0023
0024 private Vector theList = new Vector();
0025
0026 private static final int KEY_NOT_PRESENT = -1;
0027
0028
0029    public OrderedList( Class theElementClass) {
0030       super( theElementClass);
0031    } // End OrderedList constructor.
```

The *AlreadyPresentException*, imported on line 0013, is supplied by the *Generics* package with the intention that it should be thrown if an attempt is made to add an element to an *OrderedStructure* which has the same key value as an existing element. The class is declared on lines 0021 and 0022 with the encapsulated **Vector** instance, *theList*, declared and constructed on line 0024. The manifest value on line 0026 will be used to communicate the result of a search within the class, as will be explained below. The definition of the constructor follows on lines 0029 to 0031.

The design of the *add ()* action is as follows:

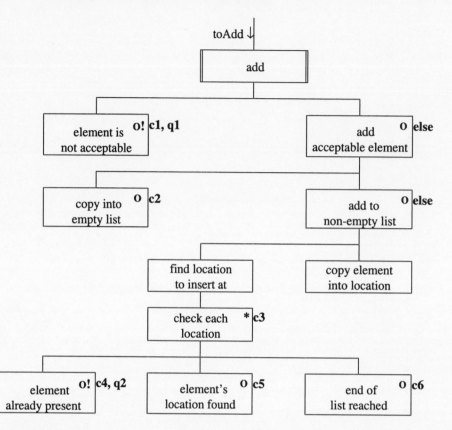

c1: If element is not of an acceptable class.
c2: If the list is empty.
c3: While the location to insert has not been reached.
q1: Explicit Generic exception.

c4: If current keys is equal to key to insert.
c5: If current key is greater than key to insert.
c6: If all elements checked.
q2: Explicit AlreadyPresent exception.

The essence of this design can be explained by considering a list of e-mail addresses and tracing the design as new addresses are added. Assume that an *OrderedList* contains the e-mail addresses shown in Figure 14.11.

If the address *dull@hopeless.com* is to be added the correct location for it to be inserted is at location 1. On the first iteration the address at location 0 will be examined and, as it is not equal to or greater than the address to be inserted, the loop will iterate to consider location 1. The address at this location is not equal to the new address but it is alphabetically greater than it, which causes the loop to terminate and the new address to be inserted at location 1, automatically moving all subsequent addresses down the list.

If the address *wally@nowhere.edu* is to be added to the list as shown in Figure 14.11 it should be added at location 3, beyond the end of the existing addresses. In this case the loop will iterate three times as none of the addresses are equal to or greater than the new address, and the new address will be appended to the list.

If any attempt is made to add an address which is equal to one of the existing addresses then an *AlreadyPresentException* will be thrown. As it is not possible to

Location	address
0	anorak@boring.com
1	geek@nowhere.edu
2	sad@lost.org

Figure 14.11   Ordered list of e-mail addresses.

examine the contents of an empty list this is treated as a special case. The implementation of this design is as follows:

```
0034        public void add(Keyable toAdd) {
0035
0036        Orderable  keyToAdd       = toAdd.keyValueIs();
0037        Orderable  thisKeyValue;
0038
0039        int        thisLocation   = 0;
0040        int        numberOfElements = theList.size();
0041        boolean    locationFound  = false;
0042
0043          if ( !isAcceptableElement( toAdd) ){
0044             throw new GenericException();
0045          } else {
0046            if ( this.isEmpty()) {
0047               theList.addElement( toAdd.copy());
0048            } else {
0049              while ( !locationFound) {
0050                 thisKeyValue = ((Keyable) theList.elementAt(
0051                                       thisLocation)).keyValueIs();
0052                 if ( thisKeyValue.keyIsEqualTo( keyToAdd)) {
0053                    throw new AlreadyPresentException();
0054                 } else if ( thisKeyValue.keyIsGreaterThan( keyToAdd) ){
0055                    locationFound = true;
0056                 else {
0057                    locationFound = (++thisLocation == numberOfElements);
0058                 } // End if.
0059              } // End while.
0060              theList.insertElementAt( toAdd.copy(), thisLocation);
0061            } // End if.
0062          } // End if.
0063        } // End add.
```

On line 0036 the key value of the element which is to be added is obtained using its *keyValueIs()* action. Assuming that the element *toAdd* is acceptable and the list is empty a copy of the element is added to the Vector in line 0047. Otherwise, lines 0050   and 0051 will control an indefinite iteration. The phrase *theList.elementAt-(thisLocation)* will return the Object stored at *thisLocation* in the Vector *theList*. This has to be cast to the *Keyable* class, which is safe as only *Keyable* objects have been stored in the list, before its *keyValueIs()* action can be applied to obtain its key value. The *Orderable* relational actions are then used on lines 0052 and 0054 to decide if an element with the same key value is already present or if the next element in the Vector has a key value greater than the value to be inserted, which would indicate that the new element should be added at the current location.

Otherwise, on line 0057, the *thisLocation* index is incremented and tested to ensure that it does not now indicate that all elements in the Vector have been examined, which would indicate that the new element should be added at the end of the list.

If the exception is not thrown on line 0053 then, after the loop has terminated, the value of *thisLocation* will indicate where in the Vector *theList* a copy of the element *toAdd* should be inserted into the list. This is accomplished on line 0060. The start of a demonstration harness which illustrates the adding of elements of the *Persons* class to a suitably instantiated *OrderedList* is as follows:

```
0001 // Filename OrderedListDemo.java.
0002 // Demonstration harness for the OrderedList class.
0003 //
0004 // Written for JOF book, chapter 14.
0005 // Fintan Culwin, v0.1, August 1997.
0006
0007
0008 import Generics.OrderedList;
0009 import Generics.GenericException;
0010 import Persons.*;
0011
0012 class OrderedListDemo {
0013
0014    public static void main(String args[]) {
0015
0016    EmailAddress demoAddress;
0017    NamedPerson   demoNamedPerson = new NamedPerson();
0018    PhonePerson   demoPhonePerson;
0019    String        demoString;
0020
0021    OrderedList demoList = new OrderedList( demoNamedPerson.getClass());
0022
0023
0024       System.out.println( "\tOrdered List Demonstration Program\n\n");
0025
0026       System.out.println( "Adding three instances to the list ...");
0027
0028       demoNamedPerson = new NamedPerson( "sad@lost.org",
0029                                          "Suzie Sad");
0030       demoList.add(demoNamedPerson);
0031
0032       demoPhonePerson = new PhonePerson( "geek@nowhere.edu",
0033                                          "Gary Geek",
0034                                          "111-2222");
0035       demoList.add(demoPhonePerson);
0036
0037       demoNamedPerson = new NamedPerson( "anorak@boring.com",
0038                                          "Andy Anorak");
0039       demoList.add(demoNamedPerson);
0040
0041
0042       System.out.println( "\nShowing the list ...\n");
0043       System.out.println( demoList);
```

The construction of the *demoList* on line 0021 is essentially identical, in concept, to the construction of the *Queue* class earlier in this chapter. Once constructed three *Persons* instances are constructed and added to the list, in reverse alphabetic order, before the list is output. The output from this part of the demonstration, which seems to indicate that parts of the *add()* action are operating correctly, was as follows:

```
                  Ordered List Demonstration Program

Adding three instances to the list ...

Showing the list ...

1  E-mail : anorak@boring.com Name : Andy Anorak
2  E-mail : geek@nowhere.edu Name : Gary Geek Phone : 111-2222
3  E-mail : sad@lost.org Name : Suzie Sad
```

The context diagram for this demonstration harness, illustrating how the various interfaces are implemented and used, is given in Figure 14.12.

14.6 ▦ The *OrderedList* remaining actions

The addition of a new element into an existing list, as described above, used a *sequential search* to locate the appropriate position for the new element to be inserted. When using an ordered structure it is possible to use a more elegant technique, known as a *binary chop search*, which is more efficient for large structures. The implementation of the *OrderedList* class has a private action called *findKey()* whose task is to

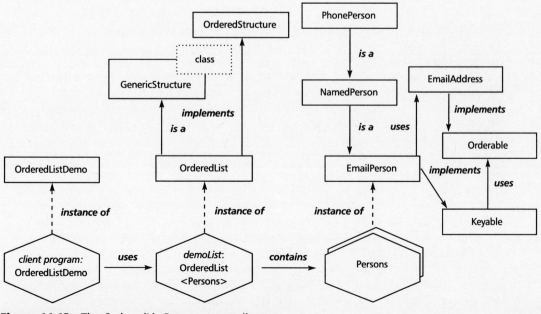

Figure 14.12 The *OrderedListDemo* context diagram.

find the location within the list of the key supplied, or indicate if it is not present. The design of this action is as follows:

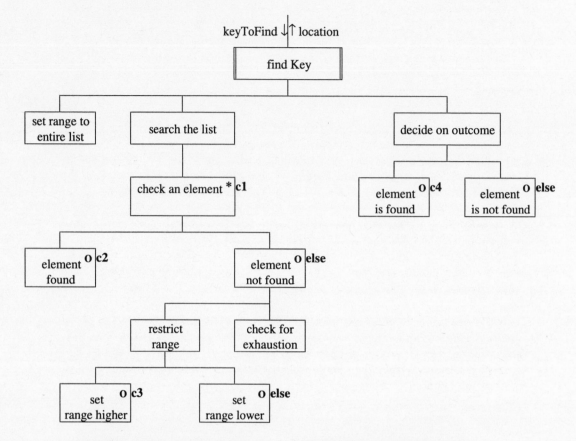

c1: While not found and not exhausted.   **c3:** If key element at this location is
c2: If element found at this location.   greater than key being sought.
                                               c4: If element has been found.

The essence of this design is to examine a range of the list for the key being sought. Initially the range consists of the entire list and the element in the middle of the list is the first to be checked. If this is the element being sought then the loop will terminate, otherwise the range of the search is restricted. As the list is ordered, if the key of the element being examined is greater than the key being sought then the sought element, if it is present, must be in the lower part of the range, otherwise it must be in the higher part of the range.

Having limited the range of the search to the lower or upper part of the current range, the loop iterates restricting the search to the appropriate part of the list. This will continue until the element being sought is located in the middle of the range, or the range has been restricted to a single element and it is not the element being sought. For example, consider the list shown in Figure 14.13.

A search for *dull@hopeless.com* would start by considering the address in the middle of the list, *geek@nowhere.edu*. This is not the address being sought, but it is alphabetically greater than it, so if *dull@hopeless.com* is in the list it must be somewhere below location 2. The second iteration would restrict the search to this part of the list and

Location	Address
0	anorak@boring.com
1	dull@hopeless.com
2	geek@nowhere.edu
3	sad@lost.org
4	wally@nowhere.edu

Figure 14.13 Ordered list of e-mail addresses.

might examine the address at location 0. This, also, is not the address being sought but is alphabetically lower than it. So, on the third iteration the search will be restricted to the part of the current range above location 0 and below location 2. This is a range consisting of a single element, which is the one sought, so the search will terminate indicating that *dull@hopeless.com* is at location 1 in the list.

Alternatively if the address *whoisit@whereisit.org* were being sought, the first iteration would examine location 2 and decide to restrict the search to the range 3 to 4. On the second iteration location 3 would be examined and the search restricted to the range 4 to 4 on the third iteration. As this is not the element sought and the range has only one element in it the search can conclude that the address is not contained in the list.

The advantage of a binary chop search over a sequential search should now be obvious. A sequential search may have to examine every entry in the list to conclude that the element being sought is, or is not, present. A binary chop search will be able to reach the same conclusion by examining far fewer elements. The implementation of this design is as follows:

```
0097        private int findKey( Orderable keyToFind) {
0098
0099        Orderable thisKeyValue;
0100        int      lowerBound    = 0;
0101        int      upperBound    = theList.size();
0102        int      thisLocation  = (upperBound + lowerBound) /2;
0103        int      nextLocation;
0104        boolean  found         = false;
0105        boolean  exhausted     = false;
0106
0107           while ( (!found) && (!exhausted) ) {
0108              thisKeyValue  = ( (Keyable)
0109                                 theList.elementAt( thisLocation)).
0110                                 keyValueIs();
0111              if ( thisKeyValue.keyIsEqualTo( keyToFind)) {
0112                 found = true;
0113              } else {
0114                 if ( thisKeyValue.keyIsGreaterThan( keyToFind)) {
0115                    upperBound = thisLocation -1;
0116                 } else {
0117                    lowerBound = thisLocation +1;
0118                 } // End if.
0119                 nextLocation = (upperBound + lowerBound) /2;
0120                 exhausted    = (thisLocation == nextLocation);
```

```
0121              thisLocation = nextLocation;
0122          } // End if.
0123       } // End while.
0124
0125       if ( found) {
0126          return thisLocation;
0127       } else {
0128          return KEY_NOT_PRESENT;
0129       } // End if.
0130    } // End findKey.
```

The implementation of the decision to terminate the search when the list has been exhaustively checked, on lines 0119 and 0120, is implemented as a check to make sure that the next location to be checked is not the same as the last location checked. It was implemented in this way to avoid obscure problems with **int**eger arithmetic.

The remaining *OrderedList* actions which are concerned with maintaining the list can now be implemented by taking advantage of the *findKey()* action, as follows:

```
0066    public Keyable obtain( Orderable keyToObtain) {
0067
0068       int location = findKey( keyToObtain);
0069
0070       if ( location == KEY_NOT_PRESENT) {
0071          throw new NoSuchElementException();
0072       } else {
0073          return ((Keyable) theList.elementAt( location)).copy();
0074       } // End if.
0075    } // End obtain.
0076
0077
0078    public Keyable remove( Orderable keyToRemove) {
0079
0080       int     location = findKey( keyToRemove);
0081       Keyable hold;
0082
0083       if ( location == KEY_NOT_PRESENT) {
0084          throw  new NoSuchElementException();
0085       } else {
0086          hold = ((Keyable) theList.elementAt( location));
0087          theList.removeElementAt( location);
0088          return hold;
0089       } // End if.
0090    } // End remove.
0091
0092    public boolean isPresent( Orderable keyToCheck) {
0093       return (this.findKey( keyToCheck)) != KEY_NOT_PRESENT;
0094    } // End isPresent.
```

For example, the *remove()* actions calls the *findKey()* action and stores the result in a local variable called *location*. If this value is equal to the manifest value *KEY_NOT_PRESENT* a NoSuchElementException is thrown. Otherwise, the element is retrieved from the **Vector** and held, whilst it is removed, before the held element is returned. The *obtain()* action is virtually identical but, on line 0073, returns a *copy()* of the element stored at *location* in *theList*. The *elementAt()* action returns an Object value which has to be cast to a Keyable value before the *copy()* action can be applied to it, requiring the brackets as shown. The remaining *OrderedList* actions, with the exception of the *toString ()* action, are implemented as calls of the equivalent *theList* Vector action:

```
0133        public Enumeration elements() {
0134            return theList.elements();
0135        } // End elements.
0136
0137
0138        public int size() {
0139            return theList.size();
0140        } // End size.
0141
0142
0143        public boolean isEmpty() {
0144            return theList.isEmpty();
0145        } // End isEmpty.
0146
0147
0148        public String toString() {
0149
0150        int          thisElement = 0;
0151        Object       fromList;
0152        StringBuffer buffer      = new StringBuffer();
0153        Enumeration  contents    = theList.elements();
0154
0155           while( contents.hasMoreElements()) {
0156              fromList = contents.nextElement();
0157              thisElement++;
0158              buffer.append( thisElement + "   " + fromList + "\n");
0159           } // End while;
0160           return buffer.toString();
0161        } // End toString.
```

The *toString ()* action uses an Enumeration object to iterate through the Vector and store each element, preceded by a sequence number, in a *StringBuffer* which subsequently has its toString() action used to return the entire String The completion of the *OrderedList* demonstration test harness will be left as an end-of-chapter exercise.

There is one possible insecurity in this generic implementation. The *Keyable* element is checked to make sure that it is of an acceptable class before it is stored in the list, and so it need not be tested when it is recovered from the list. However, no check is made upon the *Orderable* arguments. At the time of compilation Java will make sure that the actual arguments are of an *Orderable* class, but cannot check that they are of the precise *Orderable* class which should be used with the stored *Keyable* class.

For example, using an example introduced above, the *LibraryListOrderable* class is *AcquisitionNumber*. As the *AcquisitionNumber* class is an *Orderable* class Java will allow it to be passed as an argument to an *OrderedList* which has been constructed to store *Persons*. However, if an attempt is made to compare an *AcquisitionNumber* with an *EmailAddress*, the java run-time system would be unable to find a suitable action and will throw an exception.

Although the facilities which have been introduced in this chapter have been described as generic, they are really only a partial and rather cumbersome attempt to provide such facilities. Some languages, for e.g. Ada, supply a true generic facility which allows examples such as this to be implemented much more easily and powerfully. However, the advantages of using generic data structures merit the inclusion of the facilities in this chapter.

Summary

▨ Generic facilities allow a data structure to store, securely, elements from a hierarchy of classes.

▨ The generic facilities in Java are primitive compared with some other environments.

▨ An Interface declaration states the actions which a class, which declares itself to implement that Interface, must provide.

▨ A class can only extend a single class but can implement multiple interfaces.

▨ An instance of a class which implements an interface can be used as an actual argument where the formal argument specifies the interface type.

▨ A *Queue* stores elements in a *first in first out* (*fifo*) manner.

▨ A *Stack* stores elements in a *last in first out* (*lifo*) manner.

▨ An *OrderedList* stores elements according to some defined key value.

▨ A binary chop search is more efficient than a sequential search, but can only be used on an ordered structure.

Exercises

14.1 Complete the demonstration harness clients for the *Queue*, *Stack* and *OrderedList* classes and use them to increase your confidence that the classes are implemented correctly.

14.2 Produce a black box test plan for either the *Queue* or *Stack* classes and compare it with the actions you have included in demonstration harnesses from Exercise 14.1. By how much has this increased your confidence in the implementation of the class?

14.3 Revisit the *ContactList* application in Chapter 13 and reimplement it making use of an *OrderedList*. From the user's point of view are there any differences?

14.4 Using the *LibraryBook* hierarchy in Exercise 13.6 reimplement the *LibraryList* application making use of an *OrderedList*.

14.5 Produce a black box test plan for the applications in Exercises 14.3 and 14.4. Compare the two test plans and decide which aspects of the tests are testing the *OrderedList* functionality. What would this imply for the test plan of a third application which also makes use of an *OrderedList*?

Chapter fifteen

Dynamic and recursive data structures

In this chapter the consideration of data structures will be concluded with an introduction to a group of data structures known as *dynamic data structures*. These structures can grow, and shrink, as they are used, under the developer's control. This is something like the Vector and Hashtable classes introduced in Chapter 13. Those structures will reallocate space for themselves as more elements are added, but will not automatically release the space once it is no longer required. The two structures which will be developed in this chapter will dynamically obtain, and subsequently release when no longer required, the resources used to store their elements.

For small structures containing perhaps a few hundred elements, this is an insignificant consideration. But as the structures get larger, containing perhaps thousands of elements, this can become a significant consideration. The first structure which will be introduced, known as a *linked list*, is not suitable for use with large structures, but introduces the concepts and techniques which are required for the second structure, known as a *binary tree*, which is suitable. Many other dynamic data structures can be developed and used, in addition to the two which will be presented, and a knowledge of the nature, construction and characteristics of this family of structures is an essential part of learning to become a software developer.

The implementation of the binary tree structure will also introduce another technique for controlling the execution of software. In addition to sequence, selection and iteration it is also possible to use *recursive* control structures. Recursion is more cognitively complex than the three techniques used so far but for some situations it is an extremely elegant technique.

15.1 ▧ Linked lists

A linked list is a data structure which, assuming it is not empty, contains an *element* which holds the *data* being stored and a *link* which connects it to the rest of the list. The rest of the list, assuming it too is not empty, contains an element which holds the second data item being stored and a link which points to the rest of the list. This third element in the link is identical to the first two elements, and so can contain links to further elements, which themselves contain links to further elements, etc. Eventually the list will come to an end where the link in an element does not contain a reference to a further element. A linked list, containing three e-mail addresses, is illustrated in Figure 15.1.

Each element in the list, which contains the data being stored and a link which can connect it with the next, is known as a *node*. In Figure 15.1 the first node in the list

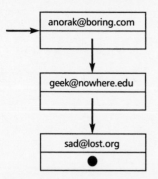

Figure 15.1   A linked list with three nodes.

contains the details of *anorak@boring.com* and a link which connects it to the second node containing *geek@nowhere.edu*. This node contains a link to the third node containing *sad@lost.org* and, as this is the last node in the list, its link is shown as a ●, connecting it to nothing. As suggested in the diagram the nodes are maintained in the list in an alphabetic sequence, so if the details of *dull@hopeless.com* were added the structure of the list would have to change to that shown in Figure 15.2.

Likewise if *abbot@monastery.org* were added it would have to be inserted into the list before *anorak@boring.com* and the link of the *abbot* node would have to connect to the *anorak* node, whose onward links would have to be undisturbed. Or if *zzz@snooze.gov* were added it would have to be linked to by the *sad* node, with its link not connecting to a further node.

When an element is removed from the list then the node containing the element will have to be removed, the links reconnecting as appropriate. For example, if *geek@nowhere.edu* were removed from the list in Figure 15.2, then the node containing *dull@hopeless.com* would have to be linked to *sad@lost.org*.

15.2 ▓ The *LinkedList* class diagrams and *ListNode* class

The class diagram for the *LinkedList* class, which implements the *OrderedStructure* interface, is given in Figure 15.3.

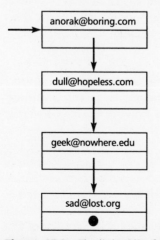

Figure 15.2   The linked list from Figure 15.1 with another node added.

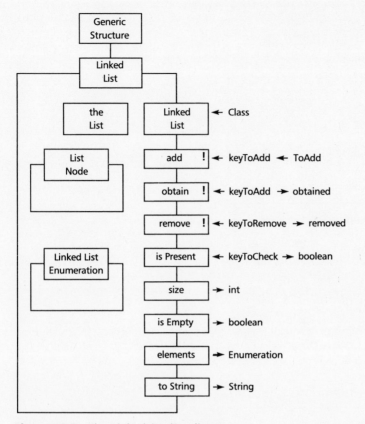

Figure 15.3   The *LinkedList* class diagram.

The diagram indicates that the *LinkedList* class is an extended *GenericStructure* class and implements the *OrderedStructure* interface. It also indicates that, besides encapsulating *theList*, it also encapsulates two further classes: a *ListNode* class to provide the nodes which form the list and a *LinkedListEnumeration* class which implements the Enumeration interface and provides the Enumeration class to traverse the list. These two classes are the sole concern of the *LinkedList* class and as such are of no use to any other classes. In order to ensure that they cannot be used by any other classes they are totally private to the *LinkedList* class. The technique for implementing this design in Java will be introduced below.

The public actions provided by the *LinkedList* class are exactly the same as those provided by the *OrderedList* class, as presented in the previous chapter. This allows a *LinkedList* to be used in any place where an *OrderedList*, or indeed any other *OrderedStructure*, is used.

The implementation of the *LinkedList* class is dependent upon the design of the *ListNode* class whose class diagram is given in Figure 15.4.

As a totally private class contained within the *LinkedList* class with all of its actions **protected**, it can only be used by the other encapsulated classes and the *LinkedList* class and is totally invisible outside the class. A *ListNode* instance contains two private attributes: *theData* which contains the data to be stored in the node and *nextNode* which contains the link to the next node in the list. The only constructor requires that both of these data attributes are supplied and there are two enquiry actions which

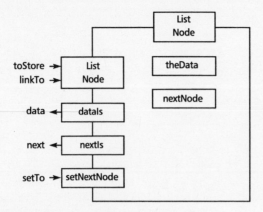

Figure 15.4 The *ListNode* class diagram.

allow their values to be retrieved. However, there is only one action which changes the value of a single attribute. So having constructed a *ListNode* it is possible to change its link but it is not possible to change the data which it contains. The implementation of this design is as follows:

```
0198 ////////////////////////////////////////////////////////
0199 // Private ListNode class, providing the nodes which    //
0200 // are linked together to implement the LinkedList.     //
0201 ////////////////////////////////////////////////////////
0202
0203
0204 class ListNode extends Object {
0205
0206 Keyable  theData;
0207 ListNode nextNode;
0208
0209
0210     protected ListNode( Keyable  toStore,
0211                         ListNode linkTo) {
0212        theData  = toStore;
0213        nextNode = linkTo;
0214     } // End ListNode constructor.
0215
0216
0217     protected Keyable dataIs() {
0218        return theData;
0219     } // End dataIs.
0220
0221
0222     protected ListNode nextIs() {
0223        return nextNode;
0224     } // End nextIs.
0225
0226
0227     protected void setNextNode( ListNode setTo) {
0228        nextNode = setTo;
0229     } // End setNextNode.
```

```
0230
0231 } // End class ListNode.
```

The line numbers indicate that this class definition is contained within another file, the *LinkedList.java* file, and follows the definition of the *LinkedList* **class** in that file. The declaration of the **class** on line 0204 does not specify the modifier **public**, meaning that the **class** is implicitly **private** and can only be seen, and used, by the other classes contained within the file. This is the Java mechanism by which the encapsulation of a class within another class is achieved.

The data attribute *theData* is declared on line 0206 as being of a *Keyable* class which is required if the *LinkedList* is to implement the *OrderedStructure* interface. On line 0207, the *nextNode* attribute is declared to be of the *ListNode* class. This data attribute is of the class which is currently being declared! Thus a *ListNode* instance contains a *Keyable* data attribute and another *ListNode*. These two attributes correspond to the upper and lower parts of the nodes shown in Figures 15.1 and 15.2. What is shown as a link on those diagrams is implemented as a *ListNode*, which itself contains a *ListNode*, which again can contain a *ListNode*, and so on. A *ListNode* which has a **null** value in its *nextNode* data attribute would correspond to the node which terminates the list. This should become clearer as the *LinkedList* class is explained.

15.3 ■ The *LinkedList* constructor and *add()* actions

The implementation of the *LinkedList* class, as far as the end of the constructor, is as follows:

```
0001 // Filename LinkedList.java.
0002 // Class to implement the OrderedStructure interface
0003 // making use of a single linked list.
0004 //
0005 // Written for JOF book, chapter 15.
0006 // Fintan Culwin, v0.1, August 1997.
0007
0008
0009 package Generics;
0010
0011 import Generics.GenericException;
0012 import Generics.OrderedStructure;
0013 import AlreadyPresentException;
0014
0015 import java.util.Enumeration;
0016 import java.util.NoSuchElementException;
0017 import java.lang.ArrayIndexOutOfBoundsException;
0018
0019
0020 public class LinkedList extends      GenericStructure
0021                         implements OrderedStructure {
0022
0023 private ListNode theList        = null;
0024 private int      numberOfElements = 0;
0025
0026
```

```
0027     public LinkedList( Class theElementClass) {
0028        super( theElementClass);
0029     } // End LinkedList constructor.
```

This implementation is very similar to that of the *OrderedList* presented in the previous chapter. There is no need for this class to import the Vector class and this has been removed from the list of imported classes. On line 0023, the data attribute *theList* is implemented as an instance of the *ListNode* class and will be used as the first node of the linked list. The default **null** value of *theList* is confirmed in the listing emphasizing that the list is currently empty.

In order to maintain a count of the number of elements in the structure an **int**eger *numberOfElements* attribute, with the initial value 0, is declared on line 0024. The constructor is implemented as a call of its parent, *GenericStructure*, constructor to record the class of elements which can be stored in the structure. The design of the *add()* action is as follows:

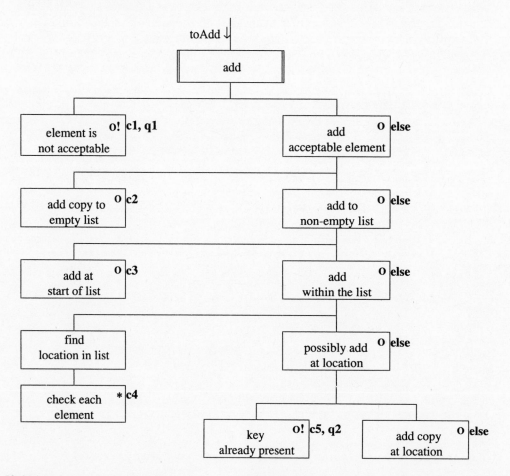

c1: If element is not of an acceptable class.
c2: If the list is empty.
c3: If new element belongs before the first node.
c4: While the location to insert has not been found.

c5: If an element with the same key has been found.

q1: Explicit GenericStructure exception.
q2: Explicit AlreadyPresent exception.

The easiest way to explain this design is to present its implementation and then to trace through the implementation as elements are added to the list. The implementation of this design is as follows:

```
0033    public void add( Keyable  toAdd) {
0034
0035    Orderable  keyToAdd    = toAdd.keyValueIs();
0036    Orderable  nextKeyValue = null;
0037    ListNode   newNode     = new ListNode( toAdd.copy(), null);
0038    ListNode   thisNode    = null;
0039    ListNode   nextNode    = null;
0040
0041      if ( !isAcceptableElement( toAdd)) {
0042        throw new GenericException();
0043      } else {
0044        if ( this.isEmpty()) {
0045          theList = newNode;
0046          numberOfElements++;
0047        } else {
0048          if ( keyToAdd.keyIsLessThan(
0049                    theList.dataIs().keyValueIs())) {
0050            newNode.setNextNode( theList);
0051            theList = newNode;
0052            numberOfElements++;
0053          } else {
0054            thisNode    = theList;
0055            nextNode    = thisNode.nextIs();
0056            if ( nextNode != null ) {
0057              nextKeyValue = nextNode.dataIs().keyValueIs();
0058            } else {
0059              nextKeyValue = null;
0060            } // End if.
0061            while( (nextKeyValue != null)                    &&
0062                   (!(keyToAdd.keyIsLessThan( nextKeyValue))) ){
0063              thisNode = nextNode;
0064              nextNode = thisNode.nextIs();
0065              if ( nextNode != null) {
0066                nextKeyValue = nextNode.dataIs().keyValueIs();
0067              } else {
0068                nextKeyValue = null;
0069              } // End if.
0070            } // End while.
0071            if ( (nextKeyValue != null)                     &&
0072                 (keyToAdd.keyIsEqualTo( nextKeyValue)) ){
0073              throw new AlreadyPresentException();
0074            } else {
0075              thisNode.setNextNode( newNode);
0076              newNode.setNextNode( nextNode);
0077              numberOfElements++;
0078            } // End if.
0079          } // End if before existing.
0080        } // End if empty list.
0081      } // End if unacceptable.
0082    } // End add.
```

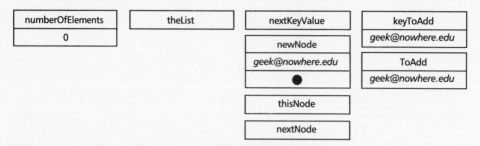

Figure 15.5   The list before adding *geek@nowhere.edu*.

Assuming that *theList* is initially empty and the *add()* action is called to add an element whose e-mail key value is *geek@nowhere.edu*, the state of the action at line 0040 can be visualized as shown in Figure 15.5.

This diagram shows, on the left, the encapsulated data attributes *numberOfElements* which has the value 0 and *theList* which is currently empty. To the right are the four local variables, of which only *newNode* has been initialized, as shown, with a copy of the element *toAdd*. On the far right the arguments to the action are shown.

Assuming that the class of *toAdd* is deemed acceptable on line 0041 the condition on line 0044 should evaluate **true** as the list contains no elements. This will cause lines 0045 and 0046 to be executed, which will cause the state of the attributes to change to that shown in figure 15.6. As the **if** condition on line 0044 was **true** control will pass to the end of the **if** structure on line 0080 and the action will terminate.

A second call of the *add()* action, adding an element whose e-mail address is *sad@lost.org*, will be traced. On this occasion the test on line 0041 will again be **false** and the test on line 0044 will be **false** causing the statements starting on line 0048 to be executed. The test on lines 0048 and 0049 uses the *keyIsLessThan()* action of the *keyToAdd Keyable* object. The argument to this action is the key value of the data stored in the *theList* node. This effectively compares *sad@lost.org* with *geek@nowhere.edu* and will evaluate **false** as *sad* is not alphabetically less than *geek*.

Execution of the statements on lines 0054 to 0060 will produce the situation shown in Figure 15.7. Line 0054 causes *thisNode* to have the same value as *theList*, and as the link in *theList* does not connect it to another node the execution of line 0055 will not initialize *nextNode*. The test on line 0056 will be false as *nextNode* is uninitialized (**null**) and so the value of *nextKeyValue* will remain **null**.

The compound condition, controlling the **while** loop, on lines 0061 to 0062 will commence by evaluating the first term, *nextKeyValue* !=**null**. As *nextKeyValue* is **null** this will be **false**, and as **false** and anything will always be **false** Java will not evaluate the second term on line 0062. This is fortunate as it would attempt to apply the *keyIsLessThan()* action to a **null** argument which would cause an exception to be thrown. As the **while** loop condition is **false** the loop will not iterate and the condition on line 0071 will be evaluated. This is a check to make sure that an attempt

Figure 15.6   The list's data attributes after adding *geek@nowhere.edu*.

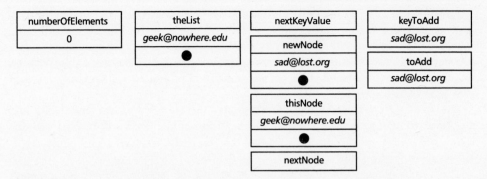

Figure 15.7   The list from Figure 15.5 during the addition of *sad@lost.org*.

is not being made to add an element whose key is already in the list and will evaluate **false**.

The statements on lines 0075 to 0077 cause the new node to be added to the list. The statement on line 0075 causes the link value of *thisNode* to point to the *newNode*. As *theList* and *thisNode* both refer to the same object this will cause the value of *theList* to change, effectively causing it to link itself to the *newNode*. The situation after line 0077 has executed and the action has terminated as shown in Figure 15.8.

Next, considering the addition of *anorak@boring.com*, this will cause the condition on line 0048 to evaluate **true** as *anorak* is alphabetically less than *geek*. The statement on line 0050 will cause the link in the *newNode* to connect it to *theList*, and through it to the rest of the list. The execution of line 0051 will cause *theList* to take the value of *newNode* which, following the execution of line 0052, will produce the situation shown in Figure 15.9.

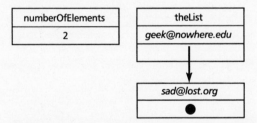

Figure 15.8   The list from Figure 15.6 after the addition of *sad@lost.org*.

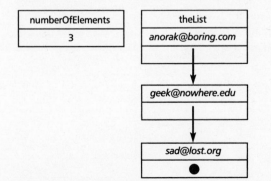

Figure 15.9   The list from Figure 15.8 after the addition of *anorak@boring.com*.

The addition of *zzz.snooze.com* will cause the **while** loop condition on line 0061 to be evaluated. On this occasion *nextKeyValue* will not be **null** as line 0055 will cause *nextNode* to refer to the node linked to *thisNode*, i.e. the *geek* node, and subsequently line 0057 will cause *nextKeyValue* to take the value *geek@nowhere.edu*. As the term on line 0061 is **true** the second term, on line 0062, will be evaluated comparing zzz with *geek* and evaluating **true**.

The loop will iterate causing the *thisNode* link to refer to the *geek* node and *nextNode* to refer to the *sad* node. The **if** condition in line 0065 will be **true** and line 0066 will cause *nextKeyValue* to have the value *sad@lost.org*. This situation is illustrated in Figure 15.10.

The loop condition will again evaluate **true** and the loop will iterate for a second time causing *thisNode* to move down the list to *sad@lost.org*, and thus *nextNode* and *nextKeyValue* to become **null**. The third evaluation of the loop condition will be **false** and the loop will terminate. Lines 0075 to 0077 will connect the new node to the list by setting *thisNode*'s link to point to the *newNode*, the *newNode*'s link to be set **null** and the *numberOfElements* to be incremented to 4. This effectively adds the *zzz* node beyond the *sad* node.

Considering Figure 15.10 and assuming that *nerd@nerdy.com* is to be added, the evaluation of the loop term on line 0062 would be **false** causing the loop to terminate. The execution of line 0075 will cause *thisNode*, the *geek* node, to become linked to the *newNode*, the nerd *node*. Line 0076 will cause the link in the *newNode* to be linked to the *nextNode*, the *sad* node, and via it to any other nodes to which it is linked, e.g. the *zzz* node.

A higher level description of the implementation of the *add()* action would be that lines 0044 to 0047 are concerned with adding an element to an empty list. Lines 0048 to 0053 are concerned with inserting an element before the first node of an non-empty list. Lines 0054 to 0070 are concerned with iterating through the list until the list comes to an end or the correct location for the new node to be inserted is found. Lines 0071 to 0074 make sure that an element with the same key is not already present and, finally, lines 0075 to 0077 insert the node into the list.

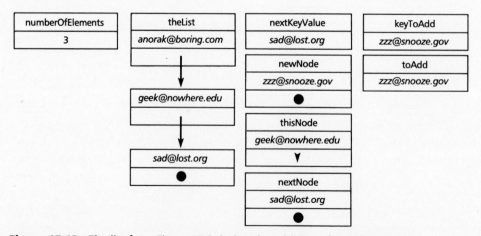

Figure 15.10   The list from Figure 15.9 during the addition of *zzz@snooze.gov*.

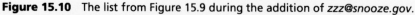

15.4 ■ The *linkedList obtain()*, *remove()* and *isPresent()* actions

These three actions are essentially very similar. Only the *obtain()* action, whose design
follows, will be described in detail.

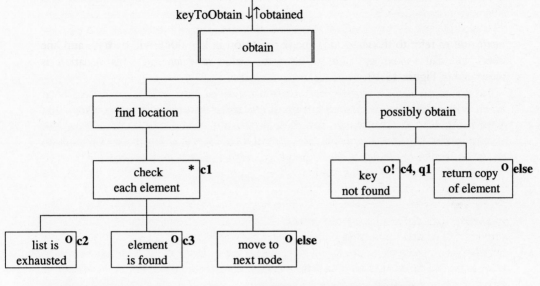

c1: While location not found and list
   not exhausted.
c2: If this node is null.

c3: If this node is to be obtained.
c4: If key was not found.
q1: Explicit NoSuchElement exception.

Again the explanation of this design will be by a trace of its implementation, which is
as follows:

```
0086        public Keyable obtain( Orderable keyToObtain) {
0087
0088        ListNode thisNode  = theList;
0089        boolean  found     = false;
0090        boolean  exhausted = false;
0091
0092          while ( !found && !exhausted) {
0093            if ( thisNode == null) {
0094              exhausted = true;
0095            } else if ( keyToObtain.keyIsEqualTo(
0096                            thisNode.dataIs().keyValueIs())) {
0097              found = true;
0098            } else {
0099              thisNode = thisNode.nextIs();
0100            } // End if.
0101          } // End while.
0102
0103          if ( found) {
0104            return thisNode.dataIs().copy();
0105          } else {
0106            throw new NoSuchElementException();
0107          } // End if.
0108        } // End obtain.
```

Assume the list in Figure 15.9 is being used and the element *geek@nowhere.edu* is wanted to be *obtain*ed. The loop condition on line 0092 evaluates **true** when it is evaluated for the first time. The *thisNode* local variable will reference *anorak@boring.com* so the condition on line 0093 will be **false** causing the condition on lines 0095 to 0096 to be evaluated, which will also be **false**. The execution of line 0099 will cause *thisNode* to move down the list to the *geek* node. The loop will iterate for a second time with the condition on line 0093 evaluating **false** again, and that on lines 0095 and 0096 **true**. This will terminate the loop as line 0097 sets the *found* flag **true**. The condition on line 0103 will be **true** causing the statement on line 0104 to return a copy of the element referenced by *thisNode*.

If the element *notinlist@nowhere.gov* were being *obtain*ed the iteration would have continued until *theNode* had moved down to the end of the list and taken the **null** value of the *sad* node's link. This would then cause the condition on line 0093 to be **true**, the *exhausted* flag would subsequently become **true** and the exception would be **throw**n on line 0106. The implementation of the *isPresent()* action is essentially identical:

```
0147      public boolean isPresent( Orderable keyToCheck) {
0148
0149      ListNode thisNode  = theList;
0150      boolean  found     = false;
0151      boolean  exhausted = false;
0152
0153         while ( !found && !exhausted) {
0154          if ( thisNode == null) {
0155             exhausted = true;
0156          } else if ( keyToCheck.keyIsEqualTo(
0157                          thisNode.dataIs().keyValueIs())) {
0158             found = true;
0159          } else {
0160             thisNode = thisNode.nextIs();
0161          } // End if.
0162         } // End while.
0163         return found;
0164      } // End isPresent.
```

The *remove()* action differs by also maintaining a *lastNode* link which always references the node before *thisNode*. If the node to be removed is *found*, the value of the *lastNode* is manipulated to remove *thisNode* from the list. The implementation of the *remove()* action is as follows:

```
0112      public Keyable remove( Orderable keyToRemove) {
0113
0114      Keyable   hold;
0115      ListNode thisNode  = theList;
0116      ListNode lastNode  = null;
0117      boolean  found     = false;
0118      boolean  exhausted = false;
0119
0120         while ( !found && !exhausted) {
0121          if ( thisNode == null) {
0122             exhausted = true;
0123          } else if ( keyToRemove.keyIsEqualTo(
0124                          thisNode.dataIs().keyValueIs())) {
```

```
0125                    found = true;
0126                } else {
0127                    lastNode = thisNode;
0128                    thisNode = thisNode.nextIs();
0129                } // End if.
0130            } // End while.
0131
0132        if ( !found ) {
0133            throw new NoSuchElementException();
0134        } else {
0135            hold = thisNode.dataIs();
0136            if ( thisNode == theList) {
0137                theList = theList.nextIs();
0138            } else {
0139                lastNode.setNextNode( thisNode.nextIs());
0140            } // End if.
0141            numberOfElements--;
0142            return hold;
0143        } // End if.
0144    } // End remove.
```

So if the *geek* node from Figure 15.9 were to be *removed*, the loop would terminate with *thisNode* referencing *geek* and *lastNode* referencing the *anorak* node. Line 0139 will cause the *anorak* node's link to point to *sad* node, isolating the *geek* node from the list, as shown in Figure 15.11.

As the *geek* node now has nothing referencing it Java will remove it, recovering its resources, in due course. The implementation of the steps on lines 0135 to 0141 *hold*s a copy of the data being removed whilst it is removed and, on line 0137, has to treat the first node in the list as a special case, before a copy of the held node is returned on line 0141.

15.5 ▨ The remaining *LinkedList* actions and the *LinkedListEnumeration* class

The remaining *LinkedList* actions are relatively straightforward:

```
0167    public Enumeration elements() {
0168        return new LinkedListEnumeration( theList);
0169    } // End elements.
```

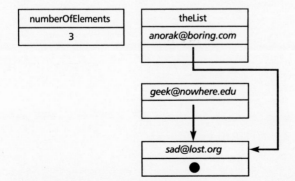

Figure 15.11   The list from Figure 15.9 during the removal of *geek@nowhere.edu*.

```
0170
0171
0172        public int size() {
0173           return numberOfElements;
0174        } // End size.
0175
0176
0177        public boolean isEmpty() {
0178           return theList == null;
0179        } // End isEmpty.
0180
0181
0182        public String toString() {
0183
0184        StringBuffer buffer      = new StringBuffer();
0185        int          thisElement = 0;
0186        Enumeration  theElements = this.elements();
0187
0188           while ( theElements.hasMoreElements()) {
0189              buffer.append( ++thisElement + "   " +
0190                             theElements.nextElement() + ".\n");
0191           } // End while;
0192           return buffer.toString();
0193        } // End toString.
```

The implementation of the *toString()* action makes use of the *LinkedList elements()* action to return an Enumeration instance of the *LinkedListEnumeration* class. Having obtained an Enumeration instance the output can be produced using the Enumeration facilities as first described in Chapter 12.

The *LinkedListEnumeration* class implements the Enumeration interface and supplies the three required actions: a constructor, *hasMoreElements()* and *nextElement()*. The implementation is as follows:

```
0235 ////////////////////////////////////////////////////////
0236 // Private LinkedListEnumeration class, implementing   //
0237 // an Enumeration to traverse the list.                //
0238 ////////////////////////////////////////////////////////
0239
0240 class LinkedListEnumeration extends    Object
0241                                 implements Enumeration {
0242
0243 ListNode currentNode;
0244
0245    public LinkedListEnumeration( ListNode startNode) {
0246       currentNode = startNode;
0247    } // End LinkedListEnumeration constructor.
0248
0249
0250    public boolean hasMoreElements() {
0251       return currentNode != null;
0252    } // End hasMoreElements.
0253
0254
0255    public Object nextElement() {
```

```
0256
0257    Object hold;
0258
0259       if ( currentNode == null) {
0260          throw new NoSuchElementException();
0261       } else {
0262          hold = currentNode.dataIs();
0263          currentNode = currentNode.nextIs();
0264          return (Object) ( ((Keyable) hold).copy());
0265       } // End if.
0266    } // End nextElement.
```

The actions of this class have to be specified **public**, even though they are totally encapsulated within the *LinkedList* class in order to comply with the Enumeration **interface** declaration and also to allow clients to access them.

The constructor requires a *ListNode* parameter which will be the first node in the list. This value is encapsulated within the class and tested for the value **null** in the *hasMoreElements()* action. The *nextElement()* action will throw a NoSuchElementException if it is called when the list is exhausted. Otherwise, it will *hold* the element at the current node and set the value of the *currentNode* to the next node in the list, which will be **null** at the end of the list, before returning a copy of the element. This involves some complicated casting as *hold* is of the Object class, but the *copy()* action can only be applied to an instance of the *Keyable* class. However, the *nextElement()* action has to return a value of the Object class, so the value in *hold* has to be cast to *Keyable* in order to be copied and subsequently recast back to an Object.

Thus a newly constructed *LinkedListEnumeration* instance will on its first call of *nextElement()* return a copy of the first element, if any, from the list; the second on the second call; and so on. When the list has been totally traversed the *hasMoreElements()* action will return **false**. This is exactly the same behaviour as required by an *Enumeration* class as described in Chapter 12.

The implementation of the *LinkedList* class can be demonstrated with exactly the same demonstration harness as was used for the *OrderedList* class in the previous chapter, with all occurrences of *OrderedList* replaced with *LinkedList*. This is possible as both classes implement the *Keyable* interface which in turn causes their key values to implement the *Ordered* interface, and demonstrates the advantages of interfaces as stated at the start of Chapter 14.

15.6 ▨ Binary trees

This part of the chapter will introduce the final data structure, binary trees. The easiest way to describe the nature of a binary tree is to show a tree being constructed from a sequence of data. Figure 15.12 illustrates the construction of a binary tree from the names *geek*, *sad*, *boring*, *zzz*, *anorak* and *dull*.

A node in a binary tree contains the data which is being stored and two links to other nodes, known as the left and the right links, either or both of which may, or may not, link the node to a further node. The first diagram in Figure 15.12 shows a tree consisting of a single node, known as the ***root node***, storing the name *geek*. When the next name, *sad*, is added to the tree it is stored in a new node which, as *sad* is alphabetically greater than *geek*, is linked into the tree as the right hand node of the

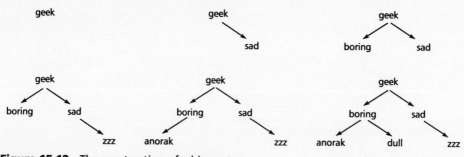

Figure 15.12 The construction of a binary tree.

geek node. Likewise the third name, *boring*, is linked as the left node of the *geek* node as it is alphabetically lower than *geek*.

The fourth name, *zzz*, needs to be added to the right of the *geek* node but the *sad* node is already in this position. So the rule is applied again, **recursively**, to the *sad* node and a new node containing the name *zzz* is linked to the right of the *sad* node. Likewise the fifth name, *anorak*, needs to be added to the left of the *geek* node, but as this is already occupied it is added to the left of the *boring* node. The final name, *dull*, needs to be added to the left of the *geek* node already occupied by *boring*. When the rule is applied to the *boring* node it is added as a new node to the right of the *boring* node, producing the final diagram in Figure 15.12.

This process could continue with the addition of more names, using the rules as described above, to produce an increasingly complex binary tree. One characteristic of the tree is that for any node, all the names which are alphabetically greater than the name at that node will be found to the right of it and all the alphabetically lower names to the left.

Another way of thinking about a binary tree is that it contains the data stored at the **root node** location and two binary trees. Each of these binary trees can be an empty tree, containing no data, or a non-empty binary tree and two further binary trees. Each of these trees can be empty or non-empty, and if non-empty they can contain two further binary trees. This definition of a binary tree contains within itself more binary trees, an example of a recursive definition. As the data structure can be described recursively it can also be constructed recursively as suggested above and implemented below.

15.7 ■ The *TreeNode* class and *BinaryTree add* action

The class diagram of the *BinaryTree* class does not differ significantly from that of the *LinkedList* class given in Figure 15.3. The encapsulated node class is known as the *TreeNode* class and the Enumeration class as the *BinaryTreeEnumeration*. The class diagram for the *TreeNode* class differs from that of the *ListNode* class by having enquiry and attribute changing actions for each of the links. Its class diagram is given in Figure 15.13.

The class diagram is incomplete, as shown by the dotted lines, for reasons which will be explained below. The implementation of this design is as follows:

```
0255 //////////////////////////////////////////////////////////
0256 // Private TreeNode class, providing the nodes which    //
0257 // are linked together to implement the BinaryTree.     //
0258 //////////////////////////////////////////////////////////
```

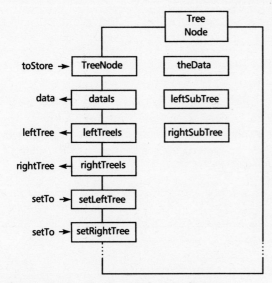

Figure 15.13   The *TreeNode* class diagram.

```
0259
0260
0261 class TreeNode {
0262
0263 Keyable   theData;
0264 TreeNode leftSubTree;
0265 TreeNode rightSubTree;
0266
0267     protected TreeNode( Keyable toStore) {
0268        theData        = toStore.copy();
0269        leftSubTree    = null;
0270        rightSubTree   = null;
0271     } // End TreeNode constructor.
0272
0273     protected Keyable dataIs() {
0274        return theData.copy();
0275     } // End dataIs.
0276
0277     protected TreeNode leftTreeIs() {
0278        return leftSubTree;
0279     } // End leftTreeIs.
0280
0281     protected TreeNode rightTreeIs() {
0282        return rightSubTree;
0283     } // End rightTreeIs.
0284
0285     protected void setLeftTree( TreeNode setTo) {
0286        leftSubTree = setTo;
0287     } // End setLeftTree.
0288
0289     protected void setRightTree( TreeNode setTo) {
```

```
0290          rightSubTree = _setTo;
0291     } // End setRightTree.
0292

...

0302 } // End class TreeNode.
```

The encapsulated *leftSubTree* and *rightSubTree* attributes of this class are themselves instances of the class being declared and so are recursively contained within it. The constructor actions are comparable with the actions of the *ListNode* class above, with the exception that a new node can only be constructed with empty (**null**) subtrees. The design of the *add()* action is as follows:

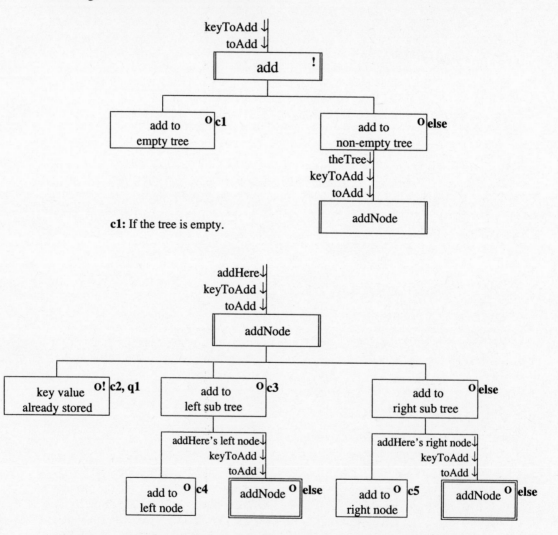

c1: If the tree is empty.

c2: If the key to add equals the key of add here.   c5: If the right subtree is empty.
c3: If key to add is less than key of add here.
c4: If the left subtree is empty.   q1: Explicit AlreadyPresent exception.

The *add()* action itself is concerned with dealing with the special case of adding to an empty tree; in all other cases it calls the **private** action *addNode()*. This action will decide, using the key of the element to be added and the key of the current node, if it is to add the element to the left subtree or to the right subtree. Assuming it is to be added to the left subtree, if this tree is empty a new node will be constructed and added to it. Otherwise, it calls the *addNode()* action passing as the *addHere* argument the left node. A similar pattern of actions happens if the new element is to be added to the right tree. The implementation of this design is as follows:

```
0034    public void add( Keyable toAdd) {
0035        if ( theTree == null) {
0036            theTree = new TreeNode( toAdd);
0037            numberOfElements++;
0038        } else {
0039            addNode( theTree, toAdd.keyToAdd(), toAdd);
0040        } // End if.
0041    } // End add.
0042
0043
0044    private void addNode( TreeNode  addHere,
0045                          Orderable keyToAdd,
0046                          Keyable    toAdd) {
0047
0048        if ( keyToAdd.keyIsEqualTo(
0049                    addHere.dataIs().keyValueIs())) {
0050            throw new AlreadyPresentException();
0051        } else if ( keyToAdd.keyIsLessThan(
0052                    addHere.dataIs().keyValueIs())) {
0053            if ( addHere.leftTreeIs() == null) {
0054                addHere.setLeftTree( new TreeNode( toAdd));
0055                numberOfElements++;
0056            } else {
0057                addNode( addHere.leftTreeIs(), keyToAdd, toAdd);
0058            } // End if.
0059        } else {
0060            if ( addHere.rightTreeIs() == null) {
0061                addHere.setRightTree( new TreeNode( toAdd));
0062                numberOfElements++;
0063            } else {
0064                addNode( addHere.rightTreeIs(),keyToAdd, toAdd);
0065            } // End if.
0066        } // End if.
0067    } // End addNode.
```

This implementation should become clearer if a trace of an addition is considered. Assuming that a tree is in the state shown in the fifth diagram of Figure 15.12, the addition of the *dull* element will proceed as follows.

As *theTree* is not empty the test in *add()* on line 0035 will be **false** and the *addNode()* action will be called passing *theList* as the *addHere* argument. Within *addNode* the test on line 0048 will be **false** and that on line 0051 **true**, as the key of the element being added, *dull*, is alphabetically lower than the element stored at the root, *geek*. The test on line 0053 will be **false** as the left subtree of the *geek* node is not empty. So the action on line 0057 will be executed, recursively calling *addNode* and passing *geek*'s left subtree as the *addHere* argument. This is a recursive call of *addNode*, as the call is made within the execution of *addNode*, and for this reason is shown in a double bounded box in the design.

On this second call *addHere* refers to the *boring* node and the condition on line 0048 will again be **false** and that on line 0051, effectively *dull < boring*, will be **false**. The condition on line 0060 will be **true** as the right hand subtree of the *boring* node is empty. Execution of line 0061 will create a new node, linked to the right of the *boring* node, containing the name *dull* and with two empty subtrees, and subsequently increment the *numberOfElements* attribute. This is the state shown in the last diagram in Figure 15.12 as expected.

At this point execution of the second call of *addNode()* will terminate and flow of control will return to the point in the first call of *addNode()* where the second call was recursively invoked. This was line 0057 and the next step in this call is to terminate, returning flow of control to the *add()* action on line 0039 which also terminates. This recursive descent and ascent of flow of control is an important consideration in the actions which follow.

The complexity of this implementation of the *BinaryTree add()* action should be compared with that of the *LinkedList add()* action. Allowing for the consideration that recursive control structures are cognitively more complex than sequence, selection and iteration, it should be clear that this action is much simpler.

15.8 ■ The *BinaryTree obtain()*, *isPresent()* and *toString()* actions

The design of the *obtain()* action is as follows:

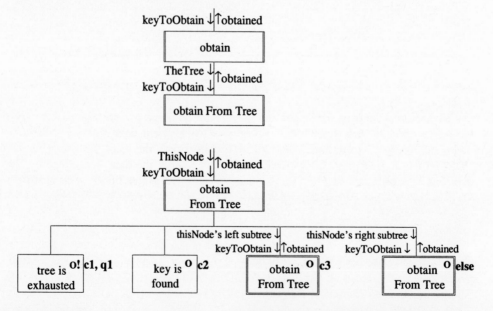

c1: If this tree is empty.   **c3:** If the key to obtain is less than the key of this tree.
c2: If the key to obtain equals the key of this tree.   **q1:** Explicit NoSuchElement exception.

The *obtain()* action consists of a call of the **private** *obtainFromTree()* action passing on *theTree* as an argument and passing back the value *obtained* from the call. The action itself raises an exception if the tree passed is empty, or returns a copy of the element stored at the current node if it is the one being sought, or recursively calls the *obtain-FromTree()* action passing either the left or right subtree depending upon the alphabetic relationship between the key being sought and the key of the current node. The implementation of this design is as follows:

```
0070        public Keyable obtain( Orderable keyToObtain) {
0071          return obtainFromTree( theTree, keyToObtain);
0072        } // End obtain.
0073
0074        private Keyable obtainFromTree( TreeNode  thisNode,
0075                                        Orderable toObtain) {
0076          if ( thisNode == null) {
0077            throw new NoSuchElementException();
0078          } else if ( toObtain.keyIsEqualTo(
0079                        thisNode.dataIs().keyValueIs())) {
0080            return thisNode.dataIs().copy();
0081          } else if ( toObtain.keyIsLessThan(
0082                        thisNode.dataIs().keyValueIs())) {
0083            return obtainFromTree( thisNode.leftTreeIs(), toObtain);
0084          } else {
0085            return obtainFromTree( thisNode.rightTreeIs(), toObtain);
0086          } // End if.
0087        } // End obtainFromTree.
```

Assume that the last tree in Figure 15.12 is being searched for the name *dull*. The *obtain()* action will call *obtainFromTree()* passing *theTree* as the *thisNode* argument. The test on line 0076 will be **false** as the tree is not empty and the test on line 0078 will also be **false** as the keys *geek* and *dull* are not equal. The test on line 0081 will be **true** as *dull* is less than *geek*, causing the *obtainFromTree()* action to be called recursively with *geek*'s left subtree passed as the *thisTree* argument.

On this call the first two tests, on lines 0076 and 0078, will again be **false** and the test on line 0081 will be **false** as *dull* is not less than *boring*. This will cause another recursive call of *obtainFromTree()* passing *boring*'s right subtree as the *thisTree* argument.

On this call the test on line 0076 will be **false** but the test on line 0078 will be **true** as *dull* is equal to *dull*. Line 0080 will **return** the element data stored at this node from this third call to the place where it was called from the second call. This is line 0083 which is itself part of a **return** statement returning the data to the place in the first call where the second call was called from. This also is line 0083 and this **return** returns the data to the place in *obtain()* where it was called from. This is line 0071 where the *dull* data, which has flown up the calls, is **return**ed as the result of the *obtain()* action.

If the search was for the name *duller*, rather than the name *dull*, then the pattern of actions would have been the same until the third call. On this call the test for equality would have been **false** and, as *duller* is considered alphabetically greater than *dull*, a fourth call of *obtainFromTree()*, passing *dull*'s right subtree, would have been made. On this call the test on line 0076 would have been **true** as *dull*'s right subtree is empty causing the NoSuchElement exception to be thrown.

The design and implementation of the *isPresent()* action are essentially identical to those of *obtain()*. Its implementation is as follows:

```
0180        public boolean isPresent( Orderable keyToCheck) {
0181          return isKeyPresent( theTree, keyToCheck);
0182        } // End isPresent.
0183
```

```
0184        private boolean isKeyPresent( TreeNode  thisNode,
0185                                      Orderable toCheck) {
0186          if ( thisNode == null) {
0187            return false;
0188          } else if ( toCheck.keyIsEqualTo(
0189                      thisNode.dataIs().keyValueIs())) {
0190            return true;
0191          } else if ( toCheck.keyIsLessThan(
0192                      thisNode.dataIs().keyValueIs())) {
0193            return isKeyPresent( thisNode.leftTreeIs(), toCheck);
0194          } else {
0195            return isKeyPresent( thisNode.rightTreeIs(), toCheck);
0196          } // End if.
0197        } // End isKeyPresent;
```

The implementation of *toString()*, which is about to be presented, does not use the Enumeration facility for reasons which will be explained below. Its design and implementation are as follows:

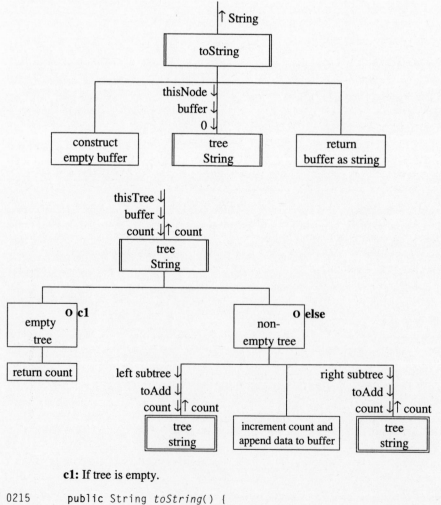

c1: If tree is empty.

```
0215        public String toString() {
0216
```

```
0217        StringBuffer buffer = new StringBuffer();
0218        int          theCount;
0219
0220          theCount = treeString( theTree, buffer, 0);
0221          return buffer.toString();
0222        } // End toString.
0223
0224        private int treeString( TreeNode      thisTree,
0225                                StringBuffer addTo,
0226                                int          soFar) {
0227
0228          if (thisTree == null) {
0229            return soFar;
0230          } else {
0231            soFar = treeString(thisTree.leftTreeIs(), addTo, soFar);
0232            addTo.append( ++soFar + " " + thisTree.dataIs() +"\n");
0233            soFar = treeString(thisTree.rightTreeIs(), addTo, soFar);
0234            return soFar;
0235          } // End if.
0236        } // End treeString.
```

Assume that this action is called to output the tree shown in the fourth diagram in
Figure 15.12. The *toString()* action will call the *treeString()* action passing *theTree*,
an empty buffer and the value 0 in the three arguments. As the tree is not empty it
will, on line 0231, recursively call itself passing *geek*'s left subtree as the *thisTree*
argument. On the second call exactly the same pattern of steps will take place, passing
boring's left subtree. This is an empty subtree so the action will return on line 0220
passing the value of *count* (0) as the returned value of the function.

Flow of control will return to the second call with the *boring* node specified as the
thisTree argument and its next action, on line 0232, is to append the pre-incremented
value of *soFar*, and the value of the data, to the buffer *addTo*. This would be "*1
E-mail : boring@etc.*". The next action is to call *treeString()* with *boring*'s right subtree
specified, the changed value of the buffer *addTo* and the incremented value of *soFar* as
the arguments. This is an empty tree so the contents of the buffer will not be changed
and the value of *soFar* will be returned unchanged. This is the last action of the *boring*
call of *treeString()* and flow of control returns to the original call of *treeString()*,
when the *geek* node was specified.

The next action of this call is to append its details to the buffer *addTo*, the pre-
incremented value of *soFar* (2) and the details stored at that node ("*geek@etc.*"). The
next action of this call is to call *treeString()* passing *geek*'s right hand subtree. This is
the *sad* node and its sequence of actions is to call *treeString()* with its left, empty,
node, which has no effect, append its details to the buffer ("*3 sad@etc.*") and then call
treeString() passing its right subtree. This call on the *zzz* node will call *treeString()*
passing its empty left node, adding its own details to the buffer ("*4 zzz@etc.*") and
calling *treeString()* passing its empty right subtree.

At this point the call on the *zzz* node will terminate, following which the call on the
sad node will terminate and then the original call on the *geek* node. If the pattern in
which the details were added to the buffer is considered it can be seen that the details
are in the sequence *boring*, *geek*, *sad* and *zzz*, each preceded by its sequence number.
When the original call, with the *geek* node specified, terminates the changed buffer will
be available and the value of *soFar* (4) returned into *theCount*. The contents of the

buffer are then returned as the String result of the *toString()* action; the value of *theCount* is discarded.

15.9 ■ The remaining *BinaryTree* actions

The remaining *BinaryTree* actions, with the exception of the *remove()* action, are as follows:

```
0200        public Enumeration elements() {
0201           return new BinaryTreeEnumeration( theTree);
0202        } // End elements.
0203
0204
0205        public int size() {
0206           return numberOfElements;
0207        } // End size.
0208
0209
0210        public boolean isEmpty() {
0211           return theTree == null;
0212        } // End isEmpty.
```

Unfortunately the *remove()* action is far more complicated. One, rather inelegant, technique is to isolate the node to be removed from the tree and then add all the elements from its left and right subtrees to the original tree.

The details of this require that the element required is first located, marked for removal and held in a local variable to be **return**ed from the action. To support this the *TreeNode* class supports a **boolean** *toBeRemoved* attribute which is **false** by default. It also supplies an action called *markForRemoval()* which sets the attribute **true** and an enquiry action called *toBeRemoved()* which returns the value of this attribute. The implementation of the *remove()* action has an associated recursive *removeFromTree()* action, comparable with the *obtainFromTree()* action as described above, which, when it locates the node to be removed, calls its *markForRemoval()* action to flag it for removal.

Having obtained the element to be removed a *trimTree()* action is called which will actually remove it, using another action called *mergeTree()* to add the contents of its left and right subtrees back to the tree. However, this would cause the *numberOfElements* data attribute to contain an incorrect value so it is stored before trimming and restored, after being decremented, before the action terminates. The implementation of the *remove()* action is as follows; the implementation of the supporting actions can be found in Appendix B.

```
0090        public Keyable remove( Orderable keyToRemove) {
0091
0092        Keyable   holdElement;
0093        int       holdCount;
0094
0095           holdElement = removeFromTree( theTree, keyToRemove);
0096           holdCount = numberOfElements;
0097           trimTree( theTree);
0098           numberOfElements = --holdCount;
0099           return holdElement;
0100        } // End remove.
```

The implementation of the *toString()* action, as described above, traversed the tree by a recursive *treeString()* action. It is not possible for such a traversal to be started and stopped as required by the *nextElement()* action of an Enumeration class. Accordingly the *BinaryTreeEnumeration* constructor extracts all the data from the tree into a Vector and iterates through this Vector in order to traverse the data in the tree. Its implementation can be found in Appendix B.

As with the *OrderedList* class, the *BinaryTree* class implements the *OrderedStructure* interface, so the same demonstration test harness as was used for the *OrderedList* in Chapter 14 can be used with this structure, once all occurrences of *OrderedList* have been replaced with *BinaryTree*.

15.10 ▓ *LinkedLists*, and *BinaryTrees* compared

The major advantage of *BinaryTrees* over *LinkedLists* is that it can be much faster to search for elements, which includes adding elements, as this is essentially a search for the appropriate location followed by the insertion. With a *LinkedList*, or indeed with a Vector, a search of the structure might have to traverse the entire list if the element being sought is not present or is the last element in the list. With a *BinaryTree* the range of the search is restricted by up to a half on each iteration and this can dramatically improve the performance for large structures. However, this is not always the case as will be demonstrated in an end-of-chapter exercise.

BinaryTrees are not as suitable when it is expected that an Enumeration traversal of the structure would be frequently required and, for this implementation, if a significant number of removals of elements from the structure were envisaged.

However, the major reasons for introducing dynamic structures before the end of this introductory book is because they are representative of a much larger number of structures which might be suitable for particular requirements. By becoming familiar with the design and implementation of dynamic structures at this stage it will be possible to approach these more advanced structures when required.

The *BinaryTree* also allows the concept, and implementation, of recursion to be introduced. Although, when it is first encountered, recursion is very difficult to comprehend, once assimilated it can be very powerful. There is always an iterative alternative to a recursive design, but in many cases the recursive design is simple and elegant whereas the iterative design is inelegant and complex. Again an initial familiarity with recursion at this stage is essential.

Summary

- ▓ Dynamic data structures can be much more efficient in their use of resources than static data structures.

- ▓ A dynamic data structure consists of a number of nodes and links which connect the nodes together.

- ▓ A class declaration file can encapsulate private class declarations within itself.

- ▓ The *LinkedList* and *BinaryTree* as presented in this chapter both implement the *OrderedStructure* interface, allowing either of them to be used wherever an *OrderedList* can be used.

- Recursive data structures contain instances of themselves, within themselves.

- Recursive actions call themselves as part of their implementation.

- Recursion is more cognitively complex than iteration but for many requirements it provides a much simpler design.

- A binary tree is more appropriate than a linked list when there is a large number of additions and searches, but a smaller number of removals and traversals.

Exercises

15.1 Revisit the *OrderedList* demonstration harness in Exercise 14.1 and reimplement it to demonstrate the equivalence of the *LinkedList* and *BinaryTree* classes as presented in this chapter.

15.2 Revisit the *ContactList* application in Exercise 14.3 and reimplement it to demonstrate the equivalence of the *LinkedList* and *BinaryTree* classes as presented in this chapter.

15.3 Trace the construction of a binary tree when the data to be stored in it is supplied in an alphabetical sequence. What does this tell you about the advantages of a *BinaryTree* over a *LinkedList*?

15.4 Revisit the black box test plans in Exercise 14.5 and consider their relevance to the *LinkedList* and *BinaryTree* structures. Produce glass box test plans for all three structures and compare the tests now required for all of them. What does this tell you about the importance of glass box considerations?

15.5 It was not possible to use a *binary chop* search to locate the position to insert a new element into a *LinkedList*, as it was not possible to determine the preceding node in the list. A *DoubleLinkedList* is made up from nodes which contain two links, one for the next node in the list and one for the previous node in the list. Implement a *DoubleLinkedList* class using a binary chop search in the *add()* action.

15.6 Adapt the demonstration harness from Exercise 15.1 to store all the integers from 1 to 1000 in a random sequence and subsequently to output them in an *OrderedList*, a *LinkedList*, a *DoubleLinkedList* and a *BinaryTree*. Execute each harness several times and calculate the average execution time in an attempt to determine which structure is the most efficient.

Chapter sixteen

Graphical user interfaces

In this final chapter the Java facilities for the construction of *g*raphical *u*ser *i*nterfaces (*GUIs*) will be introduced. The preceding chapters should have emphasized that the design and construction of quality software artefacts is a difficult, laborious and error prone task. The construction of GUIs adds further layers of complexity to this process; accordingly, this chapter can only provide an initial familiarity with some of the techniques and resources which can be used. The example in this chapter makes use of the facilities introduced by the JDK 1.1 release and is not compatible with the JDK 1.0 release.

The Java *a*bstract *w*indowing *t*oolkit (*AWT*) contains a rather primitive collection of classes which supply the various components which can be used to build GUIs. These include labels, push buttons, sliders, text boxes and menus, collectively known as *components*. Together they form the AWT class hierarchy which allows the presupplied components to be extended in order to supply a specialized functionality if required. However, these considerations are outside the scope of this book.

In previous chapters it has been repeatedly emphasized that the usability considerations are an essential part of designing an application. This is even more important with GUIs as the user has far more control over the pattern of interaction. With the text based interfaces used so far, the dialog between the user and the computer has been very largely under the control of the software which imposes a pre-determined sequence upon the pattern of interactions. GUIs give much more control to the user, offering them a collection of components and allowing the user to interact with them in any sequence.

In order to implement the software to respond to the user's actions an additional design technique, known as *s*tate *t*ransition *d*iagrams (*STDs*), will have to be introduced. In order to demonstrate these techniques a GUI for the *RoomMonitor* class, first introduced in Chapter 5, will be developed and presented.

16.1 ▧ The visual and behavioural design of the *RoomMonitorGUI*

The starting point for the development of a GUI should be a visualization of what the interface will look like when it is constructed. The visual design of the *RoomMonitorGUI* is presented in Figure 16.1.

This visual design uses location and proximity to divide the appearance into two areas: an upper *display area* and a lower *control area*. The upper area contains three rows of information which are, from top to bottom, the *current* number of people in the room, the *maximum* number of people ever in the room and the *total* number of

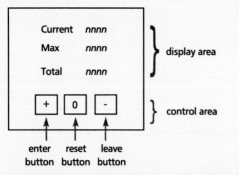

Figure 16.1   The visual design of the *RoomMonitorGUI*.

people who have entered the room. The *nnnn* associated with each of these labels indicates that the value will always be displayed using four digits, with leading zeros where necessary. The lower area contains three push buttons which will, from left to right, record the *entry* of a person into the room, *reset* the room monitor and record when a person *leaves* the room.

Having produced a visual design for the interface its behaviour can now be designed. The initial visual state of the interface, when it is first posted to the display, should be that all three displays are set to 0000. At this point the only sensible action is to record the entry of a person into the room. Accordingly only the *entry* button should be active and the other two buttons should be unavailable.

After the first person has been admitted, the displays should respond as appropriate, and all three buttons should become active. In this state pressing the *entry* button should record the entry of another person into the room. Pressing the *leave* button should record a person exiting from the room causing the *leave* button to become unavailable as, since there are no people in the room, no one can leave. Pressing the *reset* button should reset all three displays to 0000 and restore the buttons to their initial pattern of sensitivity.

During its normal operation, people will be continually entering and leaving the room causing the displays to be continually updated. From time to time the room will be empty and in this state the *leave* button should become unavailable. Likewise if the room is ever full the *entry* button should become unavailable. At all times, after the entry of the first person, the *reset* button should be available. This behavioural design of the interface can be expressed in an STD, as shown in Figure 16.2.

The diagram shows that the application has four states identified as the *reset state*, the *counting state*, the *minimal state* and the *maximal state*. The *initial state*, before the interface is posted to the display, is also considered and is represented by the solid circle at the top of the diagram. More complex applications would have a control to terminate the application and unpost the display. This state would be represented by a ringed circle with a transition leading from the interface to it.

The STD also shows the nine possible transitions in its behaviour, each of which, apart from the initial transition, is associated with some action by the user. The first transition, transition 1, is from the *initial* to the *reset* state and is not under the user's control. Its responsibility is to prepare the interface, making sure that it is in its *reset* state and then shown to the user. From this state there is a single possible transition, transition 2, to the *counting* state which will be taken when the *enter* button is pressed. The consequences of this transition are to update the displays and to set all buttons sensitive.

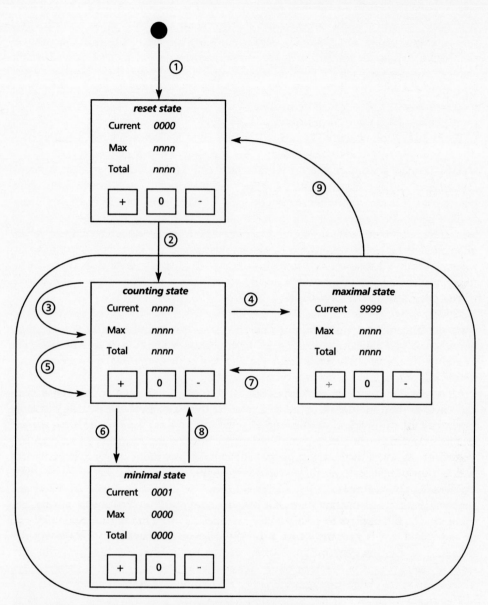

Figure 16.2 The STD for the *RoomMonitorGUI* application.

From the *counting* state pressing the *enter* button can have one of two consequences. If the value of the current number of people in the room is not one less than the maximum number of people then the effect is to return to the same *counting* state, shown as transition 3. Otherwise, if the current number counted is at its pre-maximal value, pressing the *enter* button will cause transition 4 to move to the *maximal* state, where the *enter* button becomes unavailable.

A similar pattern of events happens if the *leave* button is pressed in the *counting* state. If the current value is not one greater than the minimum value transition 5 returns to the *counting* state. Otherwise, if the value is pre-minimal, transition 6 takes the interface to the *minimal* state, where the *leave* button becomes unavailable.

Pressing the *leave* button in the *maximal* state will always cause transition 4, back to the *counting* state, to be followed. Likewise, pressing the *enter* button in the *minimal* state will always cause transition 8, back to the *counting* state, to be followed. From any of the *minimal*, *counting* or *maximal* states pressing the *reset* button effects transition 9 to the *reset* state. This is indicated by the rounded box bounding all of these states and from which transition 9 originates. These considerations can be expressed in a *state table*, as presented in Table 16.1.

The combination of the STD and state tables provides a concise and unambiguous description of the required behaviour of the interface when it is constructed. It is a specification of *what* interface is to be built and can be tested at this stage by investigations and walk-throughs to make sure that it will be effective and usable before resources are committed to building it. As with many of the examples in this book it is possibly unnecessary for an application of this complexity to be designed to this extent. However, it illustrates, and allows practise of, the design techniques which will definitely be required for more complex applications.

16.2 ■ The component instance hierarchy

The next stage in the production of this GUI is to decide upon the various components which will be required and their relationships with each other. Figure 16.3 presents a partial Java AWT class hierarchy diagram, containing the component classes which will be required for this interface.

All of the AWT components are extended from the Component class. The Button class will be used for the three push buttons at the bottom of the interface and six instances of the Label class will be used in the display area at the top: three on the left to label the values and three on the right to display the numbers. The extended Container classes have the capacity to contain other components within themselves and to control their layout. To accomplish *layout management* a class which implements the LayoutManager interface has to be used. The three classes at the bottom of the diagram, the BorderLayout, FlowLayout and GridLayout classes, are examples of such classes. The Panel class provides fundamental layout capability and its only child, the Applet class, adds the capability to post itself to the display and interact with the user.

Table 16.1 State table for the *RoomMonitorGUI* interface.

State	Action	Pre-condition	Transition	New state
initial	none	none	1	reset
reset	entry press	none	2	counting
counting	entry press	not pre-maximal	3	counting
counting	entry press	pre-maximal	4	maximal
counting	leave press	not pre-minimal	5	counting
counting	leave press	pre-minimal	6	minimal
maximal	leave press	none	7	counting
minimal	entry press	none	8	counting
counting maximal minimal	reset press	none	9	reset

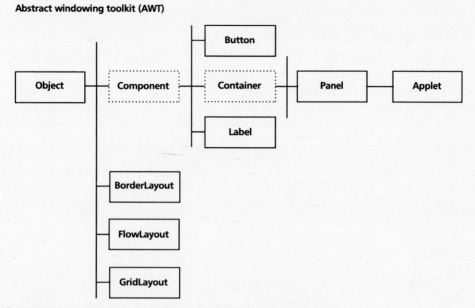

Abstract windowing toolkit (AWT)

Figure 16.3 A partial Java AWT component hierarchy diagram.

In order to obtain the visual appearance shown in Figure 16.1 a number of Panels have to be used. The display area at the top of the interface will have to have its own Panel as will the control area at the bottom. Both of these Panels will themselves be mounted upon an Applet Panel. If the intermediate Panels were not used then it would be very difficult, if not impossible, to obtain the desired, aesthetically pleasing, layout as required. The relationship between all these components is illustrated in Figure 16.4.

This diagram indicates that the six Labels providing the displays will be mounted onto a Panel which will in turn be mounted at the top of an Applet. Likewise the three Buttons providing the controls will be mounted on their own Panel which will be mounted at the bottom of the Applet. The logical relationship between these components, known as the *component instance hierarchy*, is illustrated in Figure 16.5 and also introduces names for the components.

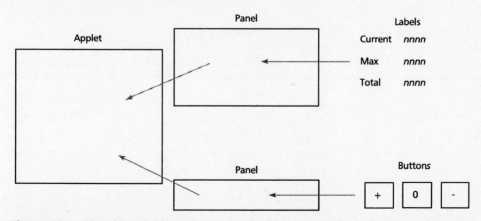

Figure 16.4 The physical relationship between the components.

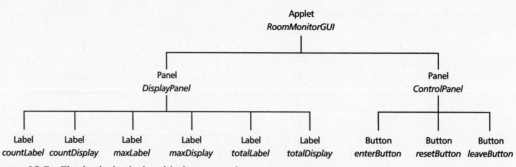

Figure 16.5   The logical relationship between the components.

16.3 ▓ Three layer GUI designs

The basis of the software design for the implementation of any application which has a GUI is to divide it into three concerns – the interface, its behaviour and the application itself – and then to implement each of these as a separate class. Here the application itself is already available as the *RoomMonitor* class in the *Counters* package. The user interface will be presented to the user as an instance of a new class called the *RoomMonitorInterface* class and the behaviour of the interface, which mediates between these two classes, is provided by an instance of a second new class called the *RoomMonitorGUI* class. The context diagram for the application is given in Figure 16.6.

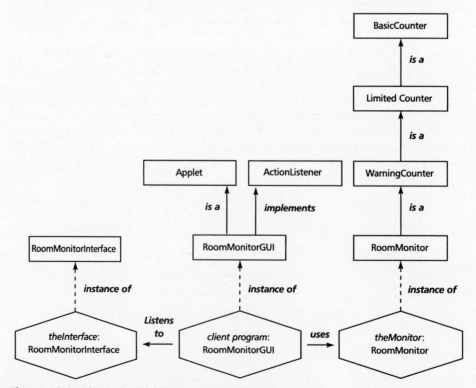

Figure 16.6   The *OrderedListDemo* context diagram.

On the right of the context diagram an instance of the *RoomMonitor* class called *theMonitor* is used by the client program which is an instance of the *RoomMonitorGUI* class. The *RoomMonitorGUI* class extends the Java **Applet** class and implements the **ActionListener** interface. This allows the client program to listen to the instance of the *RoomMonitorInterface*, called *theInterface*, on the left of the diagram. The listens to relationship between the client and the interface is central to the understanding of the implementation of GUI in the Java AWT and is illustrated in Figure 16.7.

When the user interacts with the interface, in this example by pushing its buttons, Java will generate *events* to report upon the user's deeds. These events are placed into an *event queue* from where they are retrieved in due course. At this point Java looks for the **ActionListener** object which has been registered as interested in events which originate from the component which generated the event. The events are then passed to the **ActionListener** object for it to respond to them in an application specific manner.

This event collection and dispatching facility, as well as the capability to post a top level application window onto the display, is provided by the **Applet** class. Thus by extending the **Applet** class much of the fundamental capabilities of an application is automatically provided.

In this example, when the user presses the *enter button* an event is placed in the queue and subsequently dispatched to its **ActionListener** object, the client program. When the client program receives the event it calls *theMonitor*'s *enterRoom()* action to inform it that another person has entered the room. Following this it will call its enquiry actions, such as *numberInRoomIs()*, and pass the values obtained back to *theInterface* in order that it can change its appearance in response and so provide feedback to the user on the effects of their actions. Thus the *RoomMonitorGUI* class is central to the application co-ordinating the user's actions and communicating with the application level object. However, the understanding of this class is dependent upon the implementation of the *RoomMonitorInterface* class which follows.

16.4 ■ The *RoomMonitorInterface* class

The *RoomMonitorInterface* class is responsible for constructing the interface using the logical relationships shown in Figure 16.5 and also for configuring, and reconfiguring,

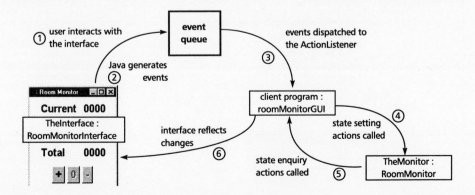

Figure 16.7 Event listening in the *RoomMonitorGUI* application.

the visual appearance of the interface as shown in the STD in Figure 16.2. Its class diagram is given in Figure 16.8.

The constructor will construct the interface installing it into the Applet instance passed to it as an argument. This instance is also used as the ActionListener destination of the Button instances in the interface; hence the implementation of the ActionListener interface shown in the context diagram. The *updateDisplays()* action requires three arguments which it will install into the three display components of the interface. The four remaining actions set the sensitivities of the three Buttons as indicated in the STDs. The implementation of this class, as far as the end of its instance declarations, is as follows:

```
0001 // Filename RoomMonitorInterface.java.
0002 // Provides an interactive interface for the RoomMonitor
0003 // class.
0004 //
0005 // Written for the JOF Chapter 16, see text.
0006 // Fintan Culwin, v0.1, August 1997.
0007
0008 import java.awt.*;
0009 import java.applet.*;
0010 import java.awt.event.*;
0011
0012 import OutputFormatter;
0013
0014
0015 public class RoomMonitorInterface extends Object {
0016
0017 private Button enterButton;
0018 private Button resetButton;
```

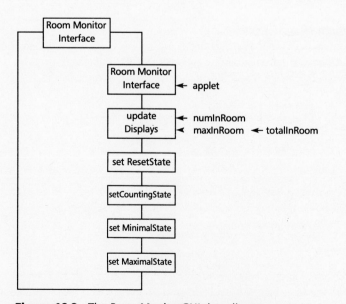

Figure 16.8 The *RoomMonitorGUI* class diagram.

```
0019 private Button leaveButton;
0020
0021 private Label countDisplay = new Label();
0022 private Label maxDisplay   = new Label();
0023 private Label totalDisplay = new Label();
```

The importation of the **awt** and **applet** classes on lines 008 to 0010 is needed to provide access to the interface facilities required for the construction of the application. On line 0012 the *OutputFormatter* class from Chapter 9 is imported and is used to format the numeric displays with leading zeros. On lines 0017 to 0020 the three **Button** instances are declared and on lines 0021 to 0023 the three **Label** instances. Only the three **Label** instances are constructed at this stage, using a constructor which does not specify a label to display. The remaining required components are created within the constructor action as follows:

```
0026       public RoomMonitorInterface( Applet applet) {
0027
0028       Panel  displayPanel = new Panel();
0029       Panel  controlPanel = new Panel();
0030       Label  countLabel   = new Label("Current ");
0031       Label  maxLabel     = new Label("Max ");
0032       Label  totalLabel   = new Label("Total ");
0033
0034          applet.setLayout( new BorderLayout( 0, 0));
0035          displayPanel.setLayout( new GridLayout(3, 2, 0, 1));
0036
0037          displayPanel.add( countLabel);
0038          displayPanel.add( countDisplay);
0039          displayPanel.add( maxLabel);
0040          displayPanel.add( maxDisplay);
0041          displayPanel.add( totalLabel);
0042          displayPanel.add( totalDisplay);
0043          applet.add( displayPanel, "Center");
0044
0045          enterButton  = new Button( "+");
0046          enterButton.setActionCommand( "enter");
0047          enterButton.addActionListener( (ActionListener) applet);
0048          controlPanel.add( enterButton);
0049
0050          resetButton  = new Button("0");
0051          resetButton.setActionCommand( "reset");
0052          resetButton.addActionListener( (ActionListener) applet);
0053          controlPanel.add( resetButton);
0054
0055          leaveButton  = new Button( "-");
0056          leaveButton.setActionCommand( "leave");
0057          leaveButton.addActionListener( (ActionListener) applet);
0058          controlPanel.add( leaveButton);
0059          applet.add( controlPanel, "South");
0060       } // End RoomMonitorInterface constructor.
```

On lines 0028 to 0032 the **Components** whose identity are only required to be known during the construction of the interface are declared and constructed. Then on line 0034 the layout policy of the **Applet** instance passed in the **applet** argument is established. The layout policy of a Panel, and thus of an Applet which is an extended Panel, determines the relationships between the Components which are added to it. The layout policy of the *applet* is set to BorderLayout. This layout policy allows up to five possible instance children, which can be added in its North, Center, South, East and West relative locations. The two arguments to the BorderLayout constructor indicate that there is to be no gap between the components.

On line 0035 the layout policy of the *displayPanel* is established as a three row by two column pattern with no (0) horizontal gap between its instance children and a 1 pixel vertical gap between them. When Components are added to this Panel they will be laid out in a top left/bottom right manner. The remaining Panel, the *controlPanel*, uses its default FlowLayout policy which will add its children in a left–right manner in a single row.

On lines 0037 to 0042 the six Label children of the displayPanel are added to it and, as explained above, will be laid out in the manner required by the visual design from Figure 16.4. Once populated the *displayPanel* is added to its instance parent, the *applet*, in its Center location.

On lines 0045 to 0048 the *enterButton* is constructed, configured and added to the *controlPanel*. The constructor, on line 0045, specifies a string which will be used to label the Button when it is displayed. On line 0046 its ActionCommand attribute is specified as "enter"; this will allow the events generated by this Button to be identified, as will be explained below. On line 0047 the ActionListener for this Button is established. The identity of the ActionListener is the *applet* argument which, as indicated in the context diagram, is of the RoomMonitorGUI class which, in addition to being an extended Applet, also implements the ActionListener interface. Thus the casting of the *applet* argument from its declared Applet class to the ActionListener class will be acceptable to Java.

Having constructed the *enterButton* it is added to the *controlPanel,* on line 0048. On lines 0050 to 0058 a similar pattern of activities first constructs and adds the *resetButton* and then the *leaveButton*. Finally, on line 0058, the *controlPanel*, now populated with its Buttons is added to the South location of the *applet*Panel.

When the *applet* is displayed it will engage in *layout negotiations* with its two child Panels. Each Panel will, recursively, engage in layout negotiations with its children. For the displayPanel it will request a height based upon the height of its three rows of children and the gaps between them; it will request a width based upon the widest combined width of the two Labels which form each of its rows. For the controlPanel it will request a height based upon the height of its single row, and a width based upon the widths of its three Buttons.

The *applet* has a BorderLayout with only its Center and South locations populated by the *displayPanel* and *controlPanel* respectively. It will, most probably, allow every Panel to have the height they have requested but will enforce the width of the broadest upon the narrowest. The final appearance of the interface is shown in Figure 16.9. This shows that the *controlPanel* has been awarded a wider area than it requested and has used the additional space by padding the left and right of its Buttons.

The implementation of the *RoomMonitorInterface updateDisplays()* action is as follows. It is passed three **int**eger arguments which it formats appropriately using the class wide *OutputFormatter formatLong()* action and installs the formatted strings into the appropriate Label components, using their *setText()* actions:

```
0063        public void updateDisplays( int numberInRoom,
0064                                    int maxInRoom,
```

Figure 16.9   The *RoomMonitorGUI* in its *reset* state under Windows 95.

```
0065                                      int totalInRoom) {
0066
0067        countDisplay.setText(
0068                  OutputFormatter.formatLong( numberInRoom,
0069                        4, true, OutputFormatter.DECIMAL));
0070        maxDisplay.setText(
0071                  OutputFormatter.formatLong( maxInRoom,
0072                       4, true, OutputFormatter.DECIMAL));
0073        totalDisplay.setText(
0074                  OutputFormatter.formatLong( totalInRoom,
0075                       4, true, OutputFormatter.DECIMAL));
0076     } // End updateDisplays.
```

The class concludes with the four *set* actions which use the Component setEnabled() action, inherited by the Button class, to specify the required sensitivity. The use made of these actions will be explained in the description of the *RoomMonitorGUI* class which follows:

```
0079     public void setResetState(){
0080        enterButton.setEnabled( true);
0081        resetButton.setEnabled( false);
0082        leaveButton.setEnabled( false);
0083     } // End setResetState.
0084
0085     public void setCountingState(){
0086        enterButton.setEnabled( true);
0087        resetButton.setEnabled( true);
0088        leaveButton.setEnabled( true);
0089     } // End setCountingState.
0090
0091     public void setMinimalState(){
0092        enterButton.setEnabled( true);
0093        resetButton.setEnabled( true);
0094        leaveButton.setEnabled( false);
0095     } // End setMinimalState.
0096
0097     public void setMaximalState(){
0098        enterButton.setEnabled( false);
```

```
0099          resetButton.setEnabled( true);
0100          leaveButton.setEnabled( true);
0101      } // End setMaximalState.
0102
0103 } // End class RoomMonitorInterface.
```

16.5 ▓ The *RoomMonitorGUI* class

The class diagram of the *RoomMonitorGUI* class is given in Figure 16.10.

The class has only three public actions which do not include a constructor; however, the *init()* action will be called during the construction of the **Applet** when it is possible for the interface to be constructed. The *main()* action is supplied in order that the program can be run as a standalone application as well as an applet within a Web browser. The *actionPerformed()* action is the only action which this class is required to supply in order for it to comply with the **ActionListener** interface. It is this *action* which will be *performed* when an event is dispatched to an instance of this class from the event queue. The implementation of this class as far as its *init()* action is as follows:

```
0001 // Filename RoomMonitorGUI.java.
0002 // Provides an interactive interface for the RoomMonitor
0003 // class.
0004 //
0005 // Written for the JOF Chapter 16, see text.
0006 // Fintan Culwin, v0.1, August 1997.
0007
0008
0009 import java.awt.*;
0010 import java.applet.*;
0011 import java.awt.event.*;
0012
0013
0014 import Counters.RoomMonitor;
```

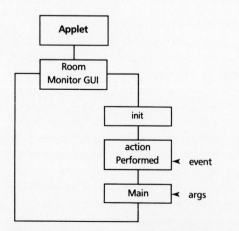

Figure 16.10   The *RoomMonitorGUI* class diagram.

```
0015 import RoomMonitorInterface;
0016
0017
0018 public class       RoomMonitorGUI
0019         extends    Applet
0020         implements ActionListener {
0021
0022 private RoomMonitor          theMonitor;
0023 private RoomMonitorInterface theInterface;
0024
0025 private static final int INITIAL_STATE  = 0;
0026 private static final int RESET_STATE    = 1;
0027 private static final int COUNTING_STATE = 2;
0028 private static final int MINIMAL_STATE  = 3;
0029 private static final int MAXIMAL_STATE  = 4;
0030 private static int       currentState   = INITIAL_STATE;
```

Following the header comments and the import clauses, lines 0018 to 0020 declare the *RoomMonitorGUI* class to be an extension of the Applet class which implements the ActionListener interface. On lines 0022 and 0023 the encapsulated *RoomMonitor* and *RoomMonitorInterface* instances are declared, in accord with the context diagram in Figure 16.6.

Lines 0025 to 0029 declare five private manifest values to reflect the five possible states of the interface, as indicated in the STD in Figure 16.2. On line 0030 a private instance variable, called *currentState*, is declared and initialized to indicate that the interface is currently in its *INITIAL_STATE*. The value of this variable will be changed always to reflect the state of the interface as presented to the user. The *init()* action is implemented as follows:

```
0033    public void init() {
0034        theMonitor   = new RoomMonitor();
0035        theInterface = new RoomMonitorInterface( this);
0036        theInterface.setResetState();
0037        currentState = RESET_STATE;
0038        theInterface.updateDisplays( theMonitor.numberCurrentlyInRoomIs(),
0039                                     theMonitor.maxEverInRoomIs(),
0040                                     theMonitor.totalNumberEnteredIs());
0041    } // End init.
```

The *init()* action will be called by Java during the construction of the Applet when it is safe for the interface to be constructed. It commences by constructing an instance of the *RoomMonitor* class designated by *theMonitor* and continues by constructing an instance of the *RoomMonitorInterface* class designated by *theInterface*. The argument supplied to this constructor is the identity of the Applet currently being constructed, for reasons explained above.

Once the *init()* action has concluded the interface contained within the Applet's Panel will be automatically posted to the user's display and their interaction with it reported via the event queue. However, before this, on line 0036, the interface is set to its *RESET_STATE* and this is recorded in the *currentState* attribute, on line 0037. The final step is a call of the *theInterface updateDisplays()* action passing the three values retrieved from *theMonitor*, in order to ensure that the interface as seen by the user accurately reflects the state of the *RoomMonitor*.

The design of the *actionPerformed()* action is as follows:

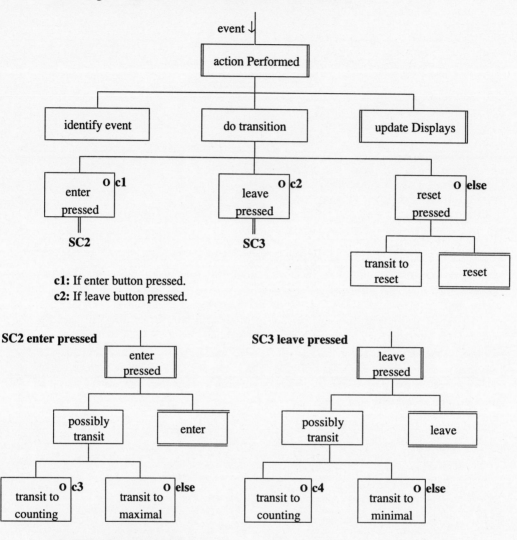

c1: If enter button pressed.
c2: If leave button pressed.

c3: If interface pre-maximal.
c4: If interface pre-minimal.

The basis of the design is to identify which button originated the event and then process it as an enter pressed, leave pressed or reset pressed occurrence; whatever way it is processed the final step of the design is to update the displays. In the case of each of the enter pressed or leave pressed situations the stages involved are possibly to transit to a different interface state and then to record the enter room or leave room occurrence with the encapsulated monitor. In the case of the reset button the transit to the reset state is always taken before the monitor is reset. The implementation of this design is as follows:

```
0044 public void actionPerformed ( ActionEvent event) {
0045
0046 String buttonPressed = event.getActionCommand();
0047
```

```
0048     if ( (buttonPressed.equals( "enter"))) {
0049         if ( (currentState == RESET_STATE))    ||
0050             (currentState == MINIMAL_STATE)) ){
0051           theInterface.setCountingState();
0052           currentState = COUNTING_STATE;
0053         } else if ( this.isPreMaximal()) {
0054           theInterface.setMaximalState();
0055           currentState = MAXIMAL_STATE;
0056         } // End if.
0057         theMonitor.enterRoom();
0058
0059     } else if ( buttonPressed.equals( "leave")) {
0060         if ( currentState == MAXIMAL_STATE) {
0061           theInterface.setCountingState();
0062           currentState = COUNTING_STATE;
0063         } else if ( this.isPreMinimal()) {
0064            theInterface.setMinimalState();
0065            currentState = MINIMAL_STATE;
0066         } // End if.
0067        theMonitor.leaveRoom();
0068
0069     } else {
0070       theInterface.setResetState();
0071       currentState = RESET_STATE;
0072       theMonitor.reset();
0073     } // End if.
0074    theInterface.updateDisplays( theMonitor.numberCurrentlyInRoomIs(),
0075                                 theMonitor.maxEverInRoomIs(),
0076                                 theMonitor.totalNumberEnteredIs()));
0077 } // End actionPerformed.
```

On line 0046 the *getActionCommand()* action of the *event*, passed by Java from the event queue as the argument to this action, is called to retrieve the actionCommand associated with the Button which originated the *event*. This was established as the interface was constructed as one of the strings "enter", "leave" or "reset" and the outer **if** structure uses the value retrieved to decide which part of the action to execute. Taking the enter branch of this **if** structure, between lines 0049 to 0057, as an example, if the interface is currently in its *RESET_STATE* or the *MINIMAL_STATE* then pressing the **enter** button will cause a transition to its *COUNTING_STATE*, effected on lines 0051 and 0052. Otherwise if the interface is in its *preMaximal* state, lines 0054 and 0055 will effect a transition to the *MAXIMAL_STATE*. Finally in this branch, on line 0057, the *enterRoom()* action of *theMonitor* is called to record the entry occurrence. To support the possible transitions to the minimal and maximal state, two supporting **boolean** actions called *isPreMinimal()* and *isPreMaximal()* are provided, as follows:

```
0082     public boolean isPreMinimal() {
0083       return ( theMonitor.numberCurrentlyInRoomIs() -
0084            theMonitor.minimumIs()) == 1;
0085     } // End isPreMinimal.
0086
0087     public boolean isPreMaximal() {
0088       return( theMonitor.maximumIs() -
```

```
0089                    theMonitor.numberCurrentlyInRoomIs()) == 1;
0090        } // End isPreMaximal
```

The remaining *RoomMonitorGUI* action, the *main()* action, will be considered in the following section.

16.6 ■ Executing the application

There are two ways in which this application can be executed, either as a standalone application or as an *applet* within a document in a World Wide Web browser. To execute within a Web browser there is no need to implement the *RoomMonitorGUI main()* action. The details of the HTML (Hyper Text Markup Language) syntax for including a Java applet within a browser are outside the scope of this book. However, a minimal HTML file might be as follows and the appearance of the applet when the HTML file was loaded by Netscape is shown in Figure 16.11.

```
<HTML>
<HEAD>
<! -- Minimal HTML document to execute the RoomMonitorGUI applet. -->
<! -- Written for the JOF book Chapter 16, see text.              -->
<! --                                                             -->
<! -- Fintan Culwin, v0.1, August 1997.
```

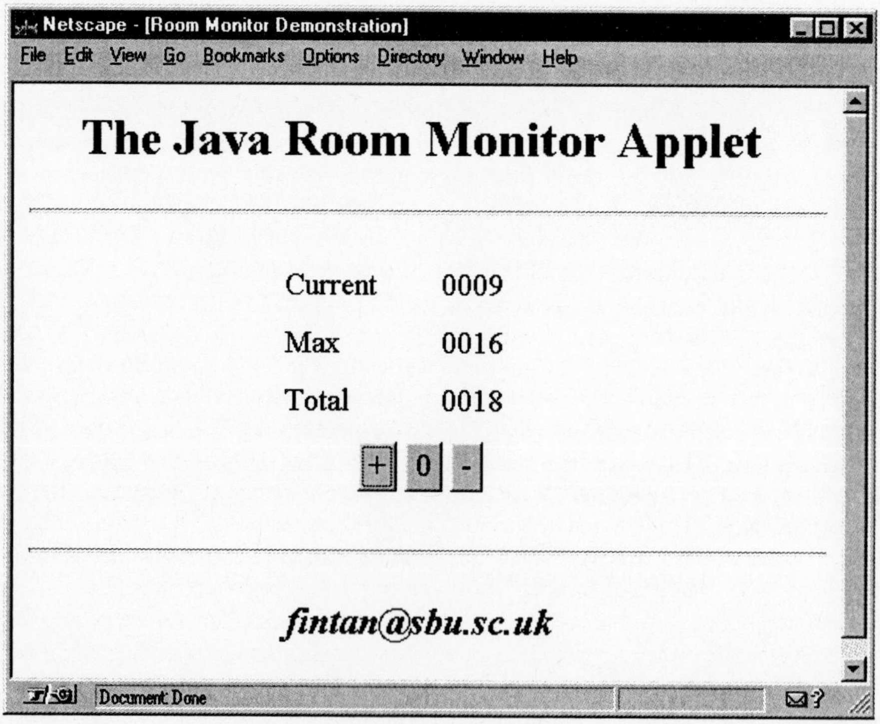

Figure 16.11 The *RoomMonitorGUI* in the *counting* state executing within Netscape 2.0.

```
<TITLE>Room Monitor Demonstration</TITLE>
</HEAD>

<BODY>
<CENTER>
<H1>
The Java Room Monitor Applet
</H1>

<P> <HR> <P>

<APPLET CODE="RoomMonitorGUI.class"
        HEIGHT=400
        WIDTH=300>
</APPLET>

<P> <HR> <P>
<H2><I>
fintan@sbu.sc.uk
</I></H2>

</CENTER>
</BODY>
</HTML>
```

By including a *main()* action in a file which extends the **Applet** class it is possible for the applet to be run outside of a browser, as well as inside a browser. The *main()* action of the *RoomMonitorGUI* class is as follows:

```
0093 public static void main( String args[]) {
0094
0095 Frame           frame         = new Frame("Room Monitor demo");
0096 RoomMonitorGUI theInterface = new RoomMonitorGUI();
0097
0098      theInterface.init();
0099      frame.add(theInterface, "Center");
0100
0101      frame.show();
0102      frame.resize( frame.preferredSize());
0103 } // End main.
```

In order to run outside of a browser the **Applet** needs to be added within a **Container Frame** instance. Consequently the main action creates an instance of the **Frame** class, called *frame*, and an instance of the *RoomMonitoirGUI* class, called *theInterface*. The default layout manager style for a **Frame** instance is **BorderLayout** and, on line 0099, *theInterface* is added into its **Center** position. Before this its *init()* action has been explicitly called in order to construct it. Finally the frame is **shown()** on line 0101 and immediately *resized()* for it to accommodate to its **preferredSize()**, based upon the preferred size of the contained *RoomMonitorGUI* instance. At this point the event dispatcher will take over, collecting the user's actions, packaging them into **Events** and passing them to the *actionPerformed()* action to be responded to. Figure 16.9 illustrates the application running as a standalone application.

Summary

- The Java AWT hierarchy supplies a collection of Components which provide the objects from which GUIs can be constructed.

- The Panel class, and so classes extended from it, have the capability of laying out their instance children.

- Layout management policies are determined by instances of classes which implement the LayoutManager interface; these include the BorderLayout, FlowLayout and GridLayout classes.

- The Applet class extends the Panel class to add the capability to interact with the user, and can be extended to produce an application's GUI.

- The design of a GUI should start with its visual appearance and continue with a design for its behaviour, expressed as a *state transition diagram* and a *state table*.

- The *component instance hierarchy* identifies, and names, the objects which will be used to construct the interface.

- When the user interacts with the interface an *Event* is dispatched, via an *event queue*, to the *actionPerformed()* action of a registered ActionListener instance.

- Applications with a GUI can be thought of as, and designed and implemented in, three layers: a presentation layer which controls the visual appearance of the interface, an application layer which supplies the application's functionality and a translation layer which implements the interface's behaviour.

Exercises

16.1 The location of the *reset* button in this interface may cause it to be accidentally pressed. Redesign the visual appearance of the interface, and then reimplement it, to mitigate this potential problem.

16.2 Design and implement a graphical user interface for the *ClickCounter* class from Chapter 3.

16.3 Design and implement a graphical user interface for the *VehicleCounter* class in Exercise 4.6.4.

16.4 When you are next using a commercial application with a graphical user interface, choose one of the dialog panels and deconstruct it to produce a component instance hierarchy. If you had the opportunity, what design changes would you make to this interface?

16.5 Design and implement a stopwatch application. When the *start* button is pressed the thread should be started and it should sleep for one tenth of a second before updating the numeric value on a label. When the *stop* button is pressed the thread should be suspended. The interface should also provide *resume* and *reset* buttons with their sensitivities changing as appropriate.

Case study: The Elephant Burger Bar

Introduction

The specification for this case study was originally used as a first year undergraduate coursework assignment at South Bank University, to be completed using Ada 95 as the implementation language. This case study was prepared by Ian Marshall who reimplemented his original designs using Java. It represents a degree of capability to which a novice developer following the contents of this book should aspire, although parts of Ian's original report have been omitted for the sake of brevity. In particular no demonstration or testing sections are included in this report. The behaviour of the program, as implemented, is described in the first section which describes the user interface.

South Bank University is located in an area of London known as the Elephant and Castle. Thus the 'Elephant' in the title of the case study indicates the geographical location of the burger bar, not the type of meat which it uses in its burgers.

Specification

The specification for this coursework is to produce a program for the operation of The Elephant Burger Bar. The Burger Bar supplies three different types of Meal: Meat, Fish and Vegetarian, which are served with a choice of Fries or BakedPotato and Coke, Lemonade or Orange. A Meat meal costs £1.50, a Fish meal £1.60 and a Vegetarian meal £1.40.

The main menu of the program should offer the operator a choice of:

- Adding a meal to the queue of meals waiting to be served.
- Serving the next meal from the queue.
- Listing the meals waiting in the queue.
- Showing the state of the cash register.
- Exiting from the program.

The menu option to add a meal to the queue should lead to a dialog where the operator indicates the options required by the customer, and the price of the meal should then be displayed. This amount is to be deposited into the Burger Bar's cash register.

The option to serve a meal should result in details of the next meal in the queue, if any, being served. The program should display details of the meal including the time at which the meal was ordered and the time at which it was served.

The option to list the meals in the queue should result in a list of all meals waiting to be served, preceded by the number of meals waiting in the queue. (The number of meals in the queue should also be displayed at the top of the main menu.)

The option to show the state of the register should indicate the number of meals (transactions) and the amount of cash in the register.

The option to exit the program should be refused if there are any meals waiting to be served.

You should reuse as many classes from the course as possible. Designs which do not make appropriate use of available resources will be penalized. The only class which might be useful which has not been introduced so far is the *TimeStamp* class.

You should start by producing an instance diagram identifying which objects you are going to reuse and which ones you are going to construct.

The *Meal* object should be constructed from a hierarchy (e.g. *SimpleMeal*, *PricedMeal*, *MealWithFriesOrPotatoes*, *MealWithDrink*, *TimeStampedMeal*). Develop this hierarchy by identifying the data attributes and actions which have to be performed upon each refinement, and using a test harness to demonstrate the actions.

You might then start by producing a program which runs the high level menu and includes the menu options as subprogram stubs. The first working version of the program might not include a cash register, only queuing and de-queuing the meal orders. (You are likely to get more marks for a program which is partially working than for a program which attempts to do everything and fails.)

User interface design

The following is the user interface definition and screen design layout for the Elephant Burger Bar main menu and submenus. Once defined, these diagrams form a 'master template' and shall be consulted during the menu implementation in Java.

Each diagram represents the screen as it will actually appear on the target machine. The ruler is used to locate individual characters and string start/end points. The bold italicized characters represent typical user inputs and are for demonstration purposes only.

There are several error messages displayed by the program. They are designed:

- To be informative – but not verbose.
- To have a common 'look' to them.
- To offer an error summary (in UPPER CASE).
- To offer a reason for the error (in lower case).

The main menu

The following is the main menu as it will appear directly after the program has started:

```
          1         2         3         4         5         6         7
0123456789012345678901234567890123456789012345678901234567890123456789012345
```

```
===============================================

Meals queued : 0

       THE ELEPHANT BURGER BAR

A.   Order a meal.
B.   Serve oldest meal.
```

```
C.    Show meal queue.
D.    Show cash register.
E.    EXIT.

PLEASE SELECT ==>
```

A requirement for this program is that the main menu displays the number of meals waiting to be served; this is displayed at the top left. From the main menu, there are five valid user inputs, each of which is now addressed separately.

Option 'A': order a meal

From the main menu, entering option 'A' invokes the main meal submenu as follows:

```
          1         2         3         4         5         6         7
0123456789012345678901234567890123456789012345678901234567890123456789012345
```

```
          MAIN MEAL OPTIONS

A.    Meat
B.    Fish
C.    Vegetarian

PLEASE SELECT A MEAL ==> A
```

Entering a valid meal option invokes the side dish submenu as follows:

```
          1         2         3         4         5         6         7
0123456789012345678901234567890123456789012345678901234567890123456789012345
```

```
          SIDE DISH OPTIONS

A.    Fries
B.    Baked potato
C.    None

PLEASE SELECT A SIDE DISH ==> B
```

Entering a valid side dish option invokes the drinks option submenu as follows:

```
          1         2         3         4         5         6         7
0123456789012345678901234567890123456789012345678901234567890123456789012345
```

```
          DRINK OPTIONS

A.    Coke
B.    Lemonade
C.    Orange
D.    None

PLEASE SELECT A DRINK ==> C
```

Entering a valid drink option leads to the redisplay of the main menu, but with the price of the requested meal displayed at the top left. For example:

```
          1         2         3         4         5         6         7
0123456789012345678901234567890123456789012345678901234567890123456789012345
```

```
=========================================
The price of the meal is 1.50
=========================================


Meals queued : 1

          THE ELEPHANT BURGER BAR

A.    Order a meal.
B.    Serve last meal ordered.
C.    Show meal queue.
D.    Show cash register.
E.    EXIT.

PLEASE SELECT ==>
```

The user is now returned to the main menu.

Option 'B': serve a meal

Following an input of 'B' from the main menu, there are two possible alternatives:

1. The meal queue is empty. The user is therefore presented with the following error message:

```
          1         2         3         4         5         6         7
0123456789012345678901234567890123456789012345678901234567890123456789012345
```

```
=========================================
SERVE MEAL COMMAND IGNORED
REASON > meal queue is empty
=========================================
```

2. The meal queue is not empty. The user is presented with the following typical information:

```
          1         2         3         4         5         6         7
0123456789012345678901234567890123456789012345678901234567890123456789012345
```

```
Meals queued : 1

=========================================
SERVING MEAL
~~~~~~~~~~~
Meal type ...... meat
Price of meal .. 1.50
Side dish ...... fries
```

```
Beverage ....... coke
Order time ..... 14:24:36
Served at ...... 14:29:12
==========================================
```

The user is now returned to the main menu.

Option 'C': show meal queue

Again, following an input of 'C' from the main menu, there are two possible alternatives:

1. The meal queue is empty. The user is therefore presented with the following error message:

```
          1         2         3         4         5         6         7
0123456789012345678901234567890123456789012345678901234567890123456789012345
```

```
==========================================
SHOW MEAL QUEUE COMMAND IGNORED
REASON > meal queue is empty
==========================================
```

2. The meal queue is not empty. The user is presented with the following typical information:

```
          1         2         3         4         5         6         7
0123456789012345678901234567890123456789012345678901234567890123456789012345
```

```
==========================================
SHOWING MEAL QUEUE
~~~~~~~~~~~~~~~~~~
Meals queued : 2

1
Meal type ...... meat
Price of meal .. 1.50
Side dish ...... fries
Beverage ....... lemonade
Order time ..... 21:38:39
Served at ...... **:**:**
2
Meal type ...... fish
Price of meal .. 1.60
Side dish ...... baked potato
Beverage ....... coke
Order time ..... 21:41:57
Served at ...... **:**:**


==========================================
```

The user is now returned to the main menu.

Option 'D': show cash register

Following an input of 'D' from the main menu, the user is presented with the following typical information:

```
          1         2         3         4         5         6         7
0123456789012345678901234567890123456789012345678901234567890123456789012345
```

```
=============================================
CASH REGISTER STATUS
~~~~~~~~~~~~~~~~~~~~~
Total transactions ....... 4
Total cash in register ... 6.10
=============================================
```

The user is now returned to the main menu.

Option 'E': exit

Following an input of 'E' from the main menu, there are two possible alternatives:

1. *There are unserved meals in the meal queue.* The user is therefore presented with the following error message:

```
          1         2         3         4         5         6         7
0123456789012345678901234567890123456789012345678901234567890123456789012345
```

```
=============================================
EXIT COMMAND IGNORED
REASON > unserved meals in queue
=============================================
```

2. *Meal queue is empty.* The program will return the user to the operating system:

```
          1         2         3         4         5         6
012345678901234567890123456789012345678901234567890123456789
```

```
Exit command accepted.
Goodbye.
```

Instance diagram

This program must make maximum reuse of available resources. Figure CS1 contains the instance diagram for the *ElephantBurgerBar* application. In the diagram boxes without shading represent classes introduced in the book which will be reused. Shaded boxes represent classes/code that do not presently exist and will be developed as part of this assignment. The *TimeStamp* class, shown with a lighter shading, has not been previously described and has been provided in order to support the time stamping of the meals. The implementation of this class is given in Appendix B.

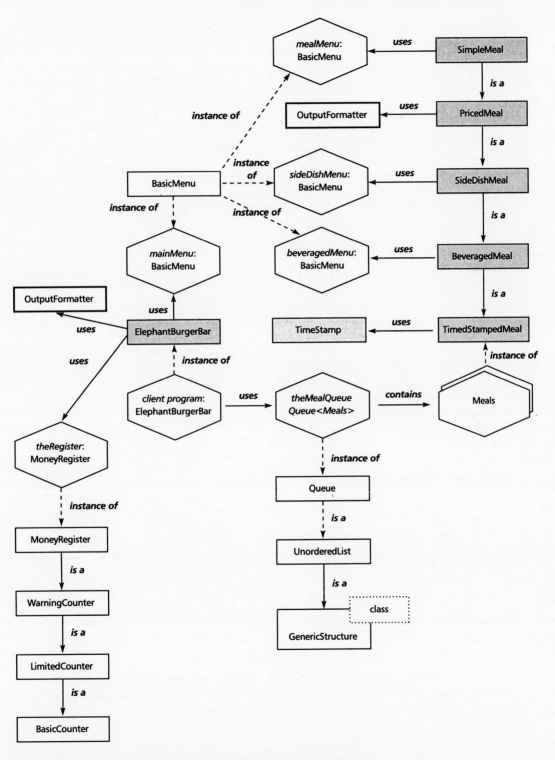

Figure CS1 Instance diagram for the *ElephantBurgerBar* application.

The *Meal* class hierarchy and class diagrams

The Meal class hierarchy is the backbone of the whole program, Figure CS2 contains its class hierarchy diagram.

The hierarchy is made up from five classes:

1. The *SimpleMeal* class, which allows a basic meal to be stored. It may be a meat, fish or vegetarian meal. Its class diagram is given in Figure CS3.
2. The *PricedMeal* class, which allows the price of the meal to be stored. Its class diagram is given in Figure CS4.

Figure CS2   The *Meal* class hierarchy diagram.

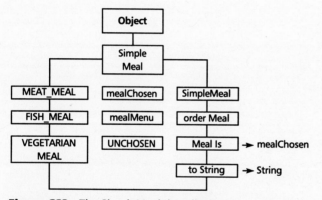

Figure CS3   The *SimpleMeal* class diagram.

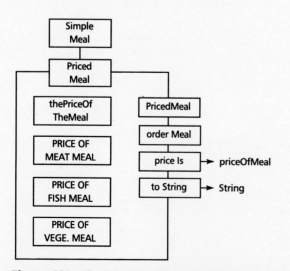

Figure CS4   The *PricedMeal* class diagram.

3. The *SideDishMeal* class, which allows an optional side dish to be stored. Its class diagram is given in Figure CS5.
4. The *BeveragedMeal* class, which allows an optional drink to be stored. Its class diagram is given in Figure CS6.
5. The *TimeStampedMeal* class, which allows meal order and serve times to be stored. Its class diagram is given in Figure CS7.

Classes

The class implementations which follow are taken directly from the class diagrams above. It is vital that class diagrams are 'frozen' once complete. This is to ensure that there is a common thread throughout development with each iterative class implementation expanding and amplifying the preceding class.

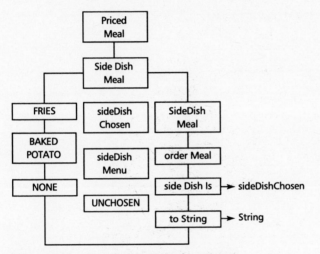

Figure CS5   The *SideDishMeal* class diagram.

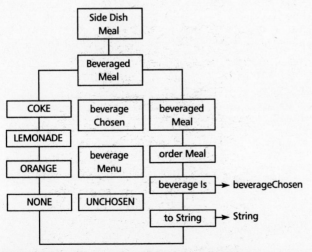

Figure CS6   The *BeveragedMeal* class diagram.

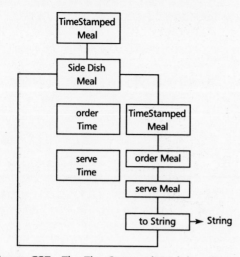

Figure CS7   The *TimeStampedMeal* class diagram.

SimpleMeal Class

```
// Filename : Meals/SimpleMeal.java
// Author   : Ian Marshall (marshaip@sbu.ac.uk)
//            2nd Year BSc(Hons) Computing Studies(Software Engineering) Student
//            South Bank University, London
// Date     : August 1997
// Version  : v1.0
// Comment  : Root type of the Meals hierarchy.
//            Introduces a basic meal.

package Meals;

import Menus.BasicMenu;

public class SimpleMeal extends Object {

    private   final static int UNCHOSEN        = 0;
    protected final static int MEAT_MEAL       = 1;
    protected final static int FISH_MEAL       = 2;
    protected final static int VEGETARIAN_MEAL = 3;

    private int mealChosen = UNCHOSEN;

    String mealOptions[] = { "Meat", "Fish", "Vegetarian"};

    private BasicMenu mealMenu = new BasicMenu( "MAIN MEAL OPTIONS",
                                                mealOptions,
                                                "PLEASE SELECT A MEAL ==>");

    public SimpleMeal() {
        super();
    } // End SimpleMeal.
```

```
    public void orderMeal() {
        System.out.println();
        mealChosen = mealMenu.offerMenuAsInt();
    } // End orderMeal.

    public int mealIs() {
        return mealChosen;
    } // End mealIs.

    public String toString() {
        StringBuffer buffer = new StringBuffer("");
        buffer.append( "\nMeal type ......");

        switch (mealChosen) {

        case UNCHOSEN:
            buffer.append( "unknown ");
            break;

        case MEAT_MEAL:
            buffer.append( "meat ");
            break;

        case FISH_MEAL:
            buffer.append( "fish ");
            break;

        case VEGETARIAN_MEAL:
            buffer.append( "vegetarian ");
            break;
        } // End switch.
        return buffer.toString();
    } // End toString.

} // End SimpleMeal.
```

PricedMeal class

```
// Filename : Meals/PricedMeal.java
// Author   : Ian Marshall (marshaip@sbu.ac.uk)
//            2nd Year BSc(Hons) Computing Studies(Software Engineering) Student
//            South Bank University, London
// Date     : August 1997
// Version  : v1.0
// Comment  : First extension of the Meals hierarchy.
//            Adds meal price functionality.

package Meals;


import OutputFormatter;
```

```java
public class PricedMeal extends SimpleMeal {

    private final static double PRICE_OF_MEAT_MEAL       = 1.50;
    private final static double PRICE_OF_FISH_MEAL       = 1.60;
    private final static double PRICE_OF_VEGETARIAN_MEAL = 1.40;
    private double thePriceOfTheMeal                     = 0.00;

    public PricedMeal() {
        super();
    } // End PricedMeal.

    public void orderMeal() {
        super.orderMeal();

        switch ( this.mealIs()) {

        case MEAT_MEAL:
            thePriceOfTheMeal = PRICE_OF_MEAT_MEAL;
            break;

        case FISH_MEAL:
            thePriceOfTheMeal = PRICE_OF_FISH_MEAL;
            break;

        case VEGETARIAN_MEAL:
            thePriceOfTheMeal = PRICE_OF_VEGETARIAN_MEAL;
            break;
        } // End switch.
    } // End orderMeal.

    public double priceIs() {
        return ( thePriceOfTheMeal);
    } // End priceIs.

    public String toString() {
        StringBuffer buffer = new StringBuffer( super.toString());
        buffer.append( "\nPrice of meal .. " +
                    OutputFormatter.formatFloat( (float) priceIs(),
                                                    2, 2, false));

        return buffer.toString();
    } // End toString.

} // End PricedMeal.
```

SideDishMeal class

```java
// Filename : Meals/SideDishMeal.java
// Author   : Ian Marshall (marshaip@sbu.ac.uk)
//            2nd Year BSc(Hons) Computing Studies(Software Engineering) Student
//            South Bank University, London
// Date     : August 1997
```

```
// Version  : v1.0
// Comment  : Second extension of the Meals hierarchy.
//           Adds side dish functionality.

package Meals;

import Menus.BasicMenu;

public class SideDishMeal extends PricedMeal {

    private   final static int UNCHOSEN     = 0;
    protected final static int FRIES        = 1;
    protected final static int BAKED_POTATO = 2;
    protected final static int NONE         = 3;

    private int sideDishChosen = UNCHOSEN;

    String sideDishOptions[] = { "Fries", "Baked potato", "None"};

    private BasicMenu sideDishMenu = new BasicMenu( "SIDE DISH OPTIONS",
                                                    sideDishOptions,
                                      "PLEASE SELECT A SIDE DISH ==>");

    public SideDishMeal() {
        super();
    } // End SideDishMeal.

    public void orderMeal() {
        super.orderMeal();

        System.out.println();
        sideDishChosen = sideDishMenu.offerMenuAsInt();
    } // End orderMeal.

    public int sideDishIs() {
    return sideDishChosen;
    } // End sideDishIs.

    public String toString() {
        StringBuffer buffer = new StringBuffer( super.toString());

        buffer.append( "\nSide dish ...... ");

        switch ( sideDishChosen) {

        case UNCHOSEN:
            buffer.append( "unknown ");
            break;

        case FRIES:
            buffer.append( "fries ");
            break;
```

```
      case BAKED_POTATO:
         buffer.append( "baked potato ");
         break;

      case NONE:
         buffer.append( "none ");
         break;
      } // End switch.
      return buffer.toString();
   } // End toString.

} // End SideDishMeal.
```

BeveragedMeal class

```
// Filename : Meals/BeveragedMeal.java
// Author   : Ian Marshall (marshaip@sbu.ac.uk)
//            2nd Year BSc(Hons) Computing Studies(Software Engineering) Student
//            South Bank University, London
// Date     : August 1997
// Version  : v1.0
// Comment  : Third extension of the Meals hierarchy.
//            Adds beverage functionality.

package Meals;

import Menus.BasicMenu;

public class BeveragedMeal extends SideDishMeal {

   private   final static int UNCHOSEN = 0;
   protected final static int COKE     = 1;
   protected final static int LEMONADE = 2;
   protected final static int ORANGE   = 3;
   protected final static int NONE     = 4;

   private int beverageChosen = UNCHOSEN;

   String beverageOptions[] = { "Coke", "Lemonade", "Orange", "None"};

   private BasicMenu beverageMenu = new BasicMenu( "DRINK OPTIONS",
                                                   beverageOptions,
                                                   "PLEASE SELECT A DRINK ==>");

   public BeveragedMeal() {
      super();
   } // End BeveragedMeal.

   public void orderMeal() {
      super.orderMeal();
```

```
        System.out.println();
        beverageChosen = beverageMenu.offerMenuAsInt();
    } // End orderMeal.

    public int beverageIs() {
        return beverageChosen;
    } // End beverageIs.

    public String toString() {
        StringBuffer buffer = new StringBuffer( super.toString());

        buffer.append( "\nBeverage ....... ");
        switch (beverageChosen) {

        case UNCHOSEN:
            buffer.append( "unknown ");
            break;

        case COKE:
            buffer.append( "coke ");
            break;

        case LEMONADE:
            buffer.append( "lemonade ");
            break;

        case ORANGE:
            buffer.append( "orange ");
            break;

        case NONE:
            buffer.append( "none ");
            break;
        } // End switch.
        return buffer.toString();
    } // End toString.

} // End BeveragedMeal.
```

TimeStamped Meal class

```
// Filename : Meals/TimeStampedMeal.java
// Author   : Ian Marshall (marshaip@sbu.ac.uk)
//            2nd Year BSc(Hons) Computing Studies(Software Engineering) Student
//            South Bank University, London
// Date     : August 1997
// Version  : v1.0
// Comment  : Fourth extension of the Meals hierarchy.
//            Adds time stamp functionality.
```

```
package Meals;

import TimeStamp;

public class TimeStampedMeal extends BeveragedMeal {

    private TimeStamp orderTime = new TimeStamp();
    private TimeStamp serveTime = new TimeStamp();

    public TimeStampedMeal() {
        super();
    } // End TimStampedMeal.

    public void orderMeal() {
        super.orderBeveragedMeal();
        this.orderTime.stamp();
    } // End orderMeal.

    public void serveMeal() {
        this.serveTime.stamp();
    } // End serveMeal.

    public String toString() {
        StringBuffer buffer = new StringBuffer( super.toString());

        buffer.append( "\nOrder Time ..... " + orderTime +
                       "\nServed at ...... " + serveTime);
        return buffer.toString();
    } // End toString.

} // End TimeStampedMeal.
```

Demonstration clients

During the iterative development of the above classes, a demonstration client was
developed at the same time. The client demonstrated the functionality offered by the
newly developed class along with the underlying hierarchy. There were, therefore, five
demonstration clients in all, but as space is limited the final client alone is reproduced
below. However, all demonstration clients are available; details can be found in
Appendix B.

TimeStampedMeal demonstration client and output

The following client demonstrates the *TimeStampedMeal* class and the underlying
hierarchy supporting it:

```
// Filename : TimeStampedMealDemo.java
// Author   : Ian Marshall (marshaip@sbu.ac.uk)
```

```
//            2nd Year BSc(Hons) Computing Studies(Software Engineering) Student
//            South Bank University, London
// Date     : August 1997
// Version  : v1.0
// Comment  : Demonstration client for the TimeStampedMeal class.

import Meals.TimeStampedMeal;

public class TimeStampedMealDemo {

    public static void main( String argv[]) {

    TimeStampedMeal demoMeal = new TimeStampedMeal();

        System.out.println( "\n\Time Stamped Meal Demonstration\n\n");

        System.out.println( "Getting the meal ...\n");
        demoMeal.orderMeal();

        System.out.println( "\n\nMeal Summary \n" + demoMeal);

        System.out.println( "Serving the meal ...\n");
        demoMeal.serveMeal();

        System.out.println( "\n\nMeal Summary \n" + demoMeal);
    } // End main.

} // End TimeStampedMealDemo.
```

This client should produce the following output:

```
            Stamped Meal Demonstration


    Getting the meal ...

            MAIN MEAL OPTIONS

    A.   Meat
    B.   Fish
    C.   Vegetarian

    PLEASE SELECT A MEAL ==> a
            SIDE DISH OPTIONS

    A.   Fries
    B.   Baked potato
    C.   None


    PLEASE SELECT A SIDE DISH ==> b
```

```
              DRINK OPTIONS

   A.   Coke
   B.   Lemonade
   C.   Orange
   D.   None

   PLEASE SELECT A DRINK ==> c


   Meal Summary
   Meal type ...... meat
   Price of meal .. 1.50
   Side dish ...... baked potato
   Beverage ....... orange
   Order Time ..... 09:37:18
   Served at ...... **:**:**

   Serving the meal ...
   Meal Summary
   Meal type ...... meat
   Price of meal .. 1.50
   Side dish ...... baked potato
   Beverage ....... orange
   Order Time ..... 09:37:18
   Served at ...... 09:37:19
```

The Elephant Burger Bar demonstration client

The design of the program is expressed in the following JSP diagrams:

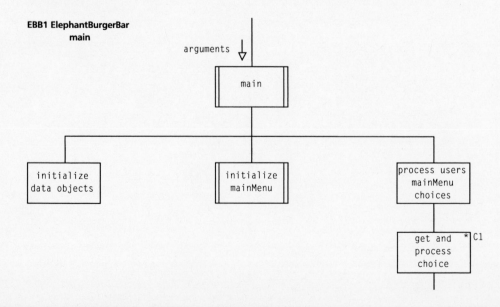

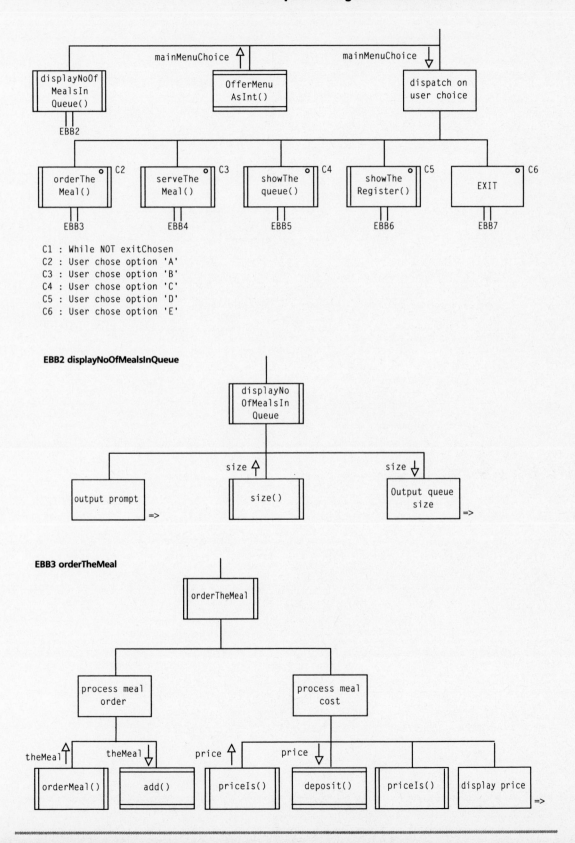

C1 : While NOT exitChosen
C2 : User chose option 'A'
C3 : User chose option 'B'
C4 : User chose option 'C'
C5 : User chose option 'D'
C6 : User chose option 'E'

EBB2 displayNoOfMealsInQueue

EBB3 orderTheMeal

EBB4 serveTheMeal

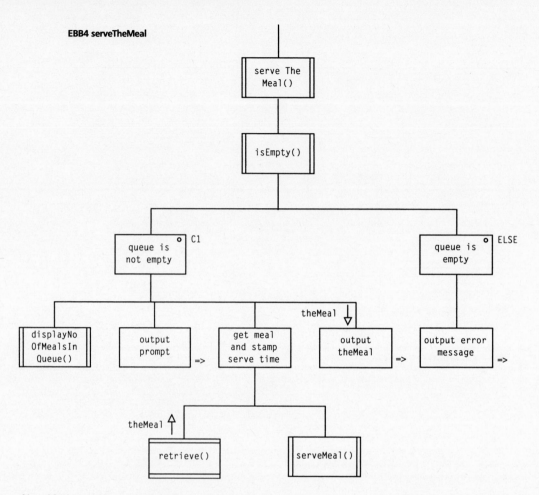

C1 : If there are unserved meals in the meal queue

EBB5 showTheQueue

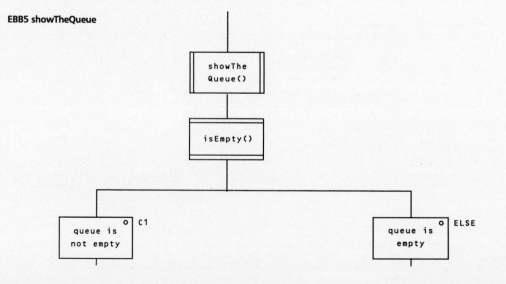

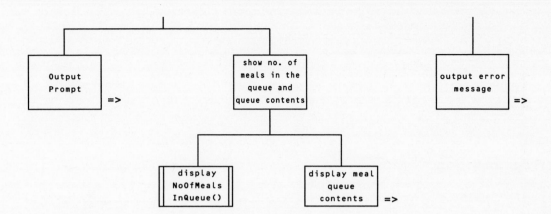

C1 : If there are unserved meals in the meal queue

EBB6 showTheRegister

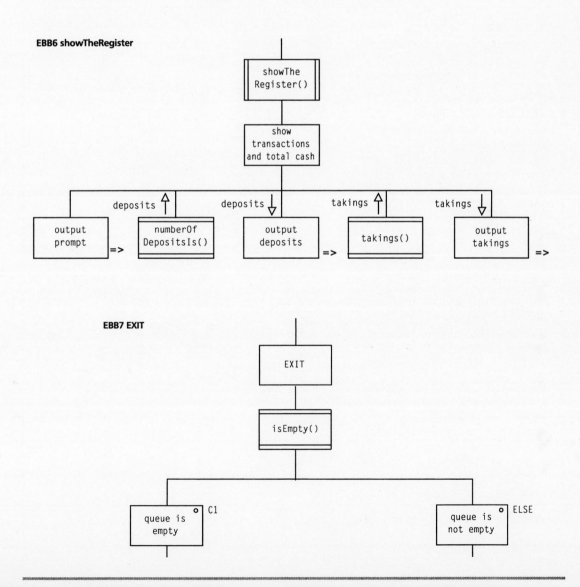

EBB7 EXIT

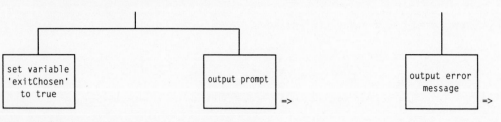

C1 : If there are unserved meals in the meal queue

Program listing

```
// Filename : ElephantBurgerBar.java
// Author   : Ian Marshall (marshaip@sbu.ac.uk)
//            2nd Year BSc(Hons) Computing Studies(Software Engineering) Student
//            South Bank University, London
// Date     : August 1997
// Version  : v1.0
// Comment  : THE "ELEPHANT BURGER BAR" DEMONSTRATION CLIENT.
//            This client addresses and implements the program
//            specification produced by Fintan Culwin.
//            The client makes full use of the Meal class hierarchy.

import Menus.BasicMenu;
import Meals.TimeStampedMeal;
import Generics.Queue;
import Counters.MoneyRegister;
import OutputFormatter;

class ElephantBurgerBar {

static TimeStampedMeal theMeal    = new TimeStampedMeal();
static Queue theMealQueue         = new Queue( theMeal.getClass());
static MoneyRegister theRegister = new MoneyRegister( 0.0);

private final static int UNCHOSEN      = 0;
private final static int ORDER_MEAL    = 1;
private final static int SERVE_MEAL    = 2;
private final static int SHOW_QUEUE    = 3;
private final static int SHOW_REGISTER = 4;
private final static int EXIT          = 5;

private static boolean exitChosen    = false;
private static int     mainMenuChoice = UNCHOSEN;

static String mainMenuOptions[] = { "Order a meal.",
                                    "Serve a meal.",
                                    "Show meal queue.",
                                    "Show cash register.",
                                    "EXIT."};

static BasicMenu mainMenu = new BasicMenu( "THE ELEPHANT BURGER BAR",
                                            mainMenuOptions,
                                            "PLEASE SELECT ==>");
```

```java
    public static void main( String argv[]) {

        while ( ! exitChosen) {

            System.out.println();
            System.out.println("=============================================");

            displayNoOfMealsInQueue();

            mainMenuChoice = mainMenu.offerMenuAsInt();

            switch ( mainMenuChoice) {

                case ORDER_MEAL:
                    orderTheMeal();
                    break;

                case SERVE_MEAL:
                    serveTheMeal();
                    break;

                case SHOW_QUEUE:
                    showTheQueue();
                    break;

                case SHOW_REGISTER:
                    showTheRegister();
                    break;

                case EXIT:
                    if (theMealQueue.isEmpty()) {
                        exitChosen = true;

                        System.out.println( "Exit command accepted.");
                        System.out.println( "Goodbye.");
                        System.out.println();
                    } else {
                        System.out.println
                                ( "=============================================");
                        System.out.println( "EXIT COMMAND IGNORED");
                        System.out.print( "REASON > unserved meals in queue");
                    } // End if
                    break;
            } // End switch.
        } // End while.
    } // End main.

    public static void displayNoOfMealsInQueue() {
        System.out.println();
        System.out.println( "Meals queued : " + theMealQueue.size());
        System.out.println();
    } // End displayNoOfMealsInQueue.
```

```
public static void orderTheMeal() {
TimeStampedMeal theMeal = new TimeStampedMeal();

    theMeal.orderMeal();
    theMealQueue.add( theMeal);
    theRegister.deposit( theMeal.priceIs());

    System.out.println( "==========================================");
    System.out.print( "The price of the meal is " +
        OutputFormatter.formatFloat( (float) theMeal.priceIs(), 1, 2, false));
} // End orderTheMeal.


public static void serveTheMeal() {
TimeStampedMeal theMeal;

    if ( ! theMealQueue.isEmpty()) {
        displayNoOfMealsInQueue();

        System.out.println( "==========================================");
        System.out.println( "SERVING MEAL');
        System.out.print  ( "~~~~~~~~~~~~~");

        theMeal = (TimeStampedMeal) theMealQueue.retrieve();
        theMeal.serveMeal();

        System.out.print( theMeal);
    } else {
        System.out.println( "==========================================");
        System.out.println( "SERVE MEAL COMMAND IGNORED");
        System.out.print  ( "REASON > meal queue is empty");
    } // End if.
} // End serveTheMeal.


public static void showTheQueue() {
    if (! theMealQueue.isEmpty()) {
        System.out.println( "==========================================");
        System.out.println( "SHOWING MEAL QUEUE");
        System.out.print  ( "~~~~~~~~~~~~~~~~~~~");

        displayNoOfMealsInQueue();

        System.out.println( theMealQueue);
    } else {
        System.out.println( "==========================================");
        System.out.println( "SHOW MEAL QUEUE COMMAND IGNORED");
        System.out.print  ( "REASON > meal queue is empty");
    } // End if.
} // End showTheQueue.
```

```
public static void showTheRegister() {
    System.out.println();
    System.out.println( "=========================================");
    System.out.println( "CASH REGISTER STATUS");
    System.out.println( "~~~~~~~~~~~~~~~~~~~~");
    System.out.print   ( "Total transactions .......");
    System.out.println( theRegister.numberOfDepositsIs());

    System.out.print( "Total cash in register ... " +
        OutputFormatter.formatFloat( (float) theRegister.takingsIs
                                                    (), 1, 2, false));
} // End showTheRegister.

} // End ElephantBurgerBar.
```

Evaluation

A lot more time was expended in analyzing the problem, designing the solution and documenting the program than actually implementing it. The idea here is that the support documentation drives the coding, which becomes almost trivial. As someone once said, 'Program code is a consequence of good design'.

I have produced working programs before, even commercially, but this is the first time I have *strictly* followed an analysis/design/code approach without reverting to hacking. This hacking usually occurs because:

- The end of the project deadline is approaching.
- Coding is well under way.
- An error is discovered.
- Initial analysis and design are not complete!

I decided from the outset that there would be little point in using an *ad hoc* approach. I had to demonstrate that I understood the development stages involved; both to my lecturer and more importantly to myself. No code was submitted to the compiler until all class diagrams and JSPs were complete and checked. There were syntax errors in the code but no logic errors – powerful proof to me that this actually works and certainly saves time in the long run.

Producing the test clients presented a dilemma. Was I going to produce five individual clients that check each class and preceding classes, or develop the client at the same time as the expanding hierarchy? I chose the former. The reason was two fold:

1. I could follow an incremental development cycle. Each part of the class hierarchy is developed and demonstrated as working before more functionality is added, by expanding the hierarchy.
2. If a fundamental design error is discovered in my hierarchy at some later stage, then I have a suite of existing test clients already produced.

The process of using dummy stubs was important during the stepwise development of the program. Each main menu option (except EXIT) has a Java action associated with it that began as a dummy stub. It simply output 'I have been called' and returned control to the caller.

The requirement specification for the Elephant Burger Bar, as issued by Fintan Culwin, was followed to the letter. All requirements were addressed fully. The only area of the requirement open to artistic licence was the user interface layout. A more user-friendly one was implemented!

Java offers a pure object oriented environment in which the novice programmer can express their designs and learn the art of software engineering. However, the novice must understand that the final implementation in any computer language is the icing on the cake. It is vital that the analysis and design stages are complete before the final abstraction of implementation. Java allows designs to be expressed in a language that is easy to learn and user-friendly to the novice and professional alike.

Certain design decisions and conventions have been used during the development of this program. Rather than producing long paragraphs of information, these decisions are summarized as follows:

- Code indentation, when required, shall be three spaces.
- Every class and client shall have a heading, with who, what, when and why.
- Comment shall only be used where it is unclear what the code is doing. Comments shall not be used where code is 'self-documenting'.
- Global variables shall be kept to an absolute minimum and their scope restricted.
- The functionality offered by existing class hierarchies shall be fully utilized.
- Appropriately named actions shall be used in the client. They shall be highly cohesive and loosely coupled.
- The client shall be as simple as possible; all complex functionality shall be moved into the meal class hierarchy.
- Error messages shall inform the user WHAT the error is and WHY it has occurred.
- Actions shall be separated by two blank lines.
- Once designed, classes shall be frozen. They shall be referred to during implementation.
- The JSPs shall be drawn and frozen before any work commences on the client. Any changes required shall be made to the JSPs and client simultaneously.
- Code shall be commented as it is developed.

Glossary

All fields of human activity have their own specialized vocabulary including common words which have a specialized meaning and words which are particular to that field. Software development is no exception and this glossary provides brief definitions of the more important specialized words and terms used in this book. The terms defined in this appendix are shown in **bold text**.

abend   Literally *ab*ortive *end*ing; where a program finishes other than when flow of control reaches the end of the main() action. Abends should be used very sparingly.

abstract   An abstract class cannot be **instantiated** and exists in a **class hierarchy** as a foundation upon which a number of non-abstract **child classes** can be built, **inheriting** the resources provided by it.

action   A class contains **data attributes** and actions which operate upon those attributes.

admit   When an **exception**al occurrence happens the admit part of a design is provided to handle the consequences.

applet   A software artefact which extends the Applet class and can therefore execute within a World Wide Web page.

application   A software **artefact** which contains a main() action and is therefore a client program.

argument   The type/identifier pairs contained in braces within an **action** declaration which specify the data flow into and out of the action.

artefact   Any Java source code component, and its compiled product, including **classes**, **interfaces**, **packages** and **client programs**.

attributes   The resources, including **data attributes** and **actions**, supplied by a class are collectively known as its attributes.

AWT   The Java *A*bstract *W*indowing *T*oolkit which supplies the facilities required to implement graphical user interfaces.

build, test, build, test...   A style of development where a class is completely designed, built and tested, before being extended.

child class   A class which is an extension of an existing class is known as its child class; there can be any number of child classes which are all **siblings** of each other.

class   A software artefact containing **data attributes** and **actions** which can operate upon those attributes, having the capability of being extended to provide **child classes**, and can be **instantiated** within a **client**.

class hierarchy All the classes extended from a particular class, or associated with it in some way, and the **parent–child** relationships are expressed in a class hierarchy diagram.

class wide attributes An attribute of a class, either a data attribute or an action, which is shared by all **instances** of that class.

client Any software artefact which makes some use of an artefact is known as its client.

client program A software artefact which contains a main() action which is where flow of control will start in a standalone **application**.

closure A user interface design principle where feedback is always provided to the user to confirm the completion of the action they have requested.

compiling The process of translating Java source code into a form which a computer can execute.

component An extension of the AWT Component class supplying the controls, and the Panels upon which they can be laid out, which are used to build graphical user interfaces.

constructor An action, with the same name as its class, which creates and initializes an **instance** of the class.

context diagram A diagram illustrating the **instances** required for an application, the relationships between them and the **class hierarchies** from which they are obtained.

data attributes A class contains data attributes and **actions** which operate upon those attributes.

data structure An artefact which can store a number of elements. Different structures are distinguished by the ways in which elements can be added and retrieved, the elements which they store and the manner in which they are stored.

demonstration harness An application which is provided only in order to demonstrate that a class appears to be working correctly.

designates A class identifier designates an **instance** of a class when it is assigned a value from a **constructor** or assigned a value which already designates an instance of the class.

dynamic dispatching Where an **overridden** action call can only be associated with an implementation of the action as the program executes.

encapsulate Where a **data attribute** is contained within a class definition.

enquiry actions Instance actions whose purpose is to return the value of a **private data attribute**.

event An instance of the Event class which reports upon the user's interactions with AWT Components.

event queue The queue of **events** waiting to be sent to their ActionListeners.

exception An unusual, but not unexpected, occurrence in a program may throw an exception. This allows a design to be divided into a **posit** part to deal with normal processing and an **admit** part to deal with exceptions. The places in the **posit** part where an exception may be thrown are known as **quits**.

explicit exception An exception which is thrown by the code being developed.

extend Defining a new **class** by adding **attributes** and/or **actions** to an existing **class**, known as development by **extension**.

garbage collection When an **instance** is no longer **designated** by anything it can be destroyed and the resources which it uses reclaimed. Java provides automatic garbage collection which relieves the developer from this tedious and error-prone chore.

generic The separation of an action declaration from the precise class of instances upon which it is designed to operate, allowing it to be used with a number of different classes. Java's generic facilities are relatively primitive.

generic structures A **data structure** which can be configured to store safely and securely **instances** of a particular class.

has a Where a class declaration **encapsulates** an instance of another class, to prevent **actions** of that class from being **inherited**.

heterogeneous A **data structure** which can contain elements from a single specific class.

homogeneous A **data structure** which can contain elements from any class in a class hierarchy.

implicit exception An **exception** which is thrown by existing code being reused.

indirection The implementation of an **action**, including **constructors**, by calling actions in the same class, or in its **parent class**.

inherit A **child class** inherits all non-**private** resources of its **parent class**.

instance Each specific **constructed** occurrence of a class.

instance attributes Where an attribute of a class, either a **data attribute** or an **action**, has one occurrence per **instance** of the class.

instance hierarchy The instances, and the relationships between them, which are required for a particular artefact. Most noticeably the Component instances required for a graphical user interface.

instantiate The act of creating an **instance** of a **class**.

interface An artefact which only declares the **signatures** of a set of **actions**. A class implementing the **interface** must provide full declarations of the actions and its instances can then be used where the instance class is specified as an **argument**.

is a A **child class** extending its **parent class** *is a*n **extension** of the parent class and **inherits** all its non-**private** resources.

iteration Zero or more occurrences of an object or action (see **repetition**).

JSP *J*ackson *S*tructured *P*rogramming notation is used to design, and document the designs of, **actions** and some **data structures**.

key The attribute of an object which determines its location in an ordered **data structure** or which can be used to identify uniquely an element in an unordered data structure.

object Class **instances** and instances of **primitive types**.

overriding An **action** in a **child class** which has the same **signature** as an action in its **parent class** and so effectively replaces the existing (overridden) declaration.

package A collection of software artefacts deemed by the developer to be collected together in some way.

parent class   A class from which a class is extended is its parent class; there can only be a single parent class.

polymorphic   An **action** name which is used by a number of different classes which have a similar semantic meaning, but different implementations. For example, the addition operator (+) adds two arithmetic values together but catenates two strings together.

posit   When an **exceptional** occurrence is considered possible the posit part of a design assumes that it will not happen.

post-increment   Unary operators on **primitive** objects which are applied after the value is referenced. For example, *anInt++* will reference the value of *anInt* before incrementing it.

pre-increment   Unary operators on **primitive** objects which are applied before the value is referenced. For example *++anInt* will increment the value of *anInt* before referencing it.

primitive   Object, such as **int**, **char** and **double**, which are pre-supplied by Java without an associated **class** definition.

primitive types   Simple numeric, character and boolean values are supplied by Java as types not **classes** solely for convenience. Equivalent classes are supplied when they are required.

private   A **resource** which is totally invisible, and so cannot be used, outside its **class** declaration.

propagate   The passing of an exception from a class **instance** where it originates, or where it is detected, to its **parent class** instance.

protected   A **resource** which is visible to its child **classes** but invisible to all other artefacts.

public   A **resource** which is totally visible, and so can be used by any artefact, outside its **class** declaration.

quit   The place in a design where an **implicit exception** or an **explicit exception** may be thrown.

recursion   The declaration of an **action**, or a **data structure**, by making reference to itself.

repetition   One or more occurrences of an object or action (see **iteration**).

resources   The **data attributes** and **actions** associated with a **class**.

run-time error   An error which occurs whilst a program is executing which results in an **implicit exception** being thrown.

semantic   The meaning of a statement as opposed to the way in which it is stated.

semantic error   A program which executes without causing a **run-time error** but does not perform according to its specification.

sibling class   All the **child classes** of a particular **parent class** are siblings of each other.

signature   The visibility modifiers, class modifiers, return type, name and arguments of an **action**.

state setting actions   Actions whose purpose is to change the value of a **data attribute**, or set of attributes.

static dispatching   Where an action call can be associated with an implementation of the action as the code is **compiled**.

STD   *S*tate *T*ransition *D*iagram illustrating the behaviour of an artefact over time as it changes from state to state. Used for the dynamics of concurrent systems and user interfaces.

stream   An ordered sequence of values containing data originating from, or entering into, an artefact.

super   A Java reserved word which designates the **parent instance** of the current instance. It can be used to indicate that an **overridden** resource of the parent instance is intended, not the **overriding** resource in the current instance.

syntax error   A statement which does not conform to Java's rules and which will be reported as an error when the source is **compiled**.

testing   A process of formal **demonstration** whose purpose is to increase confidence in the correct implementation of an artefact, but which can never provide an absolute proof of the correct implementation.

this   A Java reserved word which designates the current instance. It can be used to indicate that an **overriding** resource of the current instance is intended, not the overridden resource from the **parent instance**.

uses a   A class declaration which makes use of another class but which does not **extend** or **encapsulate** it.

Appendix A1
Java's integer types

A1.1 ▓ Primitive integer types

Java supplies four, different, primitive integer data types whose characteristics are shown in Table A1.1.

All of these types are always signed and are implemented using a 2's complement convention. Thus adding 1 to the maximum **byte** value +127 will result in the value −128, without any exception being thrown. The minimum and maximum values of each type are declared as manifest constant values in the corresponding Number class, see section A1.6. For example, the minimum and maximum **int** values are declared as java.lang.Integer.MIN_VALUE and java.lang.Integer.MAX_VALUE.

A1.2 ▓ Integer operators

The operators for integer data types are listed, with examples, in Table A1.2.

A1.3 ▓ Input and output of integer values

Simple output of integer values can be accomplished by referencing the value in the argument of a System.out.println() action. An example of this is given below, on line 0014 of the integer input code fragment.

Should more complex output formatting be required an integer value can be converted into a String by using the Integer class wide toString() action. Its simplest use is as follows:

```
String intString = Integer.toString( 42 );
```

Table A1.1 Java's primitive integer types.

type	Size (bits)	Default value	Minimum value	Maximum value
byte	8	0	−128	+127
short	16	0	−32768	+32767
int	32	0	−2147483648	+2147483647
long	64	0	−9223372036854775808	+9223372036854775807

Table A1.2 Java's integer operators. (Before each operation dis **has the value 8,** that **2 and** other **0.)**

Name	Example	dis	that	other
post-increment	dis = that++	2	3	
pre-increment	dis = ++that	3	3	
post-decrement	dis = that--	2	1	
pre-decrement	dis = --that	1	1	

The difference between a *pre-* and a *post*-operator is that with a pre-operator the reference (in this example for assignment) is made before the incrementation or decrementation. With a post-operator the incrementation or decrementation is made after the reference

addition	other = dis + that			10
subtraction	other = dis - that			6
multiplication	other = dis * that			16
division	other = dis / that			4
modular division	other = dis % that			0

The division operator gives the number of times the right hand operator divides into the left hand operator. The modular division operator gives the remainder after division. For example, *19/5* is 3, *19% 5* is 4 as 19 divided by 5 is 3 remainder 4

self-addition	other += dis;			8

Self-referential operators operate as if they were a combined operation and assignment. For example, this operation is exactly equal to other = other + dis;. Other self-referential operators include -= *= /= %= &= |= ^= >>= and <<=

bitwise or	other = dis | that			10
bitwise and	other = dis & that			2
bitwise xor	other = dis ^ that			10
bitwise negation	other = ~ dis			-9
left bitshift	other = dis << that			2
right bitshift	other = dis >> that			32
raw right bitshift	other = dis >>> that			32

All of these operators operate upon the underlying bitwise representation. Their use in general purpose programs is not very common. The difference between >> and >>> is that >> preserves the sign bit whilst >>> fills from the left with zeros

This would initialize *intString* to '42'. An overloaded Integer toString() action takes a second argument which indicates the number base which is to be used in the conversion. For example:

```
String intString = Integer.toString( 42, 16);
```

This would format the value in the String in base 16, initializing *intString* to '2A'. Having obtained a String representation of a value it can be further manipulated for formatting purposes, e.g. by padding it with leading zeros up to a specified length.

Input of integer values is best accomplished by first constructing an instance of the java.io.DataInputStream class from the pre-supplied System.in class. For example:

```
private java.io.DataInputStream keyboard =
              new java.io.DataInputStream( System.in);
```

Once constructed the class wide **java.io.DataInputStream readLine()** action can be used as the basis of a rather complex input operation, as follows:

```
0001 inputNotOK = true;
0002 while ( inputNotOK) {
0003    System.out.print( "Please type in an integer ");
0004    System.out.flush();
0005    try {
0006        integerVariable= Integer.valueOf(
0007                               keyboard.readLine().trim()
0008                                      ).intValue();
0009        inputNotOK = false;
0010    } catch ( java.lang.Exception exception){
0011        System.out.println( "cannot understand, please try again!");
0012    } // End try/ catch.
0013 } // End while.
0014 System.out.println( "Thank you input .. " + integerVariable + ".");
```

On line 0007 the phrase **keyboard.readLine()** will read a line of text from the keyboard and create a new anonymous **String** object from it. The **.trim()** term will apply the **String trim()** action to this **String** to remove leading and trailing white space. This trimmed **String** is then used as the argument of the **Integer.valueOf()** action to create an anonymous **Integer** object. Finally, on line 0008, the **Integer intValue()** operation is applied to it to produce an **int** value which is assigned to the **int** variable *integerVariable*.

This statement may cause one of two exceptions to be thrown. If an end of file is obtained from the keyboard then a **java.io.IOException** will be thrown, or if the **String** does not contain a valid integer representation a **java.lang.NumberFormatException** will be thrown. Both of these are caught on line 0010 and a message is output to the user informing them of the error and inviting them to try again. Only if a valid integer is obtained from the user will line 0009 be executed and the setting of this **boolean** variable will cause the loop to terminate, with the user's input confirmed to the user on line 0014.

It would have been preferable for the Java designers to have included this action in one of their standard packages, but for some reason it was omitted. Should an integer value ever be required in an application the code above can readily be cut and pasted to where it is required. Alternatively a simple static class containing a number of utility input actions could be produced and kept available for use.

A1.4 ▨ Casting of integer values and integer literals

Casting an integer value from a smaller to a larger representation is never dangerous, as it can be guaranteed that the larger representation can always store the value accurately. For example, none of the following can ever result in a dangerous operation and upon completion all four variables will have the same value:

```
byte  byteVariable  = someIntegerValue;
short shortVariable = byteVariable;
```

```
int    intVariable  = shortVariable;
long   longVariable = intVariable;
```

Although this is acceptable by Java it is regarded as good style to indicate always that the developer is aware that a type conversion is taking place by explicitly indicating a cast in the assignment, as follows:

```
short shortVariable = (short) byteVariable;
int    intVariable   = (int)   shortVariable;
long   longVariable  = (long)  intVariable;
```

When conversion is attempted in the other direction the Java compiler will regard it as an error. For example, the following line:

```
intVariable = longVariable;
```

will result in a compilation message such as:

```
Incompatible type for =. Explicit cast needed to convert long to int.
```

The conversion can be accomplished with an explicit cast such as:

```
intVariable = (int) longVariable;
```

However, this is only safe if the value of *longVariable* is within the limits of the **int** representation as given in Table A1.1. If the value is outside these limits only the lower 16 bits are correctly transferred, but this should not be relied upon in general purpose programs.

Integer literals in the source code are by default treated as **int** values, which are suitable for use with all integer types. If it is ever necessary to indicate explicitly that a long value is required, an 'L' can be appended to it. The attempted initialization of the *longVariable* as follows:

```
longVariable = 9223372036854775807;
```

will result in a compilation error as the literal is treated as an integer and its attempted conversion results in a error. The correct initialization would be as follows:

```
longVariable = 9223372036854775807L;
```

Literal values can be expressed in hexadecimal by prepending them with '0x', so the following assignment will result in the *intVariable* having the value −2147483648:

```
intVariable = 0xFFFFFFFF;
```

Both literal modifiers can be used if required, e.g. 0xFFFFFFFFFFFFFFFFL.

A1.5 ▒ Integer operations in the standard packages

A random **int** or **long** value can be obtained from the class wide nextInt() or nextLong() actions in the java.util.Random class. The random number package is automatically seeded from the system clock which will ensure that a different sequence of random numbers is obtained every time an instance is constructed.

The class wide **int** actions from the java.lang.Math class are listed in Table A1.3. For each of these actions there is a corresponding long action in the same class.

Table A1.3 The *int* actions in java.lang.Math.

Action	Note
`public static int round(float aFloat)`	The **int** value of the **float** value *aFloat*
`public static int abs(int anInt)`	The absolute value of *anInt*
`public static int max(int thisInt,` `                       int thatInt)`	The maximum of thisInt and thatInt
`public static int min(int thisInt,` `                       int thatInt)`	The minimum of *thisInt* and *thatInt*

Table A1.4 The actions in the java.lang.Integer class.

Manifest values

`MIN_VALUE`	The minimum Integer value
`MAX_VALUE`	The maximum Integer value

Constructors

`public Integer(int intValue)`	Constructs an Integer with the value *intValue*
`public Integer(String aString)` `        throws NumberFormatException`	Constructs an Integer with the value represented in *aString*. Throws exception if *aString* is invalid

Instance actions

`public int     byteValue()`	Obtains value as primitive **byte**, truncating if required
`public int     shortValue()`	Obtains value as primitive **short**, truncating if required
`public int     intValue()`	Obtains value as primitive **int**
`public long    longValue()`	Obtains value as primitive **long**
`public float   floatValue()`	Obtains value as primitive **float**
`public double  doubleValue()`	Obtains value as primitive **double**
`public String  toString()`	Formats value in a String
`public int hashCode()`	Supplies hash code for storing in a Hashtable
`public boolean equals(Object object)`	True if object contains same integer value

class wide actions

`public static String toString(int anInt)`	Formats *anInt* in a String
`public static String toString(int anInt,`	Formats *anInt* in a String in the number base *radix*
`public static Integer valueOf(int radix)`	Creates new Integer initialized to the value in
`                String aString)`	*aString*. Exception thrown if *aString* cannot be so
`        throws NumberFormatException`	interpreted
`public static Integer valueOf(`	Creates new Integer initialized to the value in
`                String aString,`	*aString* with regard to the *radix*. Exception
`                int    radix)`	thrown if *aString* cannot be so interpreted
`        throws NumberFormatException`	
`public static int parseInt(`	As for previous valueOf() action but returning a
`                String aString)`	primitive **int** value
`        throws NumberFormatException`	
`public static int parseInt(`	As for previous valueOf() action but returning a
`                String aString,`	primitive **int** value
`                int    radix)`	
`        throws NumberFormatException`	

A1.6 ▓ The *Integer* class

In addition to the primitive integer types Java also supplies classes which implement the **byte**, **short**, **int** and **long** types as objects; the major reason for this is to allow integers to be used with Java's utility classes. For example, if it is required to store integer values in a Vector or Hashtable then only Integer instances could be used, not primitive **int** variables.

The packages are java.lang.Number.Byte, java.lang.Number.Short, java.lang.Number.Integer and java.lang.Number.Long. Only the most important features of the Integer class are described in Table A1.4; the other classes are essentially identical.

Appendix A2
Java's floating point types

A2.1 ▦ Primitive floating point types

Java supplies two, different, primitive floating point data types whose characteristics are shown in Table A2.1.

Both of the these types conform to the IEEE 754 specification for the representation of floating point values. The minimum and maximum values of the types are declared as manifest constant values in the corresponding Number class, see section A2.5. For example, the minimum and maximum **double** values are declared as java.lang.Double.MIN_VALUE and java.lang.Double.MAX_VALUE.

A2.2 ▦ Floating point operators

The operators for the **double** data types are listed, with examples, in Table A2.2. The operators for the **float** type are essentially identical.

A2.3 ▦ Input and output of floating point values

The considerations for the input and output of floating point values are essentially identical to those for integer data types as described in section A1.3.

A2.4 ▦ Casting of floating point to and from integer values, and floating point literals

Casting a floating point value from a **float** to a **double** representation is never dangerous, as it can be guaranteed that a **double** can always store the value accurately. For example, the following can never result in a dangerous operation and upon

Table A2.1 Java's primitive floating point types.

Type	Size (bits)	Default value	Minimum value	Maximum value
float	32	0.0	1.40129846432481707e − 45	3.40282346638528860e + 38
double	64	0.0	4.94065645841246544e − 324	1.79769313486231570e + 308

Table A2.2 Java's floating point operators. (Before each operation dis **has the value 15.0, that 2.0 and** other **0.0.)**

Name	Example	other
addition	other = dis + that	17.0
subtraction	other = dis – that	13.0
multiplication	other = dis * that	30.0
division	other = dis / that	7.5

completion both variables will have the same value:

```
float   floatVariable = someFloatValue;
double  doubleVariable;

    doubleVariable = floatVariable;
```

Although this is acceptable by Java it is regarded as good style always to indicate that the developer is aware that a type conversion is taking place by explicitly indicating a cast in the assignment:

```
doubleVariable = (double) floatVariable;
```

Likewise, any integer value can be automatically or explicitly cast to either floating point type without any danger, as the floating point variable will always be able to represent it. However, the converse conversion, from any floating point type to any integer type, can be accomplished by an explicit cast but will result in an unpredictable value unless the floating point value is within the limits of the integer type's range. This can be guarded against as shown in the following fragment:

```
if ( ((long) doubleVariable) >= java.lang.Long.MIN_VALUE &&
     ((long) doubleVariable) <= java.lang.Long.MAX_VALUE ) {
   longVariable = (long) doubleVariable;
} else {
   // Value cannot be converted.
} // End if.
```

Floating point literals can be expressed in conventional (e.g. 345.678) or exponent notation (e.g. 3.45678e+02), but both mantissa and exponent must always be expressed as denary (base 10) values. By default such literals are always assumed to be of type double. Should it ever be required, a double value can be indicated by appending a D and a float by appending an F, e.g. 345.678D or 345.678F.

A2.5 ▦ Floating point operations in the standard packages

A random **float** or **double** value between 0.0 and 1.0 can be obtained from the class wide nextFloat() or nextDouble() actions in the java.util.Random class. The random number package is automatically seeded from the system clock which will ensure that a different sequence of random numbers is obtained every time an instance is constructed.

The java.lang.Math class supplies a classwide random() action which can sometimes be more conveniently used to obtain a **double** value between 0.0 and 1.0. Other actions and class wide constants in java.lang.Math are presented in Table A2.3.

Table A2.3 The floating point actions in java.lang.Math.

Manifest values

`E`	E is implemented as 2.7182818284590452354F
`PI`	Pi is implemented as 3.14159265358979323846F

Class wide general actions

`public static double abs(double `*`number`*`)`	Returns the absolute value of *number*
`public static double exp(double `*`number`*`)`	Exponential e raised to the power *number*
`public static double log(double `*`number`*`)` `        throws ArithmeticException`	Natural logarithm of *number*. Throws exception if number is less than 0.0
`public static double sqrt(double `*`number`*`)` `        throws ArithmeticException`	Square root of *number*. Throws exception if number is less than 0.0
`public static double ceil(double `*`number`*`)`	***Ceil**ing*, the smallest whole number >= *number*
`public static double floor(double `*`number`*`)`	***Floor***, the smallest whole number <= *number*

`public static double pow(double `*`this`*`,`
`                  double `*`that`*`)`
`        throws ArithmeticException`
	Power, *this* raised to the power *that*. Throws exception under various conditions

`public static int round(float `*`number`*`)`	Rounds by adding 0.5 and then returning the largest **int** value less than or equal to it
`public static long round(double `*`number`*`)`	As for **int** round() action, but using **long**
`public static synchronized` `                  double random()`	Generates a random number between 0.0 and 1.0
`public static float max(float `*`this`*`,` `                  float `*`that`*`)`	Returns greater of *this* and *that* (double version also supplied)
`public static float min(float `*`this`*`,` `                  float `*`that`*`)`	Returns least of *this* and *that* (double version also supplied)

Class wide trigonometric actions

`public static double sin( double `*`angle`*`)`	Sine value of angle (in radians)
`public static double cos( double `*`angle`*`)`	Cosine value of angle (in radians)
`public static double tan( double `*`angle`*`)`	Tangent value of angle (in radians)
`public static double asin(double `*`angle`*`)`	Arc sine value of angle (in radians)
`public static double acos(double `*`angle`*`)`	Arc cosine value of angle (in radians)
`public static double atan(double `*`angle`*`)`	Arc tangent value of angle (in radians)

For the arc variants the value of angle has to be between -1.0 and $+1.0$ and the value returned is between $-\pi/2$ and $\pi/2$

A2.6 ▨ The Float class

In addition to the primitive floating point types Java also supplies two classes which implement the **double** and **float** types as objects. The major reason for this is to allow them to be used with Java's utility classes. For example, if you wanted to store **double** values in a hash table then only Double instances could be used, not primitive **double** variables.

The two packages are java.lang.Number.Double and java.lang.Number.Float. The most important features of the Float class are described in Table A2.4; the Double class is essentially identical.

A2.7 ■ Approximations in floating point representations

The representation of floating point values on a computer may involve some non-obvious approximations. There are some numbers, e.g. $10.0/3.0 = 3.333\ldots$, which

Table A2.4 Constants and actions in the java.lang.Float class.

Manifest values	
`MIN_VALUE`	The minimum Float value
`MAX_VALUE`	The maximum Float value
`NEGATIVE_INFINITY`	Value returned by some Math actions
`POSITIVE_INFINITY`	Value returned by some Math actions
`NaN`	Not a Number, value returned by some Math actions
Constructors	
`public Float( float aFloat)`	Constructs a Float with the value *aFloat*
`public Float( double aDouble)`	Constructs a Float with the value *aDouble*
`public Float(String aString)` `        throws NumberFormatException`	Constructs a Float with the value represented in *aString*. Throws exception if *aString* is invalid
Instance actions	
`public int    byteValue()`	Obtains value as primitive **byte**, by casting
`public int    shortValue()`	Obtains value as primitive **short**, by casting
`public int    intValue()`	Obtains value as primitive **int**, by casting
`public long   longValue()`	Obtains value as primitive **long**, by casting
`public float  floatValue()`	Obtains value as primitive **float**
`public double doubleValue()`	Obtains value as primitive **double**
`public String toString()`	Formats value in a String
`public boolean isNaN()`	True if value Not a Number
`public boolean isInfinite()`	True if value is positive or negative infinity
`public int    hashCode()`	Supplies hash code
`public boolean equals(Object object)`	True if object contains same **Float** value
Class wide actions	
`Public static String toString(` `                float aFloat)`	Formats *aFloat* in a String
`public static Float valueOf(` `               String aString)` `        throws NumberFormatException`	Creates new Float initialized to the value in *aString*. Exception thrown if *aString* cannot be so interpreted
`public static boolean isNaN(float aFloat)`	True if aFloat is Not a Number
`public static boolean isInfinite(` `                float aFloat)`	True if aFloat is positive or negative infinity

cannot be represented exactly in decimal notation. Floating point values on computer systems are stored in a form of binary notation and can encounter similar problems. Some values which cannot be represented exactly in decimal can be represented exactly in binary, some values which can be represented exactly in decimal cannot be represented exactly in binary, some values cannot be represented exactly in binary or decimal and some can be represented exactly in both.

The consequences of these considerations can introduce some very subtle faults into programs. The following program illustrates this:

```
0001 // Filename SubtleFloatingPointError.java.
0002 // Illustrates a subtle fault which can occur when
0003 // using floating point values.
0004 //
0005 // Produced for JOF book Appendix A2.
0006 // Fintan Culwin, v0.1, August 1997.
0007
0008 public class SubtleFloatingPointError {
0009
0010 private static final int    ONE_HUNDRED_THOUSAND   = 100000;
0011 private static final double ONE                    = 1.0;
0012 private static final double ONE_HUNDRED_THOUSANDTH = ONE /
0013                                        ((double) ONE_HUNDRED_THOUSAND);
0014
0015    public static void main( String argv[]) {
0016
0017    int     index;
0018    double  theResult = 0.0;
0019
0020       System.out.println( "\t Illustrating a subtle floating point bug.\n");
0021       System.out.println( "Adding one hundred thousandth to itself ");
0022       System.out.println( "one hundred thousand times and seeing if the ");
0023       System.out.println( "result is equal to one... \n\n");
0024
0025       for ( index = 0;
0026             index <= ONE_HUNDRED_THOUSAND;
0027             index++ ){
0028          theResult += ONE_HUNDRED_THOUSANDTH;
0029       } // End for.
0030
0031       if ( theResult == ONE) {
0032          System.out.println( "This should be no surprise one " +
0033                                        "is equal to one!");
0034       } else {
0035          System.out.println( "This might surprise you one is equal to " +
0036                                        theResult + ".");
0037       } // End if.
0038    } // End main.
0039 } // End SubtleFloatingPointError.
```

The program declares a constant called *ONE_HUNDRED_THOUSANDTH* and then adds its value to itself 100000 times. Arithmetically this should result in the value 1.0; the **if** structure at the end of the program tests this and outputs a message indicating if this is or is not the case. The result of executing this program was as

follows:

```
        Illustrating a subtle floating point bug.

Adding one hundred thousandth to itself
one hundred thousand times and seeing if the
result is equal to one...

This might surprise you one is equal to 1.00001.
```

The value 0.00001 cannot be represented with absolute accuracy by Java. The small error in its representation causes the value of the variable *TheResult* to be very close to, but not exactly equal to, 1.0. The following program illustrates how this problem can be allowed for in the construction of programs which manipulate floating point values:

```java
0001 // Filename SubtleFloatingPointErrorAvoided.java.
0002 // Illustrates how the subtle fault which may occur when
0003 // using floating point values can be avoided.
0004 //
0005 // Produced for JOF book Appendix A.
0006 // Fintan Culwin, v0.1, August 1997.
0007
0008 import java.lang.Math;
0009
0010 public class SubtleFloatingPointErrorAvoided {
0011
0012 private static final int    ONE_HUNDRED_THOUSAND   = 100000;
0013 private static final double ONE                    = 1.0;
0014 private static final double ONE_HUNDRED_THOUSANDTH = ONE /
0015                                     ((double) ONE_HUNDRED_THOUSAND);
0016 private static final double CLOSE_ENOUGH = 0.0001;
0017
0018    public static void main( String argv[]) {
0019
0020    int    index;
0021    double theResult = 0.0;
0022
0023       System.out.println( "\t Avoiding a subtle floating point bug.\n");
0024       System.out.println( "Adding one hundred thousandth to itself ");
0025       System.out.println( "one hundred thousand times and seeing if the ");
0026       System.out.println( "result is equal to one... \n\n");
0027
0028       for ( index = 0;
0029             index <= ONE_HUNDRED_THOUSAND;
0030             index++ ){
0031         theResult += ONE_HUNDRED_THOUSANDTH;
0032       } // End for.
0033
0034       if ( java.lang.Math.abs( theResult - ONE) <= CLOSE_ENOUGH) {
0035          System.out.println( "This should be no surprise one " +
0036                                          "is equal to one!");
0037       } else {
0038          System.out.println( "This might surprise you one is equal to " +
```

```
0039                                                    theResult + ".");
0040        } // End if.
0041     } // End main.
0042 } // End SubtleFloatingPointErrorAvoided.
```

This version avoids the problem by, on line 0034, not testing the two values for strict equality but only to determine if they are sufficiently *CLOSE_ENOUGH* to each other to be considered equal. The output of this program when it was executed was as follows:

```
         Avoiding a subtle floating point bug.

Adding one hundred thousandth to itself
one hundred thousand times and seeing if the
result is equal to one...

This should be no surprise one is equal to one!
```

The general conclusion from these two programs is that it is both naïve and dangerous to test two floating point values for strict equality. Instead the degree of accuracy appropriate for the specification should be decided and a loose equality should be tested for.

Appendix 3
Java's *boolean* types

A3.1 ▦ The primitive *boolean* type and *boolean* operations

Java supplies a primitive data type called **boolean**, instances of which can take the value **true** or **false** only, and have the default value **false**. The major use of **boolean** facilities is to implement the expressions which control **if** decisions and **while** loops. As these are very largely responsible for the behaviour of programs any faults in the construction of these expressions will have dire consequences upon the correct operation of the software. Consequently **boolean** expressions should be constructed with extreme care.

There are three fundamental operations upon boolean values: **not**, **and** and **or**. The truth tables for these operations are given in Table A3.1.

The not operator (**!**) reverses the logic of a single boolean value; the other two operands combine two operators, shown on the table as *left* and *right*, together. The and (**&&**) rule is true if, and only if, both of its expressions are true. The or (**||**) rule is true if either, or both, of its expressions are true.

The relational operators equal to (=), not equal to (! =), less than (<), less than or equal to (< =), greater than (>) and greater than or equal to (> =) all result in a

Table A3.1 The fundamental boolean expressions.

	not (!)	
Value	**Result**	
true	false	
false	true	

or (||)				and (&&)		
Left	**Right**	**Result**		**Left**	**Right**	**Result**
false	false	false		false	false	false
false	true	true		false	true	false
true	false	true		true	false	false
true	true	true		true	true	true

boolean value. A set of relational operators are provided for the pre-supplied primitive integer, floating point and character types.

A3.2 ▦ Constructing and validating a *boolean* expression

It was emphasized above that boolean expressions are very largely responsible for the behaviour of a piece of software and that consequently they should be constructed with extreme care.

To explore this consideration an expression to set the value of a primitive **boolean** variable called *isAPensioner* will be set from the value of a primitive **int** variable called *personAge*, containing the age of a person and the value of a primitive **char** variable called *personGender*, containing 'M' if the person is male and 'F' if the person is female. It is assumed these are private data attributes of a class called *possiblePensioner* which has actions called *getAge()* and *getGender()* and the decision is to be implemented in a **boolean** action called *isPensioner()*.

The current UK rules for pensioner status will be used; these are that females have to be aged 60 or over and males have to be 65 or over. To support this decision and to make the rules explicit four private manifest values called *FEMALE_LIMIT*, *MALE_LIMIT*, *FEMALE* and *MALE* are declared with suitable values. The implementation of *isPensioner()* might be as follows:

```
public boolean isPensioner() {
   return ( ((personAge >= FEMALE_LIMIT) && (personGender = FEMALE)) ||
            ((personAge >= MALE_LIMIT)   && (personGender = MALE)  ) );
} // End isPensioner.
```

The validation of this expression will have to consider four possibilities: a female just below the limit, a female just above the limit, a male who is just below the limit and a male who is just above the limit; if the expression is correctly constructed then these should evaluate true, false, true and false respectively. The validation of this expression is given in Table A3.2.

The first two columns define the four conditions which will validate the expression. Column A shows the result of the first relational expression, *personAge = FEMALE_LIMIT*; and columns B, C and D the results of the remaining three relational expressions, as shown at the head of the column.

Column E shows the result of **and**ing column A with column B to indicate the result of the **and** operation on the first line of the decision. Likewise the result of the second line of the decision is shown in column F. Finally column G **or**s the contents of columns E and F together to show the overall result of the expression which will be returned from the action. This shows that the expression appears to have been implemented correctly.

There are many other **boolean** expressions which could have been constructed which would also have produced the correct pattern of results. For example:

```
public boolean isPensioner() {
   return !( (!(personAge >= FEMALE_LIMIT)) || (personGender != FEMALE)) &&
            ((personAge < MALE_LIMIT)       || (personGender != MALE)  ) );
} // End isPensioner.
```

A table similar to Table A3.2 would show that the outcome of this expression is exactly equivalent to the outcome of the previous expression. However, the previous

Table A3.2 Validation of a boolean expression.

personAge	personGender	A personAge = F_LIMIT	B personGender = FEMALE	C personAge = M_LIMIT	D personGender = MALE	E A && B	F C && D	G E || F
59	F	false	true	false	false	false	false	false
60	F	true	true	false	false	true	false	true
64	M	true	false	false	true	false	false	false
65	M	true	false	true	true	false	true	true

version is undoubtedly easier to understand. The second expression is typical of one which has been hacked around until it appears to work, rather than having been carefully constructed from a consideration of the requirements. Not only is it more difficult to validate the second expression, but it will also be much more difficult to maintain should the rules for pensioner status ever change.

The general conclusion from this section is that because **boolean** expressions are essential to the correct operation of a piece of software every one should be very carefully constructed and validated on paper before being subject to demonstration and testing. It has been shown that the largest proportion of faults in programs can be traced back to faulty **boolean** expressions. Consequently the time and effort taken to construct them carefully in the first place will be repaid in easier production and maintenance.

A3.3 ■ Input and output of *boolean* values

Boolean values can be output as a part of a System.out.print() action, being displayed as the literal 'true' or 'false'. It does not normally make sense to input a **boolean**

Table A3.3 Constants and actions in the java.lang.Boolean class.

Manifest values
```
FALSE
TRUE
```

Constructors

`public Boolean(boolean aBoolean)`	Constructs a Boolean with the value *aBoolean*
`public Boolean(String aString);`	Constructs a Boolean with the value **true** if *aString* contains the literal 'true' and **false** otherwise

Class wide actions

`public static Boolean valueOf(` `                String aString)`	Creates new Boolean initialized to **true** if the value in *aString* is 'true' and **false** otherwise

Instance actions

`public boolean booleanValue()`	Obtains value as primitive **boolean**
`public String  toString()`	Formats value in a String
`public int     hashCode()`	Supplies hash code
`public boolean equals(Object object)`	True if object contains same **boolean** value

value directly; instead a **boolean** value can be set from a relational expression or action after a value of some other type has been input. The **boolean** literals **true** and **false** are also Java reserved words.

A3.4 ▓ The *Boolean* class

As with the other primitive data types Java supplies an equivalent class for situations when an object of the type, instead of the simple variable, is required. The major actions contained in the class java.lang.Boolean are given in Table A3.3.

Appendix A4
Java's character types

A4.1 ▓ Primitive character types

Java supplies a primitive data type, called **char**, whose values include all 65535 characters of the Unicode character set. This set of characters contains not only all characters used in the English alphabet, but also characters used in other Romanized alphabets, such as the æ diphthong, and also the characters which are required for non-Romanized alphabets such as Arabic and the ideographs used by languages such as Chinese and Japanese.

The first 128 characters of the Unicode standard are exactly the same as the 128 characters of the ASCII character set, and the first 256 characters are exactly the same as the Latin-1 character set which is given in Table A4.1. Each entry in the table shows the ordinal number of the character in the range 0 to 255, the appearance of the character if any and a name for the character.

A4.2 ▓ Character operations

The only operators available for the **char** data type are the pre- and post-, increment and decrement operators which are shown, with examples, in Table A4.2.

A4.3 ▓ Input and output of character values

The raw data input stream System.in of the java.io.InputStream class supplies a read() action which can be used to obtain the next byte from the input stream. This can be cast to the **char** type and assigned to a **char** variable as follows:

```
aChar = (char) System.in.read();
```

However, in most situations it would be preferable to obtain a **char** using the java.io.DataInputStream readChar() action using techniques essentially identical to those described in Appendix A1.3 for the input of **int** values.

A4.4 ▓ Casting of integer values and integer literals

The **char** variables are represented as a 16 bit unsigned integer in the range 0 to 65535, the value determining which character from the Unicode standard it represents. It is possible to cast a **char** to a **short** or a **byte** but this might result in a negative value. Casting to an **int** or a **long** is safe as the value will always be positive.

Table A4.1 Latin-1 character table.

Code	Char	Name	Code	Char	Name	Code	Char	Name	Code	Char	Name
0		NUL	1		SOH	2		STX	3		ETX
4		EOT	5		ENQ	6		ACK	7		BEL
8		BS	9		HT	10		LF	11		VT
12		FF	13		CR	14		SO	15		SI
16		DLE	17		DC1	18		DC2	19		DC3
20		DC4	21		NAK	22		SYN	23		ETB
24		CAN	25		EM	26		SUB	27		ESC
28		FS	29		GS	30		RS	31		US
32		Space	33	!	Exclamation	34	"	Quotation	35	#	Number sign
36	$	Dollar sign	37	%	Percent sign	38	&	Ampersand	39	'	Apostrophe
40	(	Left parenthesis	41	)	Right parenthesis	42	*	Asterisk	43	+	Plus sign
44	,	Comma	45	-	Hyphen minus sign	46	.	Full stop	47	/	Solidus
48	0	Zero	49	1	One	50	2	Two	51	3	Three
52	4	Four	53	5	Five	54	6	six	55	7	Seven
56	8	Eight	57	9	Nine	58	:	Colon	59	;	Semicolon
60	<	Less than sign	61	=	Equals sign	62	>	Greater than sign	63	?	Question mark
64	@	At sign	65	A	Upper case A	66	B	Upper case B	67	C	Upper case C
68	D	Upper case D	69	E	Upper case E	70	F	Upper case F	71	G	Upper case G
72	H	Upper case H	73	I	Upper case I	74	J	Upper case J	75	K	Upper case K
76	L	Upper case L	77	M	Upper case M	78	N	Upper case N	79	O	Upper case O
80	P	Upper case P	81	Q	Upper case Q	82	R	Upper case R	83	S	Upper case S
84	T	Upper case T	85	U	Upper case U	86	V	Upper case V	87	W	Upper case W
88	X	Upper case X	89	Y	Upper case Y	90	Z	Upper case Z	91	[	Left square bracket
92	\	Reverse solidus	93	]	Right square bracket	94	^	Circumflex	95	_	Low line
96	`	Grave	97	a	Lower case A	98	b	Lower case B	99	c	Lower case C
100	d	Lower case D	101	e	Lower case E	102	f	Lower case F	103	g	Lower case G
104	h	Lower case H	105	i	Lower case I	106	j	Lower case J	107	k	Lower case K
108	l	Lower case L	109	m	Lower case M	110	n	Lower case N	111	o	Lower case O
112	p	Lower case P	113	q	Lower case Q	114	r	Lower case R	115	w	Lower case W
116	t	Lower case T	117	u	Lower case U	118	v	Lower case V	119	w	Lower case W
120	x	Lower case X	121	y	Lower case Y	122	z	Lower case Z	123	{	Left curly bracket
124			Vertical line	125	}	Right curly bracket	126	~	Tilde	127		DEL
128		Reserved_128	129		Reserved_129	130		Reserved_130	131		Reserved_131
132		IND	133		NEL	134		SSA	135		ESA
136		HTS	137		HTJ	138		VTS	139		PLD
140		PLU	141		RI	142		SS2	143		SS3
144		DCS	145		PUI	146		PU2	147		STS
148		CCH	149		MW	150		SPA	151		EPA
152		Reserved_152	153		Reserved_153	154		Reserved_154	155		CSI
156		ST	157		OSC	158		PM	159		APC
160		No break space	161	¡	Inverted exclamation	162	¢	Cent sign	163	£	Pound sign
164	¤	Currency sign	165	¥	Yen sign	166	¦	Broken bar	167	§	Section sign
168	¨	Dieresis	169	©	Copyright sign	170	ª	Feminine ordinal	171	«	Left chevron
172	¬	Not sign	173	-	Soft hyphen	174	'®'	Trade mark	175	¯	Macron
176	°	Degree sign	177	±	Plus minus sign	178	²	Superscript two	179	³	Superscript three
180	´	Acute	181	µ	Micro sign	182	¶	Pilcrow sign	183	·	Middle dot

(continued)

Table A4.1 (*continued*).

184	¸	Cedilla	185	¹	Superscript one	186	º	Masculine ordinal	187	»	Right chevron
188	¼	One quarter	189	½	One half	190	¾	Three quarters	191	¿	Inverted question
192	À	Upper A grave	193	Á	Upper A acute	194	Â	Upper A circumflex	195	Ã	Upper A tilde
196	Ä	Upper A dieresis	197	Å	Upper A ring	198	Æ	Upper AE diphthong	199	Ç	Upper C cedilla
200	È	Upper E grave	201	É	Upper E acute	202	Ê	Upper E circumflex	203	Ë	Upper E dieresis
204	Ì	Upper I grave	205	Í	Upper I acute	206	Î	Upper I circumflex	207	Ï	Upper I dieresis
208	Ð	Upper Icelandic eth	209	Ñ	Upper N tilde	210	Ò	Upper O grave	211	Ó	Upper O acute
212	Ô	Upper O circumflex	213	Õ	Upper O tilde	214	Ö	Upper I dieresis	215	×	Multiplication sign
216	Ø	Upper O stroke	217	Ù	Upper U grave	218	Ú	Upper U acute	219	Û	Upper U circumflex
220	Ü	Upper U dieresis	221	Ý	Upper Y acute	222	Þ	Upper Icelandic thorn	223	ß	Lower sharp s
224	à	Lower A grave	225	á	Lower A acute	226	â	Lower A circumflex	227	ã	Lower A tilde
228	ä	Lower A dieresis	229	å	Lower A ring	230	æ	Lower AE diphthong	231	ç	Lower C cedilla
232	è	Lower E grave	233	é	Lower E acute	234	ê	Lower E circumflex	235	ë	Lower E dieresis
236	ì	Lower I grave	237	í	Lower I acute	238	î	Lower I circumflex	239	ï	Lower I dieresis
240	ð	Lower Icelandic eth	241	ñ	Lower N tilde	242	ò	Lower O grave	243	ó	Lower O acute
244	ô	Lower O circumflex	245	õ	Lower O tilde	246	ö	Lower O dieresis	247	÷	Division sign
248	ø	Lower O stroke	249	ù	Lower U grave	250	ú	Lower U acute	251	û	Lower U circumflex
252	ü	Lower U dieresis	253	ý	Lower Y acute	254	þ	Lower Icelandic thorn	255	ÿ	Lower Y dieresis

Table A4.2 Character increment and decrement operators.
(Before each operation *that* is assumed to have the value 'A'.)

Name	Example	dis	that
post-increment	dis = that++	'A'	'B'
pre-increment	dis = ++that	'B'	'B'
post-decrement	dis = that--	'A'	'1'
pre-decrement	dis = --that	'@'	'@'

As with other casts, casting from a smaller to a larger representation, e.g from a **char** to a **long** or **int**, does not require an explicit cast. But a cast from a longer representation, e.g. to a **char** from an **int** or a **long**, always requires a cast. However, it is regarded as good style, particularly when casting from character to integer, for all casts to be performed explicitly in order to indicate that the developer is aware that a cast is taking place.

Character literals are indicated in Java source code by enclosing them within single quote characters; e.g. 'A'. A number of non-printing characters can be indicated using an escape code. These include '\n' which is new line (Unicode character 10 and/or 13) and '\t' which is tab (Unicode character 9). Any character from the Unicode sequence can be indicated by a sequence of the form '\uxxxx' where xxxx indicates the code for the sequence in hexadecimal. For example, '\u00FE' would specify the Unicode character 254 lower Icelandic thorn ('Þ').

A4.5 ▥ The *Character* class

As with the other primitive data types Java supplies an equivalent class for situations when an object of the type, instead of the simple variable, is required. The class also contains a number of classwide utility actions. The major actions contained in the class java.lang.Character are given in Table A4.3.

An example which illustrates the use of the character facilities is included in Appendix A5.

Table A4.3 Constants and actions in the java.lang.character class.

Manifest values	
`MIN_RADIX`	Minimum radix for conversions
`MAX_RADIX`	Maximum radix for conversions
Constructor	
`public Character(char aCharacter)`	Constructs a Character with the value *aCharacter*
Class wide actions	
`public static boolean isLowerCase(` `                char aCharacter)`	True if *aCharacter* is lower case
`public static boolean isUpperCase(` `                char aCharacter)`	True if *aCharacter* is upper case
`public static boolean isDigit(char aChar)`	True if *aChar* is a digit
`public static boolean isWhiteSpace(` `                char aChar)`	True if *aChar* is a white space
`public static char toLowerCase(` `                char aCharacter)`	If *aCharacter* is upper case returns lower case equivalent, otherwise returns *aCharacter* unchanged
`public static char toUpperCase(` `                char aCharacter)`	If *aCharacter* is lower case returns upper case equivalent, otherwise returns *aCharacter* unchanged
`public static int digit(char aCharacter,` `                int radix)`	Converts *aCharacter* to integer equivalent of the digit it represents with regard to *radix*, or −1
`public static char forDigit(int digit` `                int radix)`	Supplies **char** to represent digit with regard to *radix*, or null char otherwise
Instance actions	
`public char    charValue()`	Converts Character to char
`public String  toString()`	Converts Character to String
`public int     hashCode()`	Supplies hash code
`public boolean equals(Object object)`	True if *object* contains the same Character

Appendix 5
Java's *String* types

A5.1 ▨ The *String* and *StringBuffer* classes

Java does not supply or support a primitive string type, implemented as an array of **char**. Instead it supplies two String classes: the java.lang.String class provides an unchangeable String object and the java.lang.StringBuffer class provides a String which can be amended.

A5.2 ▨ The *String* constructors and actions

The String constructors are listed in Table A5.1. For some of these actions the location of a character in the String is returned or required, in such cases the first character is at location 0 and the last character is at location length() −1.

The instance actions from the String class are listed in Table A5.2.

The class wide actions are listed in Table A5.3.

A5.3 ▨ The *StringBuffer* constructors and actions

The StringBuffer constructors are listed in Table A5.4.

The instance actions from the StringBuffer class are listed in Table A5.5; the class does not have any classwide actions.

Table A5.1 java.lang.String constructors.

Constructors	
`public String()`	Constructs a new empty String
`public String(String value)`	Copies the String in *value*
`public String(char value[])`	Creates a String from the array of **char** in *value*

`public String(char value[],`
`         int offset,`
`         int count)`
	Creates a String from a slice of the array of **char** in *value* starting at *offset* and extending for *count* characters

`public String(StringBuffer buffer)`	Creates a String from the StringBuffer

Table A5.2 java.lang.String instance actions.

Instance actions

`public int length()`	The number of characters in the String
`public char charAt(int index)`	The character at location *index*

`public void getChars(`
          `int  sourceBegin,`
          `int  sourceEnd,`
          `char destination[],`
          `int  desinationtBegin)`
	Copy characters from the String starting at *sourceBegin* ending at *sourceEnd*, placing them in *destination[]* starting at location *destinationBegin*

`public void getBytes(`
          `int  sourceBegin,`
          `int  sourceEnd,`
          `byte destination[],`
          `int  desinationtBegin)`
	As for previous getChars() but casting **char**s to **byte**s

`public boolean equals(Object anObject)`	True if *anObject* contains an identical String
`public boolean equalsIgnoreCase(` `String anotherString)`	True if *anotherString* contains an identical String ignoring the case of the characters
`public int compareTo(` `String anotherString)`	Returns 0 if *anotherString* is equal, +1 if it is alphabetically greater and −1 otherwise

`public boolean regionMatches(`
          `int     toffset,`
          `String  other,`
          `int     ooffset,`
          `int     length)`
	True if *length* characters in String starting at location *toffset* matches the *length* characters in the other String starting at *ooffset*

`public boolean regionMatches(`
          `boolean ignoreCase,`
          `int     toffset,`
          `String  other,`
          `int     ooffset,`
          `int     length)`
	As for previous regionMatches() with *ignoreCase* determining if the case of the characters is to be considered

`public boolean startsWith( String prefix)`	True if the String starts with the String in *prefix*
`public boolean startsWith( String prefix,` `int    toffset)`	As for previous startsWith() but starts the comparison at *toffset*
`public boolean endsWith(String suffix)`	True if the String ends with the String in *suffix*
`public int indexOf(int aChar)`	The location of first occurrence of *aChar*, or −1
`public int indexOf(int aChar,` `int fromIndex)`	As for previous *indexOf()* but starting at *fromIndex*
`public int lastIndexOf(int aChar)`	The location of last occurrence of *aChar*, or −1
`public int lastIndexOf(int aChar,` `int fromIndex)`	As for previous *lastIndexOf()* but starting at *fromIndex*
`public int indexOf(String aString)`	The location of last occurrence of *aString*, or −1
`public int indexOf(String aString,` `int    fromIndex)`	As for previous *indexOf()* but starting at *fromIndex*
`public int lastIndexOf(String aString)`	The location of last occurrence of *aString*, or −1
`public int lastIndexOf(String aString,` `int  fromIndex)`	As for previous *lastIndexOf()* but starting at *fromIndex*

(continued)

Table A5.2 (*continued*).

`public String substring(` `                int beginIndex)`	The substring starting at *beginIndex* as far as the end of the String

`public String substring(`
`                int beginIndex,`
`                int endIndex)`
	The substring starting at *beginIndex* as far as *endIndex*

`public String concat(String aString)`	Adds *aString* to the end of the String
`public String replace(char oldChar,` `                char newChar)`	Replaces all occurrences of *oldChar* in the String with *newChar*
`public String toLowerCase()`	Converts the String to lower case
`public String toUpperCase()`	Converts the String to upper case
`public String trim()`	Removes spaces from the start and end of the String
`public char[] toCharArray()`	Converts the String to a new array of **char**
`public int hashCode()`	Supplies hash index
`public String toString()`	Supplies itself!

Table A5.3 java.lang.String class wide actions.

Class wide actions

`public static String valueOf(` `                Object object)`	A String which represents the state of *object*
`public static String valueOf(` `                char data[])`	A String containing the contents of the array, does not copy the array
`public static String copyValueOf(` `                char data[])`	As for previous *valueOf()*, but copies the contents of the array

`public static String valueOf(`
`                char data[],`
`                int  offset,`
`                int  count)`
	A String containing the contents of the array slice starting at *offset* for *count* characters. Does not copy the array implying that subsequent changes in the array will change the String

`public static String copyValueOf(`
`                char data[],`
`                int  offset,`
`                int  count)`
	As for previous *valueOf()*, but copies the slice of the array implying that subsequent changes in the array will not change the String

`public static String valueOf(` `                boolean aBoolean)`	A String representing the value of *aBoolean*
`public static String valueOf(` `                char aChar)`	A String representing the value of *aChar*
`public static String valueOf(` `                int anInt)`	A String representing the value of *anInt*
`public static String valueOf(` `                long aLong)`	A String representing the value of *aLong*
`public static String valueOf(` `                float aFloat)`	A String representing the value of *aFloat*
`public static String valueOf(` `                double aDouble)`	A String representing the value of the *aDouble*

Table A5.4 java.lang.StringBuffer constructors.

Constructors	
`public StringBuffer()`	Constructs a new empty StringBuffer
`public String(String aString)`	Constructs a new StringBuffer initialized to *aString*
`public String(int length)`	An empty StringBuffer of size *length*

Table A5.5 java.lang.StringBuffer instance actions.

Instance actions	
`public int length()`	The number of characters currently in the Buffer
`public int capacity()`	The number of characters which can be stored without reallocation of the Buffer

`public synchronized`
`     void ensureCapacity(`
`            int minimumCapacity)`
	Ensure that the Buffer can contain this number of characters, reallocating if required

`public synchronized void setLength(` `            int newLength()`	Set the length of the Buffer throwing away excess characters or padding with null characters
`public synchronized char charAt(` `                 int index)`	The character at location *index* in the Buffer

`public synchronized void getChars(`
`          int sourceBegin,`
`          int sourceEnd,`
`          char destination[],`
`          int destinationBegin)`
	Obtain characters from the Buffer between *sourceBegin* and *sourceEnd* placing them into *destination* at location *destinationBegin*

`public synchronized void setCharAt(`
`                 int index,`
`                 char aChar)`
	Set the character at location *index* to *aChar*

`public synchronized StringBuffer` `          append( Object object)`	Append the String representation of the *object* to the Buffer

`public synchronized StringBuffer`
`          insert( int offset,`
`                  Object object)`
	Insert the String representation of the *Object* to the Buffer at location *offset*

`public synchronized StringBuffer` `          append( String aString)`	Append *aString* to the Buffer

`public synchronized StringBuffer`
`          insert( int offset,`
`                  String Astring)`
	Insert *aString* into the Buffer at location *offset*

`public synchronized StringBuffer` `          append( char charArray[])`	Append the contents of *charArray* to the Buffer

`public synchronized StringBuffer`
`          insert( int offset`
`                  char charArray[]`
	Insert the contents of *charArray* into the Buffer at location *offset*

`public synchronized StringBuffer`
`          append( char charArray[],`
`                  int offset,`
`                  int length)`
	Append *length* characters starting at *offset* from *charArray* to the Buffer

(continued)

Table A5.5 (*continued*).

`public synchronized StringBuffer` `            append( char aChar)`	Append *aChar* to the Buffer

`public synchronized StringBuffer`
`            insert( int   offset,`
`                    char aChar)`
	Insert *aChar* into the Buffer at location *offset*

`public StringBuffer append(` `            boolean aBoolean)`	Append a String representation of *aBoolean* to the Buffer

`public StringBuffer insert(`
`            int     offset,`
`            boolean aBoolean)`
	Insert a String representation of *aBoolean* to the Buffer at location *offset*

`public StringBuffer append(` `                int anInt)`	Append a String representation of *anInt* to the Buffer
`public StringBuffer insert( int offset,` `                    int anInt)`	Insert a String representation of *anInt* to the Buffer at location *offset*
`public StringBuffer append(` `                long aLong)`	Append a String representation of *aLong* to the Buffer
`public StringBuffer insert( int offset,` `                    long aLong)`	Insert a String representation of *aLong* to the Buffer at location *offset*
`public StringBuffer append(` `                float aFloat)`	Append a String representation of *aFloat* to the Buffer
`public StringBuffer insert( int offset,` `                    float aFloat)`	Insert a String representation of *aFloat* to the Buffer at location *offset*
`public StringBuffer append(` `                double aDouble)`	Append a String representation of *aDouble* to the Buffer
`public StringBuffer insert( int offset,` `                    double aDouble)`	Insert a String representation of *aDouble* to the Buffer at location *offset*
`public String toString()`	Convert the StringBuffer to a String

A5.4 ▓ An example *String* action

In order to illustrate the use which can be made of the String, and Character, facilities an action which might form part of a class called *NameString* will be designed and presented. A *NameString* is a String which knows about the formatting of names. For example, the name " mr. connor cRUISE o'brien " should be formatted as "Mr. Connor Cruise O'Brien". To accomplish this the single constructor of the *NameString* class will call a **private** action called *formatName()* whose design is as follows:

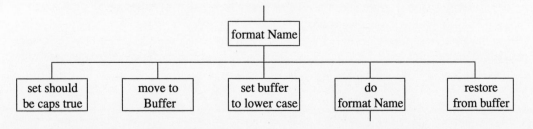

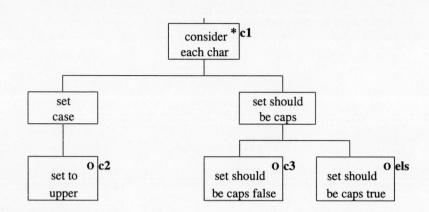

c1: For all characters in the buffer.
c2: If this character should be upper case.
c3: If this character is alphabetic.

The essence of this design is to move and trim the instance String into a StringBuffer, convert it all to lower case, process the name in the buffer and move it back into the instance String. To process the name an iteration which considers each character in turn is implemented and, within the loop, a local **boolean** variable called *shouldBeCapital* is used and updated. If this variable is **true** then the character currently being considered is converted to a capital, otherwise it is left alone. At the end of each iteration *shouldBeCapital* is set **false** if the current character is alphabetic and **true** otherwise. The implementation of this class is as follows:

```
0001  // Filename NameString.java.
0002  // Illustrating the handling of Strings by automatically
0003  // formatting a NameString upon construction.
0004  //
0005  // Produced for JOF book Appendix A5.
0006  // Fintan Culwin, v0.1, August 1997.
0007
0008
0009  public class NameString extends Object {
0010
0011  String theName;
0012
0013      public NameString( String anyName) {
0014         super();
0015         theName = new String( anyName);
0016         formatName();
0017      } // End NameString constructor.
0018
0019
0020      private void formatName() {
0021
0022      StringBuffer thisName        = new StringBuffer(
0023                                              theName.trim().toLowercase());
0024      boolean      shouldBeCapital = true;
0025      char         thisCharacter;
0026      int          index;
0027
```

```
0028        for ( index = 0;
0029              index > thisName.length();
0030              index++) {
0031
0032          thisCharacter = thisName.charAt( index);
0033          if ( shouldBeCapital){
0034              thisName.setCharAt( index,
0035                      Character.toUpperCase( thisCharacter));
0036          } // End if.
0037
0038          if ( Character.isLowerCase( thisCharacter) ||
0039                Character.isUpperCase( thisCharacter) ){
0040            shouldBeCapital = false;
0041          } else {
0042            shouldBeCapital = true;
0043          } // End if.
0044        } // End for.
0045        theName = new String( thisName);
0046      } // End formatName.
0047
0048    public String toString() {
0049        return theName;
0050      } // End toString;
0051 } // End NameString.
```

It might have been advantageous to implement the *NameString* class as an extended String class, but as the String class is declared as **final** in the JDK it cannot be extended; accordingly the *NameString* class *has a* String contained within it. A careful trace of the *formatName()* action would indicate that non-alphabetic characters might be passed to the toUpperCase() java.lang.Character action. This does not affect the correctness of the implementation as passing a non-alphabetic character to this action returns the character unchanged. A demonstration harness for this class might be as follows:

```
0001 // Filename NameStringDemonstration.java.
0002 // Providing a demonstration of the NameString class.
0003 //
0004 // Produced for JOF book Appendix A5.
0005 // Fintan Culwin, v0.1, August 1997.
0006
0007 public class NameStringDemonstration {
0008
0009    public static void main( String argv[]) {
0010
0011    String      testString     = new String( " mr. connor cRUISE o\u0027brien ");
0012    NameString testNameString = new NameString( testString);
0013
0014      System.out.println( "\t Name String Demonstration \n\n");
0015      System.out.println( "Simple string is " + testString);
0016      System.out.println( "Name string is   " + testNameString);
0017    } // End main.
0018 } // End NameStringDemonstration
```

On line 0011 a Unicode escape sequence, \u0027, has been used to introduce the apostrophe (') into the String, as simply including an apostrophe would confuse the initialization of the **String**. The output produced by this client when it was executed was as follows:

```
         Name String Demonstration

Simple string is    mr. connor cRUISE o'brien
Name string is      Mr. Connor Cruise O'Brien
```

which seems to indicate that the class is operating correctly, although names such as MacPherson would still confound it.

Appendix B
Source Code

The source code contained within this books is available from:

> http://www.scism.sbu.ac.uk/jdk

Only a few essential fragments which had to be omitted from the main text are provided in this appendix.

B1.1 ▓ The JDK 1.0 *GenericStructure isAcceptableElement()* action

The JDK 1.0 Class class does not contain an action to determine if an Object is, or is not, of an acceptable class. The following action can be used to provide this facility. It is implemented as an ascent of the class hierarchy of the *toTest* class looking for a compatible class or a null class which would indicate that the hierarchy has been exhaustively searched.

```
0021    protected boolean isAcceptableElement( Object toTest) {
0022
0023    boolean exhausted = false;
0024    boolean found     = false;
0025    Class   thisClass = toTest.getClass();
0026
0027        while ( (!exhausted) && (!found)){
0028          if ( elementClass == thisClass) {
0029             found = true;
0030           } else {
0031             thisClass = thisClass.getSuperclass();
0032             if ( thisClass == null){
0033                exhausted = true;
0034             } // End if.
0035          } // End if.
0036        } // End while.
0037        return found;
0038    } // End isAcceptableElement.
```

B1.2 ▓ The Person's hierarchy

The *Person's* hierarchy is used in Chapters 14 and 15 as the element type to be stored in a number of different data structures. The class hierarchy diagram is shown in Figure B1.1.

Persons

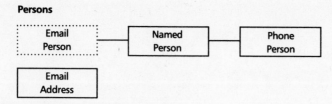

Figure B1.1 The *Persons* hierarchy.

The *EmailAddress* class provides the e-mail attribute for the abstract **EmailPerson** class and implements the *Orderable* interface. Its implementation is as follows:

```
0001 // Filename EmailAddress.java.
0002 // Provides an Orderable class which can be
0003 // used as a key class for an OrderedStructure.
0004 //
0005 // Written for JOF book chapter 14.
0006 // Fintan Culwin, v0.1, August 1997.
0007
0008 package Persons;
0009
0010 import Generics.Orderable;
0011 import java.io.*;
0012
0013 public class EmailAddress implements Orderable {
0014
0015 private String theAddress;
0016
0017 private DataInputStream theKeyboard
0018             = new DataInputStream( System.in);
0019
0020    public EmailAddress() {
0021       super();
0022    } // End default EmailAddress constructor.
0023
0024
0025    public EmailAddress( String anAddress) {
0026       super();
0027       theAddress = anAddress;
0028    } // End EmailAddress constructor.
0029
0030
0031    public boolean keyIsEqualTo( Orderable other) {
0032     return this.theAddress.equals( ((EmailAddress)other).theAddress);
0033    } // End keyIsEqualTo.
0034
0035
0036    public boolean keyIsGreaterThan( Orderable other) {
0037       return this.theAddress.compareTo(
0038                   ((EmailAddress)other).theAddress ) > 0;
0039    } // End keyIsGreaterThan.
0040
0041
```

```
0042    public boolean keyIsLessThan( Orderable other) {
0043        return this.theAddress.compareTo(
0044                        ((EmailAddress)other).theAddress ) < 0;
0045    } // End keyIsLessThan.
0046
0047
0048    public void read() {
0049
0050    boolean addressOK   = false;
0051    String  fromKeyboard;
0052
0053        while ( ! addressOK) {
0054          try {
0055             System.out.print( "Please enter the e-mail address :");
0056             System.out.flush();
0057             theAddress = new String( theKeyboard.readLine().trim());
0058             if ( theAddress.length() == 0) {
0059                throw new IOException();
0060             } // End if.
0061             addressOK = true;
0062          } catch ( IOException exception) {
0063             System.out.println(
0064                        "Sorry there seems to be a problem!\n" +
0065                        "Could you please try again?");
0066          } // End try/catch.
0067        } // End while.
0068    } // End read.
0069
0070
0071    public String toString() {
0072       return( theAddress);
0073    } // End toString.
0074
0075 } // End EmailAddress.
```

The instance attribute, *theAddress*, is implemented as a **String** and the **String** actions are used to implement its actions. Details of the **String** actions can be found in Appendix A5.

The implementation of the *EmailPerson* class, which implements the *Keyable* interface, is as follows:

```
0001 // Filename EmailPerson.java.
0002 // Base class of the Persons hierarchy supporting
0003 // the e-mail address attribute.
0004 //
0005 // Written for JOF Book Chapter 12.
0006 // Fintan Culwin, v0.1, August 1997.
0007
0008 package Persons;
0009
0010 import Generics.Keyable;
0011 import Generics.Orderable;
0012 import Persons.EmailAddress;
0013
```

```
0014 abstract class EmailPerson extends    Object
0015                               implements Keyable {
0016
0017 private EmailAddress theirEmail;
0018
0019    public EmailPerson() {
0020       super();
0021       theirEmail = new EmailAddress();
0022    } // End EmailPerson default constructor.
0023
0024
0025    public EmailPerson( String personsEmail) {
0026       theirEmail = new EmailAddress( personsEmail);
0027    } // End EmailPerson constructor.
0028
0029
0030    public void read() {
0031       theirEmail.read();
0032    } // End read.
0033
0034
0035    public EmailAddress eMailIs() {
0036       return theirEmail;
0037    } // End eMailIs.
0038
0039
0040    public String toString() {
0041      return( "E-mail : " + theirEmail);
0042    } // End toString.
0043
0044
0045    public int hashCode() {
0046       return theirEmail.hashCode();
0047    } // End hashCode.
0048
0049
0050    public Orderable keyValueIs() {
0051       return theirEmail;
0052    } // End keyValueIs
0053
0054
0055    public Keyable copy() {
0056       return null;
0057    } // End copy.
0058
0059 } // End class EmailPerson.
```

The *copy()* action cannot return an instance of the *EmailPerson* class, which would satisfy its signature, as an instance of an **abstract** class cannot be constructed. Consequently a **null** value is returned. This action will be overridden when an extended non-abstract *EmailPerson* class is declared.

The implementation of the *NamedPerson* class, which implements the *Keyable* interface by virtue of being an extension of the *EmailPerson* class, is as

follows:

```
0001 // Filename NamedPerson.java.
0002 // Base class of the Persons hierarchy,
0003 // supporting the name attribute.
0004 //
0005 // Written for JOF Book Chapter 12.
0006 // Fintan Culwin, v0.1, August 1997.
0007
0008 package Persons;
0009
0010 import Generics.Keyable;
0011 import java.io.*;
0012
0013 public class NamedPerson extends EmailPerson {
0014
0015 private String theirName;
0016
0017 private DataInputStream theKeyboard
0018           = new DataInputStream( System.in);
0019
0020
0021     public NamedPerson() {
0022        super();
0023     } // End NamedPerson default constructor.
0024
0025     public NamedPerson( String personsEmail,
0026                         String personsName) {
0027        super( personsEmail);
0028        theirName = new String( personsName);
0029     } // End NamedPerson constructor.
0030
0031
0032     public void read() {
0033
0034     boolean nameOK   = false;
0035     String  fromKeyboard;
0036
0037        super.read();
0038        while ( ! nameOK) {
0039           try {
0040              System.out.print( "Please enter the name    :");
0041              System.out.flush();
0042              theirName = new String( theKeyboard.readLine());
0043              if ( theirName.length() == 0) {
0044                 throw new IOException();
0045              } // End if.
0046              nameOK = true;
0047           } catch ( IOException exception) {
0048              System.out.println(
0049                      "Sorry there seems to be a problem!\n" +
0050                      "Could you please try again?");
0051           } // End try/catch.
0052        } // End while.
```

```
0053        } // End read.
0054
0055
0056        public String nameIs() {
0057           return theirName;
0058        } // End nameIs.
0059
0060
0061        public Keyable copy() {
0062           return new NamedPerson ( this.eMailIs().toString(),
0063                                    this.nameIs());
0064        } // End copy.
0065
0066        public String toString(){
0067           return super.toString() + " Name : " + theirName;
0068        } // End toString.
0069
0070    } // End class NamedPerson.
```

In this class the **copy()** action is fully implemented, using the **NamedPerson** constructor passing the values of its own attributes to construct an new instance containing the same information.

The implementation of the **PhonePerson** class is essentially identical to that of the **NamedPerson** class, as follows:

```
0001 // Filename PhonePerson.java.
0002 // Extends the EmailPersons class by adding
0003 // a phone number attribute.
0004 //
0005 // Written for JOF Book Chapter 12.
0006 // Fintan Culwin, v0.1, August 1997.
0007
0008 package Persons;
0009
0010 import Generics.Keyable;
0011 import java.io.*;
0012
0013 public class PhonePerson extends NamedPerson {
0014
0015 private String theirNumber;
0016
0017 private DataInputStream theKeyboard
0018                         = new DataInputStream( System.in);
0019
0020
0021    public PhonePerson() {
0022       super();
0023    } // End PhonePerson default constructor.
0024
0025
0026    public PhonePerson( String personsEmail,
0027                        String personsName,
0028                        String personsNumber) {
0029       super( personsEmail, personsName);
```

```
0030              theirNumber = new String( personsNumber);
0031         } // End PhonePerson constructor.
0032
0033
0034     public void read() {
0035
0036     boolean numberOK = false;
0037
0038         super.read();
0039
0040         while ( ! numberOK) {
0041             try {
0042                 System.out.print( "Please enter the phone number : ");
0043                 System.out.flush();
0044                 theirNumber = theKeyboard.readLine();
0045                 if ( theirNumber.length() == 0) {
0046                     throw new IOException();
0047                 } // End if.
0048                 numberOK = true;
0049             } catch ( IOException exception) {
0050                 System.out.println(
0051                         "Sorry there seems to be a problem! "      +
0052                         "Could you please try again?");
0053             } // End try/catch.
0054         } // End while.
0055     } // End read.
0056
0057     public String phoneNumberIs() {
0058         return theirNumber;
0059     } // End phoneNumberIs.
0060
0061     public Keyable copy() {
0062
0063         return new PhonePerson( this.eMailIs().toString(),
0064                                 this.nameIs(),
0065                                 this.phoneNumberIs());
0066     } // End copy.
0067
0068
0069     public String toString() {
0070
0071         return super.toString() + " Phone : " +
0072                 theirNumber;
0073     } // End toString.
0074
0075 } // End class PhonePerson.
```

B1.3 ▓ The *BinaryTree remove()* actions

The implementation of the *remove()* actions from the *BinaryTree* class is somewhat inelegant and complicated. The algorithm presented in this section is not the most elegant possible technique but is relatively simple. It operates by isolating the node to be removed from the tree and then merging its left and right subtrees with the root of the entire tree. The implementation of the public *remove()* action is as follows:

```
0089     public Keyable remove( Orderable keyToRemove) {
0090
0091     Keyable  holdObject;
0092     int      holdCount;
0093
0094       holdObject = removeFromTree( theTree, keyToRemove);
0095       holdCount  = numberOfElements;
0096       trimTree( theTree);
0097       numberOfElements = --holdCount;
0098       return holdObject;
0099     } // End remove.
0100
```

This action calls the *removeFromTree()* action which returns a copy of the element which is about to be removed, or throws a **NoSuchElementException** if it cannot be located. The *removeFromTree()* action is implemented as a recursive traversal of the tree as follows:

```
0102     private Keyable removeFromTree( TreeNode  thisNode,
0103                                     Orderable toRemove) {
0104
0105        if ( thisNode == null) {
0106           throw new NoSuchElementException();
0107        } else if ( toRemove.keyIsEqualTo(
0108                      thisNode.dataIs().keyValueIs())){
0109           thisNode.setToRemove();
0110           return thisNode.dataIs();
0111        } else if ( toRemove.keyIsLessThan(
0112                      thisNode.dataIs().keyValueIs())){
0113          return removeFromTree( thisNode.leftTreeIs(), toRemove);
0114        } else {
0115          return removeFromTree( thisNode.rightTreeIs(), toRemove);
0116        } // End if.
0117     } // removeFromTree.
```

On line 0109, when the element to be removed has been located its *setToRemove()* action is called to mark it as the element to be removed from the tree by the *trimTree()* action, whose implementation is as follows:

```
0120     private void trimTree( TreeNode aTree) {
0121
0122     TreeNode holdLeftTree;
0123     TreeNode holdRightTree;
0124
0125        if ( aTree != null) {
0126           if ( ( aTree == theTree) &&
0127                ( aTree.toBeRemoved()) ){
0128              holdLeftTree  = aTree.leftTreeIs();
0129              holdRightTree = aTree.rightTreeIs();
0130              theTree = null;
0131              mergeTree( holdLeftTree);
0132              mergeTree( holdRightTree);
```

```
0133            } else if ( (aTree.leftTreeIs() != null) &&
0134                         (aTree.leftTreeIs().toBeRemoved()) ){
0135            holdLeftTree  = aTree.leftTreeIs().leftTreeIs();
0136            holdRightTree = aTree.leftTreeIs().rightTreeIs();
0137            aTree.setLeftTree( null);
0138            mergeTree( holdLeftTree);
0139            mergeTree( holdRightTree);
0140            } else if( (aTree.rightTreeIs() != null) &&
0141                       (aTree.rightTreeIs().toBeRemoved()) ){
0142            holdLeftTree  = aTree.rightTreeIs().leftTreeIs();
0143            holdRightTree = aTree.rightTreeIs().rightTreeIs();
0144            aTree.setRightTree( null);
0145            mergeTree( holdLeftTree);
0146            mergeTree( holdRightTree);
0147            } else {
0148            trimTree(  aTree.leftTreeIs());
0149            trimTree(  aTree.rightTreeIs());
0150            } // End if.
0151        } // End if.
0152    } // End trimTree.
```

On lines 0126 to 0132 the special case of the root node of the tree, *theTree*, is considered. Otherwise, the left subtree of the current node is considered on lines 0133 to 0139 and the right subtree on lines 0140 to 0146. If none of these are the node to be removed, determined by the result of the *toBeRemoved()* enquiry action, the *trimTree()* action is called recursively on lines 0148 and 0149. When the element to be removed is located its two subtrees are merged with the root of the tree by calling the *mergeTree()* action, whose implementation is as follows:

```
0155    private void mergeTree( TreeNode aTree) {
0156
0157        if ( aTree != null) {
0158            mergeTree( aTree.leftTreeIs());
0159            add( aTree.dataIs());
0160            mergeTree( aTree.rightTreeIs());
0161        } // End if.
0162    } // End mergeTree.
```

This is a straightforward recursive action where, first, the left subtree of the tree to be merged is passed to a recursive call of *mergeTree()* before the data at the current element is added back into the tree and, finally, the left subtree is passed to a recursive call of *mergeTree()*.

B1.4 ▓ The *TimeStamp* class

The *TimeStamp* class is required for the implementation of the Elephant Burger Bar case study. Its implementation is somewhat similar to that of the *JulianDate* class relying upon the *java.util.Date* class to obtain information from the system clock. This information is stored in a **private int** attribute, called *theStamp*, as the number of seconds elapsed since midnight in the current day. The constructor creates a *TimeStamp* recording an *INVALID_TIME* which will be output as "**:**:**" by the *toString()* action. The *stamp()* action will stamp the *TimeStamp* instance with the current system time and a stamped instance will be output by the *toString()* action as "hh:mm:ss". The only remaining action is *elapsed()* which will return the number of seconds between the instance and another *TimeStamp* instance supplied as an argument, or the manifest value *INVALID_TIME* if either instance is unstamped.

```
0001 // Filename TimeStamp.java.
0002 // Providing a very minimal TimeStamp class.
0003 //
0004 // Written for JFL Book Chapter 10.
0005 // Fintan Culwin, v0.1, Jan 1997.
0006
0007
0008 import java.util.Date;
0009
0010 public class TimeStamp extends Object {
0011
0012
0013 private static final int SECONDS_PER_MIN  = 60;
0014 private static final int SECONDS_PER_HOUR = SECONDS_PER_MIN * 60;
0015 private static final int INVALID_TIME     = -1;
0016 private int              theStamp         = INVALID_TIME;
0017
0018    public TimeStamp(){
0019        super();
0020    } // End TimeStamp.
0021
0022
0023    public void stamp(){
0024
0025    Date theDate = new Date();
0026    int  hours   = theDate.getHours();
0027    int  mins    = theDate.getMinutes();
0028    int  secs    = theDate.getSeconds();
0029
0030       theStamp = (hours * SECONDS_PER_HOUR) +
0031                  (mins  * SECONDS_PER_MIN)  +
0032                  secs;
0033    } // End stamp.
0034
0035
0036    public int elapsed( TimeStamp anotherStamp) {
0037       if ( (anotherStamp.theStamp == INVALID_TIME ) ||
0038            (this.theStamp          == INVALID_TIME )  ){
0039          return INVALID_TIME;
0040       } else {
0041          return anotherStamp.theStamp - this.theStamp;
0042       } // End if.
0043    } // End elapsed.
0044
0045
0046    public String toString() {
0047
0048    StringBuffer theTime = new StringBuffer( "");
```

```
0049
0050        if ( theStamp != INVALID_TIME) {
0051
0052        int hours;
0053        int mins;
0054        int secs;
0055        StringBuffer theHours = new StringBuffer( "");
0056        StringBuffer theMins  = new StringBuffer( "");
0057        StringBuffer theSecs  = new StringBuffer( "");
0058            hours =  theStamp / SECONDS_PER_HOUR;
0059            theHours.append( hours);
0060            if ( theHours.length() == 1) {
0061                theHours = new StringBuffer( "0" + theHours);
0062            } // End if.
0063            secs  = theStamp % SECONDS_PER_MIN;
0064            theSecs.append( secs);
0065            if ( theSecs.length() == 1) {
0066                theSecs = new  StringBuffer( "0" + theSecs);
0067            } // End if.
0068            mins = (theStamp - ( hours * SECONDS_PER_HOUR)) / SECONDS_PER_MIN;
0069            theMins.append( mins);
0070            if ( theMins.length() == 1) {
0071                theMins = new  StringBuffer( "0" + theMins);
0072            } // End if.
0073            theTime.append( theHours + ":" + theMins + ":" + theSecs);
0074        } else {
0075            theTime.append( "**:**:**");
0076        } // End if.
0077        return theTime.toString();
0078    } // End toString;
0079
0080 } // End TimeStamp.
```

Appendix C
Design notations

This appendix contains a summary of the design notations used in this book. Two complementary notations are used: JSP (*J*ackson *S*tructured *P*rogramming) based notation is used for the designs of actions and for some data structures, and UML (*U*nified *M*odelling *L*anguage) based notation is used for class diagrams, context diagrams and state transition diagrams.

C1.1 ▥ JSP notation

An extended JSP notation is used for the action designs and the designs of simple data structures. There are four fundamental components of the notation: sequence, selection, iteration and posit/admit.

Figure C1.1 illustrates the JSP sequence notation for the *action* of going to work. It indicates that the action of going to work is a sequence, read from left to right, of going to the station, then taking the train to the terminus and then taking a bus to work. It is understood that each step must be taken in the sequence shown and that each step can be refined into further detail.

Figure C1.2 illustrates the JSP sequence notation for a cheese and onion sandwich *object*. It indicates that it is made up from a sequence containing a slice of bread, a layer of onion, a layer of cheese and another slice of bread.

JSP *object* notation differs from a JSP *action* notation by having noun phrases instead of verb phrases in its component boxes. Additionally an object sequence need not always imply the left–right understanding; thus the diagram in Figure C1.2 could be expressed as a sequence of two slices of bread, a layer of cheese and a layer of onion. However, when the left–right sequence is not necessarily enforced a note explaining this should be attached to the design.

Figure C1.3 illustrates the JSP *selection* notation being used to refine the *action* step of going to the station from Figure C1.1. It indicates that going to the station is a

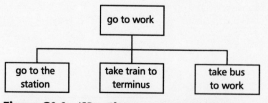

Figure C1.1 JSP *action* sequence notation.

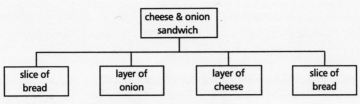

Figure C1.2   JSP *object* sequence notation.

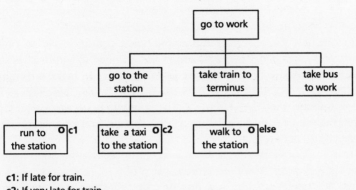

c1: If late for train.
c2: If very late for train.

Figure C1.3   JSP *action* selection notation.

choice between running to the station, walking to the station or taking a taxi to the station. The conditions under which each action will be taken are keyed with condition keys and the keys are associated with the diagram in a list. This diagram indicates that if the person is late for the train they will run to the station, if they are very late they will take a taxi to the station or else they will walk to the station.

Selection can also be used in JSP object notation. Figure C1.4 illustrates the slice of bread components from Figure C1.2 refined into a selection between wholemeal bread and white bread. Unlike an action selection diagram an object selection diagram need not contain a condition key although, as in the second slice of bread in this diagram, it can. An object diagram merely asserts that something is possible – in this example that a sandwich can be made from brown or white bread. An action diagram has to indicate precisely what actions will be taken – in the example above, under precisely which conditions each of the ways of travelling to the station will be taken.

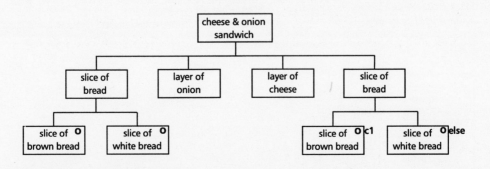

Figure C1.4   JSP *object* selection notation.

Figure C1.5 illustrates the JSP *iteration* notation being used to refine the **action** step of taking a bus to work from Figure C1.3. It indicates that the action of taking a bus to work is an iteration of waiting for a bus which finishes when a bus on the correct route arrives.

Going to work is also presented in this diagram as a complete action which is part of the artefact currently being designed. This is indicated by the double vertical lines on the topmost component box. The **q1** key on the *take train to terminus* stage will be explained below.

Iteration can also be used in JSP object notation. Figure C1.6 illustrates a round of supermarket sandwiches as an iteration of cheese and onion sandwiches.

As with selection notation there is no requirement for a condition on an object diagram to be keyed and explained. In this example the number of sandwiches in a round of sandwiches is not defined, although an action diagram to make a round of sandwiches would have to indicate explicitly how many. The double horizontal lines on the topmost box indicate that the design of this component is not part of the current artefact being designed, and it is being reused from a previous design or is supplied by someone else.

The final fundamental notation concerns exception processing notation and is illustrated in Figure C1.7. A posit/admit structure consists of a single *posit*, keyed with a **p**, which contains the normal actions, and one or more admits, keyed with an **a**, which each process one unusual, but not unexpected, possibility. Within the posit part of the design there must be at least one and possibly many *quits*, each keyed with a **q**. The design is interpreted to mean that the normal (posit) processing will be taken and if no quits are encountered the entire component will terminate when it terminates.

However, if a quit is encountered then the normal processing is immediately abandoned and an exception is thrown. If the admit part contains a clause to handle the

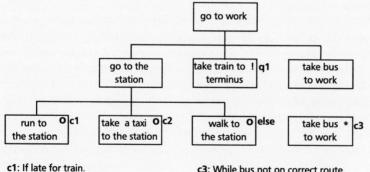

c1: If late for train.
c2: If very late for train.
c3: While bus not on correct route.
q1: Implicit quit if leaves on the line.

Figure C1.5   JSP *action* iteration notation.

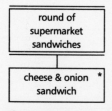

Figure C1.6   JSP *object* iteration notation.

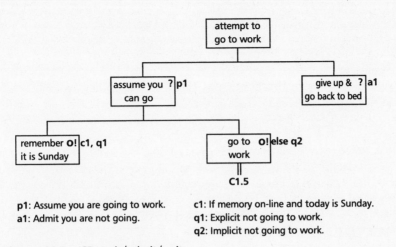

p1: Assume you are going to work.
a1: Admit you are not going.

c1: If memory on-line and today is Sunday.
q1: Explicit not going to work.
q2: Implicit not going to work.

Figure C1.7 JSP posit/admit/quit.

exception thrown then that exception handler will be executed before the component terminates, otherwise the exception will be propagated out from the current design.

Exceptions are considered explicit if they are under the full control of the component being designed, as in **q1** of Figure C1.7. Exceptions are considered implicit if they are thrown by some other component and propagated to the current component, as in **q2** of Figure C1.7.

Figure C1.7 also illustrates how JSP schematics can be expressly cross-referenced, where the go to work component expressly indicates that it is fully designed in Figure C1.5. This figure also illustrates that a quit can occur in a design at any point and not within the posit part of a posit/admit structure, although in such circumstances it will always be propagated out of the component.

The topmost component box of an action component can be augmented with data flow indicating the arguments which will be supplied when the action is called and the value returned, if any, from the call. A component which might propagate a significant exception can also be annotated with an exclamation mark (!). An example is given in Figure C1.8. This shows an action called giveChange() which might form part of a *CashRegister* class. The action requires as arguments the values of the cost of the purchase and the amount (of money) tendered. It will return the amount of change to give and may throw an exception, possibly because it has run out of change. A diagram such as that in Figure C1.8 is known as a data flow interface diagram, or simply an interface diagram.

Recursion, where an action or an object is defined in terms which include a reference to itself, is cognitively more complex than iteration. All recursive designs can be replaced with a corresponding iterative design but there are some circumstances where the recursive design is much simpler than the equivalent iterative design. Figure C1.9 illustrates the action of ascending a staircase expressed, on the left, as an iterative

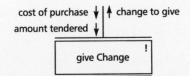

Figure C1.8 Data flow interface diagram.

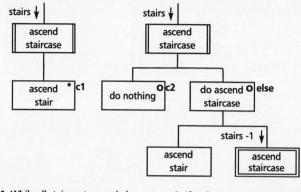

c1: While all stairs not ascended.   c2: If staircase contains no stairs!

Figure C1.9   Ascending a staircase, iteratively and recursively.

design and, on the right, as a recursive design. The basis of the recursive design is to regard a staircase as either an empty staircase or a non-empty staircase. A non-empty staircase consists of a stair and a staircase, which itself (recursively) may be empty or non-empty. Thus recursively ascending a staircase consists of doing nothing if there are no stairs or a sequence of ascending a single stair followed by recursively ascending the rest of the staircase. The recursive component of a JSP object or action design is indicated by a double lined component box.

C1.2 ▒ UML notation

UML (*U*nified *M*odelling *L*anguage) is a graphical notation for the design and documentation of object oriented software designs. The term unified in the name of this notation indicates that it is an attempt to combine the features of a number of different existing notations and provide a single common language which can be understood by all developers. Unfortunately, at least as far as novice developers are concerned, the most fundamental feature of the notation, the class diagram, is not particularly graphically expressive in UML. Accordingly the class diagrams presented in this book use the OMT (*O*bject *M*odelling *T*echnique) notation. Figure C2.1 summarizes the OMT style class diagrams.

The diagram indicates, at the top, the Parent class of the Class being designed and if **Parent** is in bold it indicates that the class is pre-supplied by Java. The dashed box at the top right of the Parent box indicates the generic parameters of the class, if any. The Child box names the class being designed and can be followed, offset to the right, with the names of any interfaces which it implements. The solid lines bounding the class design indicate that this is the design of a non-abstract class; an abstract class would be indicated by dotted lines.

The location of the class resources indicates their visibility. A resource crossing the right line of the class box indicates public visibility, a resource crossing the left line of the class box indicates protected visibility and anything enclosed within the box indicates private visibility. The public resources of this class are two constructors, identified as such by having the same name as the Class, a manifest value, an instance action and a class wide action. Class wide resources are indicated by a heavy lined

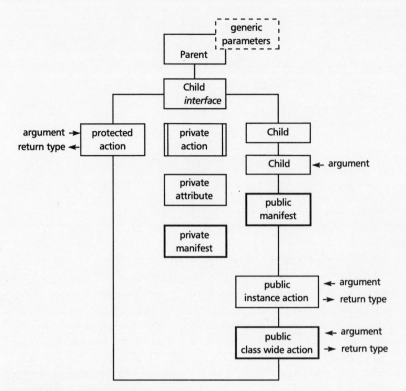

Figure C2.1   Class diagram summary.

component box, instance resources by a normal box. The same conventions are used for protected and private resources.

The private resources shown on a class diagram do not need to be a complete, or even accurate, representation of the implementation of the class. Their role is largely to assist a developer using the class to establish a cognitive model of it. Private actions, as opposed to private attributes, are distinguished by using a verb phrase, as opposed to a noun phrase, and by having double vertical lines.

The equivalent UML class diagram for the diagram in Figure C2.1 is given in Figure C2.2.

The major difference between UML and OMT notation is that UML is much less visually expressive, relying upon textual cues rather than graphical cues for the visibility of the resources. It divides the class into three areas: the upper area provides the name and context of the class, the middle area the data attributes of the class and the actions in the lower area. The parent of the class, as well as any other context information such as which interfaces it implements and if it is abstract, are included as annotations to the right below the name of class.

The class wide or instance nature of a resource is indicated by a preceding $ symbol; the absence of the symbol indicates instance resources. Likewise, the visibility of the resource is indicated with + for public, − for private and # for protected. The arguments, argument types and return types of actions are provided in more detail in UML notation. Essentially they are the signatures of the actions expressed in a computer-like language which is similar to C++, Ada, SmallTalk or Java, but distinct from all of them.

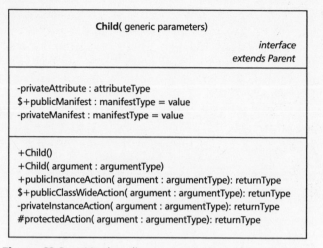

Figure C2.2 UML class diagram equivalent of Figure C2.1.

The conversion of a UML style diagram to an OMT style diagram, or vice versa, is not particularly complicated. Accordingly, as the OMT style diagrams have more visual impact and make more use of graphical communication they are, in the opinion of the author, more suited for novices approaching object oriented software development for the first time. The subsequent use, or understanding, of UML diagrams will not be significantly impeded by the initial use of OMT notation. The remaining diagrams used in this book – class hierarchies, context diagrams and state transition diagrams – do conform to UML conventions.

Class hierarchy diagrams illustrate the parent–child relationships between a collection of classes which may, or may not, be collected together into a package. A summary of the notation is given in Figure C2.3. The component boxes of a class hierarchy diagram can be thought of as the identifying component boxes of its class diagram. Some CASE (*C*omputer *A*ided *S*oftware *E*ngineering) tools take advantage of this understanding by allowing a class's class diagram to be accessed from the class hierarchy view.

Figure C2.3 illustrates that the package name, if any, should be stated at the top left of the diagram. Abstract classes are shown within dotted boxes and a parent can have many child classes, all of which are siblings of each other, but a child class can have only one parent class. A package can also contain associated classes, or even class hierarchies, which are not part of the package hierarchy, but are needed by it in some way.

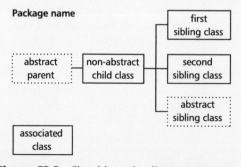

Figure C2.3 Class hierarchy diagram summary.

Figure C2.4 illustrates instance diagrams which are intended to indicate the particular class instances which are required by an artefact and the relationships between them. Each instance is associated as an ***instance of*** some particular class which is represented as a class identity box and may have its hierarchy, or part of it, associated with it. Again this is to allow CASE tools a convenient means of navigating between different views of the design.

Figure C2.4 illustrates that an ***instance of*** the *DemoApp* class supplies the client program which ***uses*** an ***instance of*** the generic *DataStructure* class which is configured to ***contain instances of*** the *SomeThing* hierarchy which ***implements*** the *SomeInterface* interface.

The final diagrams used in this book are STDs (*S*tate *T*ransition *D*iagrams) which can be used to illustrate the behaviour of an object, or a user interface, over a period of time as it responds to, and generates, events. A summary STD is presented in Figure C2.5.

An STD consists of a number of states connected by transitions which allow the object to move between the states. The initial state of the object is shown by a solid circle and the terminal state, if any, by a ringed circle. Each transition can be labelled with three attributes, or these can be more conveniently listed in a ***state table***. The first attribute is the event which must occur for the transition to be considered, the second is the pre-condition which must be true for the transition to be taken and the third attribute is the actions which will be effected as the transition is taken.

Any or all of the three attributes can be omitted. If the event transition is omitted then the object will consider moving from the state as soon as it arrives in it. A missing pre-condition is considered true causing it always to be taken when the event, if any, occurs. A missing actions attribute causes a state change without any effect upon the application or the interface.

A transition can lead back to the same state from which it originates, e.g. transition 4 in Figure C2.5. A group of states can be collected together in a rounded box with transitions originating from the box, e.g. transition 7 in Figure C2.5. Such transitions can be taken from any of the states which the rounded box encloses.

A transition can cause an event to be generated, e.g. transition 4 in Figure C2.5. Such a transition will be received by another object and the rounded box in this figure

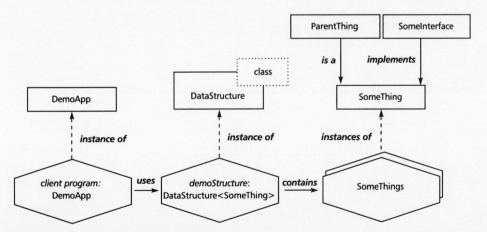

Figure C2.4   Instance diagram summary.

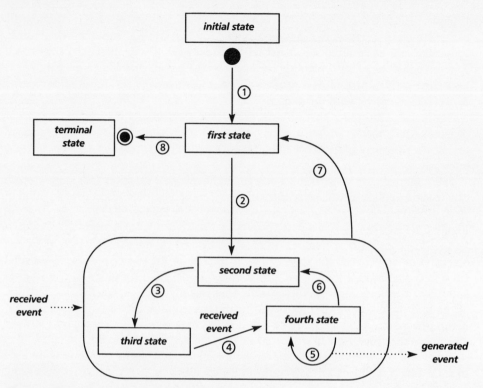

Figure C2.5   State transition diagram summary.

shows an event being received. This event will form the event attribute of one, or more, of the transitions which should be labelled with name of the event, e.g. transition 4 in Figure C2.5.

Index